Cuba and the Revolutionary Myth

Westview Replica Editions

The concept of Westview Replica Editions is a response to the continuing crisis in academic and informational publishing. Library budgets for books have been severely curtailed. Ever larger portions of general library budgets are being diverted from the purchase of books and used for data banks, computers, micromedia, and other methods of information retrieval. Interlibrary loan structures further reduce the edition sizes required to satisfy the needs of the scholarly community. Economic pressures on the university presses and the few private scholarly publishing companies have severely limited the capacity of the industry to properly serve the academic and research communities. As a result, many manuscripts dealing with important subjects, often representing the highest level of scholarship, are no longer economically viable publishing projects--or, if accepted for publication, are typically subject to lead times ranging from one to three years.

Westview Replica Editions are our practical solution to the problem. We accept a manuscript in camera-ready form, typed according to our specifications, and move it immediately into the production process. As always, the selection criteria include the importance of the subject, the work's contribution to scholarship, and its insight, originality of thought, and excellence of exposition. The responsibility for editing and proofreading lies with the author or sponsoring institution. We prepare chapter headings and display pages, file for copyright, and obtain Library of Congress Cataloging in Publication Data. A detailed manual contains simple instructions for preparing the final typescript, and our editorial staff is always available to answer questions.

The end result is a book printed on acid-free paper and bound in sturdy library-quality soft covers. We manufacture these books ourselves using equipment that does not require a lengthy make-ready process and that allows us to publish first editions of 300 to 600 copies and to reprint even smaller quantities as needed. Thus, we can produce Replica Editions quickly and can keep even very specialized books in print as long as there is a demand for them.

About the Book and Author

Cuba and the Revolutionary Myth:
The Political Education
of the Cuban Rebel Army, 1953-1963
C. Fred Judson

Showing how revolutionary myths helped develop political consciousness, this book traces the political education of the Cuban Rebel Army between 1953 and 1963. Dr. Judson demonstrates that the sources of the revolutionary myths are found in Cuba's struggle for independence in the nineteenth centry and in the political upheavals of the 1920s and 1930s. Also examining the guerrilla struggle of the 1950s in detail, he finds that these early experiences were not only an integral part of formal political education in themselves, but also became the material for new myths that mobilized the guerrillas and then sustained revolutionary morale and consciousness. Later, during the first years of the Cuban Revolution, political education for an enlarged Rebel Army was formalized, political materials developed, and instructors trained; Dr. Judson shows how the original myth of national redemption merged with that of the Rebel Army itself and with the overall Marxist-Leninist vision of socialist revolution to form the basis of political education in the Revolutionary Armed Forces in the 1960s.

Dr. C. Fred Judson is assistant professor of political studies at Queen's University, Ontario.

To the Cuban people, in this year of the 25th anniversary of the Revolution; to the Nicaraguan people, in this year of the 5th anniversary of the Sandinista Revolution; to the people of El Salvador; to those who struggle for social justice everywhere.

Cuba and the Revolutionary Myth
The Political Education of the Cuban Rebel Army, 1953–1963

C. Fred Judson

First published 1984 by Westview Press, Inc.

Published 2021 by Routledge
605 Third Avenue, New York, NY 10017
2 Park Square, Milton Park, Abingdon, Oxon OX14 4RN

Routledge is an imprint of the Taylor & Francis Group, an informa business

Copyright © 1984 by Taylor & Francis

All rights reserved. No part of this book may be reprinted or reproduced or utilised in any form or by any electronic, mechanical, or other means, now known or hereafter invented, including photocopying and recording, or in any information storage or retrieval system, without permission in writing from the publishers.

Notice:
Product or corporate names may be trademarks or registered trademarks, and are used only for identification and explanation without intent to infringe.

Library of Congress Catalog Card Number: 84-50657
ISBN 0-86531-827-1

ISBN 13: 978-0-3670-1721-7 (hbk)
ISBN 13: 978-0-3671-6708-0 (pbk)

Printed in the United Kingdom
by Henry Ling Limited

Contents

Acknowledgments.................................. xi

1   THE REVOLUTIONARY MYTH IN THE POLITICAL
    EDUCATION OF THE CUBAN MILITARY.............. 1

    Revolutionary Consciousness.................. 1
    The Political Education of the Cuban
        Military as an Object of Study.......... 3
    The Concept of Revolutionary Myth............ 8
    The Revolutionary Myth: The Case of Cuba.... 14

2   THE FOUNDATIONS OF POLITICAL EDUCATION
    IN THE CUBAN REVOLUTIONARY GENERATION........ 23

    Introduction................................. 23
    The University in the Late 1940s: Practical
        Experiences for Future Cadres........... 26
    The Batistato................................ 31
    The Generación del Centenario
        and the Moncada Assault................. 36

3   THE NEW MAMBISES: COMBAT, REPRESSION AND
    IMPRISONMENT AS POLITICAL EDUCATION FOR
    REVOLUTIONARY CADRES......................... 49

    The Moncada Defeat........................... 49
    The Trial and Revolutionary Morale........... 52
    The Trial: Propaganda Victories for
        the Rebels.............................. 54
    History Will Absolve Me...................... 55
    Political Education on the Isle of Pines.... 63

4	THE NEW <u>MAMBISES</u>: EXILE AND THE SO-CALLED SUBJECTIVIST PHASE.......................73	
	Introduction..73	
	May-July 1955..74	
	Exile in Mexico and the Training of the Expeditionaries...........................77	
	An Important Recruit: Ernesto Guevara............86	
	Final Preparations...................................94	
5	POLITICAL EDUCATION IN THE REBEL ARMY: ARMED STRUGGLE AND THE ESTABLISHMENT OF THE GUERRILLAS................................107	
6	THE POLITICAL EDUCATION OF EXPERIENCE: THE ESTABLISHMENT OF POPULAR SUPPORT IN THE GUERRILLA <u>FOCO</u> AND THE <u>TERRITORIO LIBRE</u>.....127	
	The Setting...127	
	Relations with the Rural Population..............127	
	Segundo Frente "Frank País": The Myth of Guerrilla-Peasant Worker Unity Realized in the Civil Administration of a "Territorio Libre"...........................139	
	Conclusion..149	
7	THE POLITICAL EDUCATION OF COMBAT: THE MYTH OF THE GUERRILLA STRUGGLE IN THE SIERRA....157	
	The Political Education of Combat................157	
	Opposing Morales and the Demoralization of Batista's Army..................................157	
	The Stuff of Myth: Moving the Revolutionary Project Forward...............................166	
	The General Strike and Summer Offensive.........184	
8	FALL 1958: THE EXPANSION OF GUERRILLA STRUGGLE AND THE FURTHER GENERATION OF THE REBEL ARMY MYTH..201	
	The Invasion of the <u>Llano</u>........................201	
	Rebel Leadership: The Qualities of Cienfuegos...................................209	
	The Las Villas Campaign: From Combat Into the Myth................................210	
9	THE INSTITUTIONALIZATION OF MYTHS IN THE POLITICAL EDUCATION OF THE REBEL ARMY/FAR, 1959 to 1963 225	
	Myths in the Early Revolutionary Period, 1959-1963............................225	

Institutionalization: Rebel Army
    Responsibilities and the <u>Manual</u>
    <u>de Capacitación Cívica</u> 228
Revolutionary Instructors and Schools
    of Revolutionary Instruction................238
The Role and Political Content of <u>Verde</u>
    <u>Olivo</u> in the Political Education of
    the Cuban Military..........................242
Conclusion......................................259

Selected Chronology of Events...................273
Bibliography....................................275
Index...285

Acknowledgments

I would like to express my appreciation for the support, encouragement and positive criticism from my dissertation committee at the University of Alberta, especially my supervisor Elwood Murray. Thanks is due my family, the Killam Foundation and numerous graduate students who were willing to hear and discuss ideas. I extend special thanks to Maryon McClary, whose close support was crucial to the completion of the book, and to Jan Carrick, who prepared the typescript efficiently on short notice.

C. Fred Judson

1
The Revolutionary Myth in the Political Education of the Cuban Military

REVOLUTIONARY CONSCIOUSNESS

There is nothing automatic or inevitable in the making of socialist revolutions. Objective conditions may help set the stage, but they have not of themselves moved any society into revolution. To expect that they will is to fall into the mechanism so roundly condemned by Lenin.[1] In Batista's Cuba, as in czarist Russia, human actions made history. There is a relationship between objective conditions and the human actors in social history discernible on a common-sense level. Conditions act upon people and social classes, and actions are influenced by conditions. As Marx put it in his essay on the 1851 coup in France, "men make their own history, but they do not make it just as they please; they do not make it under circumstances chosen by themselves, but under circumstances directly found, given and transmitted from the past".[2]

Marx's dictum about human beings and history contains his usual dialectical interpretation of phenomena. Human beings act upon their environment and upon "objective conditions" to change them, i.e., to make history. And yet the actors are not free subjects. There is no *tabula rasa* upon which human action may engrave history. Action occurs within a given and defined set of circumstances, the objective conditions to which Marx refers. These conditions are no more nor less than the state of property and production relations, class hierarchies and inter-class relations as embodied in the state and ideology, and the stage of development which productive forces have reached. It follows, for Marxists, that it is impossible to interpret human actions in history as pure voluntarism. If there is to be debate, it may be over the relative weight and dialectical relationship of subjective and objective factors in a given event or process. In human history there is not the one without the other but, rather, their interplay.

Revolutionary theorists of socialism in the

twentieth century have dedicated much of their attention and practice to the subjective factors, those intellectual and emotional forces which have a leading role in the making of revolutions. Much of the political genius of Lenin as a revolutionary lies in his conception of the vanguard, the subjective force incarnate.[3] It is in his theory and practice in this area that he is most directly addressing the revolutionary role of the subjective forces. Lenin's theory of the vanguard, the dedicated and disciplined body of professional revolutionaries, reflected his concern to activate subjecttive forces capable of moving beyond the restraints of objective conditions. The idea was to inject revolutionary consciousness into the mass of the population, a consciousness which would be deeper than the periodic spontaneity manifested in revolts and jacqueries.

Much of Lenin's original conception of the revolutionary vanguard grew out of the objective conditions specific to czarist Russia. Bourgeois democratic forms were truncated and obscured; police repression and censorship haunted Russian social democracy, and a history of clandestinity contributed to the atmosphere of the time. Nevertheless, the larger historical lesson has generally been confirmed by the experience of socialist insurrections in this century. It has taken a dedicated and tight-knit group to lead successful insurrections in virtually every instance. Such groups have been responsible for engendering and extending revolutionary consciousness into the larger population.

The dedication and discipline of groups which lead insurrections and the subsequent revolutions are based on revolutionary consciousness. This can be defined, on the cognitive level, as the awareness of contradictions in a society which have reached a stage, that of crisis, where a revolutionary outcome is possible. The term "revolution" here is taken to mean the radical readjustment of class relations, the overthrow of the rule of one class by another, social revolution in the classical Marxist sense. This level of revolutionary consciousness can be achieved by political practice, observation and reasoning. However, such consciousness also includes an element of faith. It includes the conviction not only that such a resolution of contradictions is possible, but also desirable, necessary and imminent. Revolutionary consciousness implies faith and belief in victory, emotional identification with the cause of social revolution, and a belief that social regeneration will be made possible by insurrection and revolution.

Socialist revolutionary consciousness, that awareness of class conflict and militant faith that action and not merely the laws of motion of capitalist development will decide the struggle in favor of the proletariat and its allies, is the prerequisite for the formation and influence of leadership cadres. From Lenin to Mao, and from Fanon to Cabral, theorists of socialist revolution insist upon this. Further, their writings commonly pose as an essential goal the extension of revolutionary consciousness to the mass of the population. They advocate nothing less than the transformation of the extant political culture into a revolutionary political culture.

Revolutionary consciousness encompasses two aspects. One may be termed the rational, in that an individual's conviction that revolution is desirable and necessary for the given society derives from an analysis of that society and of human experiences within it. Here the distinction between personal experiences and observation may be vague, just as the distinction between the perception of isolated social phenomena such as individual poverty and generalizations about class conflict or exploitation may be vague. But it is the process of coming to revolutionary consciousness that is of concern here. The rational aspect of this process involves logic in the sense that phenomena are observed and/or experienced, and conclusions drawn therefrom. But the non-rational aspect, that involving emotion and faith, is just as important in coming to revolutionary convictions, and perhaps more important in impelling revolutionary action. The present study is an inquiry into the non-rational bases of revolutionary consciousness and action in the Cuban Revolution. It is argued that non-rational elements of revolutionary consciousness are crucial to revolutions. Indeed, it will be maintained that an understanding of revolutionary movements demands attention to the non-rational bases of action.

Specifically, the object of study is the role of social myth in the Cuban Revolution. "Social myth" is conceived to be non-rational, in that adherence to myth or its acceptance as a description of reality is an act of faith. The inheritance and use of social myths from Cuban history by revolutionaries in the 1950s, the making of a new social myth, that of the Rebel Army led by Fidel Castro, and the use of social myth in the political education of the revolutionary Cuban military are the main topics of discussion.

THE POLITICAL EDUCATION OF THE CUBAN MILITARY AS AN OBJECT OF STUDY

In revolutionary Cuba, the military is the center of power. Armed struggle established the revolution and the <u>Fuerzas Armadas Revolucionarias</u> (FAR) 'Revolutionary Armed Forces', defend it and enforce it. The Cuban military is the locus of revolutionary leadership. These truths are determined largely by the historical genesis of the anti-dictatorial, anti-neocolonialist struggle during and immediately after the Batista regime of 1952-1959. The antagonistic relationship of the Cuban revolution with imperialism also determines the continuing central political role of the military.

It is a combination of factors which makes for the historical and continuing centrality of the Cuban military in the revolutionary era. The combination can be pictured as a three-tiered system of relationships developing during the twentieth century history of Cuba and culminating in the crises which produced both the objective and subjective conditions for social revolution. The basis of the system of relationships is imperialism, the international economic and political domination of monopoly capital. In the case of Cuba, United States imperialism, i.e. monopoly capitalist interests and the state apparatus which those interests dominate in the United States, embodies the first tier of the relationship system. Imperialism, then, can be seen as the fundamental independent variable for the purposes of this study. All other variables in the system derive largely, though of course not exclusively, from the basic reality of imperialist economic and political domination of Cuba until its social revolution commenced.

The second tier of variables is comprised of emanations of imperialism. In the economic sphere of Cuban society, imperialist domination resulted in dependency and underdevelopment. Following the now almost classical definition,[4] Cuban economic dependency on imperialism meant that patterns and rates of economic growth were largely dependent on decisions made outside of Cuba. Foreign corporate decision-making, guided by the needs and aims of metropolitan capitalist accumulation, exercised the determining influence over the Cuban economy. In Cuba, decisions of the United States sugar monopoly interests determined the fate of investments and production of that dominant commodity and impinged upon all other sectors of the economy. Underdevelopment or, more accurately, uneven development, has been the general result of imperialist economic domination. Uneven development, in the case of Cuba, meant distorted capitalist development. The dictates of profit produced sectoral inequality, monoculture, urban-rural discrepancies in the extreme, boom and bust cycles and chronically high underemployment and unemployment, especially among the large rural population in Cuba.

In the second tier of variables, alongside economic dependency and its consequence, uneven development, is found political dependency. Again, it is the overriding reality of imperialism which is to be considered the theoretical source of dependency, in the political as well as in the economic sphere. The basic objective of imperialism is to maintain and improve conditions for capital accumulation which benefit, primarily, the monopoly capitalist interests based in the imperialistic power. In the case of Cuba, United States imperialism maintained a "favorable investment climate" first by means of direct military intervention in the years prior to 1934, under the Platt Amendment to the Cuban Constitution. But imperialist political domination of Cuba came increasingly to mean the political and financial support of Cuban political and economic elites which would serve the interests of United States monopoly capital. This is not to say that contradictions never emerged between United States monopoly capital and sectors of the capitalist class in Cuba. Certainly the populist and nationalist elements in the policies of Cuban regimes after 1933 emerged from these contradictions. Nevertheless, in terms of constituencies, the political elites of Cuba owed first loyalty to imperialism and those economic interests in Cuba allied to foreign monopoly capital. Economic dependency produced a situation in which an independent national bourgeoisie was impossible. The Cuban capitalist class and the Cuban state remained clients in the imperialist system. A contemporary characterization of this system applies to the general nature and purpose of the imperialist-dominated Cuban state apparatus: "The basic fact is that the United States has organized under its sponsorship and protection a neo-colonial system of client states ruled mainly by terror and serving the interests of a small local and foreign business and military elite".[5]

In simple terms, imperialist economic domination of Cuba produced an oligarchy and restricted the development of an indigenous capitalist class. This truncated and dependent national bourgeoisie thus failed to develop a full system of bourgeois democratic political participation. The political duty of the oligarchy, within the imperialist system, became that of repressing the majority adversely affected by uneven and dependent capitalist development. Thus, a tendency towards militarism and dictatorship appeared early in Cuba's republican era. No group could achieve political hegemony through the institutions of liberal bourgeois democracy and still serve the vital interests of imperialism and its economic clients. The final result was the Batista dictatorship and the bankruptcy of the traditional political parties in the 1950s.

The third tier of variables is also independent in the sense that it too, as imperialism, economic and political dependency, acts upon the dependent variables - the nature of the insurrectionary forces in the 1950s, the development of revolutionary consciousness among those forces, and the process of political education among the revolutionary forces. This third tier of variables, like the first two, can be seen as a part of the overall conjuncture of objective conditions which generated social revolution and revolutionary consciousness in Cuba. These variables are the absence of a politically-organized working class movement capable of leading an insurrection and establishing a revolutionary regime and the presence, in the 1950s, of a non-traditional, radical-reformist and petit bourgeois opposition. Uneven development of the economy, repression and state control of labor organizations produced the first variable. The dependent status of the national bourgeoisie and its consequent weakness, the division and corruption of the traditional opposition parties and the repression of the Batista dictatorship produced the conditions for the emergence of the second.

The independence of the insurrectionary forces during the struggle against Batista and their leadership of the social revolution which ensued evolved from the system of relationships outlined above. After the insurrection, the lack of a revolutionary party prepared to lead a social revolution and to resist domestic and imperialist reaction and counter-revolution ensured the political leadership of the Ejército Rebelde 'Rebel Army' led by Fidel Castro. The continuing antagonism of imperialism in the face of the Cuba revolution dictated that revolutionary power would have to retain its armed character. The original guerrilla leadership which led the armed struggle has maintained its central political role in Cuba, and the military has been the most politicized element of Cuban revolutionary society.

If the system of relationships outlined above, with imperialism as its base, determined the central role of armed revolutionary force in the Cuban revolution, the same system set the stage for the development of revolutionary consciousness in the Cuban military. I have chosen to investigate this revolutionary consciousness by an examination of the political education of the insurrectionists and the FAR in the period of insurrection and consolidation of revolutionary power. Thus, the study follows the process of political education until 1963-64, when the threat of direct imperialist invasion had abated, and when most of the domestic counter-revolution had been defeated. These years saw the establishment of political education in the military in patterns which have largely been maintained since then. The revolutionary transformation of political culture which has ensued will be traced to political education in the Rebel Army. In the interest of understanding the revolutionary political culture of contemporary Cuban society, then, it is reasonable to make political education in the military an object of study.

Political education, as a concept, is open to diverse interpretations. It could include the political socialization an individual receives during childhood, in the family, the school system and in institutions

such as churches. For a sociologist, it must include
social class position and experiences such as work, influences on socialization which extend through adult
life. I will define political education here as the
taking on (passive) or inculcation (active) of values,
attitudes or ideology pertaining to the political sphere
of human existence. The word "political" here implies
power and its use for human ends, however diverse. To
become politically educated, then, is to become aware,
or conscious of human power structures and their ends.
These ends may include monopoly, equality, some conception of justice or what is good, or simple personal
pleasure. The ends of power may also be defined in
class terms, in that power is sought and exercised to
advance class interests. Becoming politically educated
is to take on some mental stance towards political behavior that organizes and explains what is observed and
experienced. Political education will shape and determine one's activity and attitudes in the political
sphere, whether that be passive support of or resistance
to a power structure, active participation in support of
a power structure, or rebellion and revolutionary activity. Clearly, no political education is neutral. Its
object is commitment, the making of choices and, in this
sense, political education is ideological.

Political education among the Cuban insurrectionaries was both rebel, in the sense explored by French
existential writers,[6] and revolutionary. It was revolutionary in that it created a world-view which assumed
class conflict and a commitment to social revolution.
It was both passive, in the sense of the impact of experience, and active, in the sense that a revolutionary
outlook was consciously pursued and inculcated. The
personal experience of individual revolutionaries became, in active political education, symbolic of class
experiences and class struggle. The figures of the
Rebel Army have had a dual role in political education.
First, their lives and personalities are the material of
political education, of the revolutionary myths and the
legends, and large numbers of Cubans relate easily to
these lives and experiences. Second, they organize the
political education and the myths themselves. They are
the stuff of an impelling and a sustaining revolutionary
mythology, and they conduct the political education,
both of the military and of the general population,
which is organized around that mythology.

THE CONCEPT OF REVOLUTIONARY MYTH

In his dual quest for the sources of heroic virtues in human history and for the spiritual renaissance of revolutionary Marxism, Georges Sorel investigated the role of the unconscious and the non-rational in human behavior.[7] As with many others at the end of the 19th century, Sorel attacked what he saw as the enthronement of rationalism and the optimism of the Enlightenment in the form of positivism: "In Sorel's time...the idea of progress was both a law of historical development, a philosophy of history and, as a consequence, also a political philosophy".[8] For Sorel, the unbounded optimism about the inevitability of human progress that positivism and the revisionist Marxism of Bernstein projected was unwarranted. Rationalism had become decadent and self-satisfied; it had become, in a word, a retrograde ideology. The whole of Sorel's work, The Illusions of Progress, is an argument against rationalism which, with capitalism, had purged the human soul of its heroic virtues. As another student of the non-rational and revolution put it, "the rationalist experience has had the effective paradox of leading humanity to the disconsolate conviction that Reason [sic] can show it no path. Rationalism has served only to discredit Reason".[9] Sorel sought to re-establish the role of the non-rational, the unconscious, as the motor force of the great movements in history. He posed pessimism against rationalist optimism as the source of energy in human movements. "The pessimist", he wrote, "regards social conditions as forming a system bound together by an iron law which cannot be evaded, so that the system is given, as it were, in one block, and cannot disappear except in a catastrophe which involves the whole".[10] The hope that illumines the "march towards deliverance" from the whole, and which anticipates catastrophe is, for Sorel, the non-rational at work in history: "A man would not go very far in the examination either of the laws of his own wretchedness or of fate, which so much shocks the ingenuousness of our pride, if he were not borne up by the hope of putting an end to these tyrannies by an effort, to be attempted with the help of a whole band of companions".[11]

Sorel was fascinated by the energy which religious conviction had lent, in history, to Christianity, to the Greeks, to Calvinism and to Judaism. Faith provided the perseverance and moral strength of these great movements: "In this warlike excitement which accompanies this will-to-deliverance the courageous man finds a satisfaction which is sufficient to keep up his ardour".[12] The will-to-deliverance Sorel saw as an ancient human drive to connect with the infinite. Rationalism had negated the infinite and left humanity without a substitute. Religious and spiritual values, that which fuelled the creative processes in war, art and industry, had been withered, and the energizing myths not replaced. In the Age of Enlightenment and since, for Sorel, "all that is best in the modern mind is derived from this 'torment of the infinite'"[13] and some new myth was required to resurrect heroic virtues. Across the world, Mariátegui, an avid reader of Sorel, agreed: "Neither reason nor science can satisfy the need for the infinite...reason itself has shown that only myth has the previous virtue of filling the deep 'I'".[14]

For Sorel, sacrifice and heroism in social movements came not from reason, but from conviction and belief. A doctrine "expressed only in words" was not enough to impel a movement. Rather, "one dies for opinions and not for knowledge, for what one believes and not for what one knows".[15] Sorel noted that "men who are participating in a great social movement always picture their coming action as a battle in which their cause is certain to triumph".[16] This element of finality and transcendence was the key to great social movements and Sorel called such convictions myths: "Such constructions I propose to call myths. The syndicalist general strike and Marx's catastrophic revolution are such myths...".[17]

The power of social myth lies in its ability to "overcome the probabilistic world of scientific fact",[18] the limitations of logical premises. Utopias are not adequate to inspire mass movements, according to Sorel, since they are purely intellectual constructs logically connected to the status quo, and can be no more than reformist.[19] Myth, on the other hand, embodies infinity in its confrontation with catastrophe. It conjures up the vision of some final struggle.

Sorel's self-appointed mission was to restore myth to Marxism, since he was convinced that "as long as there are no myths accepted by the masses, one may go on talking of revolts indefinitely, without ever provoking any revolutionary movement".[20] If socialism could recapture the elan of pre-parliamentary Marxism via a new revolutionary myth, it could effectively prepare for and force the final confrontation with the bourgeoisie. Sorel's thinking centered on "the interaction between the psychological and the material dimensions of the revolutionary mentality".[21] He was searching for the material basis of socialist revolutionary myth, and thought he found it in the production process of the worker. He envisaged industry, war and art as sharing the same roots in creativity, arguing that the worker, as a warrior or an artist, seeks to avoid incessant reproduction and to achieve improvements and innovations. Creativity and industrial discipline necessary for improvements sprang from deep psychological roots. In following the thought of Henri Bergson,[22] Sorel conceived the creative moment as an occasion on which the individual experiences the emotion of contact with the inner self. It is a moment of complete freedom, enjoyed "pre-eminently when we are making an effort to create a new individuality in ourselves, thus endeavoring to break the bonds of habit which enclose us".[23]

It was this deeper life assumed to exist in every individual that Sorel saw as responsible for creativity and heroic virtues, and which he argued was stirred by epic or by myth. The actual genesis of such moments was an impenetrable process; they lived "especially on mysteries, shadows and indeterminate nuances".[24] Sorel maintained that the production process was linked to the unconscious and the inner being and that revolutionary socialism, as the historical potential of the proletariat, was wrapped in such mystery:

> Socialism is necessarily very obscure, since it deals with production, i.e. with the most mysterious part of human activity, and since it proposes to being about a radical transformation of that region which it is impossible to describe with the clearness that is to be found in more superficial regions. No effort of thought, no progress of knowledge, no rational induction will ever dispel the mystery which envelops socialism; and it is because the philosophy of Marx recognized fully this feature of socialism that it acquired the right to serve as the starting-point of socialist inquiry.[25]

The mythic quality of Marxism was insisted upon by Sorel. He held that the power of myth was in its entirety, "which is alone important; its parts are only of interest in so far as they bring out the main idea".[26] It was useless to quibble, for example, about the ultimate accuracy of Marx's description of the conflict between the proletariat and the bourgeoisie in Volume I of <u>Capital</u>. What was important was the mythical element, "the myth in which socialism is wholly comprised, i.e. a body of images capable of evoking instinctively all the sentiments which correspond to the different manifestations of the war undertaken by socialism against modern society".[27] The descriptions of class conflict in Marxism were not meant to be assessed on their predictive qualities, Sorel argued. Rather, "the different terms which Marx uses to describe the preparation for the decisive combat are not to be taken literally as statements of fact about a determined future...Marx wishes us to understand that the whole preparation of the proletariat depends solely on the organization of a stubborn, increasing and passionate resistance to the present order of things".[28]

Sorel was not concerned with what we might currently call the validity of the revolutionary myth of socialism, since "myths are not descriptions of things, but expressions of a determination to act".[29] The crucial aspect of myth was its ability to produce action. To produce action it had to inspire faith in victory and deliverance and to provide security from all logical refutation. The myth's strength was in its call to action and not in the "details which will actually form part of the history of the future". The "heterogeneity between the ends in view and the ends actually realized"[30] was to be expected, and did not detract from the myth's historical efficacy. Sorel stressed that myth was a dynamic historical force itself. As Richard Vernon wrote in relation to this notion of Sorel's, "beliefs of the order of revolutionary projections enter so fundamentally into the situation itself that they cannot, for logical reasons, be measured against it...at the moment of adhering to such a belief, one cannot know whether it is true or not, for its truth depends on the degree of adherence which it secures".[31]

Against the positivist appropriation of Marxism and its manifestation in what Sorel called "parliamentary socialism", he saw ranged the energies of revolutionary syndicalism. It was his admiration for this vital working-class movement that led him to denote the general strike as the new revolutionary myth which could re-invigorate socialism. Myths of this kind had to be the "framing of a future, in some indeterminate time"; they had to "enclose within them all the strongest inclinations of a people, of a party or of a class, inclinations which recur to the mind with the insistence of instincts in all the circumstances of life and...give an aspect of complete reality to the hopes of immediate action by which, more easily than by any other method, men can reform their desires, passions and mental activity".[32] For Sorel, the myth of the revolutionary general strike fulfilled these qualities.

Strike activity around the turn of the century was the source of Sorel's inspiration. He felt that the organization and experience of strikes

> engendered in the proletariat the noblest, deepest and most moving sentiments that they possess; the general strike groups them all in a co-ordinated picture and, by bringing them together, gives to each one of them its maximum of intensity; appealing to their painful memories of particular conflicts, it colours with an intense life all the details of the composition presented to consciousness. We thus obtain that intuition of Socialism which language cannot give us with perfect clearness - and we obtain it as a whole, perceived instantaneously.[33]

The revolutionary socialist myth of the general strike embodied and clarified all the principles of Marxism, argued Sorel, in one indivisible whole. It expressed class conflict much better than daily experience in the work-place. Strike experience itself threw class conflict into sharper relief than the piece-work system, "but all oppositions become extraordinarily clear when conflicts are supposed to be enlarged to the size of the general strike; then all parts of the economico-juridical structure, in so far as the latter is looked upon from the point of view of the class war, reach the summit of their perfection; society is plainly divided into two camps, and only into two, on a field of battle".[34] The conception of the general strike would bring the interpretation of experience as manifestations of the class war, in every aspect of life, into sharp and permanent focus. The catastrophic and eschatological aspects of socialism ride within the idea of the general strike as the final battle against the bourgeoisie: "The general strike must be taken as a whole and undivided, and the passage from capitalism to Socialism conceived as a catastrophe, the development of which baffles description".[35]

Sorel, it has been accurately noted, used the doctrines of Marx "selectively".[36] He was more interested in the notion that class conflict moved human society forward than in the actual mechanics of socialist revolution and the nature of socialist society. Ethical and moral values for Sorel were absolute, not socially determined, as for Marx: "Sorel believed in independent and absolute moral values: the historicism of the Hegelian-Marxist tradition was never acceptable to him, still less the view that issues of basic moral or political principle can be solved by social scientists, psychologists, sociologists, anthropologists..."[37] His rejection of economism was linked to the rejection of utopias. Utopias were predictions for the future which were projected from the analysis of given situations. Thus, Sorel had little interest in Marx's practical work on revolutionary projects such as a political party or the theory of proletarian dictatorship. Such a victory of the working class, paradoxically, would deprive society of that which gave it heroic stature and creativity: the condition of struggle, the confrontation with a worthy adversary: "Only against a strong and vigorous opponent can truly heroic qualities be developed"[38] The image of a final struggle and victory inherent in every social myth was what made for an energetic creative society, according to Georges Sorel. The grand social myth of the time, for Sorel, was that of revolutionary socialism, decadent in his time, and to be revived with the myth of the general strike. Thus, as Berlin points out, Sorel's concern was not with the politics of socialist revolution, but with the vitality its myths could give to the proletariat, which he perceived as the source of creativity and as the salvation of modern society. He distrusted the total historical fulfillment inherent in Marx's scheme of class struggle and stages of history. His was a "greatly Sorelified Marx".[39] As he would have claimed, the myth was more important than its message.

The myth of the general strike, influenced by syndical practice and the independence of the syndicalist movement from parliamentary socialism, was not to be the only mobilizing myth for socialism in the twentieth century. A composite of inspiring images known as "proletarian strategy" mobilized the urban proletariat of Russia in defense of the Bolshevik Revolution during the Civil War and foreign intervention.[40] Antonio Gramsci valued Sorel's work, and conceived myth as "a political ideology which presents itself not as a cold utopia nor as a mere doctrinaire rationalization, but as a concrete creation of the imagination which acts upon a dispersed and pulverized people to provoke and organize the collective will".[41] In Peru, José Carlos Mariátegui wrote and spoke of the redemptive power of the myth of social revolution. He foreshadowed Fidel Castro's call in the 1950s for the youth of Cuba to lead the revolt against Batista and redeem the heritage of Cuba's past heroes and struggles: "The masses require unity. The masses want faith. For that reason, their soul rejects the corrosive, dissolving and pessimistic voice of those who negate and of those who doubt, and look for the optimist, cordial, young and fertile voice of those who affirm and of those who believe".[42] Mariátegui concluded that the pre-World War I philosophies of evolutionism, nationalism and historicism had undermined the rightful weapon of the proletariat, revolutionary Marxism. To break up the de facto unity of the two antagonistic classes, myth was necessary:

> What most clearly and neatly differentiates the bourgeoisie and the proletariat is the myth. The bourgeoisie now has none. It has become incredulous, skeptical, nihilistic. The proletariat has its myth: social revolution. The bourgeoisie negates, the proletariat affirms...the strength of the revolutionaries is not in their science; it is in their faith, their passion, their will. It is a religion, a mystical, spiritual force. The force of the myth.[43]

Other examples of revolutionary myth in this century are Frantz Fanon's peasant revolt and the violence of the oppressed,[44] Mao Dze-dong's "New Democratic Revolution",[45] and Amilcar Cabral's "Unity and Struggle".[46] Their common elements are their entirety, in the sense that each myth contains both the analysis of the opposing forces and the redemptive and catastrophic vision of the future that inspires action, and their pitch beyond the rational limits of extant social reality.

THE REVOLUTIONARY MYTH: THE CASE OF CUBA

I have presented the concept of revolutionary myth to this point as integral to the understanding of revolutionary consciousness. The theme of the genesis and use of revolutionary myths will be the organizing thread in the body of this study. The concept of myth should help to illuminate the frequent desperation and unpredictability of insurrections and revolutions. As one student of revolution has noted, lamenting the failure of social science literature "to capture the essence of revolutions":

> Revolutions are desperate acts; they take unpredictable turns; they can be reversed or arrested; but above all, they aim at fundamental transformation of society and of man himself. They are fuelled by ideologies which do not simply take advantage of discontent but point as well to a picture of the future. They are led by men, even when they seem most spontaneous. Revolutions occur because men want them to occur and not simply because of some general feeling of malaise...individual discontent must be translated into collective discontent, and it is this translation process which raises questions about leadership, ideas and mobilization.[47]

Sorel likely would have introduced the term "myth" into the last sentence of Kochanek's statement. Leadership, for Sorel, was a question of the ability to mobilize the masses around a myth: "For Sorel, leaders are not made by either the quantity or quality of knowledge they possess, but in virtue of how many men they can captivate and galvanize by the projection of a novel myth".[48]

The discussion of the role of myth in the Cuban revolution and, in particular, its role in the political education of the revolutionary armed forces, requires some comparisons with Sorel's conception and historical locus. Sorel's myth of the general strike was fashioned by a direct anti-capitalist struggle inside an imperialist power. Political parties professing socialism were full participants in the French parliamentary system. In Cuba, the situation was one of a national liberation struggle that had been overwhelmed and postponed by the expansion of United States imperialism. Thus, anti-imperialism was a constant element of the Cuban struggle. Direct anti-capitalism was not manifest from the beginning, entering the mobilizing myths openly only late in the revolutionary process. Further, in Cuba, it was insurrectionary practice that established the sustaining myths of the revolution, not a myth generated by organized working-class practice, as in Sorel's France.

A distinction can be made here between the mobilizing myth and the sustaining myth. The myth of the general stike never had the opportunity of becoming a sustaining myth, since no social revolution resulted from the myth in France. In Cuba, as in other countries with a successful insurrection and the subsequent establishment of a socialist regime, the role of myth is changed after victory. It must aid in sustaining the revolution, particularly in poorer countries where continuing sacrifices are required, and where imperialism and domestic capital threatens counter-revolution. Continuing revolutionary vigilance and the need for sacrifices on the part of the population result in the virtual institutionalization of revolutionary mythology in such a situation as Cuba's in the 1960s.

Historical Genesis and the Continuum of Revolutionary Myths in Cuba

Revolutionary myths in Cuba employed by Fidel Castro's M-26 and later by the revolutionary regime have deep roots in Cuba's history and culture. The cultural and historical legacy which entered into the mobilizing and sustaining revolutionary myths derived from colonialism and imperialism. An unevenly developed economy, one which, for all its statistical rankings among the top Latin American societies,[49] produced widespread unemployment, underemployment, and the usual indices of poverty and exploitation, was readily available for incorporation into revolutionary myths. Dependency and its all too apparent manifestations, both in the colonial period and, later, under United States imperialism, provided the material basis for the combination of radical analysis and non-rational futurism inherent in every revolutionary myth.

From the colonial era, slavery and the independence struggle stand out as elements available for appropriation and use in myths. Ideological and cultural forbears such as Antonio Maceo, the great military leader of the Wars of Independence, and Jose Martí, the political organizer and prophet of the nationalist movement, were only the leaders of a pantheon of heroes and nationalist figures incorporated into the myths which merged in the mid-twentieth century. After independence, the increasing weight of imperialism in Cuban life and the near-total failure of Cuban political elites to realize the promise of the nationalist movement enhanced the stature of the nineteenth century heroes. The failure of social revolution in the 1930s

and the usurpation and distortion of populist revolt by
armed gangs in the 1940s set the stage for the regeneration of the national redemptive myth with Eddy Chibás,
leader and founder of the Ortodox Party in 1947. Martyrs and heroes of the twentieth century joined those of
previous eras in the myth of unconsummated nationalism,
and eventually in anti-imperialism.

The underlying, long-term Cuban revolutionary myth
of national redemption, expressed in the phrase, <u>el
deber del cubano</u> 'the duty of a Cuban', has its roots in
fact and experience. The stuff of the national redemptive myth finds its essence in an ultimate faith in
Cuba's national destiny, in the trajectory of its history, in its people, and in the inevitability of deliverance from the legacies of colonialism and imperialism. The myth transcends the limits of probability and
rationality, proposing the creation of "another Cuba".
As one of Castro's letters from prison put it, "to revolutionize this country from top to bottom"[50] was the
non-rational, extra-logical center of this particular
myth.

The element of faith in success is essential to the
creation of daring and sacrifice in the Cuban insurrection. The inspiring myth at the beginning of armed
struggle was that of a new and redemptive revolutionary
generation, linked and identified with past martyrology,
but untainted by associations with traditional political
parties. The myth proposed that the new generation,
which called itself the Generation of Marti's Centenary,
could repeat and surpass the exploits of 1868-1898 and
the 1930s, that it was past glory reincarnated, that it
could right the wrongs in Cuban society, that it could
defeat Batista. This myth became incarnate, even in defeat, in the assault on the Moncada Barracks, July 26,
1953. Its moral pitch and the contradictions in Cuba
made the myth of a new revolutionary generation, ready
to sacrifice itself for national redemption, a material
force.

The Dynamic Quality of Revolutionary Myths in Cuba

Cuban myths appear to be cumulative. The initial
stuff of their generation is national history and the
culture produced by that history. Faith in national
redemption and Marti's vision of a prosperous and just
Cuban independence are the inspiring essence. Changes
in myths and new myths have two sources. The first can
be described as a dialectic, in that one phenomenon
calls forth an antithesis. Bourgeois and imperialist
myths and practice call forth proletarian and anti-imperialist myths and practice. Although thinkers such

as Sorel and Mariátegui argued that the bourgeoisie had in fact no myth, and that that was a symptom of its decadence and readiness for the dustbin of history, there are some elements of bourgeois and imperialist ideology which yet approach the quality of myths. An outstanding example is the notion that free market forces determine one's material lot. Another is the conviction that foreign investment equals economic development and progress. Such myths, which help sustain imperialism, elicit counter-myths when the reality of imperialist practice is contrary to its ideologies. Thus, in Cuba, when armed assaults were being launched from United States shores and the threat of direct invasion was being voiced, there arose the myth of historical Cuban anti-imperialism. Martí and Maceo were appropriated, as in the 1930s, for the myth, more of Cuba's troubles were ascribed to imperialism, and domestic resistance to social revolution was more closely linked to imperialism.

The second source of dynamism and innovation in revolutionary myths is the experience of struggle. In Cuba, for example, armed struggle, impelled by one set of myths, created new revolutionary myths. The development and transformation of myths and the genesis of new myths emerged out of the insurrectionary war and the revolutionary process which ensued. Reaction and counter-revolution, treachery, internal dissension and sectarianism, defections from M-26, the reforms of the revolutionary regime, and the development of mass institutions such as the popular militia and the Committees for the Defense of the Revolutions all had their effect on revolutionary mythology. The passage of time and the institutionalization of the Cuban Revolution[51] also had their effect. Much of the revolutionary mythology became institutionalized and, in fact, became integral to the new political culture.[52] At this point, while myths still mobilized human energies for action, they also became sustaining myths.

Sustaining myths in revolutionary Cuba have several elements. First, they are comprised of the legends of Moncada and the ensuing imprisonment of the survivors from the Generation of the Centenary, exile in Mexico, the voyage of the Granma, the guerrilla struggle in the Sierra Maestra, the invasion of the llano 'lowlands', and the final military victory over the Batista army. The leaders, martyrs and heroes of the struggle are distributed among the different social sectors of Cuban society - students, workers, peasants and declassé petits bourgeois. Second, the revolutionary regime's actions and reforms help build the sustaining myths, especially during the period of defections, the emigration of large numbers of Cubans, the literacy campaign, the Lucha contra Bandidos 'struggle against bandits', the Playa Girón invasion and the October Crisis.

Third, the official embrace of Marxism-Leninism contributed to the sustaining myths, as it accelerated the Cuban appropriation of international revolutionary culture and traditions. Proletarian and socialist international solidarity became one of the central sustaining myths. And fourth, the experience and traditions of the Revolutionary Armed Forces provided a mainstay of the sustaining mythology. The FAR represent and embody heroism, sacrifice and anti-imperialism, and are held up as a popular and revolutionary army, contrasted to the "mercenary" and anti-popular army of Batista.

Revolutionary Myths in the Political Education of the Cuban Military

Myths are the repository of revolutionary values, whatever the details of their contents. Political education in Cuba is the taking on and inculcation of those values. Both social myth and political education aim at commitment and action, the achievement of revolutionary goals, the transformation of society and individuals. Although Sorel cautioned against the examination of the parts of myths, the bulk of this study will do just that. But, here, the object is not to weaken the myths or attack them on logical grounds. Rather, the theme of myth is employed to get at the stuff and direction of political education of the Cuban military during the critical years of struggle and the establishment of the socialist regime.

There will be several stages to this inquiry into myths and political education. First, I will indulge in an extensive historical discussion of the sources of myths which motivated the left-wing Ortodoxos, students and workers who formed the Generation of the Centenary, the group which attacked the Moncada Barracks in Santiago. An attempt will be made to elucidate the forms and content of the political education of these rebels. It will be shown that much of their political education was of an experiential nature. Not only did the rebels have Cuban history to inspire their project for political and social reforms; they also came to political values through their confrontations with the repressive apparatus of the Batista regime and through their gropings for effective forms of organization and resistance.

The early period of rebellion - the attack on Moncada, with the massacre, imprisonment and exile of the survivors - is also examined as myth-making. These early experiences of what would be the core of the Rebel Army took on the characteristics of social myth in that they were compared to the exploits of past Cuban heroes and martyrs. The experiences were seen by the surviving

Rebel Army as part of the continuing Cuban duty of national redemption and as symbolic of the character and destiny of the Cuban population as a whole.

The examination of myth-making, the stuff of myth and political education which focused on myths generated from Cuban history and myths created in active struggle against Batista will be largely analytic and narrative. The materials I will be using to discuss the political education of the Rebel Army thus focus on rebel self-perceptions. As the struggle against Batista advanced and the Rebel Army grew stronger, their own myths, developed from struggle, became a more central element of political education. The chapters on the guerrilla period will attempt to convey this development.

In these same chapters, I will be examining guerrilla-peasant relations and how there developed the Rebel Army self-perception as an army united with the peasantry, fighting for agrarian reform and social gains in the benefit of rural Cuba. This self-perception assumed the characteristics of social myth during the insurrectionary war and, afterwards, in the first years of the revolution. Other equally important themes that were elements of guerrilla political education which assumed the characteristics of social myth are those of the Rebel Army as morally superior to the regular army, the Rebel Army as political vanguard and rightful leader of all resistance to Batista, the political and military supremacy of the guerrilla army in the mountains over the M-26 urban resistance, and the Rebel Army as the defender of national sovereignty.

Social myths that motivated guerrilla struggle, it is argued, were first easily appropriated from Cuban history, and then were created in the experience of insurrectionary struggle. Together, they formed the basis of political education in the Rebel Army. Political education after January 1959 to which the last chapter is devoted, employed the amalgamated myths to sustain revolutionary spirt in veterans and to arouse it in recruits. At this point Rebel Army political education began to reach a broader audience. The Rebel Army was expanded in size and the militias were created to combat counter-revolutionary bands in the mountains and to prepare against imperialist invasion. Further, the political education of an entire nation was undertaken, with these social myths as its base. More people were brought to feel part of the social myths which embody revolutionary values, in the sense that the revolutionary power sought to create the feeling that one was participating in events of historical stature. The addition of Marxism-Leninism brought a comprehensive framework to the set of social myths which comprised political education at that point. The consequent notion of the Cuban Socialist Revolution united all the social myths in political education in a coherent system.

NOTES

1. V. I. Lenin, What Is To Be Done? (1902, rpt. Beijing: Foreign Languages Press, 1975). In Chapter Two, Lenin attacks mechanistic reliance upon the contradictions of capitalism, productive forces and spontaneity for the emergence of socialism.
2. Karl Marx, "The 18th Brumaire of Louis Napoleon", in The Marx-Engels Reader, ed. Robert Tucker (New York: Norton, 1972), p. 437.
3. Lenin's What Is To Be Done? contains his thinking on this subject, and his outline for the role of the revolutionary vanguard in the preparations for the Bolshevik Revolution.
4. See Theotonio dos Santos, "The Structure of Dependency", in Readings in United States Imperialism, ed. Kuang-tih Fann and Donald Hodges (Boston: Porter Sargent, 1971), p. 226: "...a situation in which the economy of certain countries is conditioned by the development and expansion of another economy to which the former is subjected."
5. Noam Chomsky and Edward S. Herman, The Political Economy of Human Rights; The Washington Connection and Third World Fascism, Vol. I (Montreal: Black Rose Books, 1979), p. ix.
6. See Albert Camus, The Rebel, tr. Anthony Bower (New York: Knopf, 1961).
7. See Georges Sorel, The Illusions of Progress, ed. and tr. John and Charlotte Stanley (1908; rpt. Berkeley: University of California Press, 1969) and Reflections on Violence, tr. T. E. Hulme (London: Allen and Unwin, 1925), both passim. Academic studies of Sorel's thought include Irving Louis Horowitz, Radicalism and the Revolt Against Reason: The Social Theories of Georges Sorel (London: Routledge and Kegan Paul, 1961); Richard Vernon, Commitment and Change. Georges Sorel and the Idea of Revolution (Toronto: University Press, 1978); Michel Charzat, Georges Sorel et la Révolution au XXme Siècle (Paris: Hachette, 1977).
8. John and Charlotte Stanley, "Introduction" in The Illusions of Progress, by Georges Sorel, p. xiii.
9. Jose Carlos Mariátegui, El alma matinal (1925, rpt. Lima: Biblioteca Amauta, 1972), p. 23. Unless indicated otherwise, all translations in this thesis are by the author.
10. Sorel, Reflections on Violence, p. 11
11. Ibid.
12. Ibid., p. 15.
13. Reflections, p. 27
14. Mariátegui, op. cit., p. 23
15. Sorel, citing Ernest Renan, 19th century religious historian, in Reflections, p. 26.
16. Ibid, p. 22

17. Ibid.
18. Horowitz, p. 133.
19. Sorel, Reflections, p. 32.
20. Ibid.
21. John L. Stanley, "Introduction", From Georges Sorel. Essays in Socialism and Philosophy, by Georges Sorel, ed. John L. Stanley (New York: Oxford University Press, 1976), p. 40.
22. Sorel, Reflections, p. 28: "...utilizing the enlightenment we owe to the Bergsonian philosophy".
23. Reflections, p. 30.
24. Ibid., p. 159.
25. Ibid., p. 164.
26. Reflections, p. 135.
27. Ibid., p. 137.
28. Ibid., p. 148.
29. Reflections, p. 132.
30. Ibid., p. 136.
31. Ibid,. pp. 16-17.
32. Reflections, p. 133.
33. Ibid., p. 137.
34. Reflections, p. 144.
35. Ibid., p. 164.
36. Isaiah Berlin, "Georges Sorel:, in Against the Current. Essays in the History of Ideas, ed. Henry Hardy (London: Hogarth Press, 1979), pp. 296-332.
37. Berlin, p. 310.
38. Ibid., p. 313.
39. Berlin, p. 312.
40. Antonio Gramsci, Note sul Machiavelli, sulla politica e sullo stato moderno (Rome, 1971), p. 18, cited by Hugo García Salvatecci, Georges Sorel y José Carlos Mariátegui (Lima: Ubicación Ideológica del Amauta, 1979), p. 197.
41. See Leon Trotsky, Military Writings (New York: Merit Publishers, 1969), passim.
42. Mariátegui, Ideología y política (Lima: Biblioteca Amauta, 1971), p. 110.
43. Mariátegui, El alma matinal (Lima: Biblioteca Amauta, 1972), p. 27.
44. Frantz Fanon, The Wretched of the Earth (New York: Grove Press, 1964), passim. See also Lewis Coser, "The Myth of Peasant Revolt", in Coser, Continuities in the Study of Social Conflict (New York: Free Press, 1967), pp. 213-22.
45. Mao Dze-dong, "On New Democracy", in Selected Works, Vol. II (Beijing: Foreign Languages Press, 1965), pp. 339-84.
46. Amilcar Cabral, Unity and Struggle. Speeches and Writings, tr. Michael Wolfers (London: Heinemann, 1980), passim.

47. Stanley Kochanek, "Perspectives on the Study of Revolution and Social Change", *Comparative Politics*, 5, No. 3 (April 1973), pp. 318-9.

48. Horowitz, p. 136.

49. See Boris Goldenberg, *The Cuban Revolution and Latin America* (New York: Praeger, 1965), pp. 120-42 and James O'Connor, *The Origins of Socialism in Cuba* (Ithaca: Cornell University Press, 1970), pp. 12-36, on the pre-1959 economy.

50. See Robert Merle, *Moncada, premier combat de Fidel Castro, 26 juillet 1953* (Paris: Hachette, 1965), pp. 347-8.

51. The phrase is taken from *Cuban Studies*, Vol. 6, Nos. 1-2 (January and July, 1976), entitled "The Institutionalization of the Revolution".

52. See Richard Fagen, *The Transformation of Political Culture in Cuba* (Stanford: Stanford University Press, 1969), passim.

2
The Foundations of Political Education in the Cuban Revolutionary Generation

INTRODUCTION

    In the Cuba of 1952, groups of young people responded to the military coup which returned Fulgencio Batista to power. Their response, in the form of demonstrations, pamphleteering, uneven confrontations with the police and, eventually, armed assaults and sabotage, had the backing of no organized sectors of society. Neither the labor unions nor the established political parties sponsored these youths. The opposition they undertook to present developed from their own experiences, outrage and analyses of Cuban society. Once embarked on the road of resistance to dictatorship, a proportion of Cuba's youth never ceased their activity. Ultimately they were to lead an armed insurrection via guerrilla and urban struggle, and establish the conditions for the first Latin American experience of revolutionary socialism in power. In this chapter, I investigate, to some extent, the nature of this proportion of Cuban youth and suggest the specifically Cuban origins of some revolutionary myths and ideas which motivated their struggle against Batista.

    There are three questions to be addressed in a discussion of this youthful insurrectionary vanguard. First, what was the general political situation at the time the movement led by Fidel Castro was formed? Second, who were the dedicated revolutionaries? And third, what was their motivation? What, if any, was their ideology?

    The outstanding fact of Cuban politics in 1952, of course, was the coup of March 10, when Batista, fearing his electoral defeat, took power with the aid of many old proteges and cronies in the army.[1] The regime he replaced, that of President Prío Socarrás (1948-52), and its predecessor, that of Grau San Martín (1944-48), were themselves largely discredited. Wide-scale graft and corruption had accompanied both regimes.[2] The 1940 Constitution, a progressive and reformist document, had been, in practice, shelved. Opposition to the coup from the party of Prío and Grau, the Partido Revolucionario Cubano-Auténtico, generated little enthusiasm. Among the students, traditionally an active political sector, rival <u>bonches</u> 'gangs', or 'action groups'[3] prevented any real unity. In a situation where the traditional bourgeois opposition was discredited in the eyes of both the middle class and the majority population, i.e. the peasantry and the working class, the radical option was not well represented by the Communist party (the Partido Socialista Popular - PSP). Its potential was besmirched by the history of Stalinism and opportunism, which had culminated in paternalism in the trade-union movement and in a tacit alliance with Batista from the late 1930s to the opening of the Cold War.[4] The non-communist trade union movement was sunk into Mujalism (union paternalism, corruption and collaboration with the government was called "Mujalism" after the dominant leader, Eusebio Mujal) and functioned to suppress worker militancy. The Cuban bourgeoisie - large landowners, agricultural interests, bankers and industrialists - with few exceptions was compromised with Batista and with imperialism. Fatalism permeated the body politic of the potentially revolutionary sectors - the working class and petite bourgeoisie.[5] The situation has been called one of "hegemonic crisis"[6], wherein no social class is cohesive enough to impose its political control or ideology. Farber calls it a "deadlock" in which authoritarianism may flourish; he sees, in fact, a Bonapartist situation.

Those who first responded to the coup were either students themselves or were closely associated with students. The University of Havana had long been a center of politicization and agitation, particularly in the 1933 overthrow of Machado. For those who were politically conscious students in the 1944-1952 period and during the Batista dictatorship after 1952, political education leading to insurrectionism was twofold. Both formal study and daily experience provided the political education of the future cadres. These first insurrectionists of the Batista period came to a commitment to action partly through an identification with past struggles in Cuba, especially the Wars of Independence and the overthrow of Machado. This intellectual identification and patriotism became merged with the brutal realities of Cuba in their own lives. Confrontations with the police in nationalist demonstrations and the dimensions of dependent development provided a direct political education.[8] There were concrete lessons in the streets and on the campus for the future insurrectionists[9] and such lessons became a legacy contributing to the formation of the ideology of the Rebel Army and the FAR in later years.

Like much of Latin America, Cuba suffered the permanent crisis of uneven dependent development in the twentieth century. The great national problems which were motifs in the Wars of Independence were not to be resolved in the regimes after 1898. Racism, social injustice, uneven economic development, boom and bust agriculture, extremes of land tenure, chronic unemployment and underemployment, corruption of the political, judicial and law enforcement apparatuses - all remained on the immediate agenda for reforms. The national bourgeoisie was too land-oriented, too closely tied to imperialism, too involved in conspicuous consumption, and too weak as a class to take the great problems in hand.

In the Latin American societies of this century, insurrectionism intending the resolution of the major social problems via social revolution has always been able to recruit cadres from the universities, and even from the high schools. To say this is not to deny the other sources of cadres, such as the military, the clergy, professionals, the middle classes and the working class. Students and intellectuals are often the first to confront a military dictatorship on an idealist basis. This idealism and the realities of repression against the student population make the universities in Latin America an especially volatile source of urban cadres and guerrilla fighters.

In the case of Cuba, the University of Havana was a particularly fecund training ground for revolutionaries, in the 20s and 30s as well as in the 40s and 50s. The students of the 1930 generation, so instrumental in overthrowing Machado and pressing for radical reforms, left activism and radical social ideas as a legacy for those to come.[10] The sense of a continuing tradition of political involvement was deeply felt by the students of Castro's generation. In the 40s, as frustration with the Auténtico regimes grew, the themes of historical links between student generations appeared more frequently. When protesting the possibility of Grau San Martín's re-election in 1947, the Directorio Estudiantil Universitario (DEU), the student association, referred to the heroes and martyrs of the 1930 generation: "All the students raise high the glorious banner for which Mella, Trejo, Floro Pérez, Pío Alvarez, and all our heroes died, and their memory is a call to rebellion".[11] Not only the 1930 generation received homage from the students of the 40s and 50s. They also felt linked to Martí's generation. During the 1947 student campaign against the wide-spread graft, Castro and another student went to Manzanillo to bring the Bell of Demajagua, rung in 1868 to signal the start of the War of Independence, to the University of Havana.[12] The bell had been in the care of 1898 veterans, and Castro saluted their surrender of the bell to a new generation in a campus speech: "It is a great event when the veterans of the independence struggle ally themselves with the students to lead forward the liberating aims of our past. The freedom fighters of yesterday trust the young students of today; thus we are continuing their task of achieving independence and justice".[13]

THE UNIVERSITY IN THE LATE 1940s: PRACTICAL EXPERIENCES FOR FUTURE CADRES

Students were confronted not only by the unsolved problems inherited from Cuba's past; not only did they have time and the inclination to examine and discuss the politics, history and economics of their own country and others. They also were influenced by a recent period of activism, many of whose cadres were still young and articulate. A feeling of something unfinished, el deber del cubano, as yet indefinite and vague, accompanied the lives of many students in the post-war period. The influence of Spanish Republican exiles (social democrats, communists and anarchists) was felt in the academic, literary and journalistic arenas of Cuban life. Class-centered social analyses were also abroad due to the World War II alliances of the PSP and Batista, which had brought the party into his cabinet; the PSP was influential in the unions. Although the PSP held to the theory of stages (i.e., the bourgeois democratic revolution and the full development of the forces of production via capitalist industrialization would precede socialism) and was less popular in the later 40s due to zig-zags of policy and collaboration with Batista, Marxist ideas had a certain currency.[14]

In 1940, a constitution was drawn up, a quite progressive, even radical document by any standard. It contained many clauses referring to social justice, state ownership of the sub-soil, and land reform.[15] But the decade of the 40s was an era of increasingly cynical use of the national patrimony and revenues for personal enrichment. The University itself was a particularly effective route to political influence and power. Thus, the impact of radical ideas was somewhat dispersed and, by the time Castro arrived there in 1945 to study law, much of campus life was dominated by struggles between competing bonches with connections to various politicians.[16]

The outstanding factor in University life was the competition between the various bonches. They were modelled on organizations instrumental in overthrowing Machado and active in the 1930s after Batista solidified control with the support and intrigues of United States ambassadors Sumner Welles and Jefferson Caffery.[17] Permeated with opportunism and romanticism, and often close to criminal elements, such groups believed in the primacy of violent action. Many of the members of the action groups were not themselves students, and many of the leaders had close ties with highly-placed individuals in the government and the police. In particular, the three main action groups, the Movimiento Socialista Revolucionaria (MSR), the Unión Insurreccional Revolucionaria (UIR) and the Acción Revolucionaria Guiterista (ARG), also gathered together diverse political tendencies. The MSR claimed to advocate revolutionary socialism, the UIR pretended to some degree of anarchism and the ARG claimed to follow the radical ideas of a 1930s student leader, Antonio Guiteras.[18] Populist individual heroism, a sort of classically anarchist approach to politics and national problems, was combined with a desire to overthrow all dictatorships and corrupt regimes in Latin America. Gangsterism, however, and some members' involvement in corruption themselves, was a constant. Gangsterism extended into many spheres of government. Grau's regime was known to use anti-communist labor goons affiliated with the ARG in controlling the union movement.[19]

The MSR, under Rolando Masferrer, and the UIR, under Emilio Tró, engaged in the selective and, at times, indiscriminate assassination of each other's activists, on and off campus.[20] Masferrer had been with the Communists and the International Brigades in Spain, but later turned virulently anti-communist and became a very rich gang-leader, a Senator and one of Batista's main supporters. Tró accepted a position under Grau as the head of the national police investigation department, a very lucrative position.[21] Both of these groups and their respective leaders had a part in Castro's insurrectionary formation, i.e. his general political education. Though it cannot be uniquely his involvement in action groups in the 40s which led to his view that armed insurrection was the only way to overthrow Batista and address the permanent social problems, clearly his days in the action groups contributed to that conviction.

There is still a fair amount of academic and polemical controversy over whether Castro was actually involved in various action group killings, but there is no question that he did join the UIR.[22] Hugh Thomas' somewhat reserved judgement is that "perhaps to begin with against his will he joined in the extraordinary gang warfare in which against his better judgement he excelled....the action groups...were not wholly bereft of idealism and political romanticism".[23]

Whatever the extent of Castro's involvement with the action groups, and it seems that he retained his independence and had many acquaintances outside the UIR in these early years, the action orientation of Castro's experiences in the UIR did not fail to impress him.[24] However, he also sought the leadership of the law students' association and came to campaign against the gangsterism of campus life and against the manipulation of the action groups by national and government figures.25

In the summer of 1947, Castro and other students, seeking a larger cause, joined the so-called Cayo Confites expedition. Widely-known and funded by interests Castro had come to oppose in campus politics, such as Masferrer, Minister of Education Alemán, and the head of the Army, General Pérez Dámera, the invasion force was to overthrow the dictatorship of General Rafael Trujillo in the Dominican Republic. The UIR/MSR conflict notwithstanding, many UIR activists, like Castro attracted to internationalism, joined the MSR-sponsored invasion force. They trained for some three months and marked time on Cayo Confites, a small island, during the hot summer. Dominicans, veterans of the Spanish Civil War and many others who were later involved in the Caribbean Legion, a group of non-communist revolutionaries who hoped to overthrow dictators in the area, were involved in the expedition. Many of them later fought in Costa Rica in 1948 to help establish a republic.26 But the Grau government in Cuba decided not to support the invasion and the Cuban navy went to arrest the expeditionaries; Castro escaped.27

On his return to campus life, Castro was involved in numerous anti-Grau demonstrations, gaining a reputation as a lively and articulate speaker.28 It was in this year of 1947 that the ruling political party, the Auténticos, the party of Prío and Grau, split. The faction leaving was led by Eddy Chibás, a popular radio commentator and a Senator. He had a revolutionary past from the 1930s and became known as a muckraker par excellence during the Prío regime of 1948-52.29

Chibás founded the Partido del Pueblo Cubano-Ortodoxo on the themes of "administrative honesty" and anti-gangsterism.30 For many Cubans, he represented the heroic days of Antonio Guiteras, Julio Antonio Mella and other anti-Machado figures who had entered the Cuban martyrology. Many intellectuals and ex-terrorists joined the Ortodoxos, and student youth saw in Chibas a populist leader untainted by Auténtico corruption or ties to Batista. Unions dominated by Auténticos also split, and the government resorted to more gangsterism, including the assassination of Jesus Menéndez, communist sugarworkers' union leader and congressman. Castro was a speaker at the funeral for Menéndez.31

It seems that at this time Castro became increasingly disenchanted with the action groups, particularly as their violent attacks on each other were growing in ferocity and frequency. He became active in the University Committee to Fight Racial Discrimination, and in the FEU Committee on Puerto Rican Independence.32 One writer also claims that Castro was quite friendly with Lionel Soto, Alfredo Guevara, Flavio Bravo and Luís Mas Martín, all of Juventud Socialista, the PSP youth organization, discussing politics with them and beginning to read Marxist classics.33 It was with Soto that Castro achieved some notoriety by bringing the Bell of Demajagua to the campus.

On February 22, 1948, Manolo Castro, the head of the FEU, was killed. Accused of this murder by Masferrer, Castro publicly challenged the power of Masferrer's MSR on the campus. Masferrer, he said, "was trying to take over the university via coercion and violence".34 Threatened, he went into hiding and decided to attend the Bogotá Congress of Latin American Students, slated to parallel the Ninth Inter-American Conference in early April, 1948.35 There, he witnessed the "Bogotazo" after the Colombian Liberal leader Jorge Eliecer Gaitán was assassinated and apparently engaged in some street fighting against the Conservative government forces.36 Lionel Martin speculates that Bogotá "showed Fidel the divisiveness of anti-communism and bolstered his belief that imperialism was the real basis of Latin American problems", though it was not yet the issue in popular consciousness.37 In an interview with Carlos Franqui years later (probably in 1959), Castro recalled his developing anti-imperialism before Bogotá: "I came to realize more and more clearly that the policy of the United States, and its wholly disproportionate development with respect to Latin America, was the great enemy of the unification and development of the Latin American nations; the United States would always do its utmost to maintain the weakness and division on which it based its policy of directing the fate of our peoples as it pleased."38

Anti-imperialism, though inchoate, was not a novel sentiment among Cuban students in the 40s and 50s. The history of Cuba led one naturally to such a position. Martí could be easily cited.39 The students of the 20s and early 30s had developed a strong anti-imperialism based on Cuban nationalism and influenced by other Latin American nationalists.40 Even so, Castro's anti-imperialism, as he stated himself, was under-developed in these years: "In spite of having read theoretically about imperialism as a phenomenon, I did not understand it very well. I did not thoroughly appreciate the relation between the phenomenon of imperialism and the situation in Cuba".41 Castro's anti-imperialism seems to have been, at this time, a nationalist's response to underdevelopment and pro-United States dictatorships in Latin America, influenced by pan-Americanism. Aware of the history of United States military interventions in Latin America, he had not yet linked capitalism and imperialism.

Clearly, at this time Castro, as many other students, was expanding his political outlook and finding the actions of the MSR, UIR and ARG a violent dead-end. Gang warfare abated in late 1948, and many former activists turned to the Ortodoxo Party under Chibás. After returning from Bogotá, Castro joined Chibás' speaking entourage and, in 1949, had a radio program of his own on station COCO.[42] He remained active in the Ortodoxo youth movement,[43] got married, and quickly finished his law studies, opening a small practice not known for financial success. As Dubois wrote, he "dedicated his time to the defense of the poorest class, almost always without charge".[44] Castro also maintained his contacts with Juventud Socialista, joining a study group in 1949 that read Lenin's classics State and Revolution and Imperialism, having introduced himself to Marx's Capital in 1948.[45] He later remarked that what attracted him most about Marxist works at the time was "the idea that society is divided into classes with antagonistic and irreconcilable interests".[46]

Although Chibás was pro-New Deal and anti-communist,[47] Castro did not feel constrained by any Ortodoxo party line. Indeed, there was not much in the way of a party line, as entrance standards were lax and the membership heterogeneous.[48] For example, though Chibás supported the United States effort in the Korean War, Castro was opposed.[49] But Castro voted in 1948 for the Chibás-Agramonte ticket and was, himself, an Ortodoxo candidate for congressman in 1952, before the Batista coup eliminated the elections.[50]

Many future revolutionaries, both of the M-26 and of the student Directorio Revolucionario (DR), were university and secondary students during the late 40s. While few stood out as much as did Castro (the more important student leaders, like Frank País, José Antonio Echeverría, and Faure Chomón arose in the 50s, both before and after the 1952 coup), many had the opportunity to see the futility of the action groups' internecine warfare, and yet were drawn into national politics through them. The groups virtually ruled the campus, exerting influence over professors, student politics, and even marks. To achieve academic or political notoriety, one had to go through the action groups.

As their influence subsided, the populist appeal of Chibas replaced them and students would listen to his Sunday evening muckraking broadcasts.[51] Many such Chibásistas later became instrumental in the planning of the Moncada assault. And, when Chibás committed suicide in front of his radio microphone on August 5, 1951, Castro became a good muckraker himself. He audaciously reported on President Prío's questionable land-holding activities, anti-labor practices on his farms, and on his protection of a businessman who had raped a nine-year-old. Using his legal skills, Castro exposed Prío's connections to pistolero gangster groups via a court brief detailing the government botellas 'sinecures' awarded them by Prío. Castro gave the details, naming the people who picked up the cheques.[52] Significantly, one of the first measures of the revolution in 1959 was the elimination of all botellas.

The themes that Castro repeated in preparing the Moncada assault and in the Sierra Maestra, and which, indeed, have been central to the political education of revolutionary cadres and of soldiers and officers in the FAR, are evident in his student days. He clearly felt a kinship to the struggles of the past and to revolutionary students of the 1930 generation and before. In 1947, for example, the university students' federation, in condemning corruption, referred to the student martyrs of the anti-Machado struggle and pledged to fight re-election "even if the price we have to pay in the struggle is our own death".[53] Castro was one of the signatories. In some societies this reference to death would be hyperbole but, in the Cuban context, it was meant seriously. The readiness to sacrifice one's life for the fatherland was a major element in the ideology of the Rebel Army and, later, in the FAR. Patriotism generated morale.

THE BATISTATO

In the midst of rising public conern with corruption and the expectation that the Ortodoxos would win the 1952 elections, Fulgencio Batista's coup of March 10 1952 stunned the Prío regime and infuriated the students and youth of the country. Prío quickly left for Florida and Batista had full control within twenty-four hours. The working class, whose unions were characterized by state paternalism and reformist leadership, often involved in graft, had no program or organization with which to mount an effective resistance. The wave of strikes and violence in 1950-51 had only had immediate economic demands as their goal.[54] Although there was considerable anti-Batista sentiment in the working class, the proletariat did not react as a "class for itself", in Marx's term. The PSP, while respected to some extent because of its members' reputation for honesty and dedication, had been compromised by collaboration with Batista in 1939-44. It was also isolated by the Cold War spirit and hampered by its Stalinism.[55]

Batista cancelled the elections scheduled for the summer of 1952 and named himself head of state, Prime Minister and Commander-in-Chief of the armed forces. The electoral parties, already discredited by their record of corruption and their lack of programs to deal with the larger social problems of Cuba, did little more than file suits in court. The press, anticipating censorship and perhaps the arrival of cheques, remained quiescent. Only the university students and some groups within Ortodoxo youth spoke out. The FEU sent a delegation to Prío, asking for arms and pledging resistance to the coup at the university.[56] Printed declarations were handed out on and off the campus and street demonstrations began.57

Among the suits filed was Castro's. He argued that Batista had violated the constitution of 1940 and should be eligible for over one hundred years in prison.58 As with the suits filed by the Auténticos and the mainstream sectors of the Ortodoxo Party, the courts rejected the claims, arguing that "revolution is a lawful source" of authority. The government followed by dissolving all political parties and suspending constitutional guarantees. It was subsequent to these decisions that many people, especially the young, "started to consider [alternate means of] opposing Batista".59

Castro had already made many contacts with young people while a student, then as a lawyer and, finally, as a member of Juventud Ortodoxa. He had written a proclamation on Batista's seizure of power, entitled "¡Revolución no, zarpazo!" (a word implying a brutal and slick maneuver) in which he called for a "fight-back".60 He soon connected with groups advocating armed struggle against the dictatorship. The Auténticos, under Grau, began to organize conspiracies and this continued until after the overthrow of Batista. They had had a tradition of clandestinity in the 30s against Batista. The Ortodoxo Party never had such a tradition and was basically electoralist. However, elements of the Ortodoxo left wing began to combine with disparate groups of the outraged, but inexperienced youth. These groups met on the University of Havana campus, where university autonomy, though frequently violated, offered some protection. Castro now used his contacts to become a major participant in the discussions engaged in by various groups, and began to co-ordinate the activities of several such groups.61

It was at the University that Castro met Abel Santamaría, who headed a small political group.62 Abel, his sister Haydée, Jesús Montané and others began to publish an underground mimeo paper called Son Los Mismos 'They Are The Same Ones' (referring to the earlier Batista period). Santamaría, Montané and Boris Luís Santa Coloma, Haydée's fiance and another in their group, were all young accountants, working for United States subsidiaries in Cuba. Melba Hernandez, a lawyer, and Raúl Gómez García, a philosophy student and poet, helped to put out Son Los Mismos, which condemned the Batista regime. Most of these people became involved in the Moncada assault and the survivors worked in the M-26.

Castro's "Revolución no, zarpazo!" was published in Son Los Mismos and the group changed the paper's name to El Acusador 'The Accuser' at his suggestion that it would sound more militant.63 Castro became the political editor and his articles appeared in most of the limited numbers of the paper. On the first anniversary of Chibás' death, August 16, 1952, the group appeared at a mass rally of commemoration and distributed El Acusador.⁶⁴ Most of them were arrested, but Castro's article condemning Ortodoxo weakness and calling for a new revolutionary party harking to Chibás' example received exposure. Castro posed the choice for Cuban youth thusly:

> Politics is the consecration of the opportunism of those who have the means and resources. Revolution opens the way to true merit to those who have sincere courage and ideas, to those who risk their lives and take the battle standard in their hands. A revolutionary party requires a revolutionary leadership, a young leadership originating from the people, that will save Cuba.⁶⁵

This article and the more virulent "¡Zarpazo!" evidenced Castro's frustration with the established electoral parties, reflected his long-standing belief in action, and repeated the themes of Cuban national salvation. He was prophetic in his anger: "It was right to remove from office a government of murderers and thieves, and we were trying to do so peacefully with the support of public opinion and the aid of the people. But by what right do the military do so, they who have murdered and stolen without limit in the past? It is not peace but the seed of hatred that has been sown here".⁶⁶ He denied Batista's claim that it was a revolution, reminding him that Trujillo was the first to recognize the coup. Castro recalled the past, saying "Cubans! Once again there is a tyrant, but once again we shall have Mellas, Trejos and Guiterases! The fatherland is oppressed, but someday there will be freedom".⁶⁷ And appealing further to nationalism, he ended the call with the last two lines of the national anthem, called Los Bayameses after the original 1868 rebels of Bayamo in Oriente province: "To live in chains is to live sunk in shame and dishonor. To die for the fatherland is to live!"

Events were accelerating at the university and elsewhere. Student demonstrations were becoming confrontations with the police: "Historic dates and anniversaries became occasions for parading, depositing flowers on a monument, inflammatory speeches against Batista and clashes with the police, who could not resist the temptation of engaging students in open battles with sticks, stones and sometimes bullets.⁶⁸ January 28 was Martí's birthday, February 24 and October 10 were Independence War dates, December 7 marked the death of General Antonio Maceo, January 10 was Mella's death, September 30 Rafael Trejo's death, and May 20 a day to denounce the Platt Amendment. Batista's name was connected with every demonstration".⁶⁹

In Artemisa and Guanajay in Pinar del Río province, not far from Havana, a group of young workers and stu-

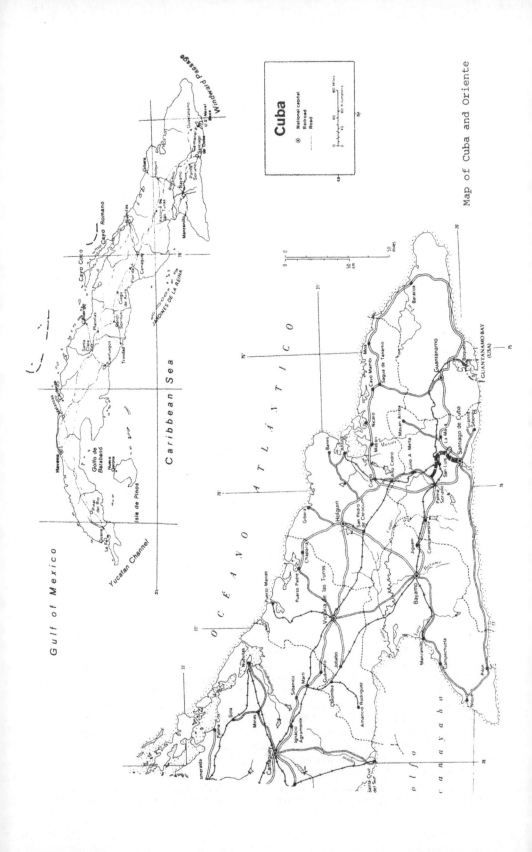

Map of Cuba and Oriente

dents had published an anti-Batista manifesto and formed a revolutionary cell. One of the leaders was a friend of Castro's and a member, like him, of Juventud Ortodoxa.[70] The friend, José Suárez, with Ramiro Valdés, Ciro Redondo, Julio Díaz and others from the Artemisa group later joined in the Moncada assault. It was Castro's multiple contacts and organizational abilities which were instrumental in pulling together the various groups into one movement independent of the established parties.

Throughout the summer and fall of 1952, opposition to Batista percolated. Rumors of Autentico invasions were abroad. By September, Castro, Abel and other Ortodoxos in the independent groups were recruiting from Juventud Ortodoxa. The latter had declared for revolutionary action, though the Ortodoxo Party itself would not.[71] A group in the Marianao suburb of Havana began organizing arms training. Many of the Artemisa group practiced shooting there and later formed the squad that attacked the Bayamo barracks while the main body of fighters attacked Moncada.[72] Castro and Abel Santamaría, in particular, were meeting with various local groups in order to build up a movement. At the same time, a philosophy professor, Rafael García Bárcena, founded the Movimiento Nacional Revolucionario (MNR). He had been a student activist in the 1930s, a founder of the Auténtico Party, and a <u>Chibásista</u>. Bárcena had also maintained contacts with some army officers.[73] Many members of the MNR went on to become M-26 activists, such as Mario Llerena,[74] Faustino Pérez, Armando Hart, Joe Westbrook, Angel Boan and Fernando Sánchez Amaya.[75] This group planned a bloodless coup, hoping to take over Campo Columbia, the main military barracks in Havana. In April of 1953 they were caught, tortured and imprisoned before anything could get underway.[76]

With the electoralist option closed indefinitely and the traditional opposition reluctant to engage in armed revolt, a significant number of people joined the "movement", as the Castro-Santamaría group was known. In late 1952 they began military training, on the university campus, in selected private homes in Havana, and in rural locales outside of Havana. Cells were organized and Castro's associates in the left wing of the Ortodoxos were usually in command.[77] The movement began to appear at demonstrations in military formation and, on January 27, 1953, a large contingent marched with thousands of youths from the campus to downtown Havana to mark Martí's birth.[78] The "<u>Generación del Centenario</u>" 'Generation of the Centenary' was taking shape.

THE GENERACIÓN DEL CENTENARIO AND THE MONCADA ASSAULT

The movement whose members paraded in military formation grew because of the failure of both the Auténtico and Ortodoxo leadership to mobilize resistance to Batista. Pedro Miret, at the time a student and, later, one of the leadership group in the Rebel Army, spoke of the rapid loss of faith in traditional parties which university students and working youth experienced: "We were always being given a date for the armed insurrection by groups like AAA[79] and by the Priístas (followers of Prío)...but they came and went".[80] The growing frustration and disgust was expressed not only in El Acusador, but in pamphlets put out by a student/worker group in Artemisa.[81] In an unpublished pamphlet entitled "Revolución sin juventud" 'Revolution without Youth', the poet Raúl Gómez García recalled past Cuban heroes and appealed to the sense of duty for Cuban youth: "We are not going to theorize, we are going to fight. We are not going to talk, we are going to act".[82]

Though a ready reservoir of students was available for recruitment, Castro's small leadership group and particularly Castro himself began to include more and more humildes 'poor' or 'lower classes'.[83] Thus, by the time that an armed action was being discussed and planned, the social composition of the assault group was largely working class and lower middle class. Hugh Thomas, in his close study of the Moncada assault, concludes that the attackers were "almost entirely lower middle class or working class...few were students...of one hundred fifty Moncada attackers, most were factory workers and shop assistants...camp followers of industrialization."[84] Significantly, there were very few who had any involvement with the 1940s action groups. The majority were between twenty and thirty years of age and had some affiliation with the Ortodox Party through Juventud Ortodoxa.[85] Many of the attackers, though not students, had joined in student demonstrations against Batista and a number had had personal confrontations with the police.[86]

Virtually all of those involved in the movement, and estimates are that some fourteen to fifteen hundred were involved in weapons training,[87] needed no prompting to join.[88] Training activities centered on arms handling and target practice, usually with .22 caliber rifles, and discipline. Political education, in this instance, can be seen as having already occurred. People came into the movement via their own experiences under the dictatorship and during the previous regimes, and via the influence of political socialization during their own upbringing. As Miret says, "we began to analyze what had produced the coup and all the previous regimes."[89]

Nonetheless, the process of training was a political education in itself and various activities, both spontaneous and organized, contributed to the raising of the political consciousness of the participants. The activists were constantly meeting in small groups, as the cell structure had been adopted early on. Frequent political discussion and the semi-clandestinity necessary to carry out arms purchases, transport and training began to mold the activists into combatants. Miret noted the growth in seriousness in the youths during the period of training; personal transformations occurred.[90]

Discretion and secrecy were also weapons. All previous attempts to mount an action against the dictatorship were either announced beforehand by the plotters or were infiltrated. Even the Santamaría group had been infiltrated while publishing El Acusador and, on one occasion, all but Castro and Melba Hernandez were surprised and arrested.[91] As a result, the movement had a tight cell structure, both civil and military leadership committees, and strict discipline. If a member was known to be drinking, provisional separation from the movement was the punishment. As well, strict sexual morality was the rule.[92] An oath of silence was taken by all members and a commission of investigations functioned to maintain discretion and avoid infiltration.[93]

The leadership was in constant contact with cell leaders, who were usually more politically aware than most members. Besides discussions and sessions of criticism and self-criticism, especially in the leadership committees, "political education was imparted by reading the works of Jose Marti."[94] Among the actual participants in the assault, many had begun to study Marxism while involved in Juventud Ortodoxa.[95] The national director of Juventud Ortodoxa, Pepe Suárez Blanco, who took part in the assault, wrote of the appeal of a radical analysis of Cuban society among Ortodoxo youths. Discussions centered around the need to eradicate latifundios and increase the workers' share of profits, educational reform to achieve mass access, and the "elimination of the professional army in the service of imperialism and reaction".[96]

Castro himself guided some of the reading within the leadership group. Both Abel Santamaría and he were avid readers of Marti[97] and Castro began to bring the former other books, more or less arranging a course of readings for his second-in-command.[98] It was in the Santamaría apartment where books were gathered and the general staff, as it were, would meet and discuss such topics as political economy, philosophy, history, military tactics, civil administration, citizen consciousness, agrarian reform and national dignity, with the focus of Martí's approach to these topics.[99] The Santamarías also built up a library for the political education of movement members. Haydée Santamaría later said that "to create that small library was a financial hardship, but it was necessary for the struggle, for the ideological culture of the future fighters.[100] It contained an encyclopedia, historical biographies, works by José Ingenieros (an Argentine Marxist), Pablo de la Torriente Brau (a Cuban poet who died fighting for the Spanish Republic), and the works of Lenin and Martí.[101] Santamaría constantly carried around a volume of Lenin's selected works,[102] and it was taken from him at his death by torture to be used as a state exhibit at the trial of the Moncada survivors.[103]

Much has been made of the taste for Marxist literature shared by the leadership of the Moncada assault, given the 1961 announcement by Castro that the Cuban revolution was Marxist. Lionel Martin noted that the leadership nucleus studied Marxism together, and draws a chain of ideology connecting the nucleus with various cell leaders who themselves had some Marxist education, trade union activities, and involvement with the PSP.[104] And Nathaniel Weyl, as representative of those who assume Castro's early recruitment by an international communist body, stresses the Castro brothers' student involvement with radical politics.[105] However, there is no solid evidence to support this view, and the considered opinion of Hugh Thomas is that Castro was "in no way a Marxist in 1953".[106]

Thomas' judgement rings true when the descriptions of leadership meetings, the court record, Castro's <u>History Will Absolve Me</u>, the Moncada Manifesto, and the biographies of participants are examined. Castro himself, when asked at the trial what books were read, replied: "We read all types of books. Anyone who was never interested in socialist literature is an ignoramus".[107] What emerges, rather than a movement motivated by orthodox Marxism-Leninism, is a group inspired by Cuban history itself. National redemption and <u>dignidad</u> [108] were outstanding motifs. Haydée Santamaría recalled that the meetings in her apartment usually centered on Martí, his critique of Cuban society, and the statutes of his Partido Revolucionario Cubano.[109] While it is true that the youths "embarked on the Moncada attack without indeed a very carefully worked-out ideology, only a desire to overthrow the 'tyrant' Batista",[110] they also engaged in a critical examination of Cuban society. In those meetings of which Haydée Santamaría retained warm memories, with frugal group meals, jokes and laughter ("Never after did a meal seem so good to us"), Cuban society was dissected. "We talked about the present and analyzed those phenomena of political corruption, the lottery, the sinecures and the embezzlement by high functionaries. We said that we could not stop there, that it was necessary to eradicate the evils but that it was also necessary to build something more. We used to talk about agrarian reform and about other crazy projects that we had".[111]

Batista, as Thomas remarked, was for the movement a symptom rather than a cause of the social problems of Cuba.[112] The movement entertained a conscious identification with Martí and his unfulfilled goals. An historical continuity was perceived and the Moncada militants, along with the movement at large, felt kinship with all heroic and frustrated attempts in Cuban history to bring about the changes Martí deemed necessary. In this sense, the movement embraced past heroes as Cubans rather than as representatives of one ideology or another, one party or another. The material and political preparations for the assault reflected these images of nationalism, historical continuity, and a redemptive generation ready to scarifice itself.

The militants shared a deep sense of commitment to the movement, which was based upon a sense of historical responsibility, on the feeling of *el deber* 'duty', and upon personalist devotion to the persuasive, energetic and charming Castro. Personal sacrifices were evident in the training period, when many had jobs. Often the militants had to travel some distance after a long day at work to practice weapons handling.[113] The procurement of weapons and other material was a painstaking process, funds being generated by the militants themselves. In court, Castro gave the details of the contributions which amounted to some $16,480. Among others, Jesús Montané had quit his General Motors position and received $4000 which he gave to the movement. Oscar Alcalde sold his laboratory and donated the $3600 procured. Renato Guitart, the only member in Santiago, gave $1000. Ernesto Tizol donated a chicken-raising business. Pedro Marrero sold his furniture. Fernando Chenard sold his photography equipment, his means of living. Elpidio Sosa sold his job; Abel Santamaría sold his car.[114]

The plan to assault the Moncada barracks, along with those at Bayamo, had some Cuban precedent. Antonio Guiteras had planned, in 1931, to assault Moncada and "precipitate a revolt throughout the province which, in turn, would cause a national uprising".[115] Castro and the small group of planners hoped to distribute weapons to the population of Santiago and to issue a call for revolt over captured radio stations. The call was to include the manifesto of July 23, 1953, written by Raúl Gómez García on Castro's instructions,[116] a recording of Chibás' last radio speech, some patriotic poems and martial music.[117]

Chibás' speech, just before he committed suicide, recalled his efforts to show Prío's embezzlement of government funds and purchases of real estate in Florida and Central America.[118] He spoke of the history of government fraud in Cuba, contrasting it with the "great destiny" which Cuba's resources and people held in promise. Finally, he called for the Cuban people to awake and achieve economic independence, political liberty and social justice.[119]

The "Manifesto of the Moncada Revolutionaries to the Nation", as it was called, was more a paying of historical respects and a statement of patriotism and principles than a detailed program. It recalled the memory of Cuban national heroes - Céspedes and Agramonte, Maceo and Martí, Mella, Guiteras and Trejo, and Chibás. It claimed that Martí's centenary found Cuba in a dialectic of "progression and regression": dictatorship and resistance, foreign control and sovereignty. The theme of generational responsibility and sacrifice was paramount: "The angry and forceful youth of the centenary stand up, in this decisive hour, having no other interest than the desire to honor the unrealized dream of Martí with sacrifice".[120] The manifesto laid claim to the program of Martí's Partido Revolucionario Cubano, his Montecristi Manifesto and the programs of Joven Cuba, ABC Radical (left-wing groups of the 30s) and the Ortodoxo Party.

The nine points contained in the manifesto purported to root "the Revolution" in Cuba's political past and identified the Revolution with no single class or caste. It did, however, stress "a new revolution, new generation and new men".[121] It declared respect for military men "who have not betrayed the nation or surrendered our glorious flag or denied our constitution" and for "workers and students, true representatives in the defense of the people's legitimate rights throughout history". The manifesto proposed economic and industrial development via planning and promised a return to the constitution of 1940. As Thomas concludes, the realization of the programs of Martí, Joven Cuba and Guiteras would have resulted in a revolution more radical than that of Cardenas in Mexico, but not necessarily a socialist one.[122] Whatever its shortcomings and its lack of definite proposals, the manifesto articulated the vision of the militants.[123]

They assembled at "El Siboney", a small farm outside of Santiago leased by the movement. The sorry collection of weapons and ammunition, plus uniforms, had been gathered there.[124] Only a handful of the militants, the leadership, knew the details of the plan, and most of the attackers had been hand-picked from among the different cells, so that few knew each other.[125] One hundred thirty-four men, with Haydée Santamaría, Melba Hernandez and Dr. Mario Muñoz Monroy acting as a medical corps, were to attack Moncada, while some twenty-eight had been sent to attack Bayamo.[126] Castro and Santamaría explained the mission and gave short exhortations. Castro's talk, later called "Este movimiento triunfará"[127]

'This Movement Will Triumph', again related the movement to 1868 and 1895. He said the movement would win regardless of the outcome, as it would impel the Cuban people by example.[128] Finally, he offered those unwilling to participate an out, and called for exemplary treatment of prisoners.

The political education of the Generación del Centenario was derived largely from their own experience and from Cuban history. Students identified with the patriots and national heroes of the independence wars, as did the young workers in the movement, and with the martyrs of the struggle against Machado, and later Batista, in the 20s and 30s. The feeling of national incompleteness was launched anew with the disappointments of the 40s governments of the Auténtico Party. The example of the early action groups had degenerated to the gang warfare of the 40s, though an element of populist heroism was retained. Government corruption and subordination to imperialism gave way to an outright military dictatorship which served up the national patrimony to itself and its domestic allies and opened Cuba to further penetration by foreign capital and criminal elements. Infused with the goals of Martí and the exhortations of Chibás, and influenced by some exposure to the more radical ideologies of the century, an element of Cuban society revolted. There was a feeling that not only did the dictatorship have to be removed, but that Cuban society itself needed a re-shaping, a regeneration. While student and worker militancy increased, the traditional parties floundered, the worker organizations failed to mount an effective resistance to the dictatorship, the PSP lacked in real influence, and the way was cleared for a non-traditional opposition.[129] Yet, it was an opposition rooted in Cuban history and an analysis of that history and the society which produced it. It was to retain the strong connection with the Cuban past and to develop further via the experience of repression and resistance. The very nature of the armed struggle this opposition took up and the impact it had upon Cuban society were to provide further political education.

NOTES

1. For a detailed account of Batista's career and the March 10 coup, see Hugh Thomas, Cuba (London: Eyre and Spottiswoode, 1971). Another discussion of the period is contained in Jorge I. Dominguez, Cuba, Order and Revolution (Cambridge: Belknap Press, 1978), pp. 110-33. A Marxist account in presented in Samuel Farber, Revolution and Reaction in Cuba (Middletown: Wesleyan University Press, 1976).

2. A description of police corruption is contained in Rolando Bonachea and Marta San Martín, *The Cuban Insurrection 1952-1959* (New Brunswick, N.J.: Transaction Books, 1974), pp. 31-4.

3. These were organized groups of students and self-styled "revolutionaries", inspired in part by similar groups of the 1930s, who dominated university politics by violence. Their motivations were confused and included, in some cases, a real adherence to the principles of 1933 revolutionaries. By the late 1940s, they "exhibited an insatiable appetite for power and wealth, and a determination to obtain both regardless of obstacles". The rivalries of the *bonches* kept politically conscious students divided until the coup. See Jaime Suchlicki, *University Students and Revolution in Cuba, 1920-1968* (Coral Gables: University of Miami Press, 1969), p. 48.

4. See Robert J. Alexander, *Communism in Latin America* (New Brunswick: Rutgers University Press, 1957), pp. 278-85.

5. See Edmundo Desnoes, *Punto de Vista* (Havana: Instituto del Libro, 1967), pp. 13-20.

6. Nelson Valdés, "Revolution and the Institutionalization in Cuba", Cuban Studies, 6, nos. 1-2 (January and July 1976), p. 6.

7. Farber, p. 16.

8. See the account of Haydée Santamaría on the youth of her brother, Abel Santamaría, one of the Moncada martyrs, in Carlos Franqui, *Diary of the Cuban Revolution*, tr. Georgette Felix, Elaine Kerrigan, Phyllis Freeman, Hardie St. Martin (New York: Viking Press, 1980), pp. 26-9.

9. See the description of demonstrations in Suchlicki, pp. 58-70; Bonachea and San Martín, pp. 42-56.

10. Bonachea and San Martin, pp. 41-2.

11. "Against the Re-election of Ramón Grau San Martín" (20 Jan. 47) in Fidel Castro, *Revolutionary Struggle, Vol. I of the Selected Works of Fidel Castro* (Cambridge: MIT Press, 1972), ed. Rolando Bonachea and Nelson Valdés, p. 131-2.

12. Thomas, p. 812.

13. "The Dignity of Our Freedom Fighters", in Bonachea and Valdés, p. 132.

14. See Maurice Zeitlin, *Revolutionary Politics and the Cuban Working Class* (New York: Harper Torchbooks, 1970), passim. See also Farber, pp. 138-42.

15. See Thomas, pp. 719-21, for an assessment of the 1940 constitution.

16. See Bonachea and San Martin, pp. 10 ff.

17. On these events, see Luis E. Aguilar, *Cuba 1933. Prologue to Revolution* (Ithaca: Cornell University Press, 1972), pp. 200-29 and Farber, p. 41: "[Welles] and Caffery found a close affinity with Bati-

sta in what became a tacit alliance against Grau [the President in late 1933] and particularly against Guiteras [the radical student leader and Minister of the Interior]".

18. See Farber, pp. 118-122.
19. Farber, p. 122.
20. See Suchlicki, pp. 51-2.
21. Bonachea and San Martin, p. 11.
22. Bonachea and San Martin, p. 11. There has never been any definitive evidence that Castro killed anyone at the University. Herbert Matthews, in Castro, A Political Biography (London: Allen Lane, The Penguin Press, 1969), pp. 24-5, rejects the notion outright. Lionel Martin, in The Early Fidel. Roots of Castro's Communism (Secaucus: Lyle Stuart, 1978), p. 54, shows that for the alleged killing of student association president Manolo Castro in 1948, no arrest warrant for Castro was ever issued. Nathaniel Weyl, on the other hand, in his Cold War classic Red Star Over Cuba (New York: Devin-Adair, 1961), credits Castro with several killings. See his chapter "Apprenticeship in Murder".
23. Thomas, p. 811. Andrés Suárez, in Cuba: Castroism and Communism, 1959-1966 (Cambridge: MIT Press, 1967), pp. 14-20, depicts Castro as a personalist gunslinger lacking in morality and erudition.
24. Castro, in Franqui, Diary, p. 9: "In those days I was quixotic, romantic, a dreamer, with very little political know-how but with a tremendous thirst for knowledge and a great impatience for action".
25. Martin, pp. 29, 35.
26. Martin, pp. 32 ff.; Thomas, pp. 812 ff.; Bonachea and San Martin, p. 12.
27. Bonachea and San Martin, p. 12.
28. Martin, p. 35.
29. See Luis Conte Agüero's political biography, Eduardo Chibás, el adalid de Cuba (Mexico, 1955).
30. Farber, p. 122.
31. Martin, p. 40.
32. Ibid., p. 70. Martin remarks that this puts the lie to Thomas' assertion that Castro was silent on racism until 1953.
33. Martin, p. 40. This claim is part of the argument that Castro was a Marxist from his university days.
34. Castro, "On the Death of Manolo Castro", in Bonachea and Valdés, p. 133. This statement was issued at a press conference.
35. This presence of Castro at the "Bogotazo" gave rise to another of the black legends cultivated about his early days after the Bay of Pigs fiasco. See Weyl, pp. 31-5.
36. Thomas, p. 816, says it is "obscure how much fighting Castro did there". See Jules Dubois, Fidel Castro. Rebel-Liberator or Dictator? (New York: Bobbs-

-Merrill, 1959), pp. 18-23 for a sympathetic account denying the allegations that Castro killed priests in Bogota.

37. Martin, p. 60.
38. Franqui, p. 9.
39. See Jose Martí, Jose Martí, Cuba, Nuestra America, y los Estados Unidos (Mexico: Siglo XXI, 1973), ed. Roberto Fernandez Retamar, passim; Jose Martí, Our America (New York: Monthly Review Press, 1977), ed. Philip Foner. For a discussion of Martí's anti-imperialism, see Emilio Roig de Leuchsenring, Martí, anti-imperialista, 2nd. ed. (Buenos Aires: Hemisferio, 1962).
40. See Aguilar, Cuba 1933, pp. 68-78.
41. Interview in Lee Lockwood, Castro's Cuba, Cuba's Fidel (New York: Macmillan, 1967), p. 139.
42. Thomas, p. 817; Martin, p.70, says that Castro spoke regularly on radio COCO during 1948-50, particularly of corruption and racism.
43. This section of the Ortodoxos was the most enamored of Chibás' proposed social reforms and return to 1933 principles.
44. Dubois, p. 26.
45. Martin, p. 64. For Martin, this reading made Castro a Marxist long before M-26 or the Bay of Pigs.
46. In Lockwood, p. 139.
47. Farber, p. 122; Martin, p. 79.
48. Farber, loc. cit.
49. Martin, loc. cit.
50. Dubois, p. 26; Thomas, p. 820.
51. Dubois, p. 26.
52. Martin, pp. 86-91. See Castro, "I Accuse", in Bonachea and Valdés, pp. 136-43. In this newspaper article, Castro outlined the stories of rape, land embezzlement, anti-labor practices and gangster botellas referred to above.
53. See "Against the Re-election of Ramón Grau San Martín", in Bonachea and Valdés, pp. 131-2.
54. Farber, pp. 130-38. Farber's notion of a Bonapartist situation, one in which no single class has political hegemony, is an apt description of Cuba in 1952.
55. See Zeitlin for a sanguine assessment of PSP influence in the working class. Farber, p. 142, questions the depth of working class support for communist ideas in the 1950s.
56. Bonachea and San Martín, p. 44, fn. 4.
57. Ibid., p. 45.
58. Castro, "Brief to the Court of Appeals", in Bonachea and Valdés, pp. 142-52.
59. Bonachea and San Martín, p. 14.
60. "Proclamation on Batista's Seizure of Power", in Bonachea and Valdés, pp. 147-49.
61. Rolando Bonachea and Nelson Valdés, "Introduction", in Bonachea and Valdés, pp. 36-7.

62. Information on this group comes from Ibid., p. 37, Bonachea and San Martín, pp. 14-15, and Thomas, p. 825.
63. Bonachea and San Martín, p. 14.
64. Bonachea and Valdés, p. 38.
65. Castro, "Critical Assessment of the Ortodoxo Party", in Bonachea and Valdés, pp. 152-3.
66. Castro, "¡Revolución no, zarpazo!", in Bonachea and Valdés, pp. 147-9.
67. Ibid.
68. Bonachea and San Martín, p. 43.
69. Ibid.
70. Comandante José Ponce Díaz, "Recuerdos del ataque", Verde Olivo, 26 July 63, p. 17.
71. Farber, p. 150.
72. Bonachea and Valdés, p. 41.
73. Thomas, p. 797.
74. An academic and later manifesto-writer for M-26. See Mario Llerena, The Unsuspected Revolution (Ithaca: Cornell University Press, 1978).
75. Thomas, pp. 867-8; Bonachea and Valdés, p. 43, fn. 119.
76. Thomas, p. 801; Bonachea and Valdés, p. 43.
77. Ponce Díaz, p. 15; Bonachea and San Martín, p. 16.
78. Melba Hernandez, "Siempre supimos que el asalto al Moncada culminaría en la victoria", Verde Olivo, 28 July 63, p. 30
79. Formed by Aureliano Sánchez Arango, an activist against the first Batista regime of the 30s, and Prío's Minister of Education. See Thomas, p. 797.
80. Pedro Miret, "Un grupo verdaderamente heróico", Verde Olivo, 29 July 62, pp. 6-7.
81. Ponce Díaz tells of using his small printing press in Artemisa to produce anti-Batista pamphlets. Díaz says he was impressed with Castro because he had no connections "to the past or to political hacks". See Carlos Franqui, The Twelve, tr. Albert Teichner (New York: Lyle Stuart, 1968), p. 25.
82. Cited in Jesús Montané Oropesa, "La Generación del Centenario libra sus primeros combates", Verde Olivo, 29 July 62, pp. 8-11.
83. It has been argued that Castro deliberately chose "peasants and men of scarce education" to maintain his control over the movement. See Carlos Alberto Montaner, Informe Secreto sobre la revolución cubana (Madrid: Ediciones Sedmay, 1976), p. 39. This appears an unfounded allegation.
84. Thomas, p. 825. See also Martin, p. 116, who argues that Castro had a "workerist" orientation at this time.
85. See Autores Varios, Mártires del Moncada (Havana: Ediciones R, 1965). The pocket biographies with-

in nearly all mention Ortodoxo links.
86. Ibid.
87. Pedro Miret, p. 7.
88. At the subsequent trial, all the defendants declared their willingness to take part in the assault with no coercion. See Marta Rojas, La Generación del Centenario en el Moncada (Havana: Ediciones R, 1964), passim. Rojas was present at the trial as a reporter and later compiled this official history via extensive interviews with the families and associates of the attackers.
89. Miret, p. 6.
90. Ibid. Interviews with families of those killed at and after Moncada also attest to this. Many parents of nineteen and twenty-year-olds speak of their sons' seriousness. See Mártires del Moncada, passim.
91. Montané Oropesa, pp. 8-11. Montané was one of the editors and is still among the top leadership of the Cuban government.
92. Jesús Montané Oropesa, "El estilo de trabajo de los combatientes del Moncada y de Bayamo", Verde Olivo, 19 July 64, pp. 8-9, 52.
93. Rojas, La Generación, p. 43.
94. Bonachea and Valdés, p. 42.
95. Raúl Castro, "VIII anniversario del 26 de julio", Verde Olivo, 16 July 61, pp. 3-10.
96. Pepe Suárez Blanco, "Relato de un combatiente del Moncada", Verde Olivo, 29 July 62, pp. 83-5.
97. Thomas, p. 828, says Santamaría was a "fanatic of Martí" and Castro claimed in court that Martí was "the intellectual author" of the Moncada assault. See Rojas, pp. 66-7.
98. Mártires, p. 271.
99. Rojas, p. 50. See Jose Martí, "Resoluciones del Partido Revolucionario Cubano" and "Manifiesto de Montecristi", in Obras Completas (Havana: Editorial Lex, 1931), I, pp. 298-353 and II, pp. 240-7.
100. Haydée Santamaría, "A once años del Moncada", in Martires, pp. 17-21.
101. Haydée Santamaría, "A once años...", p. 19.
102. Miret, p. 7.
103. Photo in appendix of Mártires.
104. Martin, p. 118. Martin argues that Castro and Santamaría were already "convinced Marxists" in 1952, but soft-pedalled ideology to avoid Cold War anti-communism.
105. Weyl, pp. 73-85, 92-7. See Herbert Matthews, Revolution in Cuba: An Essay in Understanding (New York: Scribner's Sons, 1975), p. 53, for a discussion of Raúl Castro's "flirtation" with the PSP in 1953; Thomas, p. 828.
106. Thomas, p. 829.
107. Quoted in Dubois, p. 45.

108. See John Gillin, "Ethos Components in Modern Latin American Culture", in <u>Contemporary Cultures and Societies of Latin America</u>, ed. Dwight E. Heath and Richard No. Adams (New York: Random House, 1965), p.508: "Inner integrity or worth which every person [and in this case, a nation] is supposed to have originally and which he is supposed to guard jealously".
109. Haydée Santamaría, in <u>Mártires</u>, pp. 18-19.
110. Thomas, p. 833.
111. Haydée Santamaría in <u>Mártires</u>, pp. 18-19.
112. Thomas, p. 833.
113. Many families of the Moncada dead remarked upon this to the authors of <u>Mártires</u>.
114. See Castro's testimony in Rojas, pp. 31-4.
115. Bonachea and Valdés, p. 54.
116. Text of the manifesto in Bonachea and Valdés, pp. 255-8.
117. Castro, <u>History Will Absolve Me</u> (New York: Lyle Stuart, 1961), p. 16. Castro claims he could have taken a radio station with ten men and aroused a ready population, but chose to take Moncada by surprise and secure it before the broadcast.
118. See the appendix of Castro, <u>La historia me absolverá</u> (Havana: Ediciones Populares, 1961), for the text of the speech.
119. Montaner, p. 16, thinks Castro would never have emerged had Chibás remained alive to unite the Ortodoxo factions.
120. Bonachea and Valdés, p. 157.
121. Ibid.
122. Thomas, p. 829; see also Goldenberg, p. 152.
123. For an example of their sentiments, see "Pensamientos de Jose Luis Tasende" in <u>Mártires</u>, p.94. Tasende was an electrical mechanic and had assisted Castro during his investigation of Prío's land-holdings. See also the poem by Raúl Gómez García, "Ya estamos en combate", which he recited to the group before the assault, in <u>Mártires</u>, pp. 211-13, and the "Hymn of July 26", composed several days before the attack by singer/combatant Agustín Díaz Cartaya, in Thomas, pp.833-34.
124. See Juan Almeida's impressions in Franqui (1968), p. 18.
125. See the remarks of Ponce Díaz, in Franqui (1968), p. 13.
126. Martin, pp. 138-30, argues that Bayamo was chosen for its proximity to a manganese mine known for harsh conditions and militant miners who were to be armed.
127. Text in Spanish in <u>Verde Olivo</u>, 26 July 64, p. 5. See English translation in Bonachea and Valdés,p.159.
128. Castro's faith in the Cuban people seems sincere. At the time, the PSP condemned the assault as "putschism". See Thomas, p. 842; Goldenberg, p. 153.
129. Farber's term.

3
The New *Mambises:* Combat, Repression and Imprisonment as Political Education for Revolutionary Cadres

Perhaps no single event stands out in the myths of the Cuban revolution more than the assault on the Moncada barracks. July 26 became the day on which the largest mass demonstrations and revolutions would take place. The movement which formed the Rebel Army and which conducted much of the urban civic resistance was named after the event. The image of Cuban youths throwing themselves against the regular army was held up as an example of sacrifice and patriotism to be emulated by the Rebel Army and by the Cuban people. The political education and indoctrination system set up after January 1959 produced dozens of articles and detailed histories of the events at Moncada, stressing the youth and dedication to principles of the attackers. They were seen as the vanguard of a redemptive generation worthy of comparison to the Mambises of 1868-1898 and the martyrs of the anti-Machado movements. The major political document which emerged after the events, Castro's History Will Absolve Me, remains a central element of the myths of the revolution. For Castro, it is "the seed of all the things that were done later on"[1]: the guerrilla struggle, the reforms of the first years in power and the development of socialism.

THE MONCADA DEFEAT

The assault on the Moncada barracks, as a military operation, failed dismally. As a political act, however, it was a qualified success. It took on the features of the classic propaganda-of-the-deed. A popular outcry was raised against the brutality of the repression following the attack, first in Santiago and, later, throughout Cuba, when the rest of the country learned of the dimensions of the repression. Castro and the movement of the Centenary became known. When the survivors were imprisoned, their amnesty became a cause célèbre among politicized students, liberal and radical intelligentsia and the left wing of the Ortodoxo Party. The events themselves became a part of Cuban martyrology and provided an emotional and ideological touchstone for the future Movimiento Revolucionario del 26 de Julio (M-26), the Rebel Army, and the revolutionary regime itself after 1959. It did not, however, galvanize mass working-class and peasant action at the time, nor did it succeed in creating a broad anti-Batista front.

The very intensity of the experience for the combatants and the depth of the tragedy which occurred strengthened the _esprit_ of the survivors. They became even more convinced of the moral righteousness of their cause.[2]

Militarily, they had failed for several reasons. First, they were poorly armed and far outnumbered. Second, the best-trained men were divided between Bayamo, the Moncada fortress itself, the Civil Hospital and the Palace of Justice.[3] Third, some of the assault group took a wrong turn and got lost in the streets of Santiago.[4] Castro recalled that these attackers were the best-armed and formed fully half of their forces.[5] Although the timing of government patrols had been checked by Renato Guitart, one armored patrol vehicle was late and intercepted the column of cars in which the attackers were travelling. Thus, shooting broke out before the barracks were actually penetrated.[6] Finally, because of this warning, the defenders of the gates were able to alert the troops, and the element of surprise was eliminated.[7] At Bayamo, the attack also failed when surprise ceased to be a factor.[8]

The result of errors and chance was a military defeat, followed by the torture, mutilation and massacre of prisoners. According to Castro, a frontal assault on the government troops was never planned: "It was never our intention to fight the regime's soldiers, but to take [the fortress] by surprise and capture arms, call the people...to call on the soldiers to abandon...the tyranny...turn their arms around and fire on the enemies of the people".[9] As it was, only a handful of attackers got inside one of the gates and they soon had to withdraw under fire.[10]

The brutal reaction of the dictatorship contributed to the propaganda success of the assault. In Bayamo, "over half the group of twenty-seven were shot to death after being taken prisoner".[11] In Santiago itself, a wave of torture, summary execution and repression was unleashed. By the end of the week, some eighty rebels were dead.

The rebels had lost only a handful of fighters in the Moncada assault, according to most accounts.[12] In the actual fighting, though the element of surprise was lost and vast numerical and weapons superiority defeated the rebels, the army sustained considerably more casualties. According to Castro, the army lost nineteen dead and thirty wounded.[13] Batista had announced thirty-three deaths among the rebels in a speech from Camp Columbia in Havana the day after the assault, and after the massacre had already begun.[14] It was in the afternoon of July 26 that the order came through to kill ten rebels for each dead soldier.[15] The instructions came from General Martín Díaz Tamayo, arriving in Santiago after a meeting with Batista, the head of the army, and the head of military intelligence in Havana. Tamayo is quoted as saying "it was shameful and a dishonor that the Army had three times more casualties than the attackers".[16]

The torture and killings began that afternoon in Santiago. Of the thirty-eight who fled to Siboney along with Castro, twenty surrendered early on to the army, and were tortured and executed. Those captured in the hospital or in the city were also tortured, mutilated and killed.[17] The local population of Santiago also suffered. Homes were invaded, innocents were arbitrarily arrested and even shot. Batista suspended all civil rights and instituted press censorship.[18] The regime picked up PSP members in town for the annual carnival and a member's birthday and attempted to implicate the PSP and ex-President Prío as instigators.[19]

There was a certain degree of popular support for the rebels on the day of the attack. During the various escapes, some were taken into private homes in Santiago. This became an element in Castro's defense.[20] In the hospital fighting, nurses were reloading the rebels' rifles.[21] In the mountains where Castro and a group of eighteen took refuge, some peasants helped them to evade government troops.[22] Public horror at the torture, mutilation and summary execution of the rebels reached such a pitch that it saved some lives.[23] Archbishop Pérez Serantes of Santiago "obtained the promise of Colonel Alberto del Río Chaviano, commander of the zone of operations, to spare the lives of any fugitives who surrendered, and he went personally into the countryside to accept their surrender".[24] A number of military men, both soldiers and officers, were instrumental in saving rebel lives.[25] Castro took these actions as indicative of the popular support his force would have attracted had they taken Moncada and made radio broadcasts calling for insurrection.[26]

There was some basis for Castro's optimistic assessment of popular sympathies for the rebels. In the second year of power, Batista's regime was already revealing its lack of a popular political base. Its contradictions were emerging. Though divided, the Auténticos and Ortodoxo opposition groups continued the denunciations of the regime that had begun in 1952.[27] Several plots were launched, though unsuccessful, involving arms shipments from the United States.[28] Students were demonstrating frequently, and an attempt was made by the MNR, a group of students and lecturers led by a popular university professor, García Bárcena, to attack Campo Columbia and persuade the forces there to rise against Batista.[29] The military itself was divided by animosities and intrigues.[30]

In the Catholic Church, "while some members of the hierarchy and the regular clergy would tolerate the new order only too easily, most Catholic laymen and priests would not".[31] In Santiago, where the Moncada attack took place, Castro had even more reason to hope that the regime's contradictions and lack of a solid political base could rally the population behind an audacious insurrection. Both the Church and professionals turned away en masse from Batista in the aftermath of the assault.[32]

The ferocity of the repression was indeed counterproductive for the dictatorship. Not only did it increase public sympathy for the Moncada attackers and provide additional momentum for an amnesty campaign, it also bolstered the rebels' conviction that they were morally correct in perceiving the army as a corrupt tool of the dictatorship, with few real links to the population. The repression stiffened the survivors' resolve and became an oft-repeated motif in the political education of the M-26 invasion force, the Rebel Army and the FAR. It provided concrete evidence for the perception of Batista's army as anti-patriotic and anti-popular.[33] Later on, in more coherent ideological terms, the army was seen via the Moncada experience as a vulnerable bourgeois military force, lacking in morale because it was a tool of a privileged minority, and manipulated by imperialism.[34]

THE TRIAL AND REVOLUTIONARY MORALE

The trial of the Moncada attackers was a display, in the social myths of the Rebel Army, of the moral superiority of the Generation of the Centenary over the regular army. This moral factor was conceived all through the subsequent years of struggle as more important than actual weapons.

Karl von Clausewitz, the perceptive Prussian student of war and politics, constantly urged his readers to grasp the relationship between physical and moral factors. Though moral factors are much more difficult to classify and to integrate into theory than physical factors, Clausewitz deemed it necessary to include moral factors in this theory: "One might say that the physical seems little more than the wooden hilt, while the moral factors are the precious metal, the real weapon, the finely-honed blade".[35] What he called "national feeling", i.e. "enthusiasm, fanatical zeal, faith and general temper" were exactly those moral factors that the Rebel Army relied upon in the Sierra Maestra of Cuba.

The natural qualities of bravery, adaptability, stamina and enthusiasm that Clausewitz recognized were inherent in a people's war (he had in mind popular Spanish resistance to the Napoleonic armies) come to merge with military spirit through training and experience. It is political consciousness that unlocks these qualities and makes moral and subjective factors so powerful in armed struggle for social and political change.

For the M-26 and the future Rebel Army, the combat at Moncada, subsequent repression and the trial became, via political interpretation, the foundation of its moral factors in the insurrectionary war. The physical shock of the combat, the torture and the executions left a deep impression. An eloquent expression of this personal impact is provided by Haydée Santamaría: "They were hours in which there was nothing but heroism, when everything was sacred. Life and death can be noble and beautiful when you fight for your life but give it up without compromise".[36]

Though the Generation of the Centenary which attacked Moncada or was imprisoned and exiled may have had a variety of visions for the post-Batista future, the common elements were patriotism and a sense of history, sacrifice for the nation and the humildes 'poor, lower classes', and a desire to act. The survivors, and especially the leadership, emerged from the experience with strengthened convictions, similar to those of B. Traven's character Professor, after the first battle of the Mexican rural workers' army under the banner of Tierra y libertad 'Land and Liberty': "Dulce es morir por la revolución de los pobres", remarks Professor: "How sweet it is to die for the revolution of the poor".[37]

Nothing is more central to Cuban revolutionary ideology than a sense of history. The nationalist "Generation of '23" and the anti-Machado forces looked to the Cuban past for inspiration, as did the anti-Prío students of the late 40s. It is not merely that the Moncada attackers knew and identified with Cuban history, but that they perceived that their actions were in themselves events, events that counted, actions that made history. The attack and aftermath greatly reinforced this self-perception as historical actors, particularly in Castro's History Will Absolve Me.[38] The precautions taken by the government at the scene of the trial contributed to the atmosphere. Armored cars surrounded the area and one thousand soldiers were deployed along the approaches to the courthouse.[39]

THE TRIAL: PROPAGANDA VICTORIES FOR THE REBELS

The blunders and prevarications of the Batista regime provided the attackers with numerous opportunities. First, many of the hundred-plus defendants had nothing to do with the events. The regime had claimed that ex-President Prío, other Auténtico figures, the Ortodoxos and the PSP had all conspired with Castro in Santiago to take the Moncada barracks by assault.[40] But, in the trial, all the PSP, Auténtico and Ortodoxo leaders were completely absolved of responsibility.[41] Castro and his group gained in stature, as the country realized they had acted independently. For the public, "suggestions that Castro was involved with the Auténticos were soon discounted".[42]

Second, the physical facts of torture, arbitrary arrest and the trial arrangements helped bring public attention, in the words of Hugh Thomas, to a deed which might otherwise have been forgotten.[43] Demonstrations of students were organized to protest the arbitrary arrests and the suspension of civil rights.[44] Members of the middle class, church officials, and political liberals, especially in Santiago, complained.[45] With the killings by torture, the plans to poison Castro and the efforts to keep him out of sight,[46] and the manacling of prisoners in a courtroom with more than one hundred soldiers at fixed bayonets, the events assumed historic proportions and the actors the stature of heroes. The government apparently expected some trouble, given the daily demonstrations of students, and Batista declared his readiness to use any means necessary to maintain order.[47] Castro used his few appearances, as he said, "to discredit the cowardly, base and treacherous slanders that the regime had hurled against our fighters, to reveal with irrefutable evidence the frightful, repulsive crimes that they had practiced on those of our comrades whom they captured; and to bring before the nation and the world the infinite misfortune of Cuba's people, who are now enduring the most cruel, the most inhuman oppression in all their history".[48]

The trial was a political education for Castro, for the other attackers, for individuals in the army and the justice system, and for the nation. Del Río Chaviano's charges that the attackers were well-armed and numbered up to five hundred were refuted by the testimony of Castro and the evidence of soldiers themselves.[49] The charges that the rebels had tortured soldiers and used knives and grenades were also negated. Much evidence of torture by the army was revealed and confirmed by autopsy reports.[50]

The rebels' spirits remained high, though Castro was held incommunicado for over two months. Prisoners were visited by women of the city of Santiago, who brought them food and cigarettes.[51] They occasionally hummed the Hymn of Liberty, now called the Hymn of July 26, in the courtroom.[52] The regime's machinations revealed its vulnerability to the attackers as the actions of the army had revealed its indiscipline and low morale. Hugh Thomas concluded that the experiences of combat and torture, and the proximity of death, showed Castro how distinct he was from other Ortodoxo leaders and led him to conclude that further direct action was the only path to pursue.[53] There is no evidence that Castro had resolved to undertake a guerrilla struggle or further Moncada-style assaults. He was a man too attuned to the constantly changing nature of political conflict to pre-determine his course. When released, he told interviewers he planned to "stay in Cuba and fight the government in the open, pointing out its mistakes, denouncing its faults...trying to unite the whole country under the flag of Chibás' revolutionary movement".[54] Struggle was a certainty, but armed struggle seemed an option to be determined by the actions of the regime and the traditional opposition parties.

HISTORY WILL ABSOLVE ME

Castro had barely escaped summary execution himself and had seen his group of militants savagely massacred. Only the chance fact that the lieutenant in command of the squad capturing him had known him personally saved his life.[55] It cost Lieutenant Sarriá a year in a military prison.[56] Castro was kept isolated from the other prisoners and appeared only twice in court with them, though he communicated regularly with them via written messages.[57] The regime conspired to keep Castro out of the courtroom by declaring him ill. In this they were frustrated by the examining physicians' sympathy for the rebels and by Castro's letter to the court, smuggled in and read by Melba Hernandez.[58]

It was in these circumstances that Castro's political direction of the defense was exercised. Lacking absolutely in contrition, Castro's court appearances were attacks on the regime and its false accusations. In his own separate defense after the others had been sentenced, he spoke for some hours. Later, in the Isle of Pines Presidio, Castro reconstructed bit by bit his oral defense as <u>History Will Absolve Me</u>. It was written, he maintained, in solitary confinement in lime juice between the lines of ordinary letters. Castro told Robert Taber, "you would be surprised how much trouble it was. I could write for only twenty minutes or so each evening at sunset, when the sun slanted across the paper in such a way as to make the letters visible, glistening on the paper".[59] After Melba Hernandez and Haydée Santamaría were released in 1954, they and others set to work printing and distributing twenty thousand copies within Cuba.[60] However, few copies of the pamphlet were abroad among the general public before January, 1959.

The pamphlet was aimed perhaps more at the future militants and sympathizers of M-26 rather than at the total Cuban population, although it has long since become essential political reading in schools, in the Cuban Communist Party and in the FAR. It was more radical than mainstream Cuban populism and, in Farber's judgement, "addressed to a political vanguard".[61] Though Castro spoke of "one hundred thousand copies" to be distributed, it was aimed at the more politically aware elements of Cuban society, from which Castro hoped to draw a united movement, as Martí had done. In so far as this is the case, it is important to assess the tenor of the language and arguments contained in Castro's defense. What strikes the reader first is that Castro spent much more time and energy indicting the regime than in constructing a legal defense (this is no surprise, given that the verdict and sentence were predictable). The flow of language in that hot and isolated special courtroom is intended to create a feeling of shame and outrage in every Cuban with national pride. The magistrates, themselves, are berated, in respectful terms, for having allowed the case to proceed under the conditions and falsehoods constructed by the regime: "You have publicly called this case the most significant in the history of the Republic. If you sincerely believed so, you should not have allowed the trial to be degraded, time after time, by the flouting of your authority".[62] Castro refers to his solitary confinement, the various plots to keep him from appearing in the main courtroom, and the lack of legal materials for his defense. The magistrates, indeed, had ordered Castro released from solitary and brought to the court. But, "as often as it has demanded...this court was never obeyed! One after another, all its orders were disregarded".[63] Castro concluded that "here was a regime afraid to bring an accused before the courts; a regime of blood and terror which shrank in fear at the moral conviction of a defenseless man - unarmed, slandered and isolated...what dreadful crimes this regime must have committed, to so fear the voice of one accused man!"[64]

From the beginning, all references to Batista and the dictatorship convey indignation and national shame,[65] much as in the muckraking style of Chibás' fulminations against corruption. Words like "lies, cowardly, base, treacherous, shameful, scandalous" are constantly applied to the machinations of the regime during the trial. One of the stylistic ingredients of Castro's oratory familiar to students of the Cuban revolution is apparent in this early speech: the construction of opposites and their reiteration in many forms. The Batista regime is contrasted with heroic figures of the past, with the martyrs and survivors of Moncada, and with "honorable" soldiers. Castro finishes his sketch of the attempts made to silence him by claiming the sponsorship of Martí, the absolute opposite of Batista. It makes no difference that he was denied access to legal texts and even to the writings of Martí, as "I carry in my heart the teachings of the <u>Maestro</u> and in my mind the noble ideas of all men who have ever defended the freedom of the peoples of the world".[66] It is not Castro or the rebels on trial, in his opinion. It is "Batista... Monstrum horrendum" and it does not matter that "brave and worthy young men were condemned" if tomorrow "the people will condemn the dictator and his cruel henchmen".[67]

The legal defense that Castro makes revolves around the notion of constitutionality. He was prosecuted under a statute referring to the perpetration of acts of armed uprising against the constitutional powers of the state. He reminds the court that Batista's coup was against the 1940 constitution and that he, Castro, had brought suit against such sedition, only to have it refused. As a result,

> the struggle began against this man who was disregarding the law, who had usurped power by the use of violence against the will of the people, who was guilty of oppression against the established order, and who tortured, murdered, imprisoned and prosecuted those who had taken up the fight to defend the law and to restore liberty to the people.[68]

At the time, the courts had decided that revolution is the source of law. But Castro refuses to grace the coup with the word "revolution": "The nocturnal assault of the 10th of March could never be classified as a revolution".[69]

Resistance to despots is legitimate, argues Castro. He cites the 1940 constitution's article 40: "It is legitimate to use adequate resistance to protect previously granted individual rights".[70] Then, he proceeds to marshal historical examples of resistance to despots and legal principles pertaining to the same. And the court itself is accused: "With what right do the courts send to prison citizens who tried to redeem their country by giving their own blood, their own lives?"[71] After March 10, 1952, "the courts failed to act because force prevented them from doing so. Well then, confess: this time force will oblige you to condemn me. The first time, you were unable to punish the guilty; now you will be compelled to punish the innocent. The maiden of justice twice raped by force!"[72]

It is patriotism to which Castro ultimately appeals

as he builds his case for national unity against Batista. References to Cuban history are used to compare Batista's regime with the excesses of the Spanish colonial authorities: "Future generations will be struck with horror whenever they look back on these acts of barbarity unprecedented in our history...I feel shame as a Cuban..."[73] Nor do the henchmen of Batista in charge of repression and torture escape the indictment. Colonel del Río Chaviano is compared to Spanish General Valeriano Weyler, the man in charge of punitive campaigns against the Cuban population in the War of Independence.[74]

The contrast drawn is strong. Castro repeatedly refers to the young martyrs as Cuban patriots, real men and heroes rightfully inheriting the traditions and mission of Céspedes, Agramonte, Maceo, Gómez and Martí. Though many were tortured and killed, Castro claims they are like Martí - "to die for the fatherland is to live".[75] Their redemption is not to be sought through vengeance, since their lives are priceless: "The happiness of their people is the only tribute worthy of them".[76] They were patriots nurtured by Cuban history and the Cuban people. Castro speaks for them: "We are Cubans and to be Cubans implies a duty. Not to fulfil that duty is a crime, is treason. We are proud of the history of our country...taught to venerate the glorious example of our heroes and our martyrs...we were taught that the titan Maceo had said that liberty is not begged but is won with the blade of a machete".[77] Castro reminds the court that Martí was their guide and that what they learned in school made them see their duty. Rebellion against tyranny was what they learned was a Cuban's historical duty: "We sang every afternoon a hymn whose verses say that to live in chains is to live in opprobrium...all this we learned and we will never forget, even though today in our land there is murder and prison, in this Republic where the president is a criminal and a thief!"[78] Such declarations were Castro's affirmation of his faith in the power of ideas to affect history. As he said in his letter to the court protesting his being declared ill, again quoting Martí, "a just principle from the depths of a cave is stronger than an army".[79] His expectation was that the ideas he was expressing would strike a response in a majority of Cubans and create a movement to overthrow Batista and carry out radical changes.

The theme of virility and manhood, combined with bravery, runs throughout Castro's defense. He compares the "endless stream of clean young blood" with the "endless stream of lies and slanders poured out in his [Batista's] crude, odious, repulsive language".[80] The torturers are contrasted with those who sacrificed themselves. Castro recalls that the rebels refused to recant their ideals under torture or to declare that Prío had been their paymaster: "And no complaint or begging was heard. Even when they had been deprived of their virile organs, our boys were still a thousand times more manly than all their tormentors together".[81] And Haydée is held up as an example of "the heroism and the dignity of Cuban womanhood",[82] someone whom torture and the witnessing of torture could not break.

A very important element running through much of Castro's defense is his assessment of Batista's army. His views are again laid out in a consideration of opposites: the corrupt versus the honest, the thief versus the patriot, the cowardly versus the manly, those oppressing the people for the interests of an oligarchy and those whose feelings align them with the people. Castro begins this analysis by addressing the one hundred officers and soldiers surrounding him: "I am grateful for the polite and serious attention they give me. I only wish I could have the whole army before me. I know one day this army will seethe with rage to wash away the awful, the shameless bloodstains splattered across the uniform by the present ruthless clique in their lust for power".[83] Castro separates the army mass from the clique, Batista and the oligarchy here and continued to do so through the guerrilla period. He seeks to show the rank and file that they are part of the people and have no common interest with the ruling military cliques or the oligarchy, that they are being used. He puts these words into the mouths of the clique:

> Die for the regime, soldier, give it your sweat and blood. We shall dedicate a speech to you and award you a posthumous promotion (when it no longer matters) and afterwards we shall go on living luxuriously, making ourselves rich. Kill, abuse, oppress the people. When the people grow weary and all this comes to an end, you shall pay for our crimes, while we go abroad to live like princes. And if, one day, we return, do not knock – neither you nor your children – on the doors of our mansions, for we shall be millionaires, and millionaires do not know the poor. Kill, soldier, oppress the people, die for the regime, give your sweat and blood.[84]

Castro follows the theme of the generals' falsehoods, condemning the conception of honor which ratifies the killing of prisoners. The soldiers had been told that the rebels were financed by Prío and that they had tortured captives, but neither was the case. The contrast is drawn: the rebels took prisoners and "twenty who were our prisoners have been present here and according to their own words received not even an offensive word from us. Before you, also, appeared thirty soldiers who were wounded, many in the street fighting, and none were killed by us".[85] This rebel respect for the prisoner, the opposite of army policy at Moncada, became an important political and propaganda element in the political education of the Rebel Army and the Revolutionary Armed Forces.

For whom did the Generation of the Centenary sacrifice their lives, Castro asks rhetorically. What were the chances of success? He answers with a short schema of the Cuban social structure. It is intended to show that Batista's regime did nothing to remedy the symptoms of underdevelopment and backwardness afflicting large fractions of the population. He enumerates the seven hundred thousand unemployed, the five hundred thousand agrarian workers with only four months of cane harvest employment to sustain them each year, the four hundred thousand industrial workers at the mercy of dishonest unions, employers and usurers, the one hundred thousand tenant farmers, the poorly-paid teacher corps, the twenty thousand petty businessmen plagued by corrupt officials - all these comprise "the people, the ones who know misfortune and, therefore, are capable of fighting with limitless courage".[86] The rebel traditions of Oriente made it the desired locus for the start of a popular rebellion, where "the people" meant

> the vast unredeemed, the masses, to whom all make promises and whom all deceive; we mean the people who yearn for a better, more dignified and more just nation; who are moved by ancestral aspirations for justice, for they have suffered injustice and mockery, generation after generation; who long for great and wise changes in all aspects of their life; people who, to attain these changes, are ready to give even the very last breath of their lives - when they believe in something or in someone, especially when they believe in themselves.[87]

Had "the people" been mobilized by the distribution of arms and a call to rebellion based on the Moncada program, argues Castro, the army would not have resisted as a body.

The program, radical reformist in nature but not detailed, was embodied in five "revolutionary laws": 1) a return to the 1940 constitution, "until such time as the people should decide to modify or change it"[88], with the revolutionary movement assuming legislative, executive and judicial powers.[89] 2) Land reform, establishing private property for all who farmed, with indemnifications for ex-owners based on current tax assessments, but with the new titles becoming non-mortgageable and non-transferable. 3) Profit-sharing for employees in larger enterprises. 4) Adjustments in the share of the sugar market for large and small planters to achieve a more equitable situation. 5) The confiscation of holdings gained by fraud, executed by special courts, such property to be used to set up retirement funds and to build hospitals, asylums and charities.

Such a program, Castro states, would be the minimum. Further reforms of education and agriculture would come later, as would nationalization of utilities and telephones, plus prosecution of tax evaders. Cuba would open itself to refugees from Latin American tyrants. The grand problems of under-development would be addressed, with the fundamental project being the provision of employment and a decent livelihood to all. Castro argues that the conditions of under-development come from a history of greedy oligarchies and foreign dependency. It is at this point that he comes to attack the shortcomings of capitalism directly. The state as constituted seems to him to be incapable of resolving the problems of health, education, housing, industrialization and agriculture: "Society is moved to compassion upon hearing of the kidnapping of, or the murder of, one child, but they are criminally indifferent to the mass murder of thousands of children who die every year from the lack of facilities".[90]

The attacks he levels against the abuses of individuals can be seen as a reformer's zeal. Nevertheless, there are revolutionary aspects to Castro's attacks on the status quo in Cuba which presage a Marxist position. His plans for industrialization call for a revolutionary government to "mobilize all inactive capital" (capital tied up in graft, uncollected taxes and arms purchases), since development and social problems "are not solved by spontaneous generation".[91] Here, he means that capitalism is incapable of resolving the social and economic imbalances Cuba suffers. He condemns those who believe that "absolute freedom of enterprise", "guarantees to investment capital" and "the law of supply and demand" can restructure the status quo. Such principles in fact created the problems of underdevelopment. As he says, "the future of the country and the solution of its problems cannot continue to depend on the selfish interests of a dozen financiers, nor on the cold calculations of profits that ten or twelve magnates draw up in their air-conditioned offices".[92] And the analysis of the reasons for underdevelopment, though the term is never used, links the Cuban capitalist class to international capital, much as in later dependency theory. For Castro, the limitations of the profit motive, in providing electricity to rural areas, in developing an indigenous industry, in providing housing and education, point to a weak and dependent national bourgeoisie, even a commercial and agricultural oligarchy, and a state subservient to the limitations of a dominated and dependent domestic capital.[93]

Castro then draws a picture of the potential of Cuba. Sanguine as always about the possibilities and using his style of presenting opposites, he claims

> Cuba could easily provide for a population three times as great as it now has, so there is no excuse for the abject poverty of a single one of its present inhabitants. The markets should be overflowing with produce, the pantries should be full, all hands should be working. This is not an inconceivable thought. What is inconceivable is that anyone should go to bed hungry, that children should die for lack of medical attention; what is inconceivable is that 30% of our farm people cannot write their names and that 99% of them know nothing of Cuba's history. What is inconceivable is that the majority of our rural people are now living in worse circumstances than were the Indians Columbus discovered living in the finest land that human eyes had ever seen.[94]

Castro outlines schemes for agricultural development via land reform and co-operatives, with state technical and financial assistance. Housing shortages would be solved by cutting all rents, tripling taxes on rented houses, and using mass state financing to construct housing. They would not be solved by unleashing capital or providing subsidies to developers. Education would receive priority. All these plans indeed became core projects for the revolutionary regime five years later. Funds for such plans, which would end unemployment, avoidable illness and ignorance, were to come from currently embezzled government monies, the end of corrupt officials taking kickbacks from large companies owing taxes, extensive sinecure systems, and an end to arms purchases abroad.[95]

Finally, Castro reminds the court that in the year of the Apóstol's Centenary, "his dream lives...his people are rebellious...his people are worthy...His people are faithful to his memory. There are Cubans who have fallen defending his doctrines. There are boys who in magnificent selflessness come to die beside his tomb, giving their blood and their lives so that the dream of Martí could continue to live in the heart of his country".[96]

This document, Castro's defense, is a summing up of his own political education to late 1953.[97] It contains all the elements of the political education the new Mambises, the Rebel Army, would receive in their Mexican exile and training. An amalgam of the experiences of the Moncada assault and repression, with a deep sense of history in the making and of the continuity of Cuban history, it is a prime example of Castro's gift for articulation. Hope and conviction in the face of repression, sacrifice for the future benefit of the Cuban nation, belief in the power of revolutionary ideas, and a faith in the moral superiority of the cause are embedded in the document. Such are the moral factors contained in History Will Absolve Me, factors vital to the success of the insurrection and to the coherence and continuity of the revolutionary armed forces since 1953.

POLITICAL EDUCATION ON THE ISLE OF PINES

Crucial for revolutionary morale is the conviction that one counts, that one's thought and actions are important, that one is affecting history.[98] Only through this conviction can ideas, the subjective, become a material force in history. Ideas can then be wielded by a person, a class or a people as weapons in a struggle. When ideas come together in a coherent explanatory system and are applied to objective situations or events they become at the least a certain perspective and, at best, an ideology. They become frameworks of interpretation and guides to action. Castro and the surviving leadership attempted to move the work of transforming ideas into a material force in Cuban history forward among the political prisoners on the Isle of Pines. The evolution of a revolutionary political mythology continued.

With few exceptions, the captured survivors of the Moncada assault in the Presidio on the Isle of Pines were serving sentences of ten years or more.[99] Many of those who escaped capture at Moncada had sought refuge in foreign embassies in Havana, and had left Cuba to reside in Costa Rica and, later, Mexico.[100] Morale during the trail had remained high, and those in the Boniato prison in Santiago, separated from Castro, had maintained a tight discipline among themselves.[101] It was with these twenty-eight comrades that the Rebel Army had its beginnings.

Education of these first cadres was to be both general and political. Prison itself was to be a political education, aiding in the formation of a dedicated core of revolutionaries which would later impel a broad civic movement of resistance. It was a conception of a revolutionary vanguard which Castro embraced and it had come naturally out of the experiences of preparing a movement to attack the dictatorship at Moncada. As one of the prisoners, still a member of the Cuban military and political leadership cadres in the 1980s, remembered several years after victory, "from the outset Fidel told us our imprisonment should be combative, and we should acquire rich experience that would help in the continuation of the struggle once we were freed".[102]

To carry out the educational project, a school was

set up, called the Academia Abel Santamaría, in honor of the martyred second-in-command.[103] Castro gave classes on philosophy, world history, geography and oratory. Oscar Alcalde was the mathematics instructor. Pedro Miret lectured on political economy and Jesús Montané gave classes in foreign languages, particularly English. Pepe Suárez Blanco lectured on Cuban history, while Armando Mestre was in charge of the exercise program, which included intense volleyball matches. The "faculty", with Raúl Castro included, studied Marx's Capital.[104] However, the academy was not permitted to function long. It was closed after several months when Batista paid a visit to the prison. The rebels had sung the July 26 hymn through the bars and Batista had become incensed. As a result, several prisoners were put in bartolinas 'underground holes'. The hymn's author, Agustín Díaz Cartaya, was beaten, and visits were curtailed. Castro was placed in solitary confinement.[105]

Physical conditions in the prison were harsh at the whim of the authorities, and Castro's cell had no light or water. However, as in many prisons, the guards were less than fully committed to the desires of the authorities, and Castro managed to communicate with his comrades and with sympathizers on the outside, through a voluminous correspondence. He also constructed an oil lamp in order to read.[106] He turned to books and the writing of letters.

For Castro, reading meant a chance to delve into "the author's social ideas".[107] Everything he read seemed a significant lesson in world history applicable to his own time. His encouragement of the others in their reading was based on a belief that books held ideas, and that ideas were the root of human progress: "I never stopped thinking it was worthwhile spending my time on such studies [of Cuban and world history and of socially-motivated literature] if they would help me combat existing evils".[108] Prison for Castro, as for many before and since with political lives, provided an opportunity for the development of views and reflection on the past and present: "This prison is a terrific classroom. I can shape my view of the world in here, and figure out the meaning of my life".[109]

Study and reading was required of all the rebel prisoners. Castro regarded them as "an elite. Those who learned to handle weapons are now learning to wield books for the important battles of the future. Their discipline is Spartan; their lives, their education is Spartan; everything about them is Spartan, and their faith and commitment are so unshakeable that they too will rise to the cry 'with the shield or on a shield'".[110]

The man who received most of Castro's prison letters was Luís Conte Agüero, an Ortodoxo radio commentator and long-time friend from university days.[111] The first letter, edited and released later as a "Manifesto to the Nation", was written in December of 1953.[112] It called upon Conte Agüero to organize denunciation of the massacre at Moncada: "I understand that terror paralyzed people's hearts for a long time, but now it is no longer possible to endure the mantle of total silence that cowardice has thrown on those horrendous crimes, the reaction of despicable and brutal hatred by a tyranny that defies description".[113] The letter provided descriptions of the tortures and assassinations and, as in History Will Absolve Me, compared the 1871 executions of anti-Spanish student demonstrators with the 1953 massacre. With quotes from Martí and criticism of those who cried putschism, including the PSP and the Ortodoxos, the letter is another brick in the edifice of morale and the power of righteous ideals which became the most significant weapon in the Cuban revolution.

The movement's workers and sympathizers had three tasks in 1954. First, they were to keep alive the memory of Moncada and agitate for amnesty. The political situation had lightened somewhat with Batista's announcement of November elections.[114] Castro felt the focus of Cuban politics shifting from revulsion against the 1952 coup towards the electoral path and, as is evidenced by one of the letters to Conte Agüero, felt isolated and outside the political debates in Cuba: "To be a prisoner is to be condemned to a forced silence; to hear and read what is said and written without being able to state an opinion; to be subjected to the attacks of cowards who take advantage of the situation to aggress upon those who cannot defend themselves and to make plans which would require our immediate reply, were we not physically prevented from doing so".[115]

Second, those outside had to maintain some semblance of a revolutionary network within Cuba and with the exiles. Such clandestine work involved visits to the prison and the diffusion of letters and documents. Castro wrote Melba Hernandez, stating that "propaganda cannot be abandoned for a single minute, because it is the soul of every struggle".[116]

Third, and allied with the second task, the movement was engaged in reproducing and distributing History Will Absolve Me under heavy police surveillance.[117] For Castro, it was "a pamphlet of decisive importance for its ideological content and its tremendous accusations".[118]

Castro's own political education advanced further towards a Leninist style of organization, with an adjunct of caudillismo. He rarely questioned his own fitness for leadership. He became more convinced of the need for revolutionary changes and for a core of revolutionary workers to move the project forward outside of prison. The movement for change had to achieve some unity and the "excessive number of personalities and groups" would have to be diminished. As with Lenin's conception of the vanguard organization in What Is To Be Done?, Castro's notion of a militant vanguard was developed in conditions of repression, censorship, torture and imprisonment, with no early prospects of success. He wrote that

> the indispensable conditions for the integration of a true civic movement are ideology, discipline and leadership...leadership is essential...perhaps it was Napoleon who said that one bad general outweighs more than twenty good ones. You cannot organize a movement in which everyone believes he has a right to make public declarations without consulting anyone. Neither can you expect anything from an organization full of anarchic men who, at the first difficulty, take the road they consider best, wrecking and destroying the vehicle. Organization and propaganda have to be so strong that they implacably destroy all who try to create divisions, sects or schism.[119]

Nor was a vanguard core of militants enough. Again, similar to Lenin's emphasis in What Is To Be Done? on political education, the press and a mass line, Castro asserted that "the program must contain a full, concrete and acceptable exposition of the social and economic problems which confront the country, such that it can give to the masses a truly novel and positive message".[120]

When censorship was lifted in Cuba in 1954, due to domestic and international pressure,[121], the rebels had a chance to have their ideas more exposed to the public. Details of the Moncada events and atrocities surfaced. The regime was experiencing internal conflicts, those for some degree of liberalization ranged against those favoring a continued hard line. Several members of the government approached Castro on a visit to the prison, telling him not to be impatient.[122] His response to the sally he put in a letter of March 1955 to Conte Agüero: "How strangely the regime has dealt with us! They call us assassins in public and gentlemen in private. They fight us rancorously in public and come to make our acquaintance in private. One day it is an army colonel who gives me a cigar, offers me a book, and everybody is very courteous. Another day three cabinet ministers, smiling, affable, respectful, appear".[123]

Castro refused these overtures and would make no compromises, either in his criticism of those who welcomed Batista's announcement of elections, made shortly after the Moncada trials, or in his attacks on the regime. Nonetheless, the combination of some renewed economic growth in Cuba's economy, official United States approval of Batista's uncontested 1954 electoral "victory", and a vigorous amnesty campaign led to the release of the prisoners on May 15, 1955. Prío's eternal plans for overthrowing Batista had come to naught and the Ortodoxos were confused and divided.[124] The amnesty campaign was a practical alliance. Middle-class figures like Conte Agüero had access to politicians and to the media, while Castro supporters appeared at campaign rallies to raise the amnesty issue. Perhaps it was Batista's desire to increase the legitimacy of his regime which persuaded him to grant amnesty. He felt stronger in 1955 than before.[125]

The Moncada experiences and their aftermath marked Cuban revolutionary cadres for life. There were those who were disaffected, but those who remained with Castro were bonded to his leadership and followed his guidance in ideological matters. According to one of them, Montané, they emerged convinced of and united in the decision to continue armed struggle.[126] This did not mean the movement would abjure flexibility. It meant only that there would be no denial of principles. The creation of a broad civic movement would require political adeptness and alliances, but the core of militants would remain intact. The political arena would be employed to gain mass support for the program of the movement and to gain allies, but the core would remain prepared for insurrectionary struggle. Again, the parallels of revolutionary strategy in Cuba and czarist Russia are striking, even given the vast differences in class structure and in the actual class forces which made the respective insurrections. Castro's methods recall Lenin's five propositions on the organization of professional revolutionaries.[127]

With these intensely political experiences and these few comrades, the revolutionary leadership would forge a band of insurrectionists for the second attempt to overthrow Batista and institute radical changes. The depth of the Moncada experiences cannot be underestimated. Such experiences of direct confrontation are political in the ultimate sense of politics as the development and exercise of power, the clash of forces. Force cannot be limited to its conception as armed bodies or as institutions, for that is to ignore the force to which one must always return in the study of revolutions, the force of ideas.

NOTES

1. Castro, in Lockwood, p. 141.
2. Marta Rojas, in La Generación, describes the court appearances where each defendant proudly declared, "Yes, I participated in the assault".
3. Castro, History, p. 24.
4. Jesús Montané Oropesa, "El asalto a la posta 3

el 26 de julio", in Comisión de Orientación Revolucionaria del Partido Unido de la Revolución Socialista Cubana, <u>Relatos del asalto al Moncada</u> (Havana: Ediciones Populares, 1964), p. 100. See also Raúl Castro, "En el VIII aniversario del 26 de julio", <u>Verde Olivo</u>, 16 July 61, pp. 3-11.

5. Castro, <u>History</u>, p. 29.
6. Montané, "El asalto", p. 100.
7. Ibid.
8. See Rubén Castillo Armas, "A la misma hora del Moncada en Bayamo se escribió otra página heroica", in <u>Relatos</u>, pp. 131-6. Thomas, p. 838, suggests that the army's horses were disturbed by the attackers' approach.
9. Castro, <u>History</u>, p. 27.
10. Montané, p. 88.
11. Bonachea and San Martín, p. 21. See also the account by Capt. Andrés García Díaz, "El asalto al cuartel de Bayamo", in <u>Relatos</u>, pp. 137-42.
12. Castro, <u>History</u>, p. 25: "Our losses in the battle had been insignificant"; Robert Taber, <u>M-26, Biography of a Revolution</u> (New York: Lyle Stuart, 1961), p.41: "Total rebel casualties at Moncada had come to five dead, four wounded".
13. Castro, <u>History</u>, p. 56; Taber, p. 41, gives a figure of twenty-two dead and fifty-seven wounded.
14. Castro, <u>History</u>, p. 47.
15. García Díaz, p. 137.
16. Raúl Castro, "En el VIII anniversario", p. 9.
17. The sorry and horrifying behavior of the army is recounted in Castro's <u>History</u> and in numerous witnesses' accounts. See especially those of Melba Hernandez, Haydée Santamaría, Andrés García and José Ponce Díaz in <u>Relatos</u>. See also Rojas, <u>La Generación</u>.
18. Dubois, p. 37.
19. Bonachea and San Martín, pp. 23-4, refer to the official report by Colonel del Río Chaviano.
20. Castro, <u>History</u>, pp. 26-7.
21. Melba Hernández, "Los hombres más valientes que pueda haber", in <u>Relatos</u>, pp. 77-86.
22. Alfredo Reyes Trejo, "Del Moncada a las montañas", <u>Verde Olivo</u>, 30 July 72, pp. 24-33.
23. Vilma Espín, interview in Franqui, <u>Diary</u>, pp. 62-3.
24. Taber, p. 43.
25. Castro paid tribute to them in <u>History</u>, pp.26, 59.
26. Castro, <u>History</u>, pp. 26-7.
27. See Thomas, pp. 792-800.
28. Ibid., p. 800.
29. Ibid., p. 801.
30. Ibid., pp. 798, 852.
31. Thomas, p. 793.
32. Ibid., pp. 843-4.
33. See Thomas, Ibid: "Batista's secretary,

Andrés Domingo, was telephoned by a Santiago magistrate and asked, regarding the repression, 'Are you trying to revive the epoch of Machado with all these assassinations?'"

34. See, for example, Pepe Suárez Blanco, "Relato de un combatiente del Moncada", Verde Olivo, 29 July 62, pp. 83-5; Castro's July 26, 1962 speech in Santiago, "Ante el recuerdo de nuestros muertos, juremos ser fieles a la Patria y a la Revolución", Verde Olivo, 5 Aug. 62, pp. 12-18.

35. Karl von Clausewitz, On War, ed. and tr. Michael Howard and Peter Paret (Princeton: Princeton University Press, 1976), p. 185.

36. In Franqui, The Twelve, p.74.

37. B. Traven, General From The Jungle, tr. Desmond Vesey (New York: Hill and Wang, 1974), p. 54.

38. See evidence of this perception among other participants in Franqui, The Twelve, passim.

39. Dubois, p. 41.

40. Col. del Río Chaviano's official report, cited in Bonachea and San Martín, pp. 23-4.

41. See Rojas, La Generación, pp. 81-3, 91-3.

42. Bonachea and San Martín, p. 24.

43. Thomas, p. 843.

44. Bonachea and San Martín, p. 25.

45. Thomas, pp. 843-4.

46. Ibid., p. 843; Bonachea and San Martín, p. 26.

47. See Batista's statement in Diario de La Marina (Havana), 27 July 59, pp. 1, 3.

48. Castro, History, p. 14.

49. See Rojas, La Generación, pp. 330-31.

50. Ibid., pp. 123-37, pp. 256-69.

51. Dubois, p. 41.

52. Rojas, p. 196.

53. Thomas, p. 844.

54. May 15, 1955 interview, in Franqui, Diary, p. 89.

55. Dubois, p. 38; Rodolfo Rodriguez, "Porque Fidel Castro no fue asesinado al capturarlo el ejército en Oriente", Bohemia, 8 Mar. 59, pp. 63, 112. See also "Cuando Sarría detuvo a Fidel y a sus dos compañeros", Revolución, 26 July 62, p. 15.

56. Bonachea and Valdés, "Introduction", p. 53, fn. 250.

57. Ibid., p. 55.

58. Rojas, pp. 151-8.

59. Robert Taber, foreword to History Will Absolve Me, 3rd ed. (New York: Lyle Stuart, 1961), p. 6.

60. Francisco de Armas, "Como se editó en la clandestinidad la primera edición de 'La historia me absolverá'", in Relatos, pp. 143-48.

61. Farber, p. 186.

62. History, p. 13.

63. Ibid., p. 16.

64. History, p. 16.
65. The Spanish text conveys these sentiments much better than the translation. Certain words and combinations of words have a weightier emotional impact, given their Cuban cultural and historical context: "La odiosa bandera de la tiranía" 'The Odious banner of the tyranny'; "Hay militares manchados hasta el pelo con la sangre de muchos jovenes cubanos" 'There are military men stained up to their hair with the blood of many Cuban youths'; "Batista y su cohorte de politiqueros malos y desprestigiados" 'Batista and his cohort of evil and disreputable politicos'; "[La masa] está movida por ansias ancestrales de justicia" '[The masses] are driven by ancestral longings for justice'; "[Campesinos] que no tienen una pulgada de tierra para sembrar" '[Peasants] who haven't even an inch of ground to sow'; "El país no puede seguir de rodillas implorando los milagros de unos cuantos becerros de oro" 'The country cannot continue begging on its knees for miracles from a few golden calves'; "Somos cubanos, y ser cubano implica un deber, no cumplirlo es crimen y es traición" 'We are Cubans, and to be a Cuban implies a duty; not to fulfill it is a crime and is treason'.
66. History, p. 19.
67. Ibid., p. 17.
68. Ibid., p. 63.
69. History, p. 64.
70. Ibid., p. 67.
71. Ibid., p. 77.
72. Ibid., p. 63.
73. History, p. 45.
74. Ibid., p. 58-9.
75. Ibid., p. 59.
76. Ibid.
77. History, p. 77.
78. Ibid., p. 78.
79. "Letter to the Court of Appeals" (26 Sept. 53) in Bonachea and Valdés, pp. 163-4.
80. History, p. 22.
81. History, p. 51.
82. Ibid.
83. Ibid., p. 18.
84. Castro, History, p. 31.
85. Ibid., p. 56.
86. History, p. 35. See also Goldenberg, pp. 120-42 for a review of both the achievements and failings of the pre-1959 economy.
87. Ibid., p. 33.
88. History, p. 35.
89. A broad enough proviso, easily interpreted as revolutionary and not merely reformist, if done in the name of the working class.
90. History, p. 39.
91. Ibid., p. 41.

92. History, p. 40.
93. Ibid., p. 38. Cuban "capitalists" who import rather than industrialize and foreign "monopolies" that operate only "as far as it is profitable" are blamed for backwardness.
94. History, p. 43.
95. Ibid.
96. History, p. 78.
97. In Lockwood, p. 141, Castro says: "My Moncada speech was the seed of all the things that were done later on. It could be called Marxist if you wish, but probably a true Marxist would have said it was not".
98. André Malraux, Man's Hope, tr. Stuart Gilbert and Alastair MacDonald (New York: Random House, 1938), p. 164: "History is watching us...will judge us".
99. Haydée Santamaría and Melba Hernandez served only seven months. See Rojas, p. 370.
100. See, for example, Calixto García, "Nuestro deber era permanecer firmes a la orientación trazada por nuestro comandante en jefe", Verde Olivo, 1 Dec. 63, pp. 4-5, 56. García took refuge in the Uruguayan embassy and left for Costa Rica. See also Ricardo Rojo, My Friend Ché, tr. Julian Casart (New York: Dial Press, 1968), pp. 51-2, for a discussion of Cuban exiles in Costa Rica.
101. Dubois, p. 84.
102. Jesús Montané, "Del 26 de julio de 1953 al 15 de mayo 1955 - días de combate", Verde Olivo, 28 July 63, pp. 19-23.
103. Castro, letter of Dec. 22, 1953, in Franqui, Diary, p. 68.
104. Pepe Suárez Blanco, "Relato de un combatiente del Moncada", Verde Olivo, 29 July 62, pp. 83-5.
105. Montané, p. 23.
106. Bonachea and Valdés, p. 57.
107. Interview in Franqui, Diary, p. 66.
108. Castro, letter of March 18, 1954, in Franqui, Diary, p. 72.
109. Castro, letter of Dec. 19, 1953, in Diary, p. 67.
110. Castro, letter of Dec. 22, 1953, in Diary, p. 68.
111. See Luís Conte Agüero, Cartas del presidio, anticipo de una biografía de Fidel Castro (Havana: Editorial Lex, 1959).
112. Reproduced in Bonachea and Valdés, pp. 221-230.
113. Castro, "A Letter From Prison" (Dec. 12, 1953) in Bonachea and Valdés, p. 221.
114. See Thomas, pp. 851-62.
115. Castro, "A Letter of March, 1955", cited in Dubois, p. 86.
116. Castro, "Letter to Melba Hernandez" (April 17,

1954), in Bonachea and Valdés, pp. 230-2.
117. For a description of this work, see Francisco de Armas, "Como se editó en la clandestinidad la primera edición de 'La historia me absolverá'", in Relatos, pp. 143-8.
118. Castro, "Letter to Melba Hernandez", p. 231.
119. Castro, "Letter of August 14, 1954" to Conte Agüero, cited in Thomas, p. 859.
120. Ibid.
121. Dubois, p. 85. Dubois was instrumental in this campaign to end censorship.
122. Thomas, p. 857.
123. Castro, letter to Conte Agüero, March 1955, in Bonachea and Valdés, pp. 233-8.
124. Bonachea and Valdés, pp. 60-1.
125. See Batista, Piedras y leyes, pp. 38-9.
126. Montané, "Del 26 de julio...", p. 23.
127. Lenin, What Is To Be Done?, pp. 152-3.

4
The New *Mambises:* Exile and the So-Called Subjectivist Phase

INTRODUCTION

The process of creating a new and revolutionary political culture in Cuba, aimed primarily at a potential core of cadres and secondarily at the general population, went ahead during the short period of the militants' residence in Cuba after their release from prison. Castro was concerned to use the media - radio, television and the press - to advance criticism of the Batista regime. Such criticisms centered on the themes of dishonesty and corruption, the Moncada massacre and cover-up, and the tampering with and denial of constitutional guarantees. The continuing abuses and political repression of political opposition to the regime were also subjects for agitation. Castro's writings in the Ortodoxo newspaper La Calle hammered away at such themes and helped to discredit the regime. It was an attempt to create an anti-Batista consensus in public opinion and to show potential resistance cadres that only uncompromising opposition and unity would have results. In private meetings, Castro and his close supporters advanced the argument, again, that the traditional opposition party, the Auténticos, were ineffective, that a new resistance movement was necessary.[1] Such an argument reached its most radical form in advocating co-ordinated armed struggle and mass resistance. At this point, Castro's was one among many opposition groups and the public political education he and his supporters engaged in was not aimed at a vanguard beyond the Ortodoxo Party. Castro's supporters still claimed to represent Ortodoxo youth and left-wing factions. Rather than exclusive political claims, this political education campaign attempted to create a general anti-Batista climate. It was in private that the insurrectionist theme was pursued. It would have been suicidal to announce insurrectionism before the building of a movement had progressed some way. It was easier to allow the dictatorship's repression to weaken the arguments of electoralists. At the same time, the student leaders of the FEU, especially Antonio Echeverría, began to contemplate revolutionary violence.[2]

In this brief period, Castro wasted no opportunity to claim for the "revolutionary movement" the sanction of past Cuban national heroes like Maceo and Martí.[3] All Cuban politicians of the twentieth century were accustomed to declaring themselves and their political organizations the true heirs of such patriots. Castro used them to present the Moncada assault as an insurrectionary action in the tradition of a Cuban duty to resist tyranny and to identify the Moncada combatants with the pantheon of Cuban martyrs. The Moncada group was to be seen in the new political mythology as exemplary Cuban youth, representative of a new morality, untainted by links to past regimes, willing to sacrifice their lives for high ideals. They were presented as more honorable, patriotic and virile than the corrupt and sadistic elements in the regime and in the army. Within opposition circles, Castro's group gradually succeeded in projecting the Moncada muchachos as those to be joined and emulated in a new revolutionary movement rather than those who might be recruited, adding to other groups' appeal and revolutionary legitimacy.

MAY-JULY 1955

Fidel Castro and his Moncada comrades were released from prison on May 15, 1955, to an encouraging reception. Haydeé Santamaría, Melba Hernandez and family members met the group on the Isle of Pines.[4] Reporters and cameras surrounded the group and people milled about the hotel where they spent the day before the ferry trip to the southern port of Batabano.[5] Upon arrival in Havana, a "noisy and militant" crowd awaited them, including all the representatives of the FEU and the "entire national committee of the Ortodoxo Party".[6] On May 20, a formal welcome was held at the University, where so many demonstrations had occurred.[7] Castro and the Moncada combatants were heroes and symbols to a sizeable proportion of the population, a political force in their own right.

Castro was welcomed as an Ortodoxo member and collaborated with the Party in criticizing the regime. In an interview with Bohemia magazine, he stated he had no intention of creating a new party, that he approved of Dr. Raúl Chibás' (brother of Eddy Chibás) selection as Ortodoxo leader, and that he expected to work for the unity of all anti-Batista elements.[8] However, he called for general elections, a position the majority of Ortodoxos did not share. They desired only congressional elections.[9] Nevertheless, Castro contributed to an Ortodoxo manifesto of May 21, 1955, which criticized the "economic crisis" in Cuba, blaming it on government mismanagement and corruption, and the "social crisis" of political censorship and persecution, a lack of constitutional guarantees.[10] He even made public statements that implied the abandonment of a policy of armed struggle: "Sometimes a mass movement can accomplish what an insurrection cannot"[11], but did not accept a position in the Ortodoxo hierarchy.[12]

Although the mid-1955 Cuban political climate was comparatively mild and "there was widespread feeling among Ortodoxos and middle-class professional Cubans that negotiations with Batista were both possible and really the only viable way ahead"[13], public acrimony and repression increased. The regime suspended Ortodoxo radio and television programs shortly after the release of the manifesto, and Castro was prohibited from making public speeches after his article "Chaviano, You Lie!" appeared in Bohemia.[14]

Castro had already entered the lists against Batista on May 25 when he issued a press release condemning the arrest of Pedro Miret, one of the outstanding combatants at Moncada. In it, he claimed that the Moncada prisoners saw themselves as "guinea pigs" who would "find out if there were political guarantees or not". Given the arrest of Miret, Castro saw the amnesty as a "bloody hoax played on the people and the press, who fought so much for it...[and] on those...who are trying to encourage a peaceful climate through a calm and respectful attitude". He recommended that "exiles should not return to Cuba if things continue this way".[15]

In his challenge to Chaviano[16], one of the officers responsible for the Moncada massacre, Castro directly addressed the Moncada events, questioning the government's account. In his penchant for drawing contrasts, Castro posed the Moncada group's respectful attitudes towards the army dead and the prison personnel against Chaviano's accusations of hatred, malice and the mistreatment of Moncada soldiers wounded or captured by the rebels. Castro recalled figures of dead and wounded in battles during the War of Independence and contrasted them with the appalling proportions at Moncada among the rebels, sixteen to one.[17] As before, Castro declared Martí was his guide("Martí's thought, which preaches love, not hatred"), his respect for military men who were honest, and a promise to respect and aid the families of army dead at Moncada when the "magnanimous and concerned revolution attains power".[18] Chaviano, on the other hand, he challenged to public debate on the Moncada events, claiming that "with the blood of your fallen compañeros [at Moncada] you knead a fortune of millions which all of Cuba knows about. Smuggling, vice and any murky business venture finds a magnificent entrepreneur in you".[19]

The relaxation of censorship meant the divulgation of the Moncada assassination, and Castro used the temporary freedom of the press to publish columns attacking the regime. His vehicle was La Calle, a newspaper sponsored by an Ortodoxo leader, Luis Orlando Rodriguez. In June, Rodriguez was detained, in a climate of increasing incidents of "beatings and assassinations [by the police] that was paralleled only by the terrorist activities of some opposition groups".[20] Batista made a speech, June 5, condemning "bullies or braggarts...who have received amnesty, because I do not want them to provoke our men any more".[21] In a blistering response entitled "Murderer's Hands", Castro attacked the regime's spokesmen who were using the terms "beast, gangster, murderer, nut, crazy" to describe him. Then he addressed Batista personally: "What do you want me to do? Seek refuge in a foreign embassy? To kneel down while you threaten and insult me?" Batista had spoken of the "hands" the ruling power might use. Castro condemned this provocation to violence and questioned the claim that Batista was "the only real man around".[22]

The spate of bombings also received attention in Castro's columns in La Calle. In "Against Terror and Crime" (June 11, 1955), he argued that such action only freed the regime to employ repression against the opposition: "To set off bombs...can only be the work of scoundrels without conscience who want to serve the government instead of fighting it".[23] Jorge Agostini, an ex-official of the Prio and Grau regimes, had been killed by the police, and Castro linked terrorist bombs, Batista's veiled threat to "unleash the hand" of the regime, and Agostini's death. He called for national mobilization and justice, adding Agostini to the list of martyrs "of our struggle for national liberation".[24] A particularly sinister note was added to these events. Castro was constantly shadowed by police agents, and a car riddled with bullets was allegedly prepared, within which a dead and escaping Castro would be found.[25]

In these circumstances, Castro worked on the establishment of a new revolutionary organization along Leninist lines dedicated to insurrection. On the one hand, the public arena was employed to demonstrate "the regime's inflexibility...[which made] revolution...a last resort encouraged by the enemy".[26] On the other, Castro and his Moncada comrades began to seek out new recruits for a revolutionary organization. Contact was made with Mario Llerena and others in the Movimiento de Liberación Radical, a recently-formed group.[27] Nothing substantial came of this meeting, though Llerena later joined the M-26.[28]

More rewarding were meetings with former members of Professor García Bárcena's MNR, especially Faustino Pérez and Armando Hart, and with Ortodoxo youth activists from Oriente province. Through one of the latter, María Antonia Figueroa, Castro made contact with some young radicals of Santiago, Pepito Tey and Frank País.[29] The latter two individuals had been acquainted with Renato Guitart, the sole Moncada attacker from Santiago, in the MNR.[30] Tey and País had been student activists in Santiago and País, a gifted organizer, had early on been convinced that armed action was the only path against Batista. The Moncada assault had greatly impressed him.[31] País had already had considerable experience in organization and in actions. He headed a group called Acción Nacional Revolucionaria (ANR), made up mostly of secondary and university students from Santiago. The ANR had set bombs, captured weapons and secured dynamite in the Charco Redondo mining area, known for its militant miners. They also printed revolutionary pamphlets.[32] Lester Rodriguez, a Moncada veteran, and María Antonia Figueroa were delegated by Castro to persuade País and Tey to join the nascent organization. This they accomplished in the late fall of 1955.[33]

Thus, the second incarnation of a revolutionary organization was created. In 1952-3, Castro had brought together the Santamaría group with some working-class, peasant and Ortodoxo elements. Now, the Moncada survivors were joined by middle-class individuals and more young Ortodoxos, all with some previous anti-Batista experience. As this process got underway, Castro decided on exile in order to form an expeditionary force to begin the overthrow of Batista. Castro had concluded that "all doors being closed to the people for peaceful struggle, there is no solution except that of '68 and '95".[34] The decision was based on the closing off of access to the media, the arrest of some comrades, and the increasing virulence of personal attacks on Castro by Batistiano police and military figures. Castro cited Martí's Edad de oro in order to claim spiritual sponsorship for his venture: "When there are many without honor, there are always some who have within themselves the dignity of many. Those are the ones who revolt with terrible force against those who steal the people's freedom".[35] Convinced that the dictatorship intended to remain in power for twenty years, Castro declared he would return "with the tyranny beheaded at [his] one's feet, or not at all".[36]

EXILE IN MEXICO AND THE TRAINING
OF THE EXPEDITIONARIES

Once in Mexico, Castro devoted himself to three tasks: building an invasion force of committed revolutionaries, obtaining funds for such a project, and achieving some co-ordination of groups in a broad civic resistance movement. Housing and training for the expeditionaries had to be arranged, groups and individuals approached for contributions, and political dialogues carried on with other emigré groups and with groups in Cuba. In the midst of these activities, Castro and his followers continued to comment on Cuban politics and to develop further a revolutionary ideology. Each of these three activities was a political education in itself, in that the experiences involved led to certain conclusions about the course of politics and revolutionary change in Cuba.

Fund-Raising

At first, monies were needed for the immediate housing and nutritional demands. Some Cuban exiles were already living in Mexico City when Castro arrived, including his brother Raúl and Pedro Miret. Several houses were used to lodge militant Cubans in barracks-style arrangements, each holding five to ten men, with a <u>responsable de casa</u> - someone in charge of the house - acting as leader and concierge.[37] Castro and his supporters in Mexico met and spent time with various Spanish Republican exiles in Mexico City, including the Catalan sculptor, Victor Trapote. Trapote's daughter had married Ramiro Valdés, a close friend of Castro's from the Artemisa and Moncada days. Meeting of the exiles, forming into M-26 at this stage, took place in Trapote's studio, and it appears meals and contributions were provided.[38] Further early support came from Alfonso Gutierrez, a Mexican engineer married to Cuban pop singer Orquídea Pino, from Manuel Machado, an established printer in Mexico City, and from Rafael Bilbo, a wealthy Cuban residing in Venezuela.[39] Money also came from Rómulo Betancourt.[40]

The small apparatus that was left in Cuba was also active in collecting funds. In February 1956, a representative of this underground, probably Faustino Pérez, arrived with eight thousand dollars collected in small amounts from working-class Cubans.[41] Another ten thousand dollars arrived via Reverend Cecilio Arrastia, also collected in small amounts from M-26 sympathizers.[42] The combatants training in Mexico were elated that such popular support was forthcoming and they fired their cartridges "telling ourselves each cartridge was paid for with the blood and sweat of comrades still in Cuba".[43]

The bulk of the funding, however, came from emigré communities in the United States and especially, at a crucial moment, from ex-President Prio, "always anxious to have his finger in almost any opposition activities".[44] Castro had met Colonel Alberto Bayo early after his arrival in Mexico and had asked the former career soldier to give his group military and guerrilla training.⁴⁵ It was loosely agreed that if Castro could secure money for arms, and for a training area, and more combatants, Bayo would instruct them.⁴⁶ Castro thereupon left for the United States to set up "patriotic clubs" in the emigré communities, as Martí had done some sixty years previously: "Martí worked tirelessly to raise contributions, visiting Philadelphia, Chicago, Key West, Tampa, even Mexico City, and corresponding with Cubans throughout the hemisphere to solicit funds".⁴⁷ Castro specifically identified his methods as those of Martí: "We are doing with the emigrés the things our apostle Martí taught us in a similar situation".⁴⁸ He spent much of the fall of 1955 shuttling between various United States cities, meeting with different emigré associations, speaking and attempting to raise funds and political recruits. "Patriotic Clubs of the 26th of July" were formed in New York, Washington, Bridgeport, Chicago, Philadelphia, Union City, Miami, Tampa and Key West.⁴⁹

In the United States, Castro emphasized that Cuban emigrés could and would play a major role in ending the dictatorship, as they had helped gain independence from Spain. He distinguished between the few "exiles", persons of money, and the many emigrés: "You are more than exiles, you are emigrés of hunger. The politicians do not talk about the emigrés because you do not vote. The Revolution is interested in emigrés because we are concerned not with votes but with conscience. We come to seek the moral strength of the emigrés".⁵⁰ For Castro, to solicit the "moral strength" of the emigrés itself demanded moral strength. It was precisely this quality that the Moncada attackers had gained through the assault, the massacre, the imprisonment and the amnesty campaign. Undoubtedly, the fact that most people perceived Fidel Castro and his group as representing left-wing, reformist and insurrectionist, but anti-communist Ortodoxos helped gain him a sympathetic reception.⁵¹ Castro had encouraged this perception in his "Message to Ortodoxo Militants":

> The fighters of the 26th of July await the determined support of the best Ortodoxos of the whole island. We do not constitute a tendency within the party; we are the revolutionary apparatus of <u>Chibasismo</u> which is rooted in its cadres and from which it emerged to struggle against the dictatorship when the Ortodoxo Party lay impotent and divided in a thousand pieces. We have never abandoned its ranks.⁵²

Perhaps even more important in generating the moral appeal which Castro was able to wield in his organizing and fund-raising activities was his record of incorruptibility. Castro reminded the Cuban public that he had suffered political attacks "because everybody knows that my revolutionary integrity cannot be bought for money or position, and my loyalty to an ideal is free from duplicity and vacillation".[53] He recalled that he had not taken advantage of his notoriety and popularity upon release from prison to seek political office or to join "the embezzlers". Further, he had turned down "a salary of five hundred dollars per month that an insurance company offered me, because I do not profit from my prestige — a prestige that does not belong to me but to a cause".[54] Castro continued to stress that he wrote without salary for La Calle, that in handling the money of the cause he had never taken a cent for his own use.[55] To the meetings in the United States he reported that he and the other fighters "all live very modestly" and he appealed to the emigrés in Martí's words: "We will find magnanimous aid in all honest hearts. And we will knock on all doors. And we will ask for contributions from town to town. And they will give because we will ask with honor".[56]

Castro openly called for contributions to an invasion force: "I plan to return, as our independence fighters returned whenever tyranny threw them out of Cuban territory; I shall never return any other way".[57] And funds were collected on such an open basis. As Martí had said, "it is criminal for a man to promote a war that can be avoided, and to fail to promote an inevitable one".[58] Castro added that "a revolution is the work of the people, and it is necessary that the people know beforehand what they must do in the struggle".[59]

Castro was apparently filled with optimistic feelings at the response he received in the United States. When he issued another fund-raising call to Cubans inside the country late in the fall of 1955, he enthusiastically described some of the "unforgettable scenes I witnessed among Cuban emigres to the United States: everywhere I saw Cubans standing, their hands raised high, swearing not to rest until they saw their land redeemed, and then en masse they deposited in the mambí hat the product of their sweat".[60] That Castro could draw large emigré crowds and collect funds on the basis of a public call for the preparation of an armed struggle must have provided him with a deep sense of vindication. He could not have failed to bring back to the combatants in Mexico and to all recruits there and after the Granma landing the fact that working people were making sacrifices to donate money to the cause.

In Florida, in particular, the reception Castro got was enthusiastic. A fund-raising organization was quickly set up in the capable hands of Juan Manuel Márquez, Ortodoxo ex-city councillor of Marianao, outside Havana.[61]

Money was also collected in Costa Rica, where some Moncada veterans had been spending their exile while their comrades were in prison. Castro visited San Jose in June 1956, consulting with the social democratic political party of Costa Rica and seeking funds among emigré Cubans.[62]

Castro had met early in his exile with Justo Carrillo, President of the Development Bank under Prío, and thus had some minimal contact with Auténtico circles. Carrillo later gave Castro five thousand dollars of his own and donated by the Montecristi movement of reformist military officers planning a coup.[63] With the help of Carrillo and Teresa Casuso, a Cuban exile in Mexico who was a personal friend of Prío[64], Castro slipped across the United States border in September 1956 into Texas to meet with the ex-President. Prío agreed to help the movement and immediately sent fifty thousand dollars; by the time Batista fell, he had contributed nearly a quarter million dollars.[65] This aid was solicited even though M-26 had condemned the accepting of aid from "embezzlers" and Castro had been active in muckraking reports on Prío's real estate dealings: "If the Revolution accepts aid from embezzlers who have plundered the Republic, the Revolution will be betraying its principles. If the Revolution solicits aid from vested interests, it will be compromised before it attains power".[66] But, in the summer of 1956, the guerrilla force in Mexico was already trained, and there was a threat that the Mexican police would be able to dismantle the movement. A large amount of money had to be located quickly to get the invasion underway.[67] On the other hand, by this date, M-26's political independence was solidly established and Castro had expressed indignation with the treatment Prío had received at the hands of Batista: "Batista has been merciless with Prío beyond all limits, by insults, taunts, and humiliation... when we were arrested in Mexico...Prío - a man I have fought several times - was very much a gentleman. He wrote in his capacity as former president of Cuba an open letter to the president of Mexico asking him not to deport us".[68]

Events in Cuba and the Political Stance of M-26

In the summer of 1955, the traditional opposition and middle-class leaders, including Prío, mounted a campaign for a "civic dialogue" of all Cuban political interests. Through a new organization called the Sociedad de Amigos de la República (SAR) - Friends of the Republic - these elements hoped to convince Batista to call general elections before his "term" expired in 1958: "Public meetings were organized to explain SAR's objectives, and religious and other institutions were invited to join in the effort for a prompt and peaceful transfer of power".[69] Through the end of 1955, however, the government refused to open a "civic dialogue" or to consider early elections.

The July 26th Movement, constituted at the time of Castro's departure into exile, consistently opposed the civic dialogue. It was argued that the elections under Batista the previous year "were the most scandalous and fraudulent in our republican history...can anyone make our skeptical people believe in honest elections with Batista in power?"[70] Within the Ortodoxo Party, the only major opposition force hanging back from the civic dialogue campaign, M-26 militants pressed for the adoption of an insurrectionist line. Castro's "Message to Ortodoxo Militants" was read at the August 19, 1955 national convention and the line adopted.[71] In the United States, Castro continued to condemn electoralism as the other groups in Cuba, dissatisfied with the regime's stonewalling on the civic dialogue, took up tactics of demonstrations.

The activist university students, with a new generation of leaders, formed one of these groups. The FEU was now led by José Antonio Echeverría, a talented organizer and speaker and a radical nationalist and social democrat, though anti-communist. He and the new student leaders like Frank País, Pepito Tey, Fructuoso Rodriguez and Faure Chomón, had been involved in anti-Batista demonstrations immediately after the March 10 coup.[72] During the summer of 1955, a number of FEU student leaders organized arms training on the campus in Havana with an eye to assassinating Batista.[73] When the plot failed to materialize, the FEU set up its own revolutionary apparatus, the Directorio Revolucionario (DR). The organization was to confront the regime in the streets, provide a balance between M-26 and Batista, and eventually to topple the dictator in the name of the new generation.[74]

The DR group decided in the late fall of 1955 that the time had come to step up the opposition to the regime. They planned to provoke police brutality at demonstrations by using snipers, to denounce conciliationism, and to proclaim armed struggle.[75] A series of student riots in many Cuban cities ensued, with police beatings and shootings. New martyrs fell during a month of disturbances at the end of the year, and a five-minute work stoppage called by the FEU for December 14 to protest police brutality was widespread.[76]

The level of struggle was raised considerably by a sugar workers' strike over reduced wages in December. The DR collaborated with the sugar workers, helping organize popular support and providing meeting halls at the university, moving the country close to mass resistance.[77] The DR moved ahead with arms training and plans to kill Batista, and new riots broke out in

February and April, 1956.[78]
   Within the army itself, dissent was finally developing into political action. A military conspiracy of younger reformist officers, headed by the Cuban military attache in Washington, Colonel Ramón Barquín, was organized in April, 1956. The group had support from a number of Ortodoxo figures, but was found out and broken up, and the principals were arrested.[79] At the same time, hard-liners in the army, known as tanquistas 'the tank corps' attempted to foment disorder to provoke a Trujillo-style regime. They even provided Trujillo-supplied arms to such diverse groups as Castro's, to justify their planned coup.[80]
   In this climate of disorders and plots, which culminiated in an Auténtico faction's attack on the Goicuría barracks in Matanzas province and their massacre (forcing Prío to end his eight-month return to Cuba)[81], Batista opened the "civic dialogue" with the SAR. When the Ortodoxo leadership agreed to join the talks, the M-26 made its definitive break with the party. Castro bitterly attacked the party leadership from Mexico: "The names of those who obstruct the task of liberating their country should be recorded in the same place of dishonor and shame as the names of those who oppress it".[82] He claimed that the party had done nothing to implement the revolutionary line taken at its convention in August 1955. Even so, the M-26 would not be "different from the Ortodoxo Party for the followers of Chibás"; it would be the Ortodoxo movement "without a leadership of landlords...sugar plantation owners...without stock-market speculators, without commercial and industrial magnates, without lawyers for the big interests or provincial chieftains".[83] It would be the "revolutionary organization of the humble, for the humble and by the humble...the hope of redemption for the Cuban working-class...the hope of land for the peasants".[84]
   In Cuban opposition politics, then, the M-26 consistently advanced the argument that insurrection was the only route if Batista refused to call open general elections immediately. It was not by any means the only group advocating such a line, but there was no coordination between insurrectionist groups until, in September 1956, the DR and M-26 signed the "Mexico Pact".[85] The confusion, disunity, rivalry and treachery which marked the period strengthened the M-26 leadership's convictions that their independence and insistence was correct. In particular, already-existing distrust of certain economic classes' control of opposition parties came to a head with the Ortodoxo leadership's participation in the "Civic Dialogue". Although Castro solicited funds from Prío, the idea that the only true backers of the revolution would be working people, campesinos and students was reinforced by events in Cuba during exile.

In the process of myth formation and the political education of the Rebel Army, successful fund-raising was seen as evidence of M-26 popularity. The Rebel Army recruits and later FAR members were taught that Cubans gave money out of respect they held for the Moncada rebels' example and out of hope for a revolution. The lack of a co-ordinated opposition meant that the traditional opposition was politically bankrupt. Success in fund-raising, in the myths of the Rebel Army, meant that Cubans saw the correctness of the M-26 insurrectionary line.

Training and New Recruits

Funds had been secured and weapons were being collected. M-26 was established in Cuba, though no "broad civic resistance movement" existed. Attempts to gain the sanction of the traditional opposition parties for the insurrectionist line were a fiasco, but political lessons had been gleaned and the DR's collaboration had been gained. In Mexico, military training and political education went forward. As before, certain experiences added to the formal training. In this section, the training, political education and exile experiences are discussed.

Castro planned to have his fighters thoroughly trained in the arts of war and in guerrilla tactics. Thus, he went about securing capable instructors. Bayo he had approached "after much investigation", finding him to be well-known to Latin American revolutionaries living in Mexico.[86] After securing funds in the United States, Castro returned to Mexico City with Miguel Sánchez, a Cuban who had fought in the United States Army in Korea, and who was to take part in the training of the expeditionaries.[87] But it was Bayo who took charge of the training. He already had considerable experience in training revolutionaries as guerrillas. Both young Spanish communists intending to be underground anti-Franco fighters and anti-Somoza rebels had received training from Bayo.[88]

Bayo's military career in Spain had been extensive and varied. He had fought against Moroccan uprisings in the mountainous Rif area, and had later directed schools of aviation, both in Spain and Mexico. He had come to see the worth of guerrilla tactics in the Spanish Civil War after leading the abortive mission to take the Balearic Islands, and led guerrilla groups in Castile. His political stance had not developed into Marxism, but he had been a Socialist in Spain and he remained a Popular Front Loyalist in exile. Bayo respected the discipline and courage of the Communists in Spain during the Civil War, but was never a party member.[89]

The training that Bayo organized centered on discipline, the handling of weapons and such guerrilla skills as first aid, explosives, communications, mobility and sabotage. During the first phase of training, Pedro Miret, Bayo, José Smith and Miguel Sánchez oversaw arms training at a firing range in suburban Mexico City.[90] Discipline was maintained among the expeditionaries by the organization of their residences. Small groups were housed together in rented quarters. Cooking and cleaning responsibilities were shared. No income was forthcoming for individuals and a midnight curfew was imposed. Drinking and girlfriends were apparently forbidden, while compulsory political discussions of current events in Cuba were held and the reading of Cuban periodicals was a daily duty.[91]

During this first training period, the fighters received guerrilla instruction in Bayo's classes, learning the techniques of explosives and sabotage. Drill practice was kept indoors, while meetings and movements were semi-clandestine. Precautions were justified, in that Mexican and Cuban police were aware of M-26 activities. Surveillance, infiltration and arrests were to hamper the group until their departure from Mexico. Several Cubans, including Jesús Montané and Cándido Gonzalez, Castro's bodyguard, were arrested in the early period for illegal possession of arms. They were held for a short period, undergoing the "normal disagreeable, brutal treatment of Mexican prisons".[92] In the minds of the rebels, definite co-operation existed among the Cuban embassy, Batista and the Mexican authorities. Castro would later remark: "If instead of revolutionaries, we had been Batistianos, the embassy would have protected us. But we were adversaries of the tyranny, and its mission consisted of seeking the worst for us. Persecution and defamation emanated from the embassy".[93]

The first arrests and confiscations of weapons caches in the stylish Chapultepec Hills sector of Mexico City impelled Castro to seek another training site. Bayo managed, through a certain degree of deception, to secure the unimpeded use of a large ranch, called "Santa Rosa".[94] It was extensive, with rough terrain and access to the mountains south of Mexico City.

At Santa Rosa, the training of the rebels became even more rigid and their lives were circumscribed, but it resulted in a close feeling of camaraderie and dedication. Bayo trained the group up to fifteen hours daily, with long marches through harsh countryside and exercises in guerrilla tactics.[95] The group was not permitted to have discussions with unknown people, could only leave the ranch on weekends, and was required to submit written reports on its off-ranch activities.[96] It was Bayo, himself, who insisted on such discipline: "He was inexhaustible, insistent and stern with his charges. He demanded...the utmost discipline, physical stamina, restraint from alcohol, and what amounted to almost a monastic way of life".[97]

Political instruction in Mexico City during the early phase of training was limited mainly to discussion, reading and personal pursuit of topics by the more advanced cadres. After weapons and physical training in the afternoons, Hilda Gadea, Guevara's wife, recalled, "the men met in the evenings in a kind of political circle to study Marxian works and discuss the problems of Cuba and Latin America".[98] At Santa Rosa, political instruction took the form of Bayo's talks about the Spanish Civil War, and discussion led by some of the more educated and politically experienced members of the group.[99] Guevara came to assume the role of political commissar and to direct the discussions and reading: "Ché himself chose Marxist literature for the library for our political studies", recalled Darío López.[100]

For the rebels at Santa Rosa, political education up to that point was casual and existential, with few exceptions. For Moncada veterans, the experience of combat, defeat, torture, assassination and imprisonment had been followed by a spartan existence in exile. Some of them, like Antonio "Nico" López, Mario Dalmau and Calixto García, had taken up residence in revolutionary Guatemala. There, they had been exposed to an international community of Latin American revolutionaries and had worked to some extent with the Arbenz government.[101] Experiences of these men in Guatemala and the witnessing of the United States-sponsored overthrow of the Arbenz government "contributed a new bitterness and probably a new hostility to the United States".[102] Anti-imperialism was becoming stronger among the rebels.

Newer recruits from Cuba were largely from Juventud Ortodoxa and, as such, their political education had centered around the radical nationalism of Eduardo Chibás. They were to be guided in their political education by the guerrilla training and by the discussion led by the more experienced of their comrades. Their first formal political education came at the hands of Ché Guevara at Santa Rosa.

AN IMPORTANT RECRUIT: ERNESTO GUEVARA

I turn to a discussion of the early political formation, character and contributions of this recruit to the revolutionary cause because of his profound influence on the course of the guerrilla struggle and on the Rebel Army which emerged from it. He helped to form the revolutionary political culture of the post-insurrectionary Rebel Army and, himself, became integral to that culture. His own exploits and ideas became part of revolutionary mythology after victory and are now important elements of the Cuban revolutionary traditions and myths central to political education.

Ché

One of the major themes in Donald Schulz' dissertation[103] is the process of ideological formation within individuals and within political movements. The word "process" implies constant movement, change, development and synthesis in Schulz' assessment of revolutionary ideological formation. Schulz holds that the revolutionary political culture of Cuba, like all ideologies, was born of distinct "existential environments." For him, ideologies are never "born full-grown"; rather "they develop through the process of man's interaction with the world around him and reflect his adjustment to and/or alienation from that world".[104] This existential environment with which a nascent revolutionary ideology interacts is defined as "the opportunities, pressures and constraints posed by the political, economic and social environment within which [the revolutionary] operates".[105]

I have, in a sense, been discussing the existential environment within which the Cuban revolutionary ideology was developing before the actual guerrilla struggle. I would like now to discuss the process of ideological formation in Ernesto Guevara before the guerrilla struggle and then to come to some assessment of his contribution to the Cuban revolutionary ideology and political education of the combatants as they were when the Granma set out for Cuba. This assessment will be made in the light of Schulz' judgement that a "nascent revolutionary ideology" has as its primary function the provision of a "complex of energizing ideals with which to mobilize those alienated from the existing order into a political and military movement capable of seizing state power".[106]

Ernesto "Ché" Guevara, by any measure, is second only to Castro in the pantheon of Cuban revolutionary heroes. Of those who have had their speeches, writings and exploits reproduced in the Cuban military journal Verde Olivo, Fidel Castro and Ché Guevara are far and away the most often seen. The contributions of Guevara to the Cuban revolution, through his actions and through his thought, are difficult to overestimate. Even today, children are encouraged: "Seremos como el Ché" 'We will be like Ché'.[107]

As with Fidel Castro, Guevara's early life was characterized by a generalized and clear rebelliousness.[108] According to one biographer, this seems to have been inherent to Guevara's family: "Certain things were taken for granted: a passion for justice, the rejection of fascism, religious indifference...a prejudice against money and the ways of making it. The family also had a personal rebelliousness..."[109] Guevara's mother, Celia de la Serna, has been judged to be a mixture of aristocrat and rebel: "She was a flaming rebel through and through, and she combined with her rebelliousness a fierce independence, an unwavering stubbornness, a keen intelligence and a sharp tongue".[110]

The home environment was undoubtedly the foundation for Ernesto Guevara's personal political development. The friendships with anti-fascist Spaniards, the political discussions in the home, the political content of much of the family library, which Guevara devoured as an adolescent, and his parents' involvement in anti-gorila[111] and anti-Peron activities made for an unusual middle-class upbringing.

As a youth, Guevara was attracted to travel and engaged in long journeys around Latin America. Alberto Granados, one of his erstwhile travel companions, expressed an opinion on the motivation for these travels: only after much travelling "could a correct answer be found to the question which was bothering him more and more: how could the lives of the people living on the continent be changed for the better, how could they be released from poverty and disease, how could they be freed from the oppression of the landowners, capitalists and foreign monopolies?"[112]

Guevara discussed the further radicalizing effects of one journey, wherein he and Granados worked at various leper colonies. He spoke to a meeting of doctors in Cuba, recalling that he had "dreamed of becoming a famous researcher; I dreamed of working tirelessly to aid humanity, but this was conceived as personal achievement".[113] However, these travels had changed his perspective. He came to want to change the situation of the poor, though still through personal effort: "I began to study the means of becoming a revolutionary doctor".[114] His mind, as he intimated, was still occupied by contradictory notions of the solution to Latin American miseries. Personal efforts and reformism were one side of the equation. A nebulous and chimerical social revolution, a profound change in the social system, was the other.

After completing his medical studies, Guevara undertook another trip, moving first through Bolivia. The political lesson Guevara seemed to draw from his observations in Bolivia was a harsh one. Though the government had nationalized the tin mines, set in motion an agrarian reform and created a popular militia, Guevara expressed his reservations. He saw that the living conditions for the Indian masses had changed little and that the MNR leadership was small and still bourgeois. He criticized the MNR's paternalistic, reformist approach to the problems of the Indians: "The question is one of fighting the causes and not just being satisfied

with getting rid of the effects. This revolution is
bound to fail if it doesn't manage to break down the
spiritual isolation of the Indians, if it doesn't succeed in reaching deep inside them, stirring them right
down to the bone, and giving them back their stature as
human beings".[115] Guevara later told Hilda Gadea that
he did not regard the Bolivian revolution of 1952 as a
true one, that the leadership was corrupt, and that it
would end by delivering itself to United States imperialism.[116]

Guevara arrived, after extensive travels and experiences with Latin American revolutionaries of every
persuasion, in Guatemala. It was the end of 1953, just
as the final conflict between the Arbenz government and
the various forces of United States political and economic imperialism was heating up.

The most important personal relationship Guevara
had in Guatemala was that with Hilda Gadea. She was a
Peruvian, a left-wing militant of Haya de la Torre's
APRA, "forced into exile by the military coup led by
Manuel Odria and the repression which followed".[117] An
economist, she worked for the Institute for the Development of Production, an agency of the Guatemalan government. She was established in Guatemala City and aided
numerous Latin American political exiles. Guevara and
Rojo had been given a letter of introduction to her during their stay in Peru, and they soon were introduced
to her. She facilitated their entry into pensión Cer-
vantes, where a number of political emigrés were living.[118]

Guevara and Gadea immediately launched into political discussions, finding they had common reading interests. Guevara was a debator and engaged energeti-
cally in this activity whenever he was with people:
"The chief subject of argument with his friends was the
choice of means and of forces with which the Latin Amer-
can countries could be liberated from the yoke of imperialism, exploitation and poverty".[119] Guevara seems
to have spent much of his time in Guatemala reading and
debating, clarifying his own grasp of and approach to
Marxism. Most observers who knew him at the time regarded him as a Marxist, though not necessarily a party
member. Mario Dalmau, a Moncada veteran who met Guevara in Guatemala, later recalled that Guevara "had already developed a fairly clear Marxist viewpoint. He
had absorbed the writings of Marx and Lenin and read
through volumes of Marxist literature".[120] Harold White,
an American Marxist scholar with whom Guevara worked in
Guatemala, later wrote:

> I can say that he had an exhaustive knowledge of
> Marxism. After a difficult struggle, Ernesto had
> succeeded in conquering what Goethe called the
> 'thousand-headed hydra of empiricism'. He knew

very well that history is not a purely logical process, as Hegel supposed, and that life is too varied to be compressed into an equation or a formula. But he also knew that this does not mean that there are no political, social or economic laws. If this were true, socialism would not be scientific; there would be nothing left over but utopian dreams and each country would be deprived of objective forces to defeat imperialism. Because of his experience and critical mind he was able to approach a synthesis, in about six months, an outline of the profound and comprehensive structure that makes Marxism a science.[121]

Nevertheless, he refused to join the Partido Guatemalteco de Trabajo (PGT), The Communist party, as a prerequisite to his working as a doctor.[122]

The last six months of the Arbenz regime were months of increasing tension. Rojo described the open atmosphere of conspiracy: "The cafes in Guatemala in those days were alive with rumors and American CIA agents, many of whom operated openly. There was no mystery about their headquarters and hang-outs or where and how some interesting bits of information could be sold to them for United States dollars".[123]

The United States stepped up its pressure and intrigues after the nationalization of United Fruit Company properties. Secretary of State John Foster Dulles succeeded in getting OAS sanction of intervention in Guatemala, because of the "communist danger", in March 1954.[125] Guevara refused to take a plane home to Argentina, arranged by his embassy, committing himself to the defense of the revolution. When the bombing began in May, he joined the Youth Alliance, a branch of the PGT, and stood guard duty.[127] He tried to persuade the PGT and the Arbenz regime to arm the people and form popular militias, having little faith in the ultimate loyalty of the United States-trained Guatemalan armed forces. Guevara later told Jorge Masetti, an Argentine journalist, that he had "tried to form a group of young men like myself to fight the _frutero_ [United Fruit Co.] adventurers. In Guatemala it was necessary to resist and almost no one wanted to do it".[128]

Near the end of the Arbenz regime, in June, Guevara came to various conclusions about Marxism, about the Guatemalan situation, and about revolutionary struggle. He was convinced that only a thorough social revolution could resolve Latin America's ills. A coup or elections would never bring about a true social revolution. Only an armed mass movement which would "acquaint the people with the goals of a revolution"[129] would succeed. As for the communist parties, Guevara said that he "respected them and considered their theoretical approach correct", but that they "were not developing the correct policy of solidarity with the people"; they tended to be bureaucratic.[130]

Guevara wrote a short article, never published, entitled "I Saw the Fall of Jacobo Arbenz". It showed a clear revolutionary and anti-imperialist stance.[131] He saw a world divided between socialism and imperialism, the militant Leninist view. National liberation struggles in the Third World would widen the sphere of world socialist revolution. In Guatemala, United States imperialism in the form of United Fruit, Electric Bond and Share Company and Atlantic Telephone and Telegraph had created a puppet national bourgeoisie. This class would never support a real social transformation, and third positions of such figures and parties as Betancourt, Figueres in Costa Rica and APRA were a betrayal of the anti-imperialist struggle. The struggle against imperialism and servile oligarchies would result in socialist societies in Latin America and elsewhere. Such a struggle had to be carried out by arms and have the support of the people: "He was absolutely certain that if Arbenz had armed the people his government would not have fallen".[132]

Thus, Guevara had come, via upbringing, experience and study, to a deep, personal and independent Marxism by the end of his time in Guatemala.[133] This is not to say that he had decided when and where to fight, or that he had entirely thrown off his "bourgeois values",[134] merely that he was close to a decision to fight imperialism. The last sentence of his essay on Guatemala read: "The struggle now begins".[135] He had decided, as he later said, that "to be a revolutionary doctor or to be a revolutionary at all, there must first be a revolution".[136]

Ché and M-26 in Mexico

Guevara finally had to flee Guatemala after the ovethrow of Arbenz. True to his predictions, the Guatemalan military had not supported the revolution in the face of United States Ambassador William Peurifoy's ultimatum[137] and the PGT and Arbenz' government had not been willing to arm the population. This costly mistake remained firm in Guevara's mind. In May 1955, he, Rojo and Gadea encountered José Manuel Fortuny, the general secretary of the PGT. Guevara confronted him and asked why the regime had not fought the coup. Fortuny answered that the struggle was continuing, but that the situation had been very difficult. Guevara retorted that they should have made a stand while still in power, that Arbenz should have gone into armed resistance in the countryside and used his moral stature as an elected president. The people would have rallied, in Guevara's opinion.138

While in Guatemala, Guevara had his second encounter with Cuban emigres, having met some in Costa Rica. Gadea had met several Moncada veterans, particularly Antonio Nico López, and had introduced them to Guevara.139 It was his first meeting with Moncada survivors and he took to López immediately, respecting above all that these people had taken some action.

It was in the latter half of 1955 that Guevara was introduced to Fidel Castro. Guevara heard Castro tell of his plans to invade Cuba in Oriente province, "the most militant, patriotic and revolutionary of all Cuban provinces...where I have the most supporters and friends".140 Guevara later recalled their first meeting in an interview in the Sierra Maestra:

> I spoke with Fidel a whole night. At dawn I was already the physician of the future expedition. In reality, after the experience I went through, my long walks throughout all of Latin America and the Guatemalan closing, not much was needed to convince me to join any revolution against a tyrant; but Fidel impressed me as an extraordinary man. He faced and resolved the impossible. He had an unshakeable faith that once he left he would arrive in Cuba, that once he arrived he would fight, that once he began fighting he would win. I shared his optimism. It was imperative to act, to fight, to concretize. It was imperative to stop crying and fight. It was necessary to demonstrate to the people of his fatherland that they could have faith in him, because he practiced what he preached. He said, ' in 1956 we shall be free or we shall be martyrs', and he announced that before the year ended he would land somewhere in Cuba leading his expeditionary army.141

Guevara was struck by what he perceived as superior qualities of leadership in Castro, and Castro was impressed by "Guevara's combative temperament". Castro also later recalled this meeting: "I believe that at the time I met Che Guevara he had a greater revolutionary development, ideologically speaking, than I had. From the theoretical point of view he was more formed, he was a more advanced revolutionary than I was".142

This faith in action and leadership, and the belief that a popular uprising would result from the invasion characterize what Guevara would call the "subjectivist phase" of Cuban revolution ideology. It reflected, for him, a distinct stage of social conceptualization and experience:

> Before the landing of the *Granma* a mentality predominated which to some degree might be called

'subjectivist': blind confidence in a rapid popular explosion, enthusiasm and faith in the power to liquidate Batista's might by a swift armed uprising combined with spontaneous revolutionary strikes and the subsequent fall of the dictator. The movement was the direct heir of the Ortodoxo Party, and its main slogan was 'Honor against Money', that is to say administrative honesty as the principal idea of the new Cuban government.[143]

The thought of action against an imperialist-supported dictatorship is what primarily appealed to Guevara, though certain of Castro's ideals appealed to the revolutionary in him: agrarian reform, nationalizations, and the notion that armed struggle was the key to antidictatorial movements.

Ché Guevara thus became part of the expeditionary force, and began a more clandestine life in Mexico than before. He and Hilda became targets of police surveillance, arrests and interrogations during the training period.[144]

As mentioned before, Guevara was central to the political education of the combatants during the intensive training at Rancho Santa Rosa. On the one hand he was a diligent, serious and exemplary student of guerrilla warfare. Bayo called him his best student.[145] On the other hand, he taught the barely literate "how to read and understand what you have read", choosing what would be read.[146] One of the themes consistent in Guevara's approach to education in general was that of <u>dignidad</u>. For this reason, speculates one writer, Guevara would read <u>Don Quixote</u> to the peasant recruits in the Sierra Maestra.[147] No doubt he would speak of <u>dignidad</u> to the less-educated fighters training at Santa Rosa. The themes of anti-facist heroism in Spain both he and Bayo would have shared, while Guevara's readings of Soviet novels about World War II and of the Chinese revolution would provide him with further material on <u>dignidad</u>, sacrifice and patriotism. The strong anti-imperialist feelings of Guevara, cultured in his travels and existentially reinforced by his witnessing of the recent events in Guatemala, insured that he would lead many discussions at Santa Rosa on imperialism's support for dictators in Latin America and the Caribbean.

The combatants, although there were some with higher education, were mostly "humble, ordinary people - store clerks, laborers, students at business schools or at secondary school...they were not like the revolutionaries I [Teresa Casuso] had known, but much humbler and cruder...their language was coarse..."[148] Hard data on these fighters, as Schulz writes, "is almost nonexistent".[149] Nor is there much evidence as to the content of the guided and frequent political discussions they had at Santa Rosa. Certainly, the general level of political education that the recruits brought to Santa Rosa was not high. Guevara recalled one of the Moncada veterans who saw things simply as a matter of a coup to counter the coup of Batista in 1952.[150] What is known is that there was a library of Marxist works, and that study groups were provided with the works of Martí and the M-26 manifesto.[151] Schulz chooses to call this stage of ideological development one of a "primitive ideological Weltanschauung" of ideas and values, ambiguous and overlaid with feelings of loyalty to the leadership.[152] While this may be true of many of the Granma expeditionaries, it was not the case with the Castros, Guevara, Nico López and a few others with an international perspective and a more and more committed anti-imperialism, founded either on an understanding of the theory of imperialism or on an awareness of the Guatemala experience. The combination of discipline, mutual experiences and political education at Santa Rosa did produce a dedicated group of fighters. One of them, Abilio Collado, the Granma helmsman and Moncada veteran, remembered the Santa Rosa days some seven years later: "Never have I gone through a harder discipline nor have I met a group of men where there was such a great feeling of fraternity".[153]

FINAL PREPARATIONS

There were four political experiences for the M-26 leadership and cadres in Mexico. First, there was the training itself, under Bayo. Second, there was the addition of Ché Guevara and the impact of the Guatemala events. Third, events in Cuba and the politics of other opposition groups affected the ideological position of M-26. Fourth, harassment and imprisonment in Mexico added to the political education of the cadres and in turn became part of their own revolutionary political culture, influencing the ways in which they perceived political reality, the struggle and their mission. I will discuss the last two influences in this section.

During 1955 and 1956, the political atmosphere in Cuba was confused and contradictory. There was no unity among the various opposition currents and government policies vacillated. I have already mentioned the movement for a "civic dialogue", the increased militancy of the FEU-DR, and the sugar workers' strike. One of the results of the "dialogue" movement was the final separation of M-26 from the Ortodoxo Party. A result of DR militancy was the "Mexico Pact" with M-26. The DR also continued its policy of golpear por arriba 'striking at the top', assassinating Antonio Blanco Rico, head of Batista's Military Intelligence Service (SIM), on October 26, 1956.[154] Although M-26 had made the pact with the

DR, Castro censured this attack on Blanco Rico.[155]

Various Auténtico groups were preparing in Florida and elsewhere for invasions, supported financially by Prío. And, in Cuba, the year 1956 saw several conspiracies hatched. One Auténtico group, led by Daniel Martin Labrandero, a Spanish Republican military officer, planned to attack the presidential palace and kill Batista. They were discovered, dispersed and Labrandero later killed.[156] Another Auténtico group, led by one Reynold García, made a suicidal attack on the Goicuría barracks in Matanzas province, a repeat, on a smaller scale, of the Moncada assault. The group walked into an ambush and all thirty-odd men were killed.[157] Even the dictator of the Dominican Republic, Leonidas Trujillo, got involved in a Prío scheme to land an invasion force in Oriente. Men were trained and arms secured. Finally, Trujillo withdrew his support in return for Cuban concessions on meat imports from the Dominican Republic, and some of the arms went to Frank País' Santiago M-26 organization.[158] Castro condemned the Trujillo maneuvers, equating the Cuban and Domincan dictators, and pointing out that right-wing Cuban military plotters were also in contact with Trujillo.[159]

Throughout 1956, government terror and resistance actions escalated. The M-26 urban underground bombed nightclubs and parks and attacked police patrol cars, while the DR concentrated on executing top government and police figures.[160] This tactic was not paralleled by organized working-class resistance to Batista's regime. The working class was under the "double dictatorship", as Farber put it, of Batista and Eusebio Mujal, the corrupt union boss. The PSP was ambivalent and discouraged strikes. Batista's own paternalistic economic policies and the state of the economy in 1955-57 also created ambiguities. Foreign investment increased and the world sugar price rose, relieving some of the pressures of the post-Korean War slump. Batista put money into large public works projects. However, unemployment remained chronic and high, public revenues were low due to corruption and tax evasion, and growth was hampered and uneven due to a lack of planning.[161]

The general situation can be described as a multi-layered series of crises. Long-term crises characterized the economy, which had a surface and transient prosperity. The dictatorship experienced a crisis of legitimacy before and after the "civic dialogue" attempts. This political crisis was manifested in several ways. First, Batista had to play both to disaffected middle-class and civic sectors and also to the far-right elements in the military and police. Second, certain elements were battling, both among themselves and against the dictatorship, to achieve power. Third, Batista had to try and keep some degree of working-class support. Fourth, he had to follow, to some extent, Cold War policies set up in the north. An anti-communist campaign got underway; diplomatic ties with the Soviet Union and other socialist countries were broken; the PSP was curtailed and finally outlawed. The M-26 was officially linked to communism and anti-communist literature proliferated.[162] Any policy Batista followed was bound to displease some sectors of society. Liberalization was followed by repression, relaxation by rigidity. No single class was capable of achieving political hegemony and Batista remained in an uneasy Bonapartist situation.[163]

From Mexico, Castro followed these events and the shifting fulcrums of multiple crisis in Cuba. The "civic dialogue" and Batista's attacks on him, combined with the traditional opposition's disavowal of his movement, resulted in sentiments like those expressed in the essay "Against Everyone!"[164] Castro justified his own cause of justice in Cuba by proclaiming the heroism and incorruptibility of the Moncada movement, combating the charges of gangsterism, and claiming that "the politicking opposition...[was] discredited."[165] He tried to claim the mantle of Chibás and radical Ortodoxo platforms for M-26 when the Ortodoxo Party finally rejected the insurrectionist line.[166] When the liberal military plot led by Colonel Ramón Barquín failed in April, 1956, Castro labelled them "honest military men" and the "best men of the armed forces, the officers most capable of defending the fatherland".[167]

The expeditionaries were having their own problems in Mexico in the summer of 1956. Informers had infiltrated the training camp at Santa Rosa.[168] In late June, Fidel Castro and Ramiro Valdés, a Moncada veteran, were arrested in the streets of Mexico City. Further arrests were made at one of the "safe houses" and, a few days later, Santa Rosa itself was raided and a score or so of the fighters were jailed, including Guevara and Bayo.[169] Arms were also confiscated. In the Cuban and Mexican press, the prisoners were called communists. The Cuban papers claimed that the Mexican police had "proof that Fidel Castro was not only a member of the Communist Party but the secret leader of the Mexico-Soviet Cultural Institute". The Mexican newspaper Excelsior listed Ernesto Guevara as an "international communist agitator".[170]

The day after his arrest, Castro issued a statement denying any ties with the communists or with Prío. And, some twenty days after the arrests, still in prison, Castro made some extended comments on his situation.[172] First, he condemned the lack of legal representations on their behalf by the Cuban embassy. Then, he revealed that he had been aware of several plots emanating from within the Batista regime to have him eliminated. He accused the Cuban embassy of fomenting the arrests and pointed to Mexican news items detail - the presence of Cuban SIM agents. Many of those arrested underwent torture at the hands of the Mexican Security Police, wrote Castro, and he cited articles to that effect from Excelsior.[173] The secret service had used the pozole treatment on Cándido Gonzalez, Julio Díaz and Alfonso Zelaya.[174] Hilda Gadea was also picked up and, during her interrogation, she heard someone speaking English: "It confirmed my suspicion that there was a North American among the police".[175]

Castro strongly denied any ties with the PSP:

> The accusation of my being a communist was absurd in the eyes of all who knew my public path in Cuba...I have been a militant in only one Cuban political party and that is the one founded by Eduardo Chibás. What moral authority, on the other hand, does Mr. Batista have to speak of communism when he was the communist candidate in the elections of 1940...if his pictures beside Blas Roca and Lázaro Peña [PSP leaders] are still around...?[176]

The charges against the revolutionaries were illegal possession of firearms and violation of an immigration law prohibiting conspiracy against other governments.[177] The Mexican press, which had begun coverage of the incident by reporting what the police had declared, soon changed its assessment. Articles and editorials appeared exonerating the Cubans of the "communist" charge, criticizing the arbitrary actions of the Mexican police, and attacking Batista.[178] Finally, after some weeks, public attention mounted and pressure brought to bear by Mexican public figures, such as ex-president Lázaro Cárdenas, union leader Lombardo Toledano, and artists David Siqueiros and Diego Rivera, resulted in the release of all except Guevara and Cuban Calixto García.[179] They were accused of illegal entry to Mexico, but were released after two months' captivity.[180]

In prison, spirits remained high among the combatants, who had now completed most of Bayo's intensive course. A sense of fraternity and mission was felt. Hilda Gadea recalled that "the farewells after each visit were beautiful. Prisoners and visitors gathered around together; we would sing the Cuban national anthem and the hymn of the 26th of July. The prisoners joined arms to make a solid barrier somehow symbolic of the vanguard of the people. We were all moved; all of it - prison, the fraternal feeling, our common ideals - had a deeper meaning for us...there was a communal feeling of confidence that all difficulties would be overcome".[181]

It was during the imprisonment that Teresa Casuso, well-known among the new generation of Cuban revolutionaries as a member of the Generation of 1930, made the acquaintance of Fidel Castro, Raúl Castro, Guevara and the others. She visited the prisoners and offered to help them.[182]

Casuso got perhaps more than she expected. Upon release, Castro asked to store "some things" in her home, which turned out to be a substantial arsenal.[183] She also rented the next-door building for the insurrectionists, and they practiced weapons handling under the tutelage of Pedro Miret, a future Minister of Agriculture in the revolutionary regime.[184] The various hide-outs that had been used as weapons caches had been discovered and were being watched, and the Santa Rosa operation shut down. So, after more money was located, camps were opened in Tamaulipas, Jalapa, Boca del Rio and Ciudad Victoria, all quite distant from Mexico City.

Bayo was unable to take part in these final training sessions, and his better students, including Guevara, took over instruction. Political instruction continued, with the study group format retained. Discussion centered around "Cuban problems and how they could be solved once the revolutionaries had attained power...why the revolution of 1933 had failed...the lessons that could be learned from the recent Guatemalan debacle".[186] Undoubtedly land reform, nationalization, educational campaigns, and the destruction of the Batista army and its replacement by popular militias to ensure the survival of the revolutionary government were central topics.

For the last intensive period of training, weapons purchases and the expense of a yacht for the invasion, Castro needed substantial funds. He asked Teresa Casuso to approach Prío, and she went to Miami for that purpose. A meeting between Castro and Prío was arranged for McAllen, Texas, and the money was arranged.[187]

Treachery, which became a theme in the first hard years of the Revolution, again threatened to abort the invasion plans in Mexico. Rafael del Pino, Castro's erstwhile university and Bogotá companion, was acting as one of his bodyguards. He apparently gave the Cuban embassy in Mexico City a blueprint of Casuso's home and the location of some arms caches. Suspecting that he had been found out, he left one of the training camps precipitously. Two weeks later, Casuso's home was raided and some fifty thousand dollars worth of arms and ammunition was confiscated. Casuso and Pedro Miret were jailed.[188] These events, plus continuing harassment by the Mexican authorities, precipitated the purchase of the yacht _Granma_, and the invasion was launched November 25, 1956.

With an inchoate ideology, generous measures of self-sacrifice, adventure and derring-do, the group assembled in Mexico (and many were left behind, as _Granma_ would not hold them)[189] launched an insurrection. Political education of the combatants was still haphazard and a heady mixture of idealism and patriotism. Individual and group experiences were themselves a political education and formed part of the education of those less experienced. At the time the expeditionaries left Tuxpán, Mexico for Oriente, the strands of experience, ideals and patriotism were not yet a coherent ideology. Guevara, as was mentioned, later described this stage of ideological formation as basically subjectivist.

The other strands of the Cuban revolutionary ideology were present beneath this subjectivist surface. More radical ideas about class struggle and the irresponsibility of capitalism in Cuba were present in <u>History Will Absolve Me</u>. A strong anti-American and anti-imperialist tone was supplied by Raúl Castro, Ché Guevara and the Moncada veterans who had been in Guatemala. Camilo Cienfuegos brought a new note of anti-Americanism from his experiences in the United States.[190] And a theoretical and radical Marxism, one which criticized the established communist parties, made its presence felt in the person of Guevara. The over-riding concern was to fight Batista, with an independent political position, and to know how to fight. As Castro said, "in those days these [theoretical questions] were not the questions we talked about. What we discussed was the fight against Batista, the plan for landing in Cuba and for beginning guerrilla warfare".[191] There was no coherent political education, in the sense that one developed in the Rebel Army camps in the Sierra Maestra and other parts of Oriente in 1956-58 or later in the Rebel Army/FAR after 1959. Political education was imparted by those who, it was granted, knew more or had had more political experiences.

Why they were fighting was clear enough to each combatant. But the real political dimensions of guerrilla struggle were as yet obscure and the actual form revolutionary political power would take was very vague. The process of insurrection and the course of post-insurrection struggles emerged only through experience. The existential environment in Mexico, of training; the contributions of personalities and individual experiences; the collective experiences of Moncada and its aftermath; the events in Mexico of harassment, treachery, plots, arrest, torture and imprisonment; the observation of unrest, terrorism, opposition disunity and political bankruptcy in Cuba - all these elements made experience the outstanding political educator, the revolutionary pedagogue. It would remain so until the institutionalization of the Rebel Army and, even then, it was not eclipsed by formal political education.

The experiences of exile and training became part of the myths of the Rebel Army and the Cuban Revolution in the more formal political education developed later. They were seen at times when the clear vision of Castro and the dedication, sacrifice, hardships and ingenuity of the recruits were the only guarantors of success. In an atmosphere of intrigues and powerful interests ranged against the nascent Rebel Army, the myth would hold, the unformed Cuban Revolution was moving slowly forward on the momentum of the Moncada attack and the leadership of Castro; discipline and morale based on adherence to the "Cuban duty", to the principles of Martí and Chibás, and to a love for the Cuban people and land provided the sustenance of the Rebel Army-in-training.

NOTES

1. See Bonachea and Valdés, pp. 64-6.
2. See Suchlicki, pp. 70-1.
3. It was from Antonio Maceo that the slogan, "freedom is won with the edge of a machete" came. In a letter of July 14, 1896 to Federico Perez Carbó, Maceo wrote: "Freedom is won with the edge of a machete, it is not begged; to beg for rights is worthy only of cowards incapable of exercising them". Cited by Osvaldo Dorticós in "A luchar para el triunfo final de nuestra Revolución Socialista" Verde Olivo, 10 Dec. 61, pp. 18-25. See Philip Foner, Antonio Maceo (New York: Monthly Review Press, 1977), for a readable political biography of Maceo.
4. Taber, p. 50.
5. Dubois, p. 94.
6. Ibid.
7. Thomas, p. 864.
8. Dubois, p. 95.
9. Bonachea and San Martín, p. 35.
10. Bonachea and Valdés, pp. 63-4.
11. Bonachea and Valdés
12. Taber, p. 50.
13. Thomas, p. 866.
14. Bonachea and Valdés, p. 64.
15. Castro, "Declaration on the Arrest of Pedro Miret", in Bonachea and Valdés, p. 243.
16. Castro, "Chaviano, You Lie!" (May 29, 1955), in Bonachea and Valdés, pp. 244-9. The original Spanish "¡Chaviano, mientes!", uses the familiar second person verb form, an insult in the appropriate circumstances, but otherwise friendly and intimate.
17. Ibid., p. 247.
18. Ibid., p. 248.
19. Castro, "Chaviano, You Lie!", p. 249.
20. Bonachea and Valdés, p. 64.
21. Batista's speech cited in Bonachea and Valdés,

p. 250.
22. Castro, "Murderer's Hands" (June 5, 1955), in Bonachea and Valdés, pp. 250-2.
23. Castro, "Against Terror and Crime", in Bonachea and Valdés, pp. 252-4.
24. Ibid.
25. Thomas, p. 867. Thomas adds that Raúl Castro had already been arrested on a trumped-up arson charge during the period.
26. Bonachea and Valdés, p. 65.
27. See Llerena, p. 55. The MLR, made up mostly of intellectuals, with a program of reforms in elections, education and agriculture.
28. Ibid., pp. 78-9.
29. Bonachea and San Martín, p. 38; Thomas, pp. 867-8.
30. Bonachea and San Martín, p. 39, fn. 34.
31. Eduardo Yasells, "Entrevista: recuerdos sobre Frank y Daniel", Verde Olivo, 4 Aug. 63, pp. 4-13.
32. Bonachea and San Martín, p. 39.
33. Ibid., p. 40.
34. Castro, "Against the Return of Carlos Prío from Exile", (July 10, 1955), in Bonachea and Valdés, pp. 257-9.
35. Castro, "Against the Return...", p. 259.
36. Castro, "Letter to Prominent Political Leaders" (July 5, 1955), in Bonachea and Valdés, p. 257.
37. Thomas, p. 869.
38. Ibid.
39. Bonachea and San Martín, p. 65.
40. Thomas, p. 876.
41. Faustino Pérez, "A diez años del Granma", Verde Olivo, 11 Dec. 66, p. 21.
42. Bonachea and San Martín, p. 65.
43. Juan Almeida, quoted in Franqui, The Twelve, p. 30.
44. This assessment is in Thomas, p. 876.
45. Bayo was a Hispano-Cuban with long years of residence in Spain and a military career there encompassing counter-insurgency operations in the Rif of Morocco and battles against Franco for the Republic. He was an acknowledged author on the subject of guerrilla warfare, having practiced it in Spain.
46. Dubois, p. 99.
47. Philip Foner, "Introduction", in Our America, by José Martí, ed. Philip Foner (New York: Monthly Review Press, 1977), p. 41.
48. Castro, "Speech in New York" (Nov. 1, 1955), in Bonachea and Valdés, pp. 281-4.
49. Bonachea and Valdés, p. 74.
50. Castro, "Speech at Flagler Theater" (Miami, Nov. 20, 1955) in Bonachea and Valdés, pp. 284-7.
51. Thomas, p. 869, writes that in 1955 "all close followers of Castro appear still to have been

Ortodoxos in outlook".
    52. Castro, "Message to the Congress of Ortodoxo Militants" (Aug. 15, 1955), in Bonachea and Valdés, pp. 271-7.
    53. Castro, "Against Everyone?" (December 25, 1955) in Bonachea and Valdés, pp. 292-301.
    54. Castro, "Against Everyone!", p. 293.
    55. Ibid., p. 295.
    56. Castro, "Speech in New York", p. 282.
    57. Castro, "Message", p. 277.
    58. Jose Martí, "Our Ideas" (March 14, 1892), in <u>Our America</u>, pp. 271-80.
    59. Castro, "Manifesto #2 to the People of Cuba" (Dec. 10, 1955), in Bonachea and Valdés, pp. 287-92.
    60. Ibid., p. 288.
    61. Dubois, p. 99; Bonachea and San Martín, p. 65.
    62. Bonachea and San Martín, p. 80.
    63. Thomas, p. 886.
    64. She was the widow of Pablo de la Torriente Brau, a Cuban poet killed in the Spanish Civil War. See Teresa Casuso, <u>Cuba and Castro</u>, tr. Elmer Grossberg (New York: Random House, 1961), p. 111.
    65. Dubois, pp. 133-4; Thomas, p. 888; Bonachea and San Martín, p. 66.
    66. Castro, "Manifesto #2", pp. 288-9.
    67. Or to purchase the indifference of the Mexican police, as Thomas suggests, p. 888.
    68. Castro, "Interviews in Mexico" (Aug. 7, 1956), in Bonachea and San Martín, p. 61.
    69. Bonachea and San Martín, p. 61.
    70. Castro, "Manifesto #1 to the Cuban People" (AUg. 8, 1955), in Bonachea and Valdés, pp. 259-71.
    71. Bonachea and Valdés, p. 69.
    72. Suchlicki, p. 59; Bonachea and San Martín, p. 45.
    73. Bonachea and San Martín, pp. 47-9.
    74. Suchlicki, pp. 71-3.
    75. Bonachea and San Martín, p. 52.
    76. Suchlicki, p. 69.
    77. Thomas, pp. 871-2.
    78. Suchlicki, pp. 69-70.
    79. Thomas, p. 884.
    80. Ibid.
    81. Bonachea and Valdés, p. 78.
    82. Castro, "The 26th of July Movement" (March 19, 1956), in Bonachea and Valdés, pp. 310-19.
    83. Ibid., p. 318.
    84. Ibid.
    85. This document, in Bonachea and Valdés, pp. 337-9, called for insurrection, general strike, and revolution while appealing to nationalism against Trujillo-aided plots. It also supported "honorable representatives" of the army imprisoned on the Isle of Pines.
    86. Bonachea and San Martín, p. 65.

87. Thomas, p. 876.
88. Ibid., p. 877.
89. Thomas, p. 877.
90. Calixto García, "Nuestro deber era permanecer firmes a la orientación trazada por nuestro comandante en jefe", Verde Olivo, 1 Dec 63, p. 5.
91. Bonachea and Valdés, p. 79.
92. Thomas, p. 877.
93. Castro, "Interview in Mexico" (Aug. 7, 1956), in Bonachea and Valdés, pp. 317-31.
94. Thomas, pp. 877-8; Bonachea and Valdés, p. 80.
95. A complete list of training activities is presented in Dubois, pp. 112-3.
96. Daniel James, Che Guevara (New York: Stein and Day, 1969), p. 88.
97. I. Lavretsky, Ernesto Che Guevara, tr. A. B. Eklof (Moscow: Progress Publishers, 1976), p. 72.
98. Hilda Gadea, Ernesto: A Memoir of Che Guevara, tr. Carmen Molina and Walter Bradbury (New York: Doubleday, 1972), p. 131.
99. There seems to be no record of such discussions.
100. Quoted in Lavretsky, p. 73.
101. Gadea, pp. 7-9; Lavretsky, p. 53.
102. Thomas, p. 878.
103. Donald Schulz, "The Cuban Revolution and the Soviet Union", Ph.D. diss. Ohio State University, 1977 (Ann Arbor: University Microfilms, 1977), #77-24, 698.
104. Schulz, p. 5.
105. Ibid., p. 13.
106. Schulz, pp. 5-6.
107. See Jonathan Kozol, Children of the Revolution (New York: Delacorte Press, 1978), p. 156.
108. Numerous biographies of Guevara are available. Among the best-known are those by Daniel James, Ricardo Rojo, I. Lavretsky and Hilda Gadea.
109. Rojo, p. 30.
110. James, p. 29. James remarks upon Celia de la Serna's anti-imperialism and anti-Americanism, p. 44.
111. The word "gorila" 'gorilla' is commonly applied to Latin American military dictators and their coteries.
112. Interview in Lavretsky, p. 31.
113. Guevara, "The Duty of a Revolutionary Doctor" (Aug. 21, 1960), in Guevara, Che: Selected Works of Ernesto Guevara (Cambridge: MIT Press, 1969), ed.
114. Ibid., p. 257.
115. Guevara's conversation recalled, and probably paraphrased, in Rojo, p. 28.
116. Hilda Gadea, Che Guevara: Años Decisivos (Mexico: Aguilar, 1972), p. 27.
117. Gadea, Ernesto, p. 1.
118. Lavretsky, p. 52.

119. Ibid., p. 55.
120. Dalmau quoted in Lavretsky, p. 56, and James, p. 77.
121. Harold White, in the appendix to Gadea, *Ernesto*, p. 221.
122. Gadea, *Ernesto*, pp. 38-9.
123. Rojo, p. 55.
124. On the chronology of events, see Stephen Schlesinger and Stephen Kinzer, *Bitter Fruit* (Garden City: Anchor Books, 1983); David Wise and Thomas Ross, *The Invisible Government* (New York: Random House, 1964), pp. 165-84; Jose M. Aybar de Soto, *Dependency and Intervention: The Case of Guatemala in 1954* (Boulder: Westview Press, 1978), pp. 196-274; *I. F. Stone's Weekly*, April 22, 1957. For another view, see North American Congress on Latin America, *Guatemala* (Berkeley: NACLA, 1974), pp. 48-51.
125. Lavretsky, p. 56.
126. Gadea, *Ernesto*, p. 46.
127. James, p. 80.
128. Jorge Masetti, *Los que luchan y los que lloran* (Buenos Aires: Editorial Jorge Alvarez, 1969), p. 83.
129. Gadea recalled their discussion in *Ernesto*, p. 49.
130. Ibid., p. 50.
131. What follows is a paraphrasing of Gadea's assessment of the article. Ibid., pp. 54-5.
132. Gadea, *Ernesto*, p. 54.
133. Here, I disagree with Thomas, p. 880, who concludes that Guevara was a revolutionary in late 1955 but not necessarily a Marxist.
134. Later, in Mexico, he still wanted to travel to Paris and entertained ideas of entering on a cinematic career. See Gadea, *Ernesto*.
135. Ibid., p. 56.
136. Guevara, "Duty of a Revolutionary Doctor", p. 258.
137. On Peurifoy's role, see Aybar de Soto, pp. 248-60; Wise and Ross, pp. 165-80.
138. Gadea, *Ernesto*, pp. 95-6.
139. Gadea, *Che Guevara*, p. 39.
140. Castro quoted in Lavretsky, p. 68.
141. Masetti, p. 83.
142. In Lockwood, p. 143.
143. Guevara, "Notas para el estudio de la ideología de la revolución cubana", *Verde Olivo*, 10 Dec. 60, pp. 10-14.
144. Gadea, *Ernesto*, pp. 121, 158, on the precautions they took; pp. 133-41 on her arrest and interrogation.
145. James, p. 86.
146. Lavretsky, p. 73.
147. Michael Lowy, *The Marxism of Ché Guevara*,

tr. Brian Pearce (New York: Monthly Review Press, 1973), p. 33.
    148. Casuso, p. 94.
    149. Schulz, p. 172.
    150. Cited in Schulz, pp. 215-6, fn. 127.
    151. Ibid., p. 173.
    152. Ibid., p. 4
    153. "Entrevista con Abilio Collado", *Verde Olivo* 1 Dec. 63, pp. 6-8.
    154. Suchlicki, p. 73.
    155. See Bonachea and Valdés, p. 86.
    156. Suchlicki, p. 76.
    157. Bonachea and San Martín, p. 64. Thomas, p. 885, suggests that "Batista set a trap for García in order to restrain the *tanquistas*", the military hardliners.
    158. Bonachea and San Martín, pp. 77-9.
    159. Castro, "Cuba and the Dominican Republic", (Aug. 26, 1956 letter to *Bohemia*), in Bonachea and Valdés, pp. 332-7.
    160. Suchlicki, p. 73; Bonachea and San Martín, pp. 73-5.
    161. The assessment is Goldenberg's, pp. 120-42.
    162. Lavretsky, p. 73.
    163. I am indebted here to Farber's work on the contradictions which produced a Bonapartist situation in Cuba.
    164. Castro, "Against Everyone!" (Jan. 8, 1956 in *Bohemia*), in Bonachea and Valdés, pp. 292-301.
    165. Ibid., p. 300.
    166. See Castro, "The 26th of July Movement" (April 1, 1956 in *Bohemia*), in Bonachea and Valdés, pp. 310-19.
    167. Castro and José Echeverría, "Mexico Pact", in Bonachea and Valdés, pp. 337-9.
    168. Thomas, p. 887; Lavretsky, p. 74.
    169. Bonachea and Valdés, p. 81; Thomas, p. 887.
    170. Lavretsky, p. 74.
    171. See Castro, "On the Arrest of Cuban Revolutionaries in Mexico" (June 22, 1956), in Bonachea and Valdés, p. 319.
    172. See Castro, "Enough Lies!" (July 15, 1956), in Bonacheas and Valdés, pp. 319-26.
    173. Castro, "Enough Lies!", p. 325.
    174. *Pozole* is a thick maize stew. The repeated dunking of prisoners to the point of drowning is called *pozole* by the Mexican police.
    175. Gadea, *Ernesto*, p. 137.
    176. Castro, "Enough Lies!", p. 323.
    177. Bonachea and Valdés, p. 81.
    178. Castro, "Enough Lies!", pp. 324-5.
    179. Lavretsky, p. 75; Bonachea and Valdés, p. 81.
    180. Gadea, *Ernesto*, p. 152. She claims Castro paid a considerable *mordida* 'bribe' to secure their

release.
181. Ibid., p. 150.
182. Casuso, pp. 92-5.
183. Ibid., p. 105.
184. Ibid., p. 109.
185. Bonachea and Valdés, p. 82.
186. Bonachea and Valdés, p. 82.
187. Casuso, pp. 111-2.
188. Ibid., pp. 116-7; Thomas, p. 891; Dubois, p. 135. Apparently, del Pino received $15,000 for his betrayal. He later led an abortive uprising against the Cuban government and was sentenced to thirty years.
189. Bonachea and Valdés, p. 87: "Nearly fifty... were left behind".
190. On Cienfuegos, see Gabriel Pérez Tarrau, Cronología de un héroe (Havana: Gente Nueva, 1976), and Guillermo Cabrera Alvarez, Hablar de Camilo (Havana: Instituto del Libro, 1970).
191. In Lockwood, p. 143.

5
Political Education in the Rebel Army: Armed Struggle and the Establishment of the Guerrillas

The band of rebels which established a guerrilla struggle and carried out an armed insurrection against Batista completed one set of Cuban revolutionary missions and energizing myths and created another. This is not to say that the two sets of myths are mutually exclusive. Rather, by keeping their word to invade and fight the dictatorship, Castro and the rebel group completed and personally re-lived the revolutionary myths of Cuban history. The generations of '68 and '95, of Céspedes, Agramonte, Maceo and Martí were emulated in the very style of the M-26 organization and the invasion. The revolutionary myth of social justice from Maceo's and Martí's thought was kept alive in the Sierra Maestra in the form of the Rebel Army's vision of social revolution. The legacy of the radicals of the anti-Machado and anti-Batista struggles of the 30s, and the radical nationalism of Chibás, were redeemed by a new generation in the Sierra and in the cities. And, finally, the events and personalities of the struggle created a new pantheon of Cuban revolutionary heroes and a new revolutionary myth to fuel the political process after January 1, 1959. The exploits of the M-26 and the Rebel Army came to provide new material for the continuing political education of recruits during the struggle, for the political education of the new army after 1959, and for the political education of the entire population.

In this chapter, I wish to discuss two broad processes. First, the ongoing political education within the Rebel Army in its various existential and organized forms. And, second, how the events and personalities of the struggle came to form a more mature but novel ideology and myths central to political education during the revolutionary process initiated in 1959 by the insurrection.

The object of political education in a guerrilla force is to create a discipline and morale superior to that of the enemy. There must be some explanation of realities which reflects upon the already-present experience and sentiments of the guerrillas and the recruits. The explanation must be clear and advance the rebellious outlook of the disaffected and repressed in the direction of high morale and optimism. It must identify the enemy and the reasons he is an enemy and provide both the immediate and long-term objectives of the struggle. It is a tall order, but political education, conceived as a process, is crucial in every guerrilla struggle and in every revolutionary movement. As General Giap, one of the great guerrilla leaders of the century, put it, "political work...is of the first importance. It is the soul of the army".[1]

My method here will be to refer to the course and character of the struggle in the first six months, and to the memories of the combatants to elicit, as far as is possible, the nature and themes of political education in the Rebel Army. Reminiscences and recollections of combatants provide one source of information, while journalists' reports provide another. A third source is furnished by the better secondary syntheses of the insurrection's events. Of necessity, I will be examining the leadership style of the outstanding leaders in the rebel column, as it reflects upon the daily political education of *la tropa* 'the troops'. I will try to show that political education in the Rebel Army was uniquely Cuban in content, in the sense that the pre-*Granma* experiences of the Moncada generation and the revolutionary legacy of previous generations in Cuban history formed a large part of political education. Further, the unique course of the war and daily exigencies specific to the Sierra Maestra contributed to the Cuban-ness of the political education.

Writing about the desperate military situation of the fledgling Bolshevik Revolution, John Reed observed: "People in revolt have a way of defying military precedent".[2] In Cuba, in 1957, the New *Mambises* of M-26 not only defied precedents, they also defied the realities of discovery, defeat and dispersal. The landing of the *Granma* and the anticipated uprisings in urban centers were an unmitigated military disaster. But then, the Moncada assault had also been a tragic disaster, and it did not halt the insurrectionary movement. Neither the political crisis, nor the spirit of resistance among Cubans available for recruitment to a rebel movement had changed. In fact, the example of Moncada encouraged the non-Marxist left to embrace insurrectionism. Deep emotions of Cuban nationalism were involved and, for one student of Cuban revolutionary ideology, the *Granma* invasion was born "more of emotion than of reason".[3] But the power of the revolutionary myth is that it transcends reason; it is a non-rational faith in deliverance from an oppressive system that energizes insurrection. Georges Sorel's "political philosophy of active radicalism", his faith in the power of the socialist revolutionary myth, was based "on the assumptions of irrationalism - on the superiority of the myth of projective impressions over critical judgement".[4] Castro had said "in 1956 we shall be free or we shall be martyrs"[5], and the defective yacht <u>Granma</u>, packed with men, left on an upbeat note: the rebels sang the national anthem and the "Hymn of the 26th of July".[6]

The hardships and disasters which ensued bound some of the fighters even closer together and closer to Castro's leadership than before, while some others eventually left the force. The yacht's engines were in poor repair and the weather was atrocious. All but a handful of the eighty-two on board were violently and unceasingly ill.[7] The rations on board were short, the trip longer than anticipated and, at one point, the navigator, Roberto Roque Nuñez, fell overboard for an hour or more.[8] The situation was almost desperate. As one man later recalled it, "that damned launch rolling for five days like a drunken tortoise".[9]

The political tragedy was even worse. The M-26 groups in Cuba had been organized, though imperfectly, to launch an uprising to coincide with the landing of the invasion forces, projected for November 30.[10] In Havana, the M-26 was not ready and did not know of the impending uprising in Santiago. In most areas, the little action that was mustered was isolated sabotage. The general strike which was planned failed to materialize. Unions dominated by <u>Mujalista</u> leadership and by the communists were having no part in the plans, and M-26 labor organizers in most places outside of Santiago were isolated. In Santiago, however, though he had strong doubts and pleaded for more time, Frank País combined with Pepito Tey, Haydée Santamaría and Lester Rodriguez, a Moncada veteran, to organize a strong blow against the dictatorship.[11] With a couple hundred M-26 urban militants, País planned to pin down the government's two thousand troops in Moncada with a mortar and sniper fire, attack the police stations, capture and distribute arms to the population and call for a general strike. In preparation, on November 28, to some of the assembled underground, Pepito Tey read Ernst Thälmann's call to the people of Hamburg for an uprising against the Nazis, drawing the parallel with the late 1956 terror unleashed by the Batista regime.[12] But, as with the original Moncada assault, the element of surprise was lost, and the single mortar did not come into action. Nonetheless, street fighting broke out, with the militia wearing M-26 armbands, and Santiago was paralyzed for two days.[13] This action became part of the revolutionary myths in the political education of the Rebel Army/FAR in 1959. Those who fought the Batista forces and fell in Santiago were seen as heroes of the continuous struggle beginning at Moncada. Similarly, when disputes in M-26 occurred over the course of the struggle, i.e. whether to concentrate on rural guerrilla struggle or urban insurrection with a general strike, those in the llano 'plains', 'urban areas', pointed to the relative success of the Santiago insurrection.

Castro had planned to land at Niquero, south of the city of Manzanillo, and meet up with one hundred men organized by Crescencio Pérez, a leader of precaristas 'squatters', and by Celia Sánchez, a writer from the Oriente coast.[14] The idea was to assault the Niquero barracks, distribute arms to the one hundred men and attack Manzanillo, in a campaign that would "culminate in a general strike".[15] The idea of guerrilla struggle in the Sierra Maestra, though prepared for in Mexico, was in fact a temporary alternative.

On board the Granma, the rebels heard of the Santiago uprising by radio. They felt heartened at the action, but frustrated at its defeat and their helplessness. Castro's attitude was apparently "grave, but confident, as always".[16]

As they approached the coast on December 1, weapons were uncrated, cleaned and oiled, then distributed; uniforms were put on; Castro circulated among the fighters, talking to each one. He spoke of discipline under fire, respect for the lives of the government soldiers and the need to take weapons, not their lives. He spoke of the support they would receive from the people if they had to take to the mountains, and of the thousands who would fight alongside them if weapons were secured.[17]

The landing, in the wrong place, was perilous; the coast was a mangrove swamp, the footing muddy and precarious. It took hours to cover several hundred meters. Large amounts of supplies, food, medicine and arms were abandoned.[18] In addition, it appears that Batista knew about the projected landing and had planes out searching for the Granma. It was shot up as the rebels were recovering from the exhausting disembarcation. The army moved in to surround the area and block the routes into the mountains.[19]

The hungry and exhausted group struck inland to avoid the army, which was already bombing the area. With little to eat and no contact with the small rural militia organized by the M-26, they straggled through a cane-field region in stiff new boots, poorly armed. On December 5, they halted at Alegría de Pío, the only route from their landing place to the Sierra Maestra mountains. The peasant sympathizers tried to reach them there, but they were already surrounded.[20] Due to a traitorous guide and their own evident trail, the army was in a position to ambush the group in an open area.[21]

The intense fire of the army killed and wounded a number of the rebels in a few moments. Those who surrendered were killed; some escaped. The band was dispersed and wandered in smaller groups for days.

These harsh days of the voyage, the landing and the ambush gave rise to some of the heroic quotations and stories which appear in the materials for the political education, not only of the revolutionary armed forces, but of the nation as a whole. The spirit of patriotism and sacrifice for Cuba, which was instrumental in mounting the Moncada attack, also brought individuals to the landing at Playa de los Colorados, near Niquero. A sense of history is in the words of Faustino Pérez, who took part in the invasion to "cumplir el deber de cubano 'fulfill the Cuban duty', inspired by Martí's thought:"'whoever sees his people in disorder and agony without an apparent door opening to well-being and honor should look for that door or he is not an honorable'...we came with our spirits anointed with the same constructive objectives which made Céspedes leave Bayamo and Máximo Gómez [Independence War military leader] bless the 'incendiary task'".[22]

It was at Alegría de Pío that the legend of Camilo Cienfuegos began, for those receiving their political education during and after the insurrection. Under fire at Alegría, some of the rebels shouted that they should surrender. But Camilo roared out, "here no one surrenders, damn it!"[23] Another who shouted "No surrender!" and kept firing was Juan Almeida, later the head of the FAR.[24]

The continuing legend of Fidel Castro's coolness and leadership, even in the midst of debacle, picked up tempo at the landing and in the succeeding days. Guevara recalled that when the airplanes were firing on the abandoned Granma, Castro stood up and prepared to march off, saying "hear how they are shooting at us. They're terrified. They fear us because they know we're going to finish them".[25] As they walked inland, before the Alegría disaster, Fidel Castro tried to talk to every guajiro 'peasant' they met.[26] Many were frightened and ran off before the rebels approached. Batista's planes had been strafing the area. If the rebels could find no one near the bohíos 'huts' they would leave money for what they took to eat. If the peasants remained, Castro would engage them in conversation, explaining who the rebels were, talking intently into someone's face, asking questions about their work and pay. He would say: "We have come far and seen no schools, no hospitals, only starving children... in the cities men are enriching themselves while you are hungry. It is for this we have come, to change everything and to free the land".[27] Castro was especially careful always to pay generously for things, to ask for them, to ask if the rebels were not imposing: "When they refused, we continued our march without protest... while Batista's army took everything they wanted from the bohíos, even the women, of course. Castro's people respected the guajiro's property and paid generously for everything consumed".[28]

The aftermath of Alegria de Pío was a period of confused and scattered wandering, contacts with some of the tenuous M-26 peasant network, thirst, hunger and regrouping of the survivors.[29] The handful who survived and remained in the mountains formed the core of the Rebel Army. Castro himself laid up in a cane-field for five days: "When the revolution is triumphant", he told his two companions, "we will have to erect a monument to our savior sugar cane".[30]

Demoralization struck the survivors hard. They had lost many comrades and the peasants were generally reticent, although the rebels were helped and hidden after Alegria. Some of the M-26 peasants fled: "I have to say it - there were some men we couldn't control. They fled like rabbits..why hide it?"[31]

With the help of Crescencio Pérez and his network of friends and relatives, the survivors regrouped, ate well, and headed into the Sierra. The myth of the "twelve" comes from this time.[32] The actual number of rebels is debated, but Dubois lists them as Fidel and Raúl Castro, Guevara, Camilo Cienfuegos, Calixto Morales and Calixto García, Faustino Pérez, Universo Sánchez, Efigenio Ameijeiras, Ciro Redondo, Juan Almeida and René Rodriguez.[33] With Castro claiming "the days of the dictatorship are numbered!", to the incredulity and consternation of René Rodriguez[34], they arrived in the highest massif of the Sierra, the environs of Pico Turquino.

Down in the cities of Oriente, repression had followed the Santiago uprising. Civil liberties were suspended, jails were filled, trials held, indiscriminate shootings occurred, the victims mostly young men. In Holguín, Colonel Fermín Cowley presented the people with "Batista's Christmas Gift", the bodies of twenty-nine men and boys "left littering the countryside or hanging from trees over the Yule holiday".[35] The rural Guardia was known for its whimsical violence and harassment of women, while women in the cities later recalled that "in the old days if your man was not at home, you worried that he was beaten up or dead".[36] In both Havana and Oriente, the mounting reign of police terror, as many years later in urban Nicaragua and El Salvador, brought increased resistance and attention to the rural guerrilla struggle from middle-class civic organizations and individuals".[37]

As with the Soviet World War II officer Colonel Bourdzhan Momysh-Uly[38], Castro knew that the demoralization of his little band could only be redeemed by action and victory. It was also the only way to recoup lost arms and ammunition. Combat was to be a living political education. Defeat at Alegria had been a bitter, but necessary, lesson: "Characteristic of the small group of survivors, embued with a spirit of struggle, was the understanding that to imagine spontaneous outbursts throughout the island was an illusion".[39] The initial "subjectivism", as Guevara had called it, had been radically altered.

The attack on the small coastal garrison at La Plata[40] had several ramifications and political lessons for the guerrillas. First, in taking the garrison and capturing arms without a casualty, they came to know it could be done. Indeed, it had to be done: "It was an important moment, for we had few bullets; we had to take the barracks no matter what, for otherwise we would spend all our ammunition and remain practically defenseless".[41] Second, the rebels gained experience in deception and in the brutal system of chivatos 'informers and collaborators' and the Guardia Rural, which were the strongest enemies in the struggle for influence among the guajiros of the Sierra Maestra. It was a lesson about the relationships of power and its use in the mountains, a lesson in the sociology and politics of the society in which the guerrilla had to survive, fight and thrive. They captured a man named Chicho Osorio, a notorious chivato, near La Plata, to gain information.[42] He was a mayoral 'overseer' on a large latifundio nearby and carried out a minor reign of terror over the squatters and day-laborers. The guerrillas got him to talk by taking advantage of his inebriation and posing as Guardias, and he talked of his crimes against peasants, including murder, of the good soldiers (the brutal ones), the bad soldiers (those who refrained from abuses) and of the other chivato peasants. He boasted of having helped kill some of the rebels at Alegria. In the first gunfire at La Plata, he was executed.

Thirdly, the policy of honorable treatment of enemy wounded and captured was observed from this first battle. Castro not only ordered Guevara to help the enemy wounded, but left all their medicines with the captured soldiers, so as to continue aiding the wounded.[43] This treatment became a strong moral force on the side of the rebels, as time went on: "Our attitude toward the wounded contrasted sharply with that of the army. The army not only murdered our wounded, but also abandoned their own. In time, this difference began having its effects, and constituted one of the factors in our victory".[44]

This was a time of very tentative relationships with the guajiros of the Sierra Maestra. The army, the Guardia Rural and the mayorales brought reprisals against the peasants in the Sierra for real and suspected aid to the rebels. Killings, torture, rapes, theft, burnings and aerial bombardments occurred. The area was inhabited by precaristas [45] who were continually having to fight against latifundistas, guards and mayorales to keep their plots. With the arrival of the rebels, the pressure on them increased. At the same time, the rebels were punishing chivatos and cruel mayorales like Chicho Osorio and, at La Plata, they released precaristas made prisoners by the guards. Some peasants from Crescencio Pérez' network had joined the rebels as guides and helpers after Alegría and, with the attack on La Plata and, a few days later, a successful ambush against the notorious army commander Sánchez Mosquera's troops[46], some others offered to join. They were turned down, as arms were lacking.

Guevara's views on the Sierra peasantry during this period of isolation are very perceptive. Most of the expeditionaries were urban-dwellers and had never, until the invasion and Alegría de Pío, known deep hunger. And they distrusted the peasants, having reason to fear treachery. But the generous treatment the rebels received from a number of peasants after Alegría, the example of Crescencio's party, and the hard life in the Sierra brought about a change. They began to understand how harsh life was in the Sierra: "We began to know it [hunger]...and so many things became very clear [about the peasants' condition]".[47] They understood why "still many campesinos were fleeing terrified at our presence, for fear of the reprisals the government took when it learned of even the most minimal contact between the inhabitants of the zone and our group".[48] And, here, the course of the insurrection took on a cold logic for Guevara. With the small but successful actions by the rebels, the peasants could see that the army could not end the guerrilla struggle, though it could uproot the peasants and destroy their homes, even kill them. The guerrillas were "the only force which could resist and punish the abuses, and thus to take refuge amidst the guerrillas, where their lives would be protected, was a good solution".[49]

The rebels were beset by Batista's planes and bombed several times in late January-early February. It was discovered that a trusted peasant guide, Eutimio Guerra, had been informing the army of their whereabouts. He had even been contracted to kill Castro. He was executed on the day of Herbert Matthews' (New York Times reporter) visit to the rebel camp and, at the last moment, asked the rebels to take care of his children after victory.[50]

This execution and that of Osorio were not hidden from the Sierra Maestra population. Rather, they publicized the revolutionary code of the guerrillas, who eventually became the "real and effective authority to whom the peasants referred all problems".[51] Reprisals by the army occurred when it intermittently entered the small settlements: "Every campesino was seen as a potential rebel".[52] But the guerrillas also enacted reprisals against informing and common crimes, and they remained in the area. Thus, the campesinos, if at first not out of political conviction or love for the rebels, were forced to co-operate by the dictates of survival and self-interest. However harsh revolutionary justice, it was nevertheless seen as justice and, in the absence of a legitimate authority, the guerrillas became the local authority. After the establishment of a fairly secure territory, if a guajiro was forced into the plains or killed by the Guardia of the army for co-operation with the rebels, his family was cared for from the rebel stores and cash supply. The rebels punished bandits who preyed on the guajiros.[53] Slowly, trust and cooperation were built up. A network of supplies, informers and militia was eventually created in the "Territorio Libre" 'Free Territory'.

These early months were ones of tremendous hardship for the guerrillas. Consequently, there were problems of low morale and discipline. The air attacks had further disheartened some of the men. There were some desertions. As Guevara put it, "our situation was not a happy one in those days. The column lacked cohesion. It had neither the spirit which comes from the experience of war nor a clear ideological consciousness. Now one comrade, now another, would leave us; many requested assignments in the city..."[54] Some of the talk became defeatist, and "Fidel made a short speech urging greater discipline and explaining the dangers which might arise if this discipline were disregarded. He also announced the three crimes punishable by death: insubordination, desertion and defeatism".[55]

Faustino Perez had been sent to contact the urban M-26 after the landing, to let them know of the rebels' survival, to get supplies organized, and to secure some recruits. Ten of them arrived on February 1, the day of some desertions, along with surgical supplies and new uniforms prepared by the Manzanillo underground.[56] They had still not discovered Eutimio Guerra's treachery, a cause of much of their demoralization. The new recruits were precaristas from the region and now the rebel group took on more of its peasant army aspect, though it was never, strictly speaking, a peasant army. The thrust of the Rebel Army myth was that it was an army _for_ the peasants, and included peasants, but not that _it_ was born of peasants.

The recruits brought news of the deserter Sergio Acuna's death at the hands of the army. He had bragged about his exploits and had been betrayed. For Guevara, it taught the rebels "the value of unity and the uselessness of attempting individually to feel the collective destiny".[57] The first purge followed this knowledge. Three men "of very low morale" were sent away, and two seriously wounded men were evacuated. Some of the new recruits were appalled at the lack of food, shelter and defenses in the Sierra, and also left, "a fact which was to the advantage of the troop".[58]

The <u>precarista</u> recruits brought a certain amount of superstition with them. Guevara recalled a belief that dreams could predict events such as death and bombing attacks. Since "it was part of my daily task to make explanations of a cultural or political type to the men, I explained firmly that this was not possible".[59] One of the peasants, forty-five year-old Julio Zénon Acosta, became Guevara's first literacy student, symbolic for Guevara of the nascent peasant-guerrilla unity. Zénon had "understood the enormous tasks which the Revolution would face after its victory, and....was learning the alphabet to prepare himself for this".[60]

February and March 1957 were very ambiguous times for the rebel force. They had yet to consolidate a territory or a positive relationship with the general <u>guajiro</u> population. Yet, they achieved international and national publicity and support from urban cadres began to filter through. It was a classical first stage guerrilla struggle: survival for another day was a victory in the long run. Morale was still low, but an element of indomitability was also present.[61]

Two events were important in this period beyond mere survival. First, contact was made with representatives of the urban M-26. Frank País, Vilma Espín (lawyer and later spouse of Raul Castro), Haydée Santamaría and Celia Sánchez met with the rebels in the Sierra to work out a system of supply and communications.[62] Second, a visit to the rebel camp by Herbert Matthews had been arranged, and he arrived clandestinely to conduct an interview with Castro.[63] His articles, which appeared shortly in the <u>New York Times</u> and which were reprinted in Cuban newspapers, just as censorship was temporarily lifted, were revelatory and sympathetic. Matthews was struck by Castro's "overpowering personality", finding him an "educated, dedicated fanatic, a man of ideals, of courage and of remarkable qualities of leadership".[64] It was a real coup of publicity and propaganda. The whole island knew that the rebel invaders had survived and were fighting; the glowing prose of Matthews talked of the democratic, nationalist, anti-imperialist, anti-colonialist and socialist, but still anti-communist ideals of the movement comprised of "unspoiled youth, honest businessmen, the politician of integrity, the patriotic army officer".[65] It broadcast the fact that the rebels paid for everything and that their treatment of captured and wounded army soldiers was exemplary. Castro told Matthews that "the soldiers are fighting badly; their morale is low and ours could not be higher. We are killing many, but when we take prisoners they are never shot. We question them, talk kindly to them, take their arms and equipment and then set them free...they do not want to fight, and they do not know how to fight this kind of mountain warfare. We do".66

The December repression after the failed uprisings, the continuing brutal treatment of Sierra guajiros by the Batista military and the news that Castro was alive and fighting gave a spurt of energy to the urban resistance movement which was crucial in the months of wandering in an unestablished territory. Demonstrations against police terror took place.67 A civic resistance movement began to take shape, basically co-ordinated by M-26 activists, but integrated by many non-M-26 elements. Raúl Chibás, head of the Ortodoxo Party, Felipe Pazos, a leading Cuban economist, and others became involved in collecting funds, printing pamphlets and organizing supplies.68 Middle-class and "responsible" people were engaged in moving arms and ammunition.

Persuaded at the February meeting that the guerrilla struggle was promising and deserving of aid, País organized a group of around fifty of the best urban fighters and collected arms and supplies. The fifty, including three young United States civilians living on the Guantánamo base69, arrived a few days after the abortive and bloody student DR attack on Batista's palace (March 13, 1957)70, under the command of Jorge Sotús, one of País' lieutenants in the Santiago uprising. They were driven into the area in trucks owned by Huber Matos, an Oriente rice grower who later flew arms in from Costa Rica and became a popular Rebel Army commander before his disaffection and arrest in 1959.71

The new recruits more than doubled the strength of the rebel force, but they were unprepared for the harsh life of the Sierra. Those in the mountains since the landing, or having joined since, though suffering low morale themselves,72 were more toughened: "We saw in the new troop all the defects which those who had landed on the Granma had had: lack of discipline, the inability to adjust to major difficulties, lack of decision, the incapacity to adapt to this life".73 The new recruits were not used to infrequent meals or to single daily meals, and "if the ration did not taste good they would not eat it". They also would jettison canned food from their new packsacks to reduce weight, while keeping toiletries.74

Guevara and the other veterans were upset by the lack of marching ability, and by the attitudes of Sotús. He was, according to Guevara, "a man of authoritarian spirit who could not get on with the men, and the troop in general".75 Castro reorganized the group, with a council dominated by the veterans, and imposed discipline. Turning down Guevara's suggestion that immediate combat should be undertaken to "temper the new men in battle", Castro decided to train the recruits in guerrilla warfare techniques and build their stamina in long marches through the mountains and the jungle. The column was split into squads for separate cooking, the distribution of food and medicines and ammunition, and veterans were placed in each squad to teach the recruits. It became the task of the veterans, themselves victims of low morale, to create discipline and morale in the recruits. Before, it had been Fidel or Raúl Castro, or Guevara, who tried to maintain spirits.[76]

Relations with the guajiros in the Sierra were not yet strong, though Cresencio Pérez' people, with Guillermo García and Ciro Frías, two early peasant recruits, moved through the mountains with information and food. The Batista army had been re-organized under the command of Major Barrera Perez, in the Sierra Maestra. He had re-established order in Santiago after the uprising. He and three Batista cabinet ministers instituted a civic action program for the military in the area which gained some precarista support.[77] Internal army politics soon replaced him with the brutal Major Casillas, a man responsible for killings, torture and burnings in the area since December.[78] Castro's people spent weeks moving back and forth with the recruits, establishing contacts with the peasants, food caches and information networks. When they returned to the Arroyo del Infierno, where they had been bombed and chased by Sánchez Mosquera's troops, the peasants came to tell them who had led the military there. An informer was executed.[79] The rebels began to tend to the medical needs of the peasants, adjudicate quarrels and punish wrongdoings. For Guevara, these contacts brought the rebels an awareness "of the necessity for a definitive change in the life of the people. The idea of agrarian reform became clear, and oneness with the people ceased being theory and was converted into a fundamental part of our being".[80]

In May, the rebel column was in better physical shape. Regular supplies were arriving, the precaristas were more trusting and new publicity had been achieved by CBS reporter Taber's television coverage of the troop. Andrew St. George, of Look magazine, and quite likely of the CIA,[81] was also with them for a time. Still, the rebels moved constantly to avoid detection and "our struggle against the lack of physical, ideological and moral preparation among the men was a daily one: the results were not always encouraging".[82] Again, there were some desertions and expulsions. The column tried to set various ambushes of army trucks, without success. But a new shipment of weapons from Santiago did arrive, and the knowledge that a group led by Calixto Sánchez (a World War II United States veteran and a union leader of airport workers) had landed from Florida in the yacht Corintia on the north coast of Oriente,[83] resolved Castro to mount an assault on the army.

Castro and Guevara discussed the political impact of an attack on an army outpost, at El Uvero, on the coast below the Sierra Maestra. The army had a number of such posts surrounding the Sierra, from which chivatos were sent out to reconnoitre the guerrillas.[84] Castro argued that to capture such a post would divert the army from the Corintia force and "have tremendous moral impact upon both the rebels and the Cuban nation".[85]

In a fierce fire fight of several hours, the post was taken. The rebels suffered six dead and nine wounded, while casualties on the army side were nearly double. Guevara took charge of the wounded and moved off from the main body of the guerrillas, who retreated with a truckload of arms and supplies. The effect was just as Castro had predicted: "For us this was the victory which marked our coming of age. From this battle on, our morale grew tremendously, our decisiveness and our hopes for triumph increased also".[86] But Castro knew that the capture of El Uvero and the general jubilation of the guajiros in the neighborhood would bring army troops and repression. In front of the guerrilla graves, he spoke to his column: "Very hard days await us. We have to make a great effort and sacrifices to strengthen our will. But if we make it, if we can stand it for fifteen days, we will have triumphed, we will have obtained the victory of the revolution. We have to carry this memory [of El Uvero] in our hearts and the pain for our comrades. For them we have to reach our objectives".[87] This theme of carrying on the struggle, and then the revolution, for the fallen comrades, became integral to the political education of recruits to the Rebel Army and to the FAR.

Guevara and his group were separated from the main guerrilla force for about forty days, in which time most of the wounded were healed. Their painful and slow retreat was another in the string of hardships endured in the guerrilla war which became something revered in the post-1959 Rebel Army and later in the FAR's political education efforts. During this period of recuperation, Guevara and his squad had to rely on the peasants for their survival.[88]

Guevara initiated evening discussions with the first three peasants to help them and soon numbers of them would come to the bohio at night for conversation with the rebels. Guevara talked of land reform and of collective agriculture, "of what we would do when the war was over".[89] Local superstitions and santeria (the belief in personal santos 'saints','spiritual intervenors') were also topics which Guevara handled diplomatically.[90] A system of vocal warnings, of supply and of information was arranged among the local peasantry for the support of the guerrillas.

Guevara devoted time to the political education of the recruits his group attracted during their stay with the wounded, attempting to convince them that the end of the dictatorship was insufficient, that agrarian reform and radical social change in the Sierra was imperative. It was a time in which most peasant recruits were "out to see Batista brought down",[91] but had no further plans. Some were with the guerrillas because of personal grievances against individual guards or soldiers, or because their families had been hurt by the repression after El Uvero. The government troops had arrived soon and some two thousand families were placed in the equivalent of "strategic hamlets". The troops carrying out the evacuation acted ruthlessly.[92] Guillermo García later recalled the early months of the struggle as too harsh to spend much time on political ideology: "Who had time for that? For all of us, there was only one thing on our minds. To beat Batista. We spent all our time worrying about that. How to get more guns, more men..."[93]

Nevertheless, Guevara sought to make clear in the recruits' minds the connection between the struggle against Batista and the <u>Guardia</u> and land reform. Most peasants perceived the struggle as aimed at immediate abuses. There was little conception of the range of changes and possibilities the overthrow of Batista and the destruction of the army might bring about. Likewise, as García pointed out, the immediate thrust of political education centered on developing the conviction in each guerrilla that, with arms, he could confront and defeat the <u>Guardia</u> and regular army units. It was more difficult to convince a <u>guajiro</u> that he was representative of a class. The broader perspective that was more easily developed was that of a nationalist spirit; it was easier to link a <u>guajiro</u> to the <u>Mambí</u> guerrilla fighters than to a social class.

Guevara's personal conduct impressed those recruits who stayed. Joel Iglesias recalled Guevara's absolute insistence on equal conditions and rations: "He never enjoyed anything alone, but always shared it out".[94] A whole anecdotal lore eventually built up around this personalist influence of the leaders on their troops, an influence based on conduct and example.[95]

The great enemies against which political education was aimed at this time were fear of the army, "who loomed as giants in our imagination and in the stories of the <u>guajiros</u>",[96] the reluctance to march, the lack of weapons and contact with the main guerrilla force. Another target of Guevara's political education was anti-communism, very prevalent among the peasants. The first woman recruit in Guevara's unit, Oniria Gutierrez, recalled a conversation with Guevara about her political ideas: "I answered I was Ortodoxo, like my whole family...I asked if he were religious. No, he answered, because I am a communist. For a young girl like me, it was a surprise. I said, 'you can't be one, you are very nice'. He laughed and began to explain many things that I had not known".[97] Another fighter, Marcial Orozco, remembered a discussion about communism initiated by a peasant guerrilla who said that after Batista, they would have to fight against communism. Guevara suggested it would be difficult, since one could never tell who was a communist. On another occasion, when the guerrilla struggle was in its second year, Guevara's rebel paper El Cubano Libre, contained these lines: "Communists, it would seem, are all those who take up arms because they are fed up with poverty and it does not matter which country we are discussing...those who kill the common people, men, women and children, call themselves democrats. How much the whole world resembles Cuba!"[98]

For the first six months in Cuba, then, political education was largely existential. Severe hardships and isolation from the urban support movement made for a physically desperate situation and dependence for survival upon the local peasantry. This dependence created a new concentration, for the guerrilla leaders, on the class fraction, the precaristas, among whom the guerrillas moved and fought. This early experience and the development of trust on both sides brought about a symbiotic relationship. The guerrillas defended the precaristas and imposed a revolutionary order in the area, while the peasants closed around the guerrillas and protected them. The few recruits from the peasant class fraction peculiar to the Sierra Maestra brought attitudes which political education had to address. Santería, distrust of authority, suspicion, fear of the army and anti-communist sentiments had to be addressed in people of great survival skills and natural ingenuity, but without much, if any, formal education or political experience.

The immediate goal of political education in the pedagogic sense was the creation of discipline. This depended more upon the self-discipline, morale and examples of the leadership than on the conveyance of any revolutionary myths. The dictates of survival against a vastly superior force, in a semi-hostile population, against the elements and with considerable isolation from the urban movement, were the source of themes. The personal conduct of the leaders helped to create the model of discipline and morale desired. When the guerrilla became more established territorially and when supplies, arms and communications were secured from the urban cadres, more solid encampments were set up and political education took on somewhat more formal outlines.

I have dealt here in some detail with the first few months of the guerrilla struggle in an attempt to elucidate both the intermittent, relatively unsophisticated and difficult political education in the Rebel Army and the stuff of myth. Hardship, pursuit and the establishing of a working relationship with the Sierra peasantry were the daily experiences of the guerrillas and this was their personal and corporate political education. This learning process, which they were prepared to go through largely by their own adherence to the various myths of Cuban national redemption, social revolution and the example of Moncada, developed into the myth of the Rebel Army. With moral superiority, discipline and adaptability, their activities became exploits in short order. After several months, there was a myth of the Rebel Army. It was used consciously to communicate with the llano and with the outside world, e.g. via Herbert Matthews. It was also used to inspire new recruits with the discipline and confidence necessary for guerrilla struggle. Ultimately, this new myth developed into a strong entity linked to the myths of national redemption and socialist revolution in a myth system central to political education of the Rebel Army/FAR after 1959.

The guerrillas as social revolutionaries as well as fighters: this was the dual image of the Rebel Army combatants which has been carried through in the formal political education of the revolutionary Cuban military from the days of the guerrilla struggle to the present. The "civic soldier", as Jorge Domingues has put it,[99] was developing from the first days in the Sierra, a soldier who undertook social reforms while fighting. The notion of the "civic soldier" perhaps needs the adjective "revolutionary" too, since the "civic soldier" model may also serve counter-revolutionary purposes. Nevertheless, this dual role of the Cuban guerrilla has been at the center of the Rebel Army myth from the beginning. What are we, and what are the enemy soldiers? the rebels were asked in their political education. Because of superior morale and a basis in a just cause, they could be civic soldiers, rebels with a social mission, rather than simply fighting machines. Because of the lack of a just cause, the enemy soldier was a mercenary and not capable of defending the interests of the people. Even so, the real enemy was behind the mercenary soldier, an enemy whose identity it was more difficult for the underdeveloped Rebel Army political education to convey. When the Rebel Army myth became an official myth and was linked to Cuban nationalism and to Marxism-Leninism after 1961, it achieved its full potential to mobilize and sustain revolutionary spirit.

NOTES

1. Vo Nguyen Giap, People's War, People's Army (New York: Praeger, 1962), p. 55
2. John Reed, Ten Days That Shook The World (New York: Bonie and Liveright, 1919), p. 218.
3. Schulz, p. 174.
4. Horowitz, p. 2
5. Castro, "Speech in New York" (Nov. 1, 1955), in Bonachea and Valdés, pp. 281-4.
6. Guevara, Reminiscences of the Cuban Revolutionary War, tr. Victoria Ortiz (New York: Monthly Review Press, 1968), p. 40.
7. Guevara, Reminiscences, p. 40.
8. Capt. Roberto Roque Nuñez, "Relato", Verde Olivo, 1 Dec 63, pp. 14-15.
9. Julio Cortazar Díaz, in Cuba Internacional, May-June 1970, p. 12.
10. For an account of the plans, mis-organization and uneven preparedness of the M-26 underground, see Bonachea and San Martín, pp. 78-83.
11. See Verde Olivo, 4 Aug. 63, pp. 9-10 for details of the uprising.
12. Eduardo Yasells, "Siete Años", Verde Olivo, 1 Dec. 63, pp. 9-11.
13. "Frank, el jefe del levantamiento", Verde Olivo 5 Dec 71, pp. 42-9.
14. Celia Sánchez, in Franqui, The Twelve, pp. 66-8: "From the 29th on we had transport vehicles and fuel supplies..."
15. Faustino Pérez, cited in Schulz, p. 174.
16. Taber, p. 55; see also Dubois, p. 139.
17. Taber, p. 57; Abilio Collado, in Cuba Internacional, p. 12.
18. Diary of Dr. Fernando Sánchez Amaya, cited in Taber, pp. 59-60.
19. Bonachea and San Martín, pp. 86-7.
20. Guillermo García, in Franqui, The Twelve, p. 90
21. Guevara, Reminiscences, p. 43
22. Cited in Armando Gimenez, Sierra Maestra. La Revolución de Fidel Castro (Buenos Aires: Editorial Lautaro, 1959), p. 42.
23. Hector de Arturo, "Desde el '56", Verde Olivo, 5 Dec. 71, pp. 68-70.
24. Universo Sánchez' recollection, in Franqui, The Twelve, p. 57.
25. Guevara, in Cuba Internacional, p. 13.
26. Taber, pp. 60-2.
27. Ibid.
28. Guevara, in Cuba Internacional, p. 14.
29. Guillermo García, in Franqui, The Twelve, pp. 90-2.
30. Dubois, p. 143.

31. García, loc. cit.
32. See Franqui, The Twelve.
33. Dubois, p. 144; see Thomas, p. 901, fn. 53 for a discussion of the variable figures.
34. Dubois, p. 144.
35. Taber, p. 84
36. Interview in Jose Yglesias, In The Fist of the Revolution (New York: Pantheon Books, 1968), p. 51. On the Guardia, p. 13.
37. See Taber, pp. 87-8. These organizations, especially the Resistencia Civica, included "influential professional, business and social leaders...the Lions Club, Rotarians and various cultural societies.
38. Subject and narrator in Alexander Bek, Volokolamsk Highway (Moscow: Foreign Languages Press, 1953). Excerpts from this book were later published in Verde Olivo; the book itself was made available to FAR personnel and Momysh-Uly was celebrated by the FAR on his visit to Cuba in the 60s.
39. Guevara, "Notas para el estudio de la ideología de la Revolución Cubana", Verde Olivo, 8 Oct. 60, pp. 10-14.
40. See Guevara, Reminiscences, pp. 54-9.
41. Ibid., p. 57.
42. This account comes from several guerrilla witnesses, in Cuba Internacional, pp. 34-5; see also Guevara, Reminiscences, pp. 55-8.
43. Crescencio Pérez, in Cuba Internacional, p. 35.
44. Guevara, in Cuba Internacional, p. 59.
45. See Antonio Nuñez Jiménez, Geografía de Cuba (Havana: Editorial Lex, 1959), pp. 543 ff. for a socio-economic description of the Sierra Maestra.
46. See "Infierno de Palma Mocha", in Cuba Internacional, pp. 36-7.
47. Guevara (Obra Revolucionaria #24, 1960), cited in Thomas, p. 902.
48. Guevara, in Nuñez Jimenez, p. 576.
49. Guevara, "Notas", p. 12.
50. Guevara, Reminiscences, p. 70.
51. Bonachea and San Martin, p. 91.
52. Guevara, in Cuba Internacional, p. 14.
53. Taber, p. 92.
54. Guevara, Reminiscences, p. 65.
55. Guevara, Reminiscences, p. 65.
56. Ibid., pp. 67-8.
57. Ibid., p. 71.
58. Guevara, Reminiscences, p. 70.
59. Ibid., p. 71.
60. Ibid, p. 73.
61. Guevara wrote to Gadea late in January: "They will never succeed in surrounding us. The battle is not over yet, we still have a lot of fighting to go, but the scales are already tilted to our side and with every day more weight is added to our advantage". Cited in Gadea,

Ché Guevara, p. 199.
62. Guevara, Reminiscences, pp. 76-7.
63. The first article appeared in the New York Times, 24. Feb. 57. See Herbert Matthews, The Cuban Story (New York: George Braziller, 1961).
64. Matthews, The Cuban Story, p. 36.
65. Ibid., p. 44.
66. Ibid., p. 37.
67. Thomas, p. 912. On January 4, 1957, five hundred women demonstrated in Santiago over the death by torture and gunshot of William Soler, a boy of fourteen.
68. Ibid., pp. 917-8.
69. Charles Ryan, Victor Buehlman and Michael Garvey. Only the first stayed, to fight at El Uvero in May, 1957. The others left when the CBS TV team led by Robert Taber visited the rebels.
70. See Suchlicki, pp. 75-81, and Bonachea and San Martín, pp. 106-32, for the most detailed accounts of the action in English.
71. Guevara, Reminiscences, p. 87.
72. See the account of Efigenio Ameijeiras in Franqui, The Twelve, pp. 139-57, for a description of hardships, hunger and bickering.
73. Guevara, Reminiscences, p. 87.
74. Ibid.
75. Ibid.
76. They were fairly successful. See Ameijeiras, in Franqui, The Twelve, p. 150.
77. Thomas, pp. 924, 935.
78. Ibid., p. 936.
79. Guevara, Reminiscences, pp. 75-6.
80. Guevara, Reminiscences, p. 102.
81. See Thomas, pp. 938, 967.
82. Guevara, Reminiscences, p. 107.
83. They did not know that the action had met with disaster. Trained by Bayo and financed by Prío, the group was caught and executed after torture. See Bonachea and San Martín, pp. 134-8.
84. Guevara, Reminiscences, p. 111.
85. Ibid., p. 110.
86. Recalled by Crescencio Pérez in Cuba Internacional, p. 46.
87. Castro, in Cuba Internacional, p. 46.
88. Guevara, Reminiscences, pp. 120-5.
89. Joel Iglesias, "Junto al Ché", Verde Olivo, 13 Oct. 68, pp. 37-42. Iglesias joined the rebels at the age of fifteen in May 1957 and became an outstanding fighter.
90. Ibid., pp. 39-40. On santería among the rebels, see Bonachea and San Martín, p. 132. Many wore red, white and blue beaded necklaces sent to the Sierra by believers.
91. Alfredo Beccles, Rebel Army fighter, to José

Yglesias, *In The Fist of the Revolution*, p. 49.

    92. Bonachea and Valdés, p. 97: "A barrage of demands forced the government to put an end to its action."

    93. In Lockwood, p. 53.

    94. Iglesias, p. 40.

    95. For examples of the Guevara anecdotes, see Ernesto Cardenal, *Cuba*, tr. Donald D. Walsh (New York: New Directions, 1974), p. 110.

    96. Guevara, *Reminiscences*, p. 131.

    97. In *Cuba Internacional*, p. 19.

    98. Orozco and *El Cubano Libre*, cited in Lavretsky, pp. 101-2.

    99. Dominguez, pp. 341-78.

6
The Political Education of Experience: The Establishment of Popular Support in the Guerrilla *Foco* and the *Territorio Libre*

THE SETTING

The initial period of guerrilla nomadism ended with the taking of the El Uvero army post in May of 1957. In the summer of 1957, the army mounted company-sized forays into the Sierra, but no large troop movements were undertaken. The guerrillas were able to consolidate their forces, create more settled encampments, and move freely into a number of Sierra villages. The arms, men and supplies received from the urban M-26 organizations, especially that of Santiago, led by Frank País, had been crucial in supporting this military and territorial consolidation. Guevara's unit, consisting of those wounded at El Uvero and new peasant recruits, rejoined the main body of guerrillas in late June. On the march to rejoin Castro's tropa, Guevara had come across abandoned army trenches, which he took as "a sign of the retreat of the repressive column, making a total qualitative change in operations in the Sierra. We now had sufficient strength to surround the enemy and oblige him, under the threat of annihilation, to withdraw".[1] Life in the Sierra began to change, as a result: "A truly liberated zone existed; precautionary measures were not as necessary and there was a certain freedom to talk at night, to stir in one's hammock; authorization was given to move into villages of the Sierra and establish a closer relationship with the people".[2]

RELATIONS WITH THE RURAL POPULATION

In the first six months of the guerrilla struggle, the mutual distrust between the Sierra Maestra peasantry and the largely-urban revels was broken down. The aid given to the rebels in the desperate days after the Alegría de Pío disaster and the supplies and messenger services provided by Crescencio Pérez' group of precaristas helped to establish some confidence. As described in the previous chapter, the very survival of the rebels in the face of army pursuit demanded some cooperation on the part of the peasants, who had to choose between the powerful and hated Guardia-army-mayoral elements and the stern, suspicious but honest rebels. That the rebels were outlaws in an area already rife with outlaws was an advantage. Fugitives from lowland justice and drug smugglers had frequented the Sierra for decades and traditional negative attitudes toward governmental authority were shared by many.[3] Much as in revolutionary Mexico, distrust of the government was based on experiences of corruption, arbitrariness and brutality at the hands of the authorities.[4] Another group of outlaws could expect to receive some of this latent sympathy for the pursued.[5] At the same time, such an atmosphere bred treachery, bribery and suspicion. In a situation where much poverty and some desperation exists, the primacy of money and individual opportunism approach dangerous levels. Thus, the outlaw tradition of the Sierra Maestra both aided and hindered the guerrillas.

To overcome treachery and opportunism, in fact to survive, strict measures against chivatos were applied by the rebels in the first months. But, as the rebels began successfully to attack the rural Guardia and army units, there was more peasant confidence in the ability of the guerrillas to defend the peasantry against depredations. Rebel security was increasingly guaranteed by a friendly and respectful population, which reported the identity of peasant chivatos and informed of army and and Guardia movements. Eventually, the rebels became the benefactors of the peasantry and the de facto authority throughout the Sierra Maestra.

It has been suggested that much of the peasant support for the guerrillas was of a negative quality, a reaction to the repression Batista unleashed.[6] It is true that the bombing, napalm attacks, evacuation of peasant areas and other reprisals had their effect. Peasant escopeteros 'M-26 shotgunners' who patrolled the highways and guarded the approaches to the Sierra Maestra in 1958 told one journalist of the Guardia and army attacks that they had suffered.[7] Reactively, and to survive, they had joined the rebel cause and were assigned to the escopetero squads. In the bombed and strafed areas of Oriente that the journalist Jorge Masetti travelled through, he found the same sentiments. Reprisals, after the establishment of the guerrillas in the Sierra, produced pro-guerrilla sentiments and actions.[8]

But it was not merely reaction against Batista which won peasant support in the Sierra. The positive actions of the guerrillas were crucial. That they fought the army and the Guardia was important, but the revolutionary justice administered, the livestock confiscated and distributed, the schools built and the medical care brought to the countryside all contributed to increasing peasant support. During Masetti's 1958 visits to the Sierra, "little by little I was discovering that the adherence of the <u>campesinos</u> to Fidel Castro was not based solely on the absurd and criminal policies of Batista's <u>Guardias</u>, but in great measure on the concrete realizations of revolutionary ideals...the <u>campesino</u> who joins the Rebel Army does it not simply for self-defense...but as a means to conserve the gains which are already his own and which no one will ever be able to take away from him".[9] Masetti's interlocutors spoke of the small schools and medical treatment facilities built and staffed by the Rebel Army and M-26, the distribution of expropriated cattle and land, and of bread from small bakeries established in the area.

These gains to which Masetti refers began with the application of revolutionary justice in the Sierra, a matter of survival for the guerrillas. Informing, desertion and insubordination among the guerrillas was severely punished. Crimes by guerrillas against the peasantry, such as theft, brutality or sexual assault were dealt with implacably.[10]

The establishment of revolutionary justice became even more imperative in the summer of 1957, when Batista's commanders decided to evacuate some of the Sierra population to create a large no-man's-land. It was to be "completely banned to all except the army. The army would shoot at sight without troubling to see whether the peasant concerned was a friend or a foe. The air force would also be able to bomb the jungle indiscriminately".[11] Except for intermittent column penetrations, such as those led by Sánchez Mosquera, the army and the <u>Guardia</u> left the area. In the first several months of the struggle, Batista and his general staff apparently thought Castro dead; they refused to accept the evidence of Herbert Matthews' report.[12] Batista does not say exactly what prevented the army from entering the Sierra in force in 1957. However, with hindsight, he cites the "communist tactic" of the Rebel Army slogan, 'the rebels fight against Batista, not against the army', as the evil hand of Judas which subverted "some officers and chiefs".[13] Further, the conciliatory, democratic attitudes that Batista's government took throughout the struggle, he maintains, were used by the unscrupulous opposition to create terror and uncertainty.[14] This campaign of terror and clever slogans affected members of business and in the agricultural establishment, who criticized Batista and contributed funds to the warchest that international communism had created for Castro. Batista points to the confusion and uncertainty created in the army by criticism of his regime emanating from United States officials and by support for Castro among certain United States sectors.[15]

In an interview on March 19, 1959, Batista gave what he considered definitive reasons why his army had not annihilated the rebels in 1957:

> The reasons can be found in the fact that we wanted to maintain peace without bloodshed, in the complicity of certain high officers of the Army and in the lack of arms....The regular forces mobilized after treachery in the face of a noble gesture cost us tens of lives: Castro's mother had asked...for a truce for her son, withdrawing our patrols from the places we thought him to be, so that he could leave the country in some way....We withdrew our platoons to the coast, expecting the results of our gesture. One morning...Castro appeared with a group and killed some of a platoon in cold blood....Later he organized guerrillas and began to receive arms on the coast and by air. The arms of the Army were old, acquired at the beginning of the century, and a few from World War II...[16]

Reading between the lines of Batista's writings and interviews, it seems that he recognized the ephemeral nature of his political base in Cuba and feared both public sympathy for the rebels and the possibility of military conspiracies and desertions. He hoped the rebels would disappear if certain concessions were made to the civic opposition. He later accused "certain officers" of collusion with the rebels or of having no great concern over the existence of a guerrilla foco.[17]

In the Sierra, the virtual absence of authority gave rise to "bands of marauders who, under the pretext of revolutionary activities, indulged in looting and banditry and a host of other offenses".[18] The guerrillas had already begun to deal with various forms of banditry which traditionally plagued the area, but this surge of bandit groups was a problem with political overtones. If not controlled, they would destroy the fragile and partial confidence of the peasantry that had painstakingly been built up. As in the struggle against the chivato-Guardia-mayoral system of informers, it was an issue of power, and its resolution was a direct political education for the guerrillas, as well as for the Sierra residents.

The first case dealt with by the rebels in the summer of 1957 was that of a peasant named Aristidio. He had been a member of the rebel column before El Uvero, but dropped out, sold his revolver and declared openly that he would seek reconciliation with the army once the guerrillas left his home area. Guevara held an inquiry and had him executed, based on the following reasoning:

War is harsh, and at a time when the enemy's aggressiveness is on the rise, it is not possible to tolerate even the presumption of treason. He could perhaps have saved his skin, had this happened several months earlier, since the guerrilla movement was still insecure, or several months later, when we were much more firmly in control. But Aristidio had the bad luck to rat at the precise moment when we were sufficiently strong to punish pitilessly such an offense as his, but not strong enough to inflict any other kind of punishment, since we had no jail or facilities for any other kind of penalty.[19]

Aristidio had not gone so far as to attack other peasants, and that was the more serious threat to the still tenuous campesino-guerrilla understanding. "El Chino" Chang led a gang which, under the name of the Revolution, had confiscated supplies, tortured and murdered peasants in the area.[20] The rebels sent a platoon under Camilo Cienfuegos to chase him down. He was captured, tried in a peasant hut with witnesses, and shot. Others of his gang, young peasants and city boys "seduced by the prospect of a carefree, prodigal life dangled before them by Chang", were tried, and most acquitted. Three endured a mock execution (They were condemned to death, had their eyes covered, were bound and stood against trees. A firing squad then shot into the air.) and joined the Rebel Army. Another man, pretending to be a guerrilla messenger, had raped a young girl, and he was executed with Chang.[21]

Other similar abuses were punished during this period.[22] Two early guajiro supporters, instrumental in the unmasking of the traitor Eutimio Guerra, had been appropriating supplies sent up from the cities. One of them had used his guerrilla connections and prestige to take over three houses, in each of which he set up a woman and a food supply. He and a young man who had organized a small rebel band and terrorized the population were both tried and executed. In addition, a man who had passed himself off as "Dr. Guevara" and raped a young girl seeking medical care was executed. The trials and executions were witnessed by guerrillas and area peasants with all but two of the sentenced men, spies for Santiago boss Rolando Masferrer, "proclaiming their commitment to the Revolution"[23] after the trials and before execution.

Guevara later was careful to point out that many fell prey to such indiscipline and petty individualism. Had the times been different, their lives would have spared, "but that moment called for an iron fist. We were obliged to inflict exemplary punishment in order to curb violations of discipline and to liquidate the nuclei of anarchy which sprang up in areas lacking a stable government".[24] Such guerrilla sweeps of the "liberated territory" were made periodically during the insurrectionary period, with progressively more order established each time. Eventually, a peasant militia was initiated, with police duties as one of its functions. The Catholic and Autentico lawyer, Dr. Humberto Sori Marin, participated in these early tribunals, becoming Advocate-General in the Sierra, and codifying the Rebel Army penal code. It was based on the Mambi military code from the War of Independence.[25]

The meting out of such stern justice was not the only way in which a revolutionary code was established in relations with the peasant population. The rebels banished the middlemen who bought up the peasants' market crops like coffee and sugar. They had been the "immediate exploiters" of the guajiro farmers.[26] The guerrillas also took part in field work in the Sierra. Urban recruits who came of their own volition were put to work, in return for lodging, on small guajiro farms, while awaiting arms and training.[27] As Sartre put it,

> In order for the peasants to become rebels, the rebels became peasants and took part in field chores. It was not enough to know the need and poverty of rural people. It was necessary to suffer from these hardships and at the same time to combat them. A neat swing of the machete, cutting the stalks like a pro, will do more than a long speech.[28]

In establishing revolutionary justice, the Rebel Army spoke of controlling "anti-social elements". Discipline within the guerrilla force had to parallel the severity of revolutionary justice being imposed in the Sierra. Desertion and mistreatment of peasants were summarily dealt with by execution: "The execution of anti-social individuals who exploited their position of strength in the district in order to commit crimes was, unfortunately not infrequent in the Sierra Maestra."[29] Guevara used one episode of desertion to instruct his column; the goal was "to increase our usefulness and effectiveness in combat".[30] A fighter named "El Chino" Wong had deserted with his weapon. Of the two sent after him, one was a friend of Wong and tried to convince the second to desert, also. The second, seeing the first marching off, shot him when the order to halt was not obeyed. Guevara took his column to see the body:

> I explained to our men what they were going to see and what it meant; I explained once again why desertion was punishable by death and why anyone who

betrayed the Revolution must be condemned...many of the men had never seen death before and were perhaps moved more by personal feelings for the dead man and by political weakness natural at that period than by disloyalty to the Revolution...These were difficult times and we used this man as an example...a young, poor peasant from the vicinity."[31]

Lesser infractions by rebels were dealt with much less severely. Arguments or fist-fights were matters punished by demotion,[32] the taking of a fighter's weapon for a certain period, or "when the crime was serious enough, a prisoner guilty of a lack of discipline would be deprived of food for a day or two. This was indeed a punishment that struck home".[33] One fighter named Julio Castellanos, in Guevara's column, spent movement money meant for food on some gifts for girlfriends. He was forced to reclaim the gifts and return them to the store, and was demoted from his position as squad leader.[34]

In the summer of 1957, as in the spring, discipline and morale were central issues. A disciplinary commission was set up to enforce "respect for the rules of vigilance, general discipline, cleanliness and revolutionary morality".[35] It was soon abolished after a particularly volatile and unfortunate incident. One group of rebels was resisting the commission's activities and the commission redoubled its efforts. A squad leader and an effective fighter, Captain Lalo Sardiñas, held a gun to the head of "an undisciplined comrade", and it went off accidentally, killing the man. Guerrilla law prohibited corporal punishment and Sardiñas had previous infractions. A number of rebels called for his execution. A long meeting of the one hundred forty-six present ensued, with Castro and Guevara defending the life of Sardiñas. Castro outlined the lack of discipline extant and explained that "in the end this indefensible act had been committed in defense of the concept of discipline".[36] By a slight voting margin, Sardiñas was spared, demoted and sentenced to redeem himself by fighting alone. A number of those dissatisfied with the decision left the column: "This group included many elements of questionable trustworthiness, but there were some pretty good boys among them".[37]

This incident revealed the continuing problem of low political consciousness and the severity of rebel life in the Sierra. Lack of weapons and supplies and irregular eating kept the fighters on edge. The enemy's creation of a no-man's-land made the shipping of food by mules a risky affair. In the first months of nomadic existence, eating was dependent upon finding a peasant to buy from or it was a "meagre ration of the vegetables of the Sierra",[38] even stray cats or snakes,[39] or edible roots. As one rebel fighter recalled, "the agony of the Sierra was food. What a job it was every day to eat in the Sierra! Sometimes the guerrilla went into combat with his belly so empty that it made more noises than the bullets".[40]

The food supply for increased numbers of fighters, and for the pre-guerrillero groups set up to train recruits while they awaited arms, depended increasingly on the Sierra peasantry. As the rebels achieved control over the Sierra territory, several arrangements were made. In the small towns of the Sierra and on its outskirts, the rebels "came to terms with certain merchants...for the supplying of foodstuffs and equipment".[41] Mule teams were organized to bring the supplies. At other times, the peasant network would cook a meal for the rebels: "At the battle of Pino del Agua all the food the rebels had was toasted maize. And that maize...we ourselves toasted it in our house".[42] Supplies were also bought from the army itself. Corruption and low army morale helped the guerrillas eat.[43] Finally, the rebels contracted certain crops with some of the peasants: "We arranged that they should plant beans, corn, rice, etc. which we guaranteed to purchase".[44] Some peasants kept chickens and pigs, but cattle were very scarce. What was available came from expropriations from corrupt mayorales on latifundios of absentee landlords, from large ranches owned by Batista supporters, and from army stocks. The appropriated cattle would be divided equally between the rebels and the peasants: "There they killed a steer and one part was for the camp and the other for the peasants. They gave all the peasants their piece of meat, their ration, so that they would eat, too, because everyone there had to live from the same".[45] In the summer of 1958, during the one great Batista offensive in the Sierra, a food blockade was imposed. The rebels appropriated thousands of head of cattle from the large ranches around the Sierra and distributed them among the population. Now, for the first time "the guajiros of the Sierra, in that region particularly pauperized, enjoyed well-being; campesino children drank milk and ate beef for the first time".[46]

Food equality was observed within the tropa as well as between the rebels and the campesinos. A nickel worker who joined the rebels in early 1958 recalled that "in the monte 'the mountains' the life we led was of such complete equality it was like communism".[47] Guevara and Cienfuegos were notorious for their insistence upon food equality. Horacio Gonzalez Polanco, who was in Cienfuegos' "Antonio Maceo" Column in the fall of 1958, recalled that "when we finished eating nobody wanted to save the leftovers. Camilo used to collect it in a large pot he always carried. He would throw it over his shoulder and carry it everywhere. When the tropa was hungry, he would pull it out and divide up the food".[48] Guevara "always liked us to come out equal in everything".[49] The meal would be distributed and he took his portion last: "I remember one day Ché arrived and asked if everyone had eaten. When we said yes he began to eat. Because he would say that the leader was the last to eat. That if some comrade did not get to eat it had to be the leader".[50]

Such shared hardships tightened the bonds of comradeship in the Sierra among the guerrillas and between them and the campesino population. It was not that there was any pre-determined plan to create bonds in such a way, just as there was no detailed plan of land reform when the Granma landed. Rather, the specific characteristics of Sierra life became the rebels' daily experience and the requisites of their survival and their relationships with the peasantry became a part of their revolutionary political outlook. The rebels relied on the peasantry for food, information and communications. The network of messengers was invaluable in making of the Sierra a sanctuary, however imperfect.[51] Experience of the peasant life and hardships combined in the rebel leadership with an analysis of the socio-economic realities of the Sierra. Unlike the llano and the less remote areas, squatting and subsistence plots were the rule in the Sierra. No settled agricultural proletariat and few prosperous market farmers were to be found. Coffee was grown almost clandestinely on land wrested from the forest. Land-grabbing by latifundistas assisted by the army and the Guardia was the constant enemy of the Sierra precarista. Guevara summed up the situation thusly:

> on the first territory of our Rebel Army, made up of the survivors of the defeated Granma column, there is precisely a peasantry of different social and cultural roots, different from those which can be found in the conditions of large, semi-mechanized Cuban agriculture. In effect, the Sierra Maestra, locus of the first revolutionary column, is a place where those peasants, who, fighting hard against the latifundio, go in search of a new piece of ground which they wrench from the state or from some voracious latifundista in order to create their own small wealth. They have to struggle constantly against the exactions of the soldiers, always allied with the latifundistas, and their horizons are those of property title. Concretely, the campesino recruit to our first guerrilla army, comes from that social class which displays most aggressively its love for the land and its possession, i.e., what can be called the petit bourgeois spirit; the campesino fights because he wants land; for himself, for his children, to manage it and improve it for sale and to enrich himself by means of work.[52]

This desire for landownership, as Guevara noted, could only be met by a radical land reform in the Sierra, one which would conflict with the interest of the <u>latifundistas</u> in sugar and cattle production. It was a situation which called for land reform in immediate, practical terms, to be backed up by armed force. For Castro, it was more than <u>Realpolitik</u>; it was a philosophical principle: "Demands, in one manner or another, represent needs...man's need is his fundamental right over all others".[53]

Among the rebels, political consciousness regarding socio-economic realities in the Sierra was uneven:

> The best among us felt deeply the need for an agrarian reform and an overturning of the social system, without which the country could never achieve health. But they always had to drag behind them the weight of those individuals who came to the struggle out of nothing but a hunger for adventure or in the hope of winning not only laurels but economic advantage.[54]

Consciousness of a debt to the Sierra and its inhabitants is common among the surviving leadership of the Cuban Revolution:[55] "It was logical that the Sierra Maestra, where the revolutionary spirit of our leaders was forged and where the will and decisions to change the political, economic and social panorama of Cuba (and not just a change of functionaries, of men) was tempered, would vibrate from its roots in support of the Revolution".[56]

The land reforms instituted during the guerrilla struggle arose out of the pre-invasion ideals of the leadership and the exigencies of life in the Sierra. Guevara told Masetti in 1958, "Much of what we are doing we had not even dreamed of. You could say that we became revolutionaries in the revolution. We came to overthrow a tyrant, but we discovered that this enormous peasant zone, wherein our struggle is being prolonged, is the area of Cuba which most needs liberation".[57]

Once permanent camps were set up, like the one at La Mesa occupied by Guevara's column for over a year, some land reforms were instituted in the Sierra. Government lands and that belonging to <u>latifundistas</u> collaborating with Batista were expropriated and distributed, along with animals: "We calculated via a census the area of land necessary for a family with two, four or more children, and suggested the best crops for the land, supplying seed and technical assistance".[58] Initially, there were problems with the livestock. Peasants were killing milk cows for meat: "I came to the conclusion that the majority of the <u>campesinos</u> had killed their cow because they preferred the immediate benefit of being able to eat it to the longer range value of having the milk".[59]

The rebels responded by making the peasants sign a declaration that they would not kill milk cows.[60] Even then, "they would come and tell us that the cow had fallen down the hill or that it had had an accident".[61] Finally, the rebels decided that sale or consumption of dairy cattle meat would be punished by the removal of rights to the land, itself distributed to the most needy and most responsible peasants.[62] Such individualism and fatalism in the usufruct of land and consumption of cattle was a point of consternation for some of the leadership, who entertained a more collectivist vision: "This [behavior] naturally fortified my conviction that the land of the latifundistas should not be divided but should be organized into co-operatives".[63] Nonetheless, in the worst times, during the 1958 summer offensive by the army, peasants did preserve the animals and work together to protect them and secure common pasturage, "establishing what were in effect co-operatives in their efforts...it is a new miracle of the Revolution that the staunchest individualist, who zealously protected the boundaries of his property, joined, because of the war, the great common effort of the struggle".[64]

The building of positive relations with the Sierra peasantry was an irregular, slow and often harsh process. But, once a degree of mutual confidence was established, the benefits were many. First, the attitudes of the rebels were deeply influenced by the experience. The prolongation of the struggle and the special socioeconomic characteristics of the Sierra Maestra population forced the rebels to address the local problems. There could be no waiting for victory to institute some reforms or impose authority. To solidify peasant support, the rebels had to deal in the present. As Guevara told Masetti, "we are not fighting for them [the peasants] in the future, we are fighting now and we consider that every meter of the Sierra that is ours...is more theirs than ours".[65] The campesinos responded with vigilance and information, aid in communicating with the plains and the cities, arms and labour-power. Anyone approaching the rebels' camps in the Sierra was scrutinized by the peasants and led into investigatory ambushes if deemed untrustworthy.[66] Messengers carried out a crucial and dangerous function, linking the rebel units with each other and with urban and rural M-26 militants. As one messenger saw his mission, "at times a message was worth ten soldiers because it warned of an attack, prepared an ambush or ordered an assault".[67] Only a peasant could hope to pass easily through army lines and hope to carry copies of Rebel Army papers like El Cubano Libre or medicines from the cities. And some of the best couriers were women, like "Lydia", remembered by Guevara: "Within the Rebel Army, among those who fought and sacrificed themselves in those anguished days, the memory will live forever of the women who, by the risks they took daily, made communications with the rest of the island possible".[68]

The peasant population also contributed arms to the guerrillas, plagued until the very last days with weapons shortages. One peasant messenger-fighter recalls Guevara's instructions on rounding up arms: "He told me others had asked the people for arms roughly, saying they would be arrested and so on...I was to ask for assistance for M-26 politely".[69] Arms were not to be requisitioned from peasants, but solicited for the Revolution.

By the time permanent camps were established in the fall of 1957, relations with the precaristas and guajiros of the Sierra were strong enough to count on voluntary labor. Peasants like Polo Torres built much of the La Mesa camp used by Guevara's column: "He asked me to build a hospital, fabricating or inventing the materials myself".[70] The primitive industry set up at La Mesa - bakery, sewing machines, bomb and mine fabrication, shoe repair and print shop, were all tended by peasant workers and rebel fighters: "We built a warehouse, not just for the guerrillas, but for the campesinos, too, who had their food supplies cut off by the army blockade. The mule trains, with their foodstuffs, came up often and the warehouse was always full of necessities".[71]

Thus, relations with the Sierra peasantry were a process of political education. It was not limited to the rebels; the peasantry learned, also. Castro, Sartre wrote,

> had noticed in the [peasant] neighborhoods that he wouldn't win the total support of the masses unless the revolution were to become their common interest...no one else could change the life of these unfortunates,...it would be changed every day by themselves. Thus, he set out to...have them discover their own needs. They quickly understood: latifundios, tenant farming, limited jobs, single crop - in a short time they saw these as the origin of their troubles. Reform wasn't presented as a gratuituous gift of the future government to the people. The urgency and national necessity of it was ceaselessly explained to them...the reform venture gave them confidence in the rebel army; the military successes gave them confidence in the reform...In this new phase of the war, the peasants were transformed, these meek people took over the responsibility for the plans of the insurgents, made them their own demands, and in a certain

fashion, it was they who would 'radicalize' the rebels.[72]

To the rebels, relations with the peasants were first based on survival and the myths of peasant support they carried with them from Moncada and Mexico. Unlike the Chinese revolutionary experience of the 1920s,[73] the urban rebels of Cuba did not move from defeat in the cities to areas of an aroused, aware and organized peasantry. M-26 fighters had to start at a more primitive political level in the Sierra. As they gained the trust, respect and admiration of the peasants, they themselves assimilated the concerns and problems of Sierra life and began to act upon them in a revolutionary manner. The strict rebel code of conduct regarding relations with the peasantry, reminiscent of the Chinese Communist's "Three Main Rules of Discipline and the Eight Points for Attention"[74] was the basis for rebel successes with the peasants. Honesty about victories and defeats, circumspect personal behavior admitting of no theft, extortion or sexual assault, and prompt, generous payment for supplies and food were the rule. The peasant-rebel unity created in this process became the main basis of political support for the young revolutionary regime. The political education of revolutionary experience and action in the Sierra further radicalized the rebels and achieved the mass support necessary for the anti-imperialist and anti-capitalist measures taken once power was seized. By 1958 Castro could say, when asked about programs to be implemented once the revolution was in power, "much of what we would do, we are already doing in the Sierra".[75]

SEGUNDO FRENTE "FRANK PAIS": THE MYTH OF GUERRILLA-PEASANT WORKER UNITY REALIZED IN THE CIVIL ADMINISTRATION OF A "TERRITORIO LIBRE"

On March 10, 1958, Raúl Castro crossed the Central Highway north of the Sierra Maestra with sixty-five rebel fighters. His mission, as newly-appointed Comandante of Column Six, was to operate in northern Oriente province. In an area larger than Massachusetts, he was to impose his command on all guerrilla groups operating there, apply the rebel penal code to "anti-social" elements, attack Batista's forces, sabotage government communications, and establish revolutionary administration.[76] This new column, like that of Juan Almeida, sent to operate north of Santiago, and the squad of Camilo Cienfuegos, operating near Holguín, was part of the campaign to wrest Oriente province from government control: "Rebel patrols are moving in all directions through the entire province and...the action of armed patrols will intensify throughout the nation".[77] Castro had openly announced on March 12 the stepping-up of the armed insurrection ("the struggle against Batista has entered its final stage"), the imminence of a general revolutionary strike, to be backed by military action, and a quarantine on highway and rail traffic in Oriente. He gave government soldiers until April 5 to desert, rebel or join the guerrillas. After that, a campaign of attacking and disarming them would begin. Judicial personnel were warned to resign, public office was to be abandoned, and no taxes were to be paid to the Batista regime.[78] These decrees would have more impact if more of Oriente was "<u>territorio libre</u>", which may in part explain the launching of separate columns at this time. On the other hand, the struggle in the Sierra had become static and some initiative was needed to break the deadlock.

The experiences of Raúl Castro's Column Six is important in assessing the political education of the revolutionary forces, for many of the commanders in the area became officers in the FAR and early members of the Cuban Communist Party.[79] Northern Oriente was the scene of a considerable number of combat encounters and the area with the most developed civil administration mounted by the rebels, in many ways a model of the national revolutionary regime established after January 1959. It was a situation radically different from that of the Sierra Maestra. The Sierra Cristal itself, the major mountain range in the area, was only one of half a dozen ranges between the north coast and the Guantanamo-Santiago area in the south, and the guerrillas could move more freely than in the Sierra Maestra and still have sanctuary nearby. More of the land was cultivated and the forests were not so thick, improving access and mobility. The economy was much more diversified and developed than in the Sierra Maestra. The north and east coast was dominated by nickel and manganese mining. The major portion of the Cuban coffee crop was grown in the region, with substantial amounts of cane, sugar refineries, produce farming and a timber industry. Settled agricultural valleys alternated with mountain ranges. Large ranches completed the economic panorama.[80]

The resulting social structure was also much more complex than in the Sierra Maestra. An agricultural and industrial proletariat of some size existed, largely unionized and working the cane-fields, refineries and mines. More of a middle class existed as professionals, small businessmen and private farmers, and the bourgeoisie was more in evidence than in the Sierra, owning ranches, service industries, mines, sugar mills and plantations. Foreign monopoly capital was present in strength, in the shape of such large companies as the United Fruit Sugar Company, the Nickel Processing Corporation, and the Moa Bay Mining Company.[81]

The organizational achievements of the Segundo Frente "Frank País" were the basis of its successful administration of much of Oriente during the April-December 1958 period. The experience of Guevara in organizing the El Hombrito and La Mesa strongholds in the Sierra Maestra was a precedent, but in the Estado Libre del Segundo Frente Oriental "Frank País" the 'Free State of the Second Oriente Front 'Frank País', as it was known, social organization and civil administration were expanded much further.

The strength of Raúl Castro's organizations lay in his ability to involve peasants, agricultural workers and industrial workers. Their mobilization centered on immediate concerns: land tenure, wages, education, health and defense against abuses and attacks by the police, army, Guardia and such semi-official private armies as that of Rolando Masferrer.[82] Régis Debray remarks that, in Cuba, "the most important form of propaganda [was] successful military action"[83], attacks on outposts and patrols. The organization and involvement of the Oriente population depended on the destruction of their fear and respect for the forces of repression. Raúl Castro's objective was two-fold: to provide a secure civilian base of support for the guerrilla column, and to carry out social reforms. What resulted was a provisional state, one based on peasant committees, unions and the guerrillas, with urban supporters of a largely agrarian administration.

The first group to be approached and organized by the guerrillas was the peasantry, since it was upon them that the guerrillas relied most, especially during the first two months, when the new territorio libre was being created. The guerrillas moved through the countryside taking rural army posts one by one "under swift and devastating night attacks".[84] Food, communications and supply deliveries depended upon peasant co-operation. In the first several days, and continuing thereafter, "committees of revolutionary peasants of the M-26" were created in each locality of peasant population. They were comprised of three members: a secretary to head the effort, a civilian, and a military delegate. Their task was to secure supplies for the rebels, establish a messenger and communications network so that the rebels would know of government troops, and organize a ten-man patrol to maintain order when the army withdrew from the area.[85] When the area had been cleared of the army, the committees became the "police force of the Rebel Army".[86]

Peasant associations were organized, once the territorio libre was established. They were mass organizations, "free of sectarianism, which united all the campesinos of the area, in order to help the Ejército Rebelde...they gave their best sons to fill the rebels ranks and constituted the secure rear guard of the Revolutionary Army and an indispensable instrument of information and vigilance".[87] These two sets of organizations were built around agrarian reform. At meetings and countless conversations, Raúl Castro and other Rebel Army members stressed that the overthrow of Batista would be followed by agrarian reform. As in the Sierra Maestra, not only the promise of land reform secured peasant support. Guerrilla success in forcing out the army, enforcing revolutionary justice in cases of banditry and assault, adjudicating disputes, and bringing services such as schools, teachers and medical care were all necessary to the consolidation of relations with the peasantry.

As in the Sierra Maestra, the guerrillas were very strict in the establishment of revolutionary authority. Small groups of <u>pandillas</u> 'gangs' masquerading as M-26 units, pillaging and raping, were rounded up, summarily tried and executed.[88] Peasants who were stealing cattle or looting stores, along with Masferrer's paramilitary force, were also executed, with peasant witnesses.[89] The situation was complicated by the presence of hundreds of "men from adjacent towns who had fled to the nearby hills seeking some shelter from the repressive measures adopted by the regular army in Oriente".[90] Their desperation increased incidents of theft and looting.

As more territory was liberated from army control by the guerrillas, it was divided into military regions, each with a guerrilla column. Each column, named for a martyred revolutionary fighter, was led by a comandante and contained several companies under a captain or lieutenant.[91] Revolutionary justice was organized along these regional divisions. A Department of Justice was set up under M-26 Santiago lawyer Augusto Martinez Sanchez, and each column came to have a lawyer to administer the laws and regulations of the Segundo Frente. The rebel penal code and a civil code were established by military orders emanating from Raúl Castro.[92] By May, lawyers were being supplied to each column by the urban M-26 organizations and, eventually, lawyers and/or law students were working at the company level. A system of identification cards was instituted for the entire Segundo Frente to increase both guerrilla and residents' security.[93] The peasant associations, operating much like the Committees for the Defense of the Revolution after 1960,[94] kept track of all individuals in the area and brought crimes and infractions to the attention of the legal representatives.

As in the Sierra Maestra, the Segundo Frente had considerable support from urban M-26 groups in Santiago, Guantanamo and Mayarí. Three column commanders, Belarminio Castilla, Antonio Lussón Battle and Félix Pena Díaz, came from the Santiago organization, while doctors, lawyers and dentists also joined the Segundo Frente administration.[95] The successor to Frank País as

M-26 national action and sabotage chief, René Ramos Latour, funnelled urban fighters to the Segundo Frente after they were in action at Puerto Boniato during the April 1958 general strike.[96] They were formed into Column 17 "Abel Santamaría" and saw considerable action in the fall of 1958.[97]

Supplies from the cities and from peasant associations were not the only sources of material for the Segundo Frente. As in La Mesa, shops and small factories were established, and the Rebel Army planted some of its own crops.[98] Peasants, agricultural workers and industrial workers took part in production, and Raúl Castro saw to it that peasants, especially, "were taught different tasks in the small production lines of rebel factories", producing war material, shoes, clothing, building schools and hospitals, and repairing machinery: "Many peasants learned techniques they were later to use in peace".[99]

The rebels secured the participation of peasants, agricultural and industrial workers by providing an opportunity for self-help in developing services and by taking on recruits. Having local fighters in rebel units and basing promotion strictly on morale, discipline and fighting effectiveness, usually meant enthusiastic local support. The expansion of services was especially impressive. The Education Department reopened some two hundred schools in the area that had ceased functioning, and built three hundred new ones. They were staffed with teachers and students from the cities and by members of the Rebel Army. By the fall of 1958, three times the previous normal number of pupils were attending the classes of primary instruction, texts were being printed and conferences on education held.[100] The first literacy campaign in Cuba was launched in the Segundo Frente territory, both among the tropa and for peasants.[101]

In the area of health care, impressive gains were registered also. A group of doctors and nurses organized and ran the twelve hospitals and eight clinics built by the Rebel Army's Department of Health. Medical students operated the clinics, and doctors who accompanied the rebel units attended the campesino population. Nuñez Jimenez writes that infant mortality dropped from 40% to 5% in the areas where hospitals were built.[102]

The guerrillas also set up a Department of Public Works to build roads and airfields, and a Department of Propaganda which broadcast to the Cuban population, established radio communications with the Sierra Maestra, Venezuela, Mexico and Miami M-26 groups, and published a rebel newspaper, El Surco, distributed by peasant couriers.[103] They took advantage of the natural tax base to cover some of the costs of administration. Money came from the cities, but was also collected from land-

owners and sugar and mining companies.[104] Employees of
the Moa Bay Mining Company supplied bulldozers, tractors, jeeps, office and communications equipment, and
medicines.[105] An accounting system was set up under
Felix Pena Díaz to administer funds and expenses efficiently.[106]

The Segundo Frente forces quickly became the de
facto authority over a large area of Oriente. They employed the peasant associations, headed by PSP member
José Ramirez (later head of the National Association of
Small Farmers) as organs of political education to prepare for agrarian reform. The Agrarian Bureau of the
Rebel Army was the co-ordinating body and acted in the
interests of peasant associations vis-à-vis <u>latifundistas</u> and commercial middlemen. It organized the first
Peasant Congress, attended by four hundred peasants
from the rural areas around Guantánamo.[107] Unions of
agricultural workers were also organized, and the Segundo Frente acted on their behalf in imposing wage increases and improvements in working conditions on the sugar
companies. Worker conventions were held, as forums for
political education about the goals of the revolution,
and to unite for immediate gains.[108] Agricultural workers, miners and <u>campesinos</u> were brought together in the
administrative bodies and in the Rebel Army as fighters.

The guerrillas themselves had a Department of Revolutionary Instruction under José Nivaldo Causse and
Jorge Risquet. A "José Marti School for Troop Instructors" was established at Tumbasiete, which became a model for FAR schools of revolutionary instruction. Most
recruits to Segundo Frente forces went through a "crash
program of political instruction before being incorporated into a guerrilla unit"[109] and the instructors
were, increasingly, graduates of the Tumbasiete school.
The students of the school were "exemplary fighters"
drawn from the different rebel columns of the Segundo
Frente. At first, they felt badly at having been withdrawn from the fighting, according to G. Duvallon.[110]
They felt that the fight against Batista was their primary purpose, and "they had no clear conception of the
mechanics and course of a true revolution".[111] The student-fighters were given three months of instruction,
each of the several courses lasting fifteen days. There
were intensive courses on Cuban history, geography, economics, civics, Martiana - the writings and political
thought of Jose Martí - , "problems and objectives of
the Cuban Revolution", and constitutional law. The last
course was later replaced by one on agrarian reform.
Few texts were available, so mimeographed materials were
used, including Nuñez' <u>Geografía de Cuba</u>, Blás Roca's
<u>Fundamentos del Socialismo</u>, and historical pamphlets by
Emilio Roig de Leuchsenring.[112] The main instructional
method was that of round-table discussion of the materials and themes introduced by instructors. The staff

eventually started its own History of Cuba text, "a Marxist interpretation without a word of Marxism", in the phrase of Lionel Martin.[113]

The first graduates returned to their units to lead "courses of civic capacitation" - civic training - and to work as moderators of local labor disputes. Official accounts of the Tumbasiete school point up its importance in creating revolutionary consciousness, crucial in the period of defections and counter-revolutionary activity in the early 1960s.[114] Duvallon maintains that when Batista fled the country and the regime fell, "those who had not taken the Tumbasiete course showed their happiness with extraordinary jubilation, but in the graduates the news was received more measuredly... they were calculating what could happen now and preparing for the great tasks of peace, making the actual social revolution".[115]

The intensive experience of organizing and maintaining an extensive civil administration created cadres prepared to take over when the Batista regime collapsed, though M-26 as a whole was not prepared to assume national administration alone. It also taught the rebel soldiers who were responsible that peasant-worker-guerrilla unity was imperative. The actual armed struggle against the Batista army contained other lessons. The first was that of confidence. The Segundo Frente had great success in its military operations in rural areas, which gave it confidence to move out of the hills into the larger villages and towns and adopt a more conventional style of warfare in the fall of 1958. The "Mau Mau" of the Segundo Frente, as they were called by the peasants and by one another,[116] engaged the Batista forces extensively: "These guerrilla columns encountered the regular army over 247 times; captured six airplanes, intercepted five ships carrying supplies; captured twelve trains, conducted thirty six commando operations; burned, destroyed or captured thirty-one army posts; shot down three fighter-bomber planes; and led eleven raids against patrol boats".[117] The rebels claimed to have killed nearly two thousand government soldiers, incorporated forty-five deserters, and captured twelve hundred weapons.[118] In the final offensive of November-December 1958, they took fourteen garrisons in two weeks.[119] A motorized column under Efigenio Ameijeiras was developed and roads built so that it could move in one day across the entire Segundo Frente territory, while a march would last over a week.[120]

The military success of the rebels was based on a political success. They had come to the area with a nascent revolutionary myth, the myth of the people united against a dictatorship. They had communicated that myth to the bulk of the population of the area. The political crisis of the dictatorship and the conditions

of underdevelopment and uneven growth in the Oriente
countryside provided the objective conditions for a rapid growth of rebel sentiment. Whereas the image of
the rebels in the mountains might have been romantic
and doomed to many people in the cities, in the countryside of Oriente the image was more concrete and positive: effective administration, the establishment and
maintenance of order, social reforms, and defense
against the army and exploiters. The slogan, <u>el pueblo
unido jamás será vencido</u> 'the people united will never
be defeated' typified the experience of the Segundo
Frente and became a sustaining revolutionary myth in
the political education of the post-1959 armed forces.

The second outstanding lesson of armed struggle in
the Segundo Frente was not as advanced as the first,
that of confidence and unity. It was a lesson regarding imperialism's support of repression and dictatorship in a client state: there was growing resentment
among the guerrillas that United States-supplied arms
were being used by the Batista forces against the civilian population and the Rebel Army. The M-26 was not
clearly characterized by anti-imperialism, either in the
urban organizations or in the guerrilla forces, as it
was by nationalism and a demand for non-corrupt government. The most that can be said is that there were
strong anti-imperialist tendencies among the rebel leadership and a feeling of revolutionary kinship with
anti-imperialist figures in Cuban history such as Mella
and Martí. But, the experience of the Segundo Frente
advanced the M-26, especially the guerrillas, towards a
clear anti-imperialism.

In the spring of 1958, the crisis of the Batista
dictatorship mounted. Sabotage in the cities and countryside increased; rebel attacks on government forces
mounted; Castro declared "total war on the tyranny";
Raúl Castro and Juan Almeida led columns out of the
Sierra Maestra sanctuary. In response, Batista's forces and supporters engaged in more torture and punitive
actions against the population of both rural and urban
areas. The air force began to bomb rural areas of
Oriente more severely; Colonel Jesús Sosa Blanco, <u>Masferristas</u> and Colonel Fermín Cowley's men committed further atrocities against civilians in Oriente. The
Catholic Church raised its voice in protest, calling for
a change in government. Middle-class and business circles and civic organizations became more vocal in their
criticism of the Batista regime.[121] The United States
government and private investors in Cuba began to seek
an alternative to Batista and the mounting pressure in
Congress resulted in the imposition of an arms embargo
on March 14, 1958.

In this context Batista mounted his offensive,
starting in April-May with army columns striking into
Segundo Frente territory and with aerial bombardment of

rural areas in Oriente. The columns were ambushed and turned back by May 10,[122] but the bombing continued. Napalm and incendiary bombs were being dropped on civilian areas and air-to-ground rockets fired. Some of the Segundo Frente area peasants had taken to caves to escape the air raids, and some feared the presence of the Rebel Army, since it could mean more attacks.[123] Bombs stamped with "Made in USA" of the "Mutual Aid" logo were dropped from United States-supplied planes and, according to Robert Taber, anti-United States sentiment already present among some guerrillas increased during Nixon's abortive trip to Latin America in 1958, when he was stoned and jeered in Caracas and Lima.[124] Airborne troops had been sent to Guantánamo during the trip "as a precautionary measure".

In June, Cuban planes which were bombing in Oriente were seen being refuelled at Guantánamo and the M-26 man in the Cuban Embassy in Washington, Angel Saavedra, obtained documents regarding the delivery of three hundred rocket warheads to the Batista forces via Guantánamo, two months after the embargo was declared.[125] Raúl Castro obtained some photograpsh of Cuban planes being loaded with bombs at the United States base and, while in a cave with some campesinos during a bombing raid, he decided to act, independently of Fidel Castro.[126] He ordered Belarmino Castilla's Column 9 "José Tey" to capture a number of United States civilians and military personnel from various enterprises, in order to protest United States collusion with the dictatorship's attacks on civilians. The idea was to show the captives what United States bombs were doing.[127] On June 26, a number of United States citizens were taken from the Moa Bay Company installation after a fire fight with a Batista garrison there, from the Nicaro Nickel Company, and from the United Fruit Sugar Company installation at Guaro. Some two dozen United States Marines, returning to the base after liberty in the city of Guantánamo, were captured when their bus was ambushed along the highway.[128] Including a couple of Canadians, some forty-nine persons were taken captive.

The civilian captives were taken to a rebel base, "where they were shown some of the bomb damage and fragments of the bombs that had been dropped".[129] Dubois later interviewed Raul Castro and asked why the kidnappings had been ordered and why some equipment had been taken from Moa and Nicaro. The latter answered:

> We were obliged to detain the North American citizens in order to attract world attention in general and that of the United States in particular to the crime that was being committed against our people with the arms which the United States government had supplied to Batista for continental de-

fense. In one of the clauses of the treaty is the express prohibition that said arms be used in the domestic questions of the respective countries [The presence of United States citizens would] deter the criminal bombardments, with incendiary bombs, rockets and even napalm bombs, which in those moments were being carried out against our forces and above all against the defenseless towns of the campesinos. [Equipment was taken because] if the United States of North America supplies arms to the government of Batista, we believe we have a certain right to make use of equipment from some properties of the North American government... we have already told these companies we will not again touch their properties, that upon the triumph of our cause we will pay them for the damage caused.[130]

Immediately after the kidnappings, United States Vice Consul Grant Wollam flew to Santiago to make contact with the rebels. On his way out to the hills in a jeep, Batista planes strafed and rocketed the vehicle. The Vice Consul was unhurt.[131] He met with the "international witnesses" who told him they were well-treated. The rebels protected them from irate peasants, notified their families, and supplied them with small American luxuries. There was even a July 4th party thrown for them by the rebels.[132] When Wollam, who spoke little Spanish, berated Raúl Castro, some of the captives intervened and backed up the rebel arguments. Wollam was persuaded by them to apologize for his outburst and his outright denial of United States supplies of arms, even when he had been confronted with a napalm shell stamped "property of the United States Air Force".[133] Some of the captives, engineers and executives for the mining companies and servicing firms, sent letters to the United States government and to their own employees condemning the shipments of arms to Batista.

Journalists from the United States began to arrive to interview the rebels and the captives. Finally, Radio Rebelde in the Sierra Maestra broadcast a message and order from Fidel Castro, ordering the release of the captives. Castro condemned the bombings and the shipment of arms, but claimed not to have received any official report of the kidnappings.[134] The last of the captives were released on July 18, and immediately thereafter the area was savagely bombed.[135]

The incident showed that anti-imperialist and anti-United States government sentiment was growing in the Rebel Army in the Segundo Frente. They were willing to confront the United States government over its support of what Chomsky and Herman call "benign, constructive terror".[136] Even so, the rebels did not respond to what they considered a provocation when the United States moved a squad of Marines out of the base to "protect" the oil pipeline. Raúl Castro considered that world opinion, which was critical of the United States action, had not been adversely affected by the kidnappings. He saw the affair as a constructive political education for both the Rebel Army and for the campesinos. All could see that United States arms were being used against the rebels and the civilian population. All could see that the bombing was suspended while United States citizens were in the target area. And all could see that the attacks resumed as soon as the captives were released.[137] It was as though this sequence of events confirmed what many militants of M-26 and guerrillas already believed, that, in the words of the State Department's Director of the Office of Caribbean and Mexican Affairs, William A. Wieland, "I know Batista is considered by many as a son of a bitch...but American interests come first...at least he is our son of a bitch; he is not playing ball with the Communists".[138]

CONCLUSION

The myth of the readiness of the Cuban peasantry to join a revolutionary effort to overthrow the dictatorship was present in the Generation of the Centenary when they attacked the Moncada barracks. Fidel Castro entertained even then the possibility of guerrilla struggle being supported by Oriente guajiros. Combined with the plans for land reform, the notion of peasant support for a just struggle was an integral part of the political education of the Granma expeditionaries in Mexico. In the Sierra Maestra, the specific socio-economic characteristics of the population and the nature of the actual guerrilla struggle pushed the Rebel Army to create peasant-guerrilla unity in reality. Survival depended upon peasant trust and co-operation and the actions the guerrillas took painstakingly achieved that trust and cooperation. Land reform in the territorio libre came long before the guerrillas might have thought it would. Such plans, in the beginning, were likely to be reserved until the overthrow of Batista and the establishment of something between a bourgeois liberal democracy and a popular front government. The direct political education of life and armed struggle in the Sierra Maestra brought about a more immediate praxis in regards to peasant-guerrilla unity.

Building upon the experience of the Sierra Maestra, the Segundo Frente Oriental "Frank País" and, later, Guevara's and Cienfuegos' columns in the central provinces, further developed peasant-guerrilla unity. The different socio-economic panorama in northern Oriente and the organizational skills of the Segundo Frente leadership enabled the guerrillas to move far towards realizing another mobilizing revolutionary myth, that of worker-peasant-guerrilla unity.

In each case, the objective conditions for social revolution were addressed by cadres informed and motivated by revolutionary myths which inspired them to action and sacrifice. They had faith in the ultimate victory and in the justice of their cause; faith, as Sorel might have said, in the face of what reason and logic might have shown to be insurmountable odds.

The rebels arrived in Cuba with mobilizing revolutionary myths. The myths were developed and even transformed through experience. And sustaining revolutionary myths were generated and drawn from their experiences, myths which inspired new recruits and which helped to establish Rebel Army legitimacy as rightful heir to power after the fall of Batista. The myths of unity, of a revolution made by and for the humildes, the poor, the humble, and the working masses of Cuba, and of historically redemptive nationalism and anti-imperialism combined with experiences after January 1959 to sustain and generate revolutionary ardor. The myths of the Rebel Army formed the core of the new and revolutionary political culture and formed the basis of political education in the FAR. There was continuity between the political education of insurrectionary cadres, the political education of the experience of armed struggle and civil administration, and the political education of the armed forces once revolutionary power was attained.

The revolutionary myth of anti-imperialism gained strength through redemptive nationalism and the historical identification of the Rebel Army with previous Cuban heroes and martyrology. The leadership sought that identification consciously and undoubtedly felt it. Formal political education of the tropa by convinced anti-imperialists such as Guevara increased the mobilizing role of anti-imperialism, while experiences such as the bombing and kidnapping incidents in the Segundo Frente had a similar effect. Gradually, anti-imperialism was assuming the stature of the other mobilizing myths; it came fully into its own as a material force in Cuban history and in the revolutionary process only through further experience after January 1959.

NOTES

1. Guevara, Reminiscences, p. 132.
2. Guevara, Reminiscences, p. 133.
3. Gil Carl Alroy, "The Peasantry in the Cuban Revolution", in Rolando Bonachea and Nelson Valdés, eds. Cuba in Revolution (New York: Doubleday, 1972), pp.3-17.
4. See B. Traven's novel Rebellion of the Hanged, passim.

5. Guevara, Reminiscences, p. 193: "The peasantry recognized those lean men whose beards...were beginning to flourish, as companions in misfortune, fresh victims of the repressive forces".
6. Alroy, p. 11.
7. Masetti, p. 57.
8. Ibid., p. 91.
9. Masetti, p. 72.
10. Bonachea and San Martín, p. 100. On p. 189 there is a photograph of a guerrilla being prepared for execution in 1958; see also Cuba Internacional, May-June 1970, p. 84, for testimony by guerrilla fighters in Guevara's Column Four regarding the execution of a deserter who was robbing peasants and committing rape in the name of M-26.
11. Thomas, p. 950.
12. Fulgencio Batista, Cuba Betrayed (New York: Vantage Press, 1962), p. 52.
13. Batista, Piedra y Leyes (Mexico: Ediciones Botas, 1962), p. 43.
14. Ibid., pp. 40-45.
15. Ibid., p. 42.
16. Batista, Respuesta (Mexico: Ediciones Botas, 1960), p. 257.
17. Ibid., p. 167.
18. Guevara, Reminiscences, p. 178.
19. Guevara, Reminiscences, p. 179.
20. Account in Guevara, Reminiscences, pp. 180-1.
21. Photographs of the revolutionary tribunal in session and of an execution are found in Bonachea and San Martin, p. 101.
22. Guevara, Reminiscences, pp. 181-3.
23. Guevara, Reminiscences, p. 182.
24. Ibid., p. 183.
25. Bonachea and San Martín, p. 100.
26. Bonachea and San Martín, p. 100.
27. See the personal experience of Comandante Antonio Sánchez Pinares, in "Días de Lucha", Verde Olivo, 13 Oct. 68, pp. 27-33.
28. Jean-Paul Sartre, Sartre on Cuba (New York: Ballantine Books, 1961), pp. 50-1.
29. Guevara, Reminiscences, pp. 167-8.
30. Guevara, Reminiscences, pp. 167-8.
31. Ibid., p. 142.
32. See the account taken from the 1958 diary of Teniente Osvaldo Herrera, in Cabrera Alvarez, Hablar de Camilo, p. 85.
33. Guevara, Reminiscences, p. 169.
34. Sergio Rodriguez, "Una infraccion", in Cuba Internacional, p. 85.
35. Guevara, Reminiscences, p. 167.
36. Ibid., p. 170.
37. Guevara, Reminiscences, p. 171.
38. Guevara, in Cuba Internacional, p. 76.

39. See the account of Rafael Verdería Lién, in *Cuba Internacional*, p. 66.
40. Roberto Castro, in *Cuba Internacional*, p. 76.
41. Guevara, *Reminiscences*, p. 203. See also the recollections of Marta Paredes, Sierra resident and storekeeper, in *Cuba Internacional*, p. 76: "We kept a store in Santa Ana like a little boat on a great sea. Sánchez Mosquera suspected us, but as we served him what he wanted..."
42. Elena Garcés, Sierra resident, in *Cuba Internacional*, p. 76.
43. See the account of Juan Corria, Sierra peasant, in *Cuba Internacional*, p. 76: "At times the supplier was the army itself. Everything...ended up in the stomachs of the rebels".
44. Guevara, *Reminiscences*, p. 203.
45. Linnia Garcés, *Cuba Internacional*, p. 76.
46. Guevara, "Proyecciones sociales del Ejército Rebelde" (January 1959 speech), in *Obra Revolucionaria*, ed. Roberto Fernandez Retamar (Mexico: Ediciones Era, 1967), pp. 285-93.
47. Alfredo Beccles, in Yglesias, p. 49.
48. In Cabrera Alvarez, p. 58.
49. Account of Marzo Orozco, from Guevara's Column Four, in *Cuba Internacional*, p. 77.
50. Rigoberto Garcés, *campesino* and rebel fighter, in *Cuba Internacional*, p. 75.
51. On this network, and the role of women and children in it, see "El papel del mensajero", *Cuba Internacional*, pp. 70-3. It is comprised of recollections of various *campesino* couriers.
52. Guevara, "Cuba: excepción histórica o vanguardia en la lucha anticolonialist?" (April, 1961), in *Obra Revolucionaria*, pp. 515-26.
53. From a conversation in Sartre, p. 134.
54. Guevara, *Reminiscences*, p. 172.
55. In Lockwood, p. 53, Guillermo García recalled the process of learning, of coming to see the needs of Sierra *campesinos*: "La Sierra Maestra. Nuestra maestra". 'The Sierra Maestra. Our teacher.'
56. Castro, in *Cuba Internacional*, p. 76. This is an official view which articulates the thrust of the myth of the Rebel Army in political education after 1959.
57. Masetti, p. 135.
58. Guevara, in Masetti, p. 131.
59. Castro, in Lockwood, p. 90.
60. Guevara, in Masetti, p. 132.
61. Castro, in Lockwood, p. 90.
62. Guevara, in Masetti, p. 132.
63. Castro, in Lockwood, p. 90.
64. Guevara, *Reminiscences*, p. 195.
65. Masetti, p. 135.
66. See the account by "Pelencho" Teodoro Naranjo,

a peasant messenger, in Cuba Internacional, p. 105.
67. Ibid.
68. Guevara, Reminiscences, p. 150.
69. Rigoberto Garces, in Cuba Internacional, p. 105.
70. Polo Torres, in Cuba Internacional, p. 105.
71. Comandante Luis Orlando Rodriguez, in Cuba Internacional, p. 107.
72. Sartre, pp. 51-2.
73. See Harold R. Isaacs, The Tragedy of the Chinese Revolution, 2nd re. ed. (Stanford: Stanford University Press, 1961) and Selected Works of Mao Tse-tung, Vo. I (Peking: Foreign Languages Press, 1965), "Report on an Investigation of the Peasant Movement in Hunan", pp. 23-59, and "Why Is It That Red Political Power Can Exist In China?", pp. 63-72.
74. Selected Works of Mao Tse-tung, Vol. IV, pp. 155-6.
75. In Masetti, p. 150.
76. Fidel Castro, "Communicado de la Comandancia General del Ejército Rebelde", Bohemia 19 June 59, pp. 42-6.
77. Castro, "Total War Against the Tyranny" (March 12, 1958 Manifesto), in Bonachea and Valdés, pp. 373-8.
78. Castro, "Total War...", pp. 373-8.
79. Among others, Efigenio Ameijeiras, Carlos Iglesias, Antonio Lusson Battle, Felix Pena Diaz, Belarmino Castilla Mas, Demetrio Montseny. See also Herbert Matthews, Revolution in Cuba: An Essay in Understanding (New York: Scribner's Sons, 1975), p. 103, and Jose N. Causse, "Relato: El Segundo Frente Oriental 'Frank Pais'", Verdo Olivo, 24 Mar. 63, pp. 5-6. Causse asserts the organizational and political education experiences of the Frente made the fighter of that area better equipped to deal with the class struggles which sharpened after January 1959.
80. See Nuñez Jimenez, pp. 543 ff.
81. Bonachea and San Martin, p. 196.
82. See Taber, pp. 82-3, on Masferrer.
83. Régis Debray, Revolution in the Revolution? (New York: Grove Press, 1967), p. 56.
84. Taber, p. 252.
85. Raúl Castro, "Diario de campaña", in Edmundo Desnoes, La Sierra y el llano (Havana: Casa de las Americas, 1961), p. 213.
86. Bonachea and San Martin, p. 193.
87. Nuñez Jimenez, p. 603.
88. Hector de Arturo, "Desde el '56", Verde Olivo, 5 Dec. 71, p. 69.
89. Bonachea and San Martin, p. 190.
90. Bonachea and San Martin, p. 190.
91. José N. Causse, "Relato", p. 5.
92. Bonachea and San Martin, p. 195.

93. Ibid., p. 193.
94. See Marta Harnecker, Cuba: Dictatorship or Democracy? (Westport, Connecticut: Lawrence Hill, 1980), pp. 56-71.
95. Bonachea and San Martín, p. 191.
96. See Nydia Sarabia, "René Ramos Latour, Comandante en la ciudad y en la Sierra", Verde Olivo, 4 Aug. 63, pp. 25-6, 43-6.
97. Antonio Lussón Battle, "Relato de la Columna 17 'Abel Santamaría'", Verde Olivo, 24 Mar. 63, pp. 7-8.
98. Nuñez Jimenez, p. 603.
99. Bonachea and San Martín, p. 197.
100. Nuñez Jimenez, p. 599.
101. Bonachea and San Martín, p. 195.
102. Nuñez Jimenez, p. 602.
103. Nuñez Jimenez, p. 602.
104. Bonachea and San Martín, p. 194.
105. Ibid., p. 193.
106. Causse, p. 5.
107. Causse, p. 5; Nuñez, p. 603; Bonachea and San Martín, p. 195.
108. Causse, p. 5.
109. Bonachea and San Martín, p. 195.
110. G. Duvallon, "Tumbasiete: una escuela revolucionaria", Verde Olivo, 27 Mar. 60, pp. 12-15.
111. Duvallon, p. 14.
112. Blás Roca, a long-time PSP leader; Roig, a Marxist historian publishing from the 20s on: e.g. Los problemas sociales en Cuba (Havana: Imprenta el Ideal, 1927), Conclusiones fundamentales sobre la guerra libertadora cubana de 1895 (Mexico: Colegio de Mexico, 1945).
113. Martin, p. 220. He claims some instructors were PSP members. Duvallon, p. 16, lists the instructors as Vilma Espín, Manuel Cruz Muñoz, Dr. Juan Escalona, Dr. Zoila Ibarra, Dr. Asela de los Santos, Teniente Jorge Risquet, Ramona Ruiz, and Capitán José Causse, director.
114. See Gonzalez Tosca, "Escuelas", Verde Olivo, 5 Dec. 71, p. 84.
115. Duvallon, p. 15.
116. Taber, p. 278.
117. Bonachea and San Martín, p. 191.
118. Ibid.
119. Nuñez Jimenez, p. 604.
120. Causse, p. 6.
121. See Thomas, pp. 975-87; Dubois, pp. 211-33.
122. Taber, p. 256.
123. Raúl Castro, "Operación anti-aérea", p. 38.
124. Taber, p. 257.
125. Ibid.
126. Raúl Castro, "Operación anti-aérea", p. 38.
127. Capitán José L. Cuza, "Combate del Centro In-

dustrial de Moa", <u>Verde Olivo</u>, 14 July 63, pp. 18-24.

128. See Capitán José Q. Sandino Rodriguez, "Operación Captura", <u>Verde Olivo</u>, 15 Sept. 63, pp. 10-15. The Marines were shown the effects of the incendiary and napalm bombing.

129. Dubois, p. 270.
130. In Dubois, pp. 274-5.
131. Taber, p. 259.
132. Raúl Castro, "Operación anti-aérea", p. 37.
133. Raúl Castro, "Operación ...", p. 35.
134. See F. Castro, "On the Arrest of United States Citizens" (July 3, 1958), in Bonachea and Valdés, pp. 383-4.
135. Cuza, p. 24.
136. Chomsky and Herman, Vo. I, Ch. 3 "Benign Terror", Ch. 4, "Constructive Terror".
137. R. Castro, "Operación...", p. 38
138. Quoted in Thomas, p. 977.

7
The Political Education of Combat: The Myth of the Guerrilla Struggle in the Sierra

THE POLITICAL EDUCATION OF COMBAT

The purpose of the guerrilla foco in the Sierra Maestra was not merely survival and the conduct of a political campaign ("The Cuban civil war had been really a political campaign in a tyranny, with the campaigner being defended by armed men".)[1] Combat was necessary for survival itself, for the defense of the Sierra peasantry and, most importantly, for the destruction of Batista's army: "The defeat of the mercenary army, allowing the people to seize its weapons...".[2] As corrupt as it was, the army was not about to disintegrate on its own. It took rebel combat operations to accelerate the demoralization of the army and to bring about its full identification, in the eyes of the population, with the Batista regime. Combat created an effective force with which to replace the destroyed army after the seizure of power and to protect the revolutionary regime.

OPPOSING MORALES AND THE DEMORALIZATION
OF BATISTA'S ARMY

The roots of demoralization in Batista's army existed before the insurrectionary struggle. Promotion based on favoritism, instrumental in promoting the "Sergeant's Revolt" of 1933,[3] was again present after Batista's 1952 coup: "Batista recalled former military associates and relied heavily on politically inspired promotions within the officer ranks".[4] This created tensions between professional career officers and political appointees. Advancement through favoritism was common at all levels of the army, particularly in the Sierra, as the struggle developed: "Batistiano NCOs sought to ingratiate themselves with commanders by excess of zeal and brutality, knowing from experience that ingratiation with these officers led to results. Cowardly actions by privates led on occasion to promotions to corporalcies and sergeantcies".[5]

Promotion by favoritism undoubtedly contributed to internal tensions in the army. Competence was no guarantee of promotion and incompetence meant little success in campaigns against the guerrillas. Tensions between professional and political appointees combined with ideological differences to produce a string of military revolts and conspiracies during Batista's dictatorship. Some came from the professional officers interested in civic reforms and disturbed at the erosion of regime legitimacy.[6] Others emerged out of right-wing tanquista (tank corps) elements who desired a Dominican-style authoritarian regime.[7]

Corruption contributed to the undermining of army morale. Friends and relatives of the corrupt Chief of Staff, General Francisco Tabernilla, received rural Guardia commands, adding to "the network of protection rackets and gambling dens which they had organized throughout the country".[8] Colonel del Río Chaviano was accused by another officer of "running a big gambling and protection racket in Santiago...almost daily drunken orgies in the barracks...and vast profits from smuggling."[9] Corruption extended to those officers and units charged with fighting the guerrillas. In the latter part of 1958, Castro's forces were able to buy arms clandestinely from the army. Carleton Beals was told that [Castro] "had a regular scale of payment for Batista's cartridges, pistols, rifles, machine guns and grenades".[10] Corruption split the armed forces of Batista from top to bottom: "Officers regarded commands merely as a means of enrichment by the use of intimidation...Batista's officers, both of the police and of the armed services, spent their leisure at casinos or night clubs and enriched themselves by exacting protection money and other graft".[11]

The drive for money extended into the rank and file. Mostly drawn from the peasantry, recruits were traditionally the poor and unemployed, seeking a regular paycheck. In rural towns and outposts, the extortion of the surrounding population supplemented pay. This was the pursuit of a minority, but it kept such peasant recruits divided from the population.[12]

The breakdown of morale in the Batista army was also due to the brutality employed against the guerrillas, the urban resistance and the rural population. The ethics of brutality and torture which produced the Moncada atrocities under General Tabernilla and Colonel del Río Chaviano continued in the insurrectionary war. In the cities, the repression against the urban resistance was such that the harsh life in the Sierra was seen as almost a sanctuary. Vilma Espín, an important part of the Santiago M-26 apparatus, recalled that "going into the Sierra was a relief for us. When one of us was exhausted, he took a few days'vacation in the Sierra. If there was a message to carry, it was given to the one most in need of rest".[13] It was to escape urban repression that urban militants would enter the Sierra, to fight again but in a different fashion. Carleton Beals recalled the Havana atmosphere of mid-1957:

> When I reached the island, two or three police killings occurred daily in Havana, as well as others elsewhere. Day after day, I saw murdered victims on the main streets of Havana, posed on their knees, a noose around their necks, suspended from a miniature cross and sometimes sardonically provided with crepe and a bunch of flowers.[14]

In the Sierra Maestra, peasants rather than guerrillas were more often the object of army and Guardia abuses, but when guerrillas were captured, they expected to be tortured and killed. A fighter named Guillermo Geilín,"twice wounded and knowing what would happen to him if he were to fall into the hands of these thugs, committed suicide".[15] Guevara was unequivocal about the need to rescue wounded guerrillas: "The guerrilla must not leave a wounded comrade to the mercy of enemy troops since his fate will be, almost certainly, death".[16]

The depredations of the army and the Guardia in the countryside facilitated the drawing of contrasts. While the army bombed, burned and strafed peasant settlements thought to be collaborating with the rebels, the guerrilla force punished chivatos, built schools and hospitals and attacked army columns entering the Sierra. One of the most effective army commanders in the Sierra, Colonel Sánchez Mosquera, was also quite brutal and destructive. His policy was to burn and destroy all campesino huts, confiscate their livestock and, if possible, to remove the population from the area.[17] Other commanders well-known for excesses were Colonel Fermín Cowley, Major Merob Sosa Blanco, and Rolando Masferrer.

The Batista army collapsed as much from internal disintegration as from defeat at the hands of the rebels. From the failed summer offensive in 1958, the army's decline was sharp and rapid. The hatred of the population, the presence of a civilian resistance, corruption and the black market operating at higher levels made the rank-and-file soldier cynical about the reasons for fighting. In Cuba, units began to surrender to the rebels in the summer of 1958, to avoid combat, or even to change sides.

Batista blamed the failure of the summer offensive on the United States arms embargo, "which caught the Armed Forces with obsolete equipment",[18] on army staff problems,[19] on rumors of military coups and negotiations with the rebels,[20] and on the campaign of terror, sabotage, extortion and subversion he saw mounted by the communist front M-26.[21]

In contrast to the corruption, brutality and reticence which characterized Batista's army, the rebel commanders attempted to build a revolutionary morale. The first element of such a morale was to be a radically distinct treatment of the peasant population, reminiscent, as remarked above, of Mao's dictum to the infant Red Army. The second was the treatment afforded captured and wounded enemy soldiers, the "soldiers of the tyranny", as they were called. The rebels were constantly reminded that they were the opposite of the government troops. The government troops often abandoned their own wounded,[22] though told by their officers that dire consequences awaited the man captured by the rebels.[23] But the rebel leaders told the guerrillas, some of whom wished to mete out the same treatment to government soldiers as they, themselves, would receive if captured, that the goal of the struggle was not to kill all the soldiers but to overthrow their commanders. It was necessary to demoralize them by fighting hard, but "what we must do is kill the top dogs, the ones who order the rank and file about. These government soldiers are unfortunates who are earning a wage; they have no ideals".[24]

Some of the leaders of Batista's army, such as those who tried to institute a civic action program in the Sierra after the Granma landing, were aware that the war was also being fought in the psychological arena, the arena of morale and discipline. But the norm of army and Guardia behavior towards the peasantry undermined what credit there existed and helped to disintegrate army morale. The guerrillas, on the other hand, though experiencing frustration and bitter incidents of betrayal and treachery at the hands of some peasants, relied on consistently honest treatment, and on sincerity. It was an "element of the mystique of the guerrillas"[25] that they were forthright about their losses and lack of arms. Announcements of defeats or lacks of supplies on Radio Rebelde in 1958 resulted in contributions from both peasants and urban sympathizers.[26]

The battle of contrasting morales was joined early on. Batista's soldiers were impressed by the exemplary treatment received at the hands of the rebels when captured. The commander at the El Uvero army post, Carrera, recalled: "The treatment that the rebel tropa extended us, one must say, was commendable. They furnished us with everything we needed to be able to leave, to evacuate the zone without fear. They promised they would take the unwounded soldiers to their camps and release them at the disposition of the commander".[27] True to the rebels' word, the soldiers were released and came to tell their officers about the respectful treatment.

The Military Intelligence Service told Carrera not to discuss the affair.[28]

The corruption, brutality, indiscipline and failing morale of Batista's army were confronted by the leaders of the Rebel Army and a theory of contrasting morales began to emerge. Discipline, it was argued, was of two kinds. External discipline was that of "militarist regimes", based on mechanical responses to training and commands, and on rigid patterns of behavior: "Any small error in a soldier of a regular army is controlled by the closest comrade-in-arms".[29] Internal discipline, on the other hand, was basically an individual matter. It was not produced by mechanical and repeated patterns. Rather, it was a self-control "born of the profound conviction of the individual, of a need to obey a superior, in order to maintain not only the effectivity of the armed force in which he is integrated, but also to defend one's own effectiveness".[30] External discipline can tolerate minor errors of individuals, but the exigencies of guerrilla struggle, where each individual fighter is a unit, demand a closer discipline in each: "No one can commit the slightest mistake, since his life and that of his comrades depend upon it".[31]

This internal discipline is informal, lacking in the external manifestations present in a "mercenary army". In the Rebel Army, no repressive apparatus or intelligence service was necessary, "to control an individual in the face of temptation". Temptation, as Guevara defined it, was that of theft, drink, brutality, duplicity and sexual assault, activities which characterized Batista's army, police and Guardia. The guerrilla, in contrast, "did not drink, not because his superior officer would punish him but because he knew he should not drink, because his morale imposed abstinence on him, and his internal discipline strengthened that morale imposed by the [rebel] army".[32]

The distinction between the two forms of discipline was based upon the concept of morale. Morale, for Guevara, was a historically and class-determined quality: "Ethical morale has changed with the passage of time, in accordance with the prevailing ideas of a given society".[33] The ethical morale of Batista's army was clearly seen as retrograde, based as it was on the interests of decadent elements of society. Morale also depended on "that combative drive, that faith in the final victory and in the justice of their cause".[34] Like Sorel and Clausewitz, Guevara stressed the faith in the final victory which carried a fighter of high morale through every encounter. Guevara claimed that heroic morale, that faith in a cause, "is just what the mercenary army lacked in its confrontation with the guerrilla deluge", because there was no cause arousing the government soldiers. They were thus unprepared, for the most part, to die for the Batista regime, and could only fight "to preserve certain sinecures...for the right to plunder, to play the thief in uniform",[35] for personal loyalties, or to preserve their own lives. He claimed that this lack of a cause created soldiers who "will fight only up to a certain point: until the sacrifice of their life is demanded of them".[36] In a sense, Guevara was stating that Batista's soldiers had no myth.

The Rebel Army, on the other hand, did have a myth. Rebel fighters "felt genuinely the forceful words of our national anthem: ' to die for the fatherland is to live'".[37] They felt the words, while the mercenaries, according to Guevara, merely knew them. They felt a duty to risk and sacrifice life for the cause, while the Batista soldier did not know why he was fighting. The Batista soldier felt alienated from the population, while the guerrilla was taught and, through experience, came to feel, part of the people: "That is the reason for his strength, his triumph, in the long and short run, over whatever power tries to oppress him: the base and substratum of the guerrilla struggle is in the people".[38]

It is in this link to the people and their needs that the revolutionary guerrilla finds morale, according to Guevara. The guerrilla struggle is not that of a small group against a powerful army. Rather, it is "the war of the entire people against the dominant oppressor".[39] Indeed, the guerrillas cannot exist without popular support. They fight because, at base, they are the "vanguard" of the people; they are "social reformers. The guerrilla takes up arms as a protest of the people against its oppressors and he fights to change the social system which maintains all his disarmed brothers in poverty and misery".[40] Because the fighter is of the people, he knows them and the land better than the mercenary and can rely on their support: "However more uncomfortable he is, however much deeper the rigors of nature, the more the guerrilla feels at home, the higher is his morale, the greater his feeling of security".[41]

The Rebel Army, for Guevara, was made up of people with a cause, the "cause of the poor and of all the people". The guerrillas, in effect, would be the guarantors of what classical Marxists would call the "universal interests" of the Cuban people. This made "social researchers and judges" of the fighters. The realities with which they dealt on a daily basis made them agrarian revolutionaries: the guerrillas needed a remote zone in which to operate, "and in remote and lightly-populated places, the popular struggle for rights is situated almost exclusively on the plane of the social composition of land tenure; thus the guerrilla is fundamentally and before all else, an agrarian revolutionary".[42] The agrarian revolution becomes the cause, the mobilizing myth the rebel will die to achieve and die to defend. And to come to an awareness of and fidelity to the cause, experience is helpful but political education is necessary. Morale and discipline, then, are fostered by "revolutionary instructors who are disseminating among the mass of our army the great national goals".[43]

Finally, Guevara contrasted the Rebel Army's superiority in morale and discipline with the "mercenary" troops of Batista. Guerrilla superiority was derived from a class indentification of the fighter with the poor, oppressed and exploited. The enemy, on the other hand,

> is the junior partner of the dictator, the man who receives the last of the crumbs which the next-to-last of the privileged has left him, from a long chain beginning on Wall Street and finishing in him. He is disposed to defend his privileges but ...in the same measure as they are important... they are never worth his life.[44]

The Rebel Army was able to wield superiority in morale and discipline in several ways during the insurrectionary war. First, it helped to create what Bonachea and San Martín call their "mystique". A popular image developed, one of the heroic embattled revolutionary of conscience. The term _guerrillero_ completed its odyssey in Cuban culture from its origins in "those defenders of the Spanish slave regime who took up arms to defend the crown" [45] early in the nineteenth century through the Cuban Independence fighters to the M-26 guerrillas. Even for those Cubans who doubted that the guerrillas would succeed in toppling Batista, the rebels projected a romantic image of fighters prepared to die for a cause: "They were compared to the _Mambises_ of the Wars of Independence".[46] It was an underdog image of Cuban crusaders destined to die as heroes.

Second, the rebels took advantage of poor army tactics to mount repeated ambushes.[47] The guerrillas adopted the practice of "always aiming at the head of the marching troop, in an attempt to kill the first one or the first few, thus immobilizing the enemy force".[48] Eventually, this policy accumulated weight, to the point that, by early 1958, the army ceased its forays into the Sierra, "and the soldiers even refused to march in the advance guard".[49] The mistakes and disorganization of the Batista command structure, in large part due to rivalries and frequent changes of personnel, resulted in army units entering the same ambushes which had previously caught another unit. This was particularly true during the 1958 summer offensive. Separate units were not advised of each other's engagements or the location of guerrilla ambushes, while government radio announcements gave out absurd figures on rebel casualties.[50] Castro described the costs of deception and incompetence on Radio Rebelde after the summer offensive had been decisively turned back:

> The soldiers easily fell into the same errors which had had costly consequences for other soldiers. They fell into similar traps and even into the very same ones other troops had fallen into days before. No unit command ever received the slightest news regarding the experience that other commands had undergone...the General Staff lies deliberately; it lies to the people and to the army; it lies to avoid demoralization in the ranks because it refuses to acknowledge before the world its military incapacity, its condition of mercenary commanders sold out to the most dishonest cause that could be defended.[51]

Third, the guerrillas used their morale and discipline superiority for propaganda and psychological warfare. Propaganda was conceived to be a weapon wielded offensively and defensively. Political indoctrination of rebel fighters was considered necessary to help create morale and devotion to the cause, while propaganda was aimed both at the mass of the population and at the ranks of the Batista army. Thus, in discussing the summer offensive on Radio Rebelde, Castro aimed to cut through censorship and government deception. He accounted for the guerrillas' ability to repulse the attack by ten thousand troops by referring to the differences in morale:

> The mercenary rifles of the tyranny were smashed against the rifles of the idealists, who take no pay. All of their military technique, their military academies and their most modern weapons were to no avail. The trouble is that when the militarists do not defend their country but attack it, when they do not defend the people but enslave them, they cease being the armed forces and become an armed gang; they cease being military men and become evildoers; they no longer deserve the salary that they tear from the sweat of the people; with dishonor and cowardice they are bleeding the land even the sun that shines on them.[52]

With the start of Radio Rebelde broadcasts from the Sierra on February 24, 1958, the rebels were able to enter directly into the propaganda war. Castro considered the radio broadcasts "a factor of utmost importance".[53] Before it was "Radio Bemba" 'the grapevine' and clandestine M-26 publications that informed the mass of the population of the rebels' activities. Now, Radio Rebelde came into direct competition with government accounts of the struggle. Radio Rebelde "soon had the highest ratings of any of Cuba's radio stations and Batista was jamming its broadcasts".[54] Castro used it to advance the notion of rebel morale superiority over Batista's army, concentrating on the themes of treatment of wounded and the release of prisoners:

> Ever since we landed from the Granma, we have followed an invariable policy in dealing with the adversary and that line has been strictly kept, maybe as it has been rarely kept in all history... more than six hundred members of the armed forces have been captured by us in the Sierra Maestra alone. With the natural pride of those who follow an ethical standard, we can say that without exception the combatants of the Rebel Army have complied with the law regarding the treatment of prisoners. No prisoner has ever been deprived of his life. No wounded have ever been left unattended. But we can say more; no prisoner has ever been beaten up. And more still: no prisoner has ever been insulted. All officers who have been our prisoners can attest to the fact that none of them has been submitted to questioning, out of respect to their condition as men and as military men.[55]

One of the most stunning victories in the struggle between the two morales was registered during the summer offensive. Castro used psychological warfare to defeat the already demoralized battalion led by Major José Quevedo, whom Castro had known at the university. It was surrounded and successive attempts to break out were quashed, and it was cut off from water and supplies. The rebels set up loudspeakers around the battalion and called for its surrender: "Castro spoke personally and addressed himself to Quevedo recalling their university days and lamenting the necessity to fight against him. None of the propaganda broadcast from the front lines contained any insults to the troops or their officers".[56] Supplies dropped from the air were gathered up by the rebels. Castro sent a captured soldier to Quevedo, proposing a truce of four hours. The prisoner was living evidence of humane treatment, contrary to the General Staff's propaganda that "if a soldier is taken prisoner, he will be tortured, castrated or killed...everything that they do at army and police headquarters, everything that they have seen done to the revolutionaries".[57] Quevedo accepted the truce and the army soldiers approached the rebel positions, asking for water and food, and tobacco. Castro recalled: "We gave them what they asked. Amazed by this gesture, the soldiers embraced our men, crying with emotion".[58]

Such fraternization, and the demoralization of Quevedo's battalion, resulted in its surrender and Quevedo's virtual defection. He gave his troops the liberty to defect, an idea which they received "with enthusiasm".[59] In fact, they did not enter rebel ranks, but were given medical attention and were turned over to the Red Cross. The rebel policy on treatment of government soldiers, followed since Moncada, was bearing fruit. Castro had been careful to distinguish always between "honorable and patriotic" soldiers and the corrupt and "mercenary" elements:

> We have repeatedly proclaimed that we are not at war against the armed forces, only against the tyranny. But the unheard-of barbarities of certain officers and members of the army responsible reach a degree in which a military man in active service today could find it hard to justify his freedom from guilt for what had been happening and prove that only the unlimited ambitions of an unscrupulous dictator, plus the treason of a few officers of the 10th of March movement, led the army to assume the unconstitutional, undemocratic and undignified role it is now playing.[60]

With the exposure of large numbers of soldiers to the realities of the guerrilla struggle - better-armed and more determined rebels than they had thought, humane treatment, and popular support for the guerrillas in the Sierra - the process of army demoralization quickened after the summer offensive. By the time of the last two months of fighting around major cities of Oriente, Las Villas and Camagüey provinces, the army had "completely lost its combat power. Desertions to the enemy increased daily...many towns in the hands of the enemy after the surrender of the garrisons without a single shot being fired".[61]

THE STUFF OF MYTH: MOVING
THE REVOLUTIONARY PROJECT FORWARD

In the most crucial sense, the armed struggle in the Sierra Maestra was the key to the deadlock of political consciousness in Cuba in 1957-58. Reformism's grip on M-26 urban cadres, middle-class civic organizations and the population at large, was only to be decisively loosened by the growing success of the Rebel Army. The romantic image of embattled crusaders against tyranny, engaged in a Sisyphean task predestined to ultimate defeat, had to be transformed. The cycles of repression and concession on the part of the Batista regime, its corruption, demoralization and the intrigues within its ruling circles helped to defeat reformism. The disapprovel, however intermittent and uneven, of

Washington and the United States business community in Cuba weakened the regime, especially when military aid was cut. But none of these factors actually destroyed the regime or opened the door to the "true, real revolution", as Schulz put it, a revolution "more far-reaching by far than anything that had yet been seen in Latin America, more extreme even than any program that the Cuban Communists believed either possible or desirable".[62]

Such a "true" revolution could only come about if that part of the bourgeois state apparatus which guaranteed the status quo of class and production relations was destroyed. The revolution, as Engels observed about the 1871 Commune, had to "do away with all the old repressive machinery previously used against itself".[63] In other words, the army, the police and the Guardia had to be defeated and then destroyed, or at least socially and politically transformed, which amounts to the same result in class terms, for the revolutionary project inherent in the mobilizing myths of the Rebel Army to move forward. In the language of revolutionary Marxism, it was the repressive force of the Cuban dependent capitalist order which blocked the rapid development of class contradictions, contradictions which could generate the energy necessary to realize the "total" objectives to which Schulz refers. Combat was the only experience which could provide body to the myth of a redemptive, nationalist social revolution in the Cuban context - both for the rebel fighter and for the minds dominated by reformism.

Regis Debray explored the role of combat in Revolution in the Revolution? For the rural population in which a guerrilla foco is established, the defeat of the repressive forces in their area and the arming of the population is far more effective in creating the living myth of social revolution than a political harangue: "The destruction of a troop transport truck or the public execution of a police torturer is more effective propaganda for the local population than a hundred speeches. Such conduct convinces them of the essential: that the Revolution is on the march, that the enemy is no longer invulnerable".[64] It is the idea that insurmountable obstacles to change, i.e. the presence of repressive forces guaranteeing the status quo, are permanent that combat addresses. By fighting, the revolutionary can show to himself and to the doubters that in fact such forces, the block against radical changes, are not invulnerable: "In order to destroy the idea of unassailability - that age-old accumulation of fear and humility vis-à-vis the patrono, the policeman, the guardia rural - there is nothing better than combat".[65] For it is as Debray points out: the basis of a system of repression is psychological. It is the potential of actual repression, the threat of force which lends "prestige" to the repressive forces: "This prestige constitutes the principal form of oppression: it immobilizes the discontented, silences them, leads them to swallow affronts at the mere sight of a uniform. The neocolonial ideal is still to show force in order not to have to use it, but to show it is in effect to use it".[66]

Combat in the Sierra and Relations with the Llano M-26

During the establishment of the guerrilla _foco_ in the Sierra Maestra in the first six months of 1957 and its consolidation through the rest of the year, the Rebel Army was highly dependent upon arms and supplies from the urban M-26 organizations, especially that in Santiago headed by Frank País. Such supplies and arms were intermittent in their arrival, since "the army's cordon was sometimes extremely difficult to pass",[67] and the guerrillas were forced to take new weapons in combat and to rely on the peasants for some of their supplies. But there were difficulties beyond geographic isolation and army vigilance. The urban M-26 organizations were not averse to the strategy of armed struggle, but many urban cadres thought that the fight against Batista's repressive apparatus should be concentrated in the cities. Rural guerrilla _focos_ were to play a secondary and harassing role in support of armed urban insurrection and general strike. Frank País worked diligently in Santiago to restructure the M-26 organization shattered during the November 30, 1956 uprising at the time of the _Granma_ landing. He planned to open a second guerrilla front in the Sierra Cristal of Oriente.[68] At the same time he worked to organize a civic resistance, not only in Oriente but throughout the country, to restructure the urban underground, and to prepare for a general strike, tentatively set for the fall of 1957.[69]

The plans of País and the restructuring of M-26 would clearly keep the Sierra Maestra guerrilla front in a secondary position. Castro already had to be "constantly involved in sharp discussions to get equipment to us. The only substantial shipment made to us during that first year of struggle, except for what the combatants brought with them, was the remainder of the arms used in the attack on the Palace".[70] In fact, that shipment had been destined for a Santiago group of underground fighters led by René Ramos Latour, who were to set up a second guerrila front. Castro "Opposed this idea and only allowed a few arms for the second front, giving us orders that all possible weapons be brought up to reinforce us".[71] Apparently, Castro's plan to attack El Uvero in May 1957 convinced País to release some of the weapons to the Sierra Maestra guerrillas.[72] Castro reluctantly agreed that Latour's group would attack a fortified sugar mill outside of Santiago to gather weapons, but even the arms for that foray were confiscated by the police, and M-26 organizer Faustino Pérez was arrested.[73] The attack went ahead, but was only minimally successful. A few arms were captured, but the group was forced to retreat and had to bury the arms. País criticized the disorganization and failure of Castro's <u>tropa</u> to come to their aid.[74] Those in the Sierra, on the other hand, felt vindicated in their conviction that forces should not be divided at that point in the struggle: "The correctness of his [Castro's] position was clearly demonstrated by the capture of the arms, and we devoted ourselves to fortifying the Sierra Maestra as a first step in the expansion of the guerrilla army".[75]

Retrospectively, Debray and Guevara advanced a thesis to explain the tension between the different urban and Sierra M-26 strategies of insurrection. Debray postulated that the Sierra guerrilla leaders more quickly shed their urban, petits bourgeois notions and committed what Amilcar Cabral called "class suicide", under the influence of relations with the peasants and in the heat of armed struggle. This "transubstantiation" converted the Sierra into the vanguard of the revolution: "Power is seized and held in the capital, but the road that leads the exploited to it must pass through the countryside".[76] The "process of revolutionary maturation", as Guevara called it, was much more advanced among Sierra fighters and residents. Debray cites Castro's last letter to País of July 21, 1957, wherein Castro expressed wonder at the realization of the revolutionary ideal of guerrilla-peasant unity:

> Now we are living it, we are experiencing it in every sense, and it is truly unique...here the word 'people' which is so often utilized in a vague and confused sense, becomes a living, wonderful and dazzling reality...Force cannot defeat them. It would be necessary to kill them all, to the last peasant, and that is impossible; this, the dictatorship cannot do; the people are aware of it and are daily more aware of their own growing strength.[77]

What was developing at this point was Castro's conviction that the Rebel Army <u>foco</u> in the Sierra Maestra, because of its survival, because of its confrontation with the army, and because of its revolutionary consciousness, should have the national direction of the movement. There was considerable circumstantial encouragement in the Sierra for this view. While the urban apparatus was "largely staffed by men and women of the middle class, more moderated, better educated, of higher socio-economic background", the Rebel Army was formed increasingly of "precisely those groups...who had the least stake in the existing socio-economic order and would prove most receptive to the appeals of messianism and radical change".[78] In the Sierra, Castro's personal charisma had more immediate impact, and the leaders around him, like Raúl Castro and Guevara, supported the notion that the Sierra was the vanguard: "The Sierra was already confident [in 1957] of being able to carry out the guerrilla struggle, to spread it to other places and thus, from the countryside, to encircle the cities held by the dictatorship; by strangulation and attrition to provoke the breakup of the regime".[79] In Guevara's view,

> during this stage the llano comrades constituted the majority [of M-26 national leadership' and their political background, which had not been very much influenced by the process of revolutionary maturation, led them to favor a certain type of 'civil' action, and to a kind of resistance to the caudillo they saw in Fidel and to the 'militarist' faction represented by us in the Sierra.[80]

Such differences were more acrimonious later on. The paradox is that it was precisely in the cities where the Batista forces of repression were much more in evidence and in control. Groups like the DR and the Havana M-26 were the object of brutal repression in the cities and for many llano cadres it was more important to concentrate arms, men and resources there to resist the dictatorship. This situation was what helped convince the Sierra leadership of just the opposite, that the political and military direction of the movement should be theirs. The repressive apparatus was too effective in the cities to allow successful clandestine activities. Security against infiltration was easier in the Sierra's developing territorio libre. A single military command, situated in the mountains, would avoid the dispersal of forces and resources. What was emerging was a myth of guerrilla superiority, a myth which, as it turned out, guided the Sierra leadership to a successful military campaign against the regime. Castro wrote that "the city is a cemetery of revolutionaries and resources"[81], and he campaigned throughout 1957 on the slogan "all guns, all bullets, all resources to the Sierra".[82]

In País' efforts at restructuring M-26, which included an attempt to subordinate the military struggle to an urban political directorate and the organization of a nation-wide network for the general strike, he proposed ideological definition. In a July 7, 1957 letter to Castro, he wrote he was overseeing the drafting of a program with "serious, precise, clear and attainable positions" and invited Castro's contributions.[83] This was necessary, in his opinion, because the lack of any plan since Castro's Mexico Pact with the DR (September 1956) "made people want to know the true capacity of our leaders to exert changes and to know if we deserve their trust for such ends".[84]

At the same time, forty-five civic institutions, including the Catholic Church, issued a call for a truce, government "good faith by deeds" and elections.[85] In this context, Raúl Chibás, the brother of Eddy Chibás and head of the Ortodoxos, and Felipe Pazos, a respected economist, journeyed to the Sierra Maestra.[86] They were, as Guevara remarked, "big names in the country",[87] and were in the Sierra "as a gesture, a commitment of maturity to the armed struggle".[88] After some days of discussions between the two and the Castro brothers, a "Sierra Manifesto" was issued on July 12, 1957.[89]

There are various interpretations of the discussions and manifesto. Bonachea and San Martín see the manifesto as a "coup aimed at discouraging the political and economic programs that were being drafted under Frank País' instructions",[90] a maneuver to re-assert Castro's control of M-26. Bonachea and Valdés see it similarly as a momentary alliance of Castro with Pazos and Chibás to achieve "respectability, stature and importance" and as a door to "an accommodation with old political leaders and professional groups which eventually would be converted to the idea of insurrection".[91] Thomas noted that the manifesto was "less radical than that written by Llerena in Mexico, less radical also than Castro's own statements in Mexico, certainly less radical than the proposals in History Will Absolve Me, and less radical than Pazos' lectures".[92] He concluded that the manifesto involved "dissimulation" on Castro's part. Guevara's view, colored by hindsight and the build-up of the myths of the Rebel Army, was critical and almost cynical. He had little respect for the two "troglodyte and insensitive mentalities",[93] and saw their presence as opportunism. Pazos was looking for the provisional presidency, and Chibás was of "absolute mediocrity". In Guevara's assessment, Castro had to "make efforts to make the document truly militant, to give it a basis as a declaration of principle".[94] It was a compromise document,"no more than a small halt along the way", since "we guerrillas would have to continue the fundamental task of defeating the oppressing army on the battlefield".[95]

The manifesto was to be moderate but nationalist and aimed at a popular front to be formed with other opposition forces. It called for a constitutional democratic regime to be established by elections, a civic revolutionary common front, a provisional president, non-intervention in Cuban affairs by outside powers, an end to arms shipments by the United government, reforms of the judiciary, civil service and education, and an agrarian reform with prior indemnification for landholders. Basically it was a call for unity, a rejection of elections under the Batista regime, and the instalment of the 1940 Constitution, a position much like that of Castro before Moncada. Guevara, with hindsight, saw it thusly:

> We were not satisfied with the compromise but it was necessary; at that time, it was progressive. It could not last beyond the time when it became a brake on revolutionary development, but we were willing to go along with it. By their treachery the enemy [the bourgeois opposition] helped us to break uncomfortable bonds and to show the people their true intentions. We knew that it was a minimal program, a program which limited our efforts, but we also knew that it was not possible to assert our will from the Sierra Maestra and that we had, for a long time, to count on 'friends' who tried to use our military force and the confidence which the people felt for Fidel for their own macabre devices. Above all they wanted to maintain the rule of imperialism in Cuba through its commercial bourgeoisie, which was tightly linked to the Northern masters.[96]

Only in the interstices of the document did the suggestion of a "true" revolution and the guiding myths of the Rebel Army appear. It pointed up repeatedly the role of the rebel fighters in creating a "revolutionary bulwark of the Sierra Maestra". Reference was made to the intelligence, courage and civic spirit of Cuban youth and to sacrifices made to fulfill Cuba's "high destiny", the "beautiful ideal of a free, democratic and just Cuba".

The issuance of the manifesto, unsigned by Frank País, did not halt the increasingly virulent debate with the llano. País was convinced that the low level of M-26 organization and of political consciousness in the working class regarding a general strike and armed insurrection had been overcome: "Now that situation has changed, and it is clear that a general strike is possible and necessary".[97] His conviction was unhappily proven true, at least in Oriente. The police caught up with him on July 30, 1957 and he was abruptly killed in the streets of Santiago. Demonstrations and a general strike broke out in protest, largely spontaneous. The new United States Ambassador, Earl Smith, was witness to a demonstration of women being brutally attacked by the police.[98] The strike paralyzed Santiago for nearly a week. Shops and stores remained closed. The United

States government-owned nickel mines at Nicaro were closed. Guantánamo, Holguín and other Oriente cities felt the strike. In the first week of August, some strike activity spread to Havana. Government censorship and repression ended the action after one week.[99] It had no prior planning, except for the organizational embryo of plans initiated by País. Dubois saw it as a "spontaneous expression of repudiation of daily brutality, tortures, killings and a protest against corrupt government and equally corrupt labor leaders who had become multi-millionaires within a few years, notably Eusebio Mujal, secretary-general of the Cuban Labor Confederation".[100]

Much of the M-26 national leadership in the cities, after País' untimely death, continued to concentrate their efforts on armed insurrection and a general strike. To this end, urban M-26 members collaborated with junior naval officers and Prío's Organización Auténtica (OA) in a plot to overthrow Batista via a coup and popular insurrection: "The barracks at Havana, Cienfuegos, Mariel and Santiago de Cuba were to be taken, while civilians were to attack police stations and urge the citizenry over a major radio station to go on a general strike".[101] Discontent with favoritism in the officer corps and disgust with the brutality being unleashed on the civilian population motivated many of the navy conspirators.[102]

The plans for the coup and uprising were detailed, having been initiated by navy officers after the attack on the Presidential Palace in March 1957, and elaborated for several months after.[103] The Havana and Cienfuegos M-26 organizations were involved from the beginning and were to supply hundreds of militants for the action on the morning of September 5. The army was celebrating the twenty-fourth anniversary of the 1933 "Sergeants' Revolt" and most barracks were expected to be unprepared.

From Havana, the ambitious plan was called off by several key naval officers, and all centers but Cienfuegos were notified. There, the mutineers, the OA and M-26 took the city and the military bases after several hours of fighting.[104] Censorship and a purchased press kept most of the country unaware of the uprising. Government forces attacked the city from the air and arrived in armored columns, and a bloody battle ensued. The city's population, by all accounts, had greeted the uprising enthusiastically,[105] but, despite this popular support, the revolt was crushed in a particularly brutal fashion. Taber writes of six hundred bodies "flung into a mass grave", live burials, torture, summary executions of suspects, and other atrocities.[106]

For Guevara, the tragedy of Cienfuegos was evidence of the errors of the M-26 *llano* viewpoint.[107] The leaders of the urban insurrection in Cienfuegos had not been sufficiently aware or confident of the possibilities of guerrilla struggle. Thus, they had retained their forces in the city, waiting for the army's frontal assault: "At first they were in control but they committed the tragic mistake of not heading for the Escambray mountains, only a few minutes distant from Cienfuegos, at a time when they controlled the entire city and had the means to form a solid front in the mountains".[108] Guevara echoed Castro's remark about the city as a cemetery:

> The lesson for the future is: he who has the strength dictates the strategy. Large-scale killings of civilians, repeated failures, murders committed by the dictatorship in various aspects of the struggle we have analyzed, point to guerrilla action on favorable terrain as the best expression of the technique of popular struggle against a despotic and still strong government, the least grievous for the sons of the people. After the guerrilla force was set up, we could count our losses on our fingers - comrades of outstanding courage and tenacity in battle, to be sure. But in the cities it was not only the resolute ones who died, but many among their followers who were not total revolutionaries, many who were innocent of any involvement at all. This was due to greater vulnerability in the face of repressive action.[109]

The Development of Sierra Hegemony

The Cienfuegos uprising was the culmination of Cuba's 1957 equivalent to the "long hot summer". Batista's regime was in political crisis. In the United States Congress, increasing criticism was heard in the aftermath of the Ambassador's experiences in Santiago in July and regarding Batista's use of hemispheric defense weapons to combat rebellion. United States government agencies had been aware of the uprising in Cienfuegos and approved it.[110] Sabotage and attacks on police in the cities increased, and in the Sierra the guerrillas consolidated their hold on territory. To mark the July 26 anniversary, they mounted several combat operations, halting army forays into the Sierra and descending to attack villages and outposts on the western perimeter of the Sierra.[111] Their tactics were to create a provocation or let word out of their itinerary so that government troops would approach. Operating in separate squads, the guerrillas would set ambushes for the pursuing army unit.

The fall of 1957 was characterized by the increasing military activity of the guerrillas in the Sierra and by the stepped-up urban support for the Sierra via the Civic Resistance Movement.[112] Castro took a decision to burn the 1958 sugar crop,[113] thus emulating the "incendiary task" of Máximo Gómez during the Independence War in 1895.[114] In this context, representatives of various Cuban opposition groups in exile met in Miami on October 15, 1957, to plan some co-ordination of activity. Exile leaders from the Auténticos, the Ortodoxos, FEU, DR, Directorio Obrero, Prío's OA and the M-26 were present. For M-26, Felipe Pazos, the signer of the Sierra Manifesto, and Lester Rodriguez, in charge of arms acquisitions in the United States, were semi-official representatives(the M-26 National Directorate, without informing Castro, granted vague credentials.)[115] The result of the talks was the establishment of the Junta de Liberación Cubana, ostensibly a common front. It issued a "Document of Unity of Cuban Opposition to the Batista Dictatorship" which called for a united effort to overthrow Batista, the establishment of a provisional government leading to a constitutional regime after eighteen months, and the institution of the 1940 constitution.[116] It was a mild and reformist program that was proposed in the document, not very different from the Sierra Manifesto.

In the midst of consolidating the <u>territorio libre</u> of the Sierra Maestra, and convinced that M-26 was strong enough to declare political independence, Castro rejected and denounced the Miami document. Writing to the Junta on December 14, 1957,[117] he first reminded them that the guerrillas had been fighting for nearly a year, "with no support other than the dignity with which one should fight for a cause that one loves with sincerity and conviction, a cause worth dying for".[118] The news of the Miami Pact, which "binds the future conduct of the Movement [M-26] without even the consideration of having consulted its leaders and fighters" was "highly offensive". Castro argued that no official credentials had been granted M-26 representatives in Miami to negotiate with other organizations and that no help for military operations had been forthcoming from the latter. Furthermore, the National Directorate of M-26 had not been consulted for its approval of the document before the signing. Castro was thus "confronted with an accomplished fact", since the document had been published.

Castro asserted the independence of M-26 and claimed that it was the maker of the "real Revolution", fighting in Cuba, while the leaders of the organizations in Miami "are abroad carrying out an imaginary revolution". He objected to "the sacrifice of certain principles fundamental to our conception of the Cuban Revolution". First, the failure of the document to condemn "any kind of foreign intervention in the internal affairs of Cuba is evidence of lukewarm patriotism and a self-evident act of cowardice". The document had called for an end to arms shipments, butthis was not sufficient for Castro. He also ojbected to the failure of the document to refuse any kind of "provisional military rule".

By the time the Miami document was signed, Castro and the guerrillas were convinced by experience that they were a revolutionary vanguard. As such, the "M-26 claims for itself the function of maintaining public order and reorganizing the armed forces of the Republic". Castro rejected the Miami document's proposal that "revolutionary forces" be incorporated into the existing armed forces. By experience, the guerrillas had come to one of Engels' laws of social revolution in the age of capitalism: the priority of the replacement of the repressive apparatus. The Rebel Army and M-26 militias, argued Castro, should be the effective maintainers of order, and ensurers of justice, because of their record of struggle, their discipline and morale, and their treatment of army prisoners and wounded.

Castro then launched into a criticism of the Junta's lack of a military strategy. He considered the Junta as controlled by the Auténticos and prone to urban putschism. The Junta had underestimated the importance of the role of the guerrilla struggle in the Sierra and had not understood the "state of absolute rebellion" in the countryside of Oriente. He intimated that the old-line politicians in Miami wished only a new division of the spoils of public office in Cuba, and stockpiled arms while the guerrillas and peasants desperately needed them.

Because of this ignorance of the real struggle and for suspicion of the motives behind the Miami meeting, Castro rejected any direction of the military struggle from outside the mountains:

> The leadership of the struggle against the tyranny is and will continue to be in the hands of the revolutionary fighters in Cuba...exiles should cooperate in this struggle, but it is absurd for anyone to try to tell us from abroad what peak we should take, what sugar-cane fields we should burn, what sabotage we should carry out, or at what moment, in what circumstances and in what form we should call a general strike.[119]

Castro called for support of M-26 actions by the Junta and for co-ordination of "specific plans and concrete acts". The general strike plans by the M-26 should be joined by all in a non-partisan fashion.

Finally, Castro turned to plans for the provisional government. It was to be non-partisan, reconstitute the judicial system, and be headed by a judge of the Oriente

Appeals Court, Dr. Manuel Urrutia Lleó. This was a surto the Junta, which had been considering Pazos. The right of selection was justified because "only M-26" had been consistently active in the struggle and because the civic organizations had been slow to name someone. If necessary, the M-26 would continue to fight alone.

Castro's rejection of the Miami document caused confusion and uproar in the Junta. The DR, which had mounted a sabotage and execution campaign, tried to assassinate Batista and lost many fighters, was infuriated at Castro's claim that M-26 alone had created conditions of revolt. Faure Chomón, the DR leader and representative in Miami, wrote to Castro recalling DR co-operation and sacrifices in struggle, and condemning the "coup de grace against the revolutionary unity achieved in Miami".[120] Some Auténticos, Manuel "Tony" de Varona and Enrique Cotubanaba Henriquez, replied that the Granma had been purchased with Prío's money.[121] But the outcome was the virtual dissolution of the Junta de Liberación.

Military Consolidation and Political Formation in the Sierra Maestra

As Castro had written to the Junta, the fall of 1957 was marked by the growing frequency of combat encounters, until a "state of armed truce with Batista" was achieved: "His men did not go up into the Sierra and ours hardly ever went down".[122] After months of consolidating relations with the peasantry and establishing revolutionary order in the Sierra, the Rebel Army had taken to using its expanded numbers to attack army columns and outposts. Action was what many fighters desired: "Fighting was not the thing. The hardest thing was to gain the physical endurance you had to have for the hard life in the Sierra. There was sufficient morale for combat and that for us was like a caramel. It was the easiest thing and the sweetest in the Sierra".[123] Combat was a chance to earn a weapon, to interrupt the constant marches, to ignore hunger, and to attack the enemy: "Ché, when he saw that morale was getting low, he'd arrange an attack. It seemed like the people would forget their hunger with shooting. A few shots and withdraw, get away from the casquitos 'little helmets'."[124]

It was in this period that the Rebel Army, as young and as small as it was, could come to say that it had a tradition. Castro referred to the "army in active service with over twenty victories over the enemy"[125] in his letter to the Junta. These experiences had produced martyrs, from the day of the landing when Antonio Ñico López and others were killed, to the encouter at Mar Verde in late November, when Ciro Redondo, one of the Moncada originals, was killed. A number of fighters were wounded in these encounters, such as Guevara, Juan Almeida and Joel Iglesias, the teen-age Lieutenant, with consequent scars attesting to battle experience. The Rebel Army honored its martyrs by naming new columns after them, just as later schools, hospitals and factories were to bear their names. Within the Rebel Army itself, the martyred were held up as examples of morale and sacrifice. Thus, in one of the early numbers of El Cubano Libre,[126] the Rebel Army newspaper begun by Guevara, Ciro Redondo was eulogized:

> Ciro Redondo is dead; in him the Revolution has lost one of its most valiant captains. A very brave man, daring and with initiative, he fell like those of his kind: heroically. Untiring fighter, he helped in the last five years to organize and took part in the assault on Moncada, suffered prison and the bitterness of exile, where he was jailed for his love of Cuban freedom. A disciplined fighter, he captured the admiration and sympathy of the men under his command by his bravery and decisions in combat, where he was always in the first line.[127]

The eulogy centered first on his dedication, effectiveness and bravery, and then took up the theme of a struggle by the humildes for the humildes (the poor and exploited):

> Of humble extraction, he knew and felt the needs of his people, the urgency of struggle, to live and suffer, and if necessary, to die in order to give bread to the hungry, work to the unemployed, culture to the illiterate and above all, to die so that Cuba would not wait for a solution from abroad, so that could feel and be truly free and independent.[128]

All the elements of the revolutionary myth, of a social revolution with "total objectives", one which would redeem Cuba's past and fulfill the destiny Martí and all Cuban revolutionaries had envisioned, are contained in this short excerpt. Ciro Redondo is told posthumously that his comrades, "from the field of battle", will make his dreams reality and his death not in vain. Such deaths were bitter experiences for the small Rebel Army, which lived and fought in close quarters. Redondo's body was found mutilated, some days after the battle, which increased the impact of his loss. His example was used to contrast, again, the two morales: "The captains of the people die at the head of their troops and not hiding behind a human wall of recruits [a reference to Sánchez Mosquera]".[129]

The combats also produced heroes, whose exploits were recognized by promotion, the award of the better captured arms,[130] and by new assignments. A reputation for skill and valor was building up, within the Rebel Army itself, among the rural population, in the towns and cities of the llano, and among Batista's troops. The Rebel Army constantly compared itself to the Mambises, both in El Cubano Libre and in the political education of the tropa. The military techniques of the Mambises under Gómez and Maceo were emulated. The leaders, especially Castro and Cienfuegos, read and reread Martí and chronicles of the struggle for independence, such as those by Manuel de la Cruz and Jorge Mañach.[131] Both the burning of the cane-fields and the invasion of the central and western provinces from guerrilla strongholds in Oriente were features of the War of Independence. Castro reminded the American reporter, Andrew St. George, that "once before, Cubans burned their cane, razed their very towns, to wrest freedom from Spain".[132] And in his order to Camilo Cienfuegos regarding the invasion westward which began in August 1958, the column was named "Antonio Maceo" to honor "the glorious warrior of Independence".[133] Cienfuegos addressed his tropa before their departure: "Remember that this task was already carried out once by the Bronze Titan [Maceo]. Thus it is our obligation to fulfill this duty".[134]

Thus, by the end of 1957, the Rebel Army, inspired in its formation by a set of mobilizing myths which drew upon Cuban history and upon the experiences and perceptions of the combatants, had begun to build its own myth, that of the guerrillas as revolutionary vanguard. Its elements were superior morale and discipline, the overcoming of physical hardship, unity with the peasantry, the need to defeat the army, and the implementation of reforms. The very survival of the infant guerrilla force itself became legendary, a common motif in the political education of new recruits[135] and in propaganda aimed at llano M-26 comrades and at the population in general. The combat exploits of the rebels, especially their ability to outwit and confront units superior in numbers and weaponry, became part of the myth of the invincible guerrillas. Likewise, the development of military/political leaders such as Guevara, Cienfuegos, Raúl Castro and René Ramos Latour gave a personalist attractiveness to the rebel force.

Armed with its young tradition, its sense of history and a belief that it was the revolutionary vanguard, the Rebel Army moved from the breakdown of the Junta de Liberación to increased confrontations with the Batista army in 1958. They spent much of the late fall of 1957 and the winter of 1957-58 in a "sedentary, fixed-encampment period"[136], one of consolidation. It was a period of more settled camp life, with radio news broadcasts heard in the morning, often with Castro's political monologues following some commentary, a meal and a day-long march.[137] Castro's permanent headquarters were set up at La Plata, high on the southern Sierra slopes, in a bohío, where "a constant stream of messengers coming and going, visitors from the cities arriving for political consultations, unit commanders reporting for orders, underground leaders requiring instructions, all occupied him from early morning until far into the night".[138] Guevara established his permanent camp during this period at La Mesa and began publishing El Cubano Libre, setting up Radio Rebelde and training new recruits for the coming expansion of hostilities.

Both the school for recruits at Las Minas del Prío and El Cubano Libre deserve some comment, since they were vehicles of political education for the tropa and since they form part of the myth of the guerrillas as political vanguard. El Cubano Libre was conceived to be a weapon which would cut through government censorship and broadcast "the existence of our troops and their fighting determination...throughout the Republic."[139] El Cubano Libre, begun in November 1957, with a mimeograph laboriously brought into the Sierra, was edited at first by Guevara, and later by Luís Orlando Rodriguez, a guerrilla comandante, and Carlos Franqui, a Havana journalist. Two students from Havana, Gionel Rodriguez and Ricardo Medina, assisted.[140] El Cubano Libre was of small circulation (six hundred) and was often difficult to read ("You had to read it by day or by a bright lantern at night"; "If you did not have good eyesight you couldn't understand it very well".)[141]

The paper was meant for the rebel soldiers, first of all, and "for our people, the organizations of that time, the M-26 and all organizations which were fighting against the regime".[142] It was read to the illiterate rebel soldiers and smuggled down into the towns around the Sierra. The tone of its editorials, often written by Guevara, was militant and ironic. Its first edition announced "the beginning of the end of the tyranny", despite the crushing of the Cienfuegos uprising. The Sierra had served as the "unbreachable bulwark against the mercenary army" and the Rebel Army was now readying itself to expand into the plains. This expansion would be based on the burning of the sugar crop - "which will weaken the economic roots of the regime" - and a general revolutionary strike - "which will be the final blow and signify victory over the repressive forces". The Sierra counted on mass support for sugar sabotage; otherwise it could not succeed, and indeed, after protests by canecutters the burning of fields was halted in favor of the burning of warehouses. This action would be downstream of the livelihood of cane-cutters.[143] In referring to the general strike, El Cubano Libre urged the urban resistance to organize "in the closest detail, fitting the distinct class interests to the great revolutionary truth: there is nothing worse than Batista. All united to defeat him...no spontaneous or partial strike; it will be organized, general and revolutionary; it will be victory".[144] Like the sugar sabotage, the general strike was not carried out fully in 1958. The general revolutionary strike only came about after Batista's flight on January 1, 1959.[145]

The internationalism and anti-imperialism of Guevara were evident in his contributions to El Cubano Libre. Under his pseudonym Francotirador 'Sniper', "Sharpshooter', he posed the spectacle of United States animal-lovers protesting the Soviet use of dogs in space against the lack of demonstrations about attacks on Cuban peasants with United States-supplied planes and weapons: "Is a Siberian dog worth more than one thousand Cuban guajiros?"[146] In the January 1958 issue, Francotirador drew attention to Cuban media coverage of "disorders and deaths" in Cyprus, Algeria and Malaya. All the events were similar in that each government "inflicted numerous casualties on the rebels", there were no prisoners taken, and "communist aid to the rebels" was certain. "How Cuban the world seems! Everything is the same", he responded, "they kill a group of patriots, whether they are armed' or not...and call them communists".[147]

El Cubano Libre was followed by Surco in Raúl Castro's Segundo Frente "Frank País", by Patria, published in the Escambray Mountains after Guevara arrived there, and by Milicianos, aimed at the popular militia which was organized by M-26 in Las Villas province. They were all aimed at militancy and the political education of Rebel Army and M-26 members. They reported on military encounters, losses, deaths and victories. They included articles on socio-economic groups like the peasantry of the Sierra Maestra, on revolutionary programs like agrarian reform, and on particularly brutal individuals in the Batista forces, like Sánchez Mosquera and Fermín Cowley. The tone was uncompromising: "No Zafra [cane harvest] with Batista", "This insane executioner of the usurper regime made up of a gang of vulgar killers who have taken over the civil and military command of the nation". There was the conviction of ultimate victory: "There is no repressive organization which can defeat it [a general strike] when it is carried out in an organized and enthusiastic fashion", "...everywhere, as in Cuba, against brute force and injustice the people will have the last word, that of victory".[148]

The school for recruits, which trained them for the summer offensive by the army, and which prepared cadres to lead the expected invasion of the llanos, was set up by Guevara at Minas del Frío at the request of Castro. The director was Capitán Evelio Lafferté, a recent graduate of the army's Academy, captured in his first engagement: "He expected at least to be tortured. But little by little, he was convinced we were not as his officers had said".[149] The school dealt with basics, from March to May 1958: recruits from the llano often did not know how to shoot, to march through the mountains, or to set up ambushes: "All the young recruits that we could not incorporate for lack of arms go to the school. They are submitted to a regimen of strict discipline and severe training. We hope to get some good officers out of them in a short time".[150]

In addition to new recruits, fighters and officers were selected from all rebel units and sent to Minas del Frío. This produced the paradox pointed out by Lafferté: "It bothered us [there was another army deserter there as instructor in addition to several effective Rebel Army commanders] to be instructing people who had been defeating us, when we were on the other side...we felt somewhat demoralized to be teaching people who in practice had shown that, though they had not studied in a school, they knew tactics instinctively".[151]

The school at Minas del Frío was a harsh experience. There was little food and, when it was available, it was often limited to black beans and cans of condensed milk. Guevara imposed a very strict discipline with a fixed schedule, though the latter was impossible to maintain. Conditions were harsh enough to produce some desertions and some dismissals. Batista's air force discovered the encampment early on, which the fighters and recruits had to build themselves, and the school was submitted to daily air attacks for more than two months. This produced what Guevara called pendejitis aguda 'acute cowardice', which he could not stand; it served as the "best purifier of our Rebel Army".[152] At times, the students were called upon to join some combat in which the main columns were involved.

Guevara and Comandante Moisés Pérez, an experienced fighter, took on the task of ideological instruction and the introduction of reading skills to the largely illiterate group. It consisted mainly of commentaries on the radio news, the reading and discussion of El Cubano Libre, and talks on the history of the M-26 movement, relations with the peasants, Cuban history, and agrarian reform. The harsh experience of the camp helped to produce the discipline necessary to withstand the large-scale offensive of Batista's forces starting in May and finally defeated in August. As Guevara recalled, "between the educational task, the political education, and the lesson of the bombs, we were educated for victory. We all forged ourselves there, we learned to see the enemy for the weakness he suffered despite his strengths; we understood that there were things more important than arms; there were forces stronger than the force of arms; that victory would be of the people; our morale grew in those days".[153]

Shift in the Balance of Forces

With the raids along the Manzanillo-Bayamo highway,[154] attacks on the Veguitas barracks,[155] and the February elimination of one of the last remaining army posts in the Sierra at Pino del Agua,[156] all occurring after the new year, the Rebel Army moved into a stage of expansion. As Marzo Orozco put it, "at the beginning of 1958 things changed. Then it was we who pursued the *guardias*. In 1957 we were not looking for them, but running from them. In 1958 it got to the point where if someone came to the *guardias* asking for permission to go into the Sierra, they would say: 'we give permission up to the river; beyond that, you will have to get it from the rebels'".[157]

From the Sierra, there came a flood of statements and propaganda against the regime, which was experiencing great problems of legitimacy domestically and abroad. New interviews with United States journalists, especially those by Andrew St. George, were published.[158] Under United States pressure, and encouraged by the dissolution of the Miami Junta de Liberación, Batista relaxed censorship.[159] Castro planned the attack on the Pino del Agua barracks because he felt "it was important to strike a resounding blow to take advantage of the fact that censorship had now been lifted".[160]

The dictatorship, though the Junta had collapsed in Miami, was facing renewed opposition domestically; its measures of repression and terror were producing revulsion among civic institutions. Members of the business community joined the Civic Resistance Movement, a front organization of the M-26.[161] Lawyers began to file writs to have political prisoners released. The Church hierarchy entered the fray, issuing a statement on February 28 which condemned the violence and called for a government of national unity.[162]

Preparing to launch new columns towards northern Oriente under Raúl Castro and towards Santiago under Juan Almeida, Castro responded to the Catholic statement. In a letter to a radio station,[163] he rejected any participation in Batista's "Conciliation Commission", which had been set up in response to the Church protest: did the Church hierarchy "consider it possible that any dignified and self-respecting Cuban is disposed to sit down in a Council of Ministers presided over by Fulgencio Batista?" He asked the Church to clarify what it meant by a "government of national unity" and asked for Cuban reporters to be allowed into the Sierra. He also announced that M-26 was about to launch "the final watchwords of the struggle".

There was a flurry of civic opposition activity in March. First came the Episcopate's appeal for a political solution. Then, a number of judges and magistrates sent a letter of protest to the Havana Court of Appeals: "The administration of justice has never been so mocked, ridiculed and abused as it has been recently". Judges had been attacked and prisoners killed, while gambling and prostitution flourished, they wrote, and measures to restore order were mandatory.[164]

Finally, and as a result of Batista's actions, a large number of civic institutions, ranging from professional associations to the Church and fraternal lodges, called for the "termination of the regime and the abdication of those in executive power and the dissolution of Congress".[165] Authors of the document had to flee the police squads after its publication.[166]

A proclamation was issued at this time from the Sierra Maestra. "Total War Against the Tyranny",[167] discussed in a previous chapter, resulted from a meeting of the M-26 national directorate in the Sierra. It confirmed the strategy of general strike backed by military action. Increased sabotage and harassment of highways and communications in Oriente, plus the activities of the new front in northern Oriente, were to support the general strike and bring down the dictatorship.

THE GENERAL STRIKE AND SUMMER OFFENSIVE

There is debate as to whether Castro actually thought a general strike would succeed. Thomas writes that "it is obscure whether Castro really wanted this strike, and it has been said, without evidence, that Faustino Peréz, then effectively in control of M-26 outside the Sierra, brought pressure on him to do it."[168] Nonetheless, various statements from the Sierra had all included reference to a general strike. The first number of El Cubano Libre, for example, had specifically referred to a strike, as had Castro's "Letter to the Junta de Liberación". Bonachea and San Martín maintain that, indeed, the strike was demanded by the Sierra rebel leaders and impressed upon the llano M-26, which was unsure.[169] Guevara implied that the guerrillas were reluctant to see a general strike for fear it would be improperly organized in the cities, but that they wholeheartedly supported the strike when it occurred.[170] The issue is perhaps not whether the guerrillas wanted a strike, but whether they wanted the one which occurred.

What seems certain is that the March 7-10, 1958 meetings of the M-26 National Directorate in the Sierra decided for the widening and radicalization of the struggle against the dictatorship. The urban representatives were impressed with the gains and confidence of the guerrillas. They endorsed the March 12 manifesto declaring "total war". For their part, the guerrillas were not fully counting on a general strike to be successful. Debray writes that the strike was "one of the few actions that the city was able to propose and impose",[171] and that the guerrillas were wary. They "agreed...and collaborated in all good faith and to the utmost of their ability", but Castro wrote a letter on March 23, 1958, in which he expressed both his doubts about the strike and his confidence in the guerrillas' capacity to fight: "If he [Batista] succeeds in crushing the strike, nothing would be resolved. We would continue to struggle and within six months his situation would be worse".[172] The strike, then, would be an opportunity for an early overthrow of Batista, and at least a major coordination of efforts between the guerrillas and the llano. Pressure in the cities would enable the guerrillas to make more strikes from their Sierra bases.

There was some doubt among urban cadres about the extent of preparedness and organization in the cities, expressed by René Ramos Latour, País' successor. Santiago and Oriente were well-enough organized for the strike, but as it turned out, Havana and other areas were not properly prepared. The government spent time, effort and money preparing itself for the confrontation. Batista declared a state of emergency and assumed absolute powers in all areas of government. The police were essentially given carte blanche to exercise all force they deemed necessary. Seven thousand new soldiers were recruited. Decrees were issued purging judges who might act against Batista's unleashed police. Arms were purchased from Somoza and Trujillo after the United States embargo was imposed.[173] Workers were authorized to kill to defend the right not to strike.[174] New patrol cars for the cities were imported by the hundreds and army troops transferred to police control. A hard-line officer, Pilar García, was given the command of the national police in Havana. Almost unnoticed was Batista's announcement of the postponement of elections until November 3, 1958.[175]

Batista was confident that the strike would be crushed easily.[176] It seems that he considered the urban militants and sabotage as irritating but not powerful, as they had no real control over the unions. The Frente Obrero Nacional, Frank País' creation, "had very few organized cells within the labor movement and [was used] mainly as a propaganda channel...not as an arm of revolutionary action and organization within the working class".[177] M-26 had more influence among the urban middle class and within Protestant circles,[178] while the CTC, headed by Eusebio Mujal, Batista's man, refused to endorse the strike. Mujal had said in December 1957 that workers had no need to strike, since Batista had raised minimum wages: "As long as I live there will be no general strike".[179] The communists, with a base of minority support in the labor movement, seem to have vacillated. Thomas writes that they were initially willing to join the strike, but were rejected by M-26 urban cadres, especially in Havana.[180] On the day of the strike, April 9, most communists in Havana did not join it, and they later denounced the "unilateral call" issued by Faustino Pérez.[181]

The strike itself was a fiasco, more of an uprising than a work stoppage. The police, Masferristas and SIM were waiting to rush to work places and cruise the streets to attack those who struck.[182] The strike had been called one hour before the agreed time, noon, when a two-hour break would release workers and close stores and banks. Urban fighters were thus in action in the streets, attempting to capture weapons and engage in sabotage, while workers were still in work places. Street fighting did not encourage them to come out. There was a great lack of arms, and far too few M-26 militants were actually mobilized, available and in action. Meetings the night before had decided that organization was lacking, but that bravery and sacrifice should be demonstrated.[183] When the strike call came, communications lapses and tight security limited the actual receipt of the call. In essence, the strike or, rather, uprising, was crushed swiftly and brutally. Some two thousand patrol cars and commandeered private vehicles patrolled the streets, gunning down strikers, militants and students. Prisoners were not to be taken and summary executions were carried out all day in Havana and other cities.[184] In Santiago, the strike lasted five days, but also ended in defeat and repression.

In the Sierra, the rebels apparently did not know the exact date of the strike. Jorge Masetti, in Castro's camp when the news of the strike came, reported that there was jubilation and quick orders for attacks and ambushes were given.[185] Bonachea and San Martín claim that Castro had promised major attacks on cities from the Sierra, but that the bulk of the guerrillas never moved.[186] Camilo Cienfuegos, at the head of a small unit, was engaged in sabotage and harassing attacks near Bayamo, the first guerrilla incursions into the llano,[187] and Guevara claimed that "the revolutionary commanders...not able to prevent the strike...went to the llano to help out".[188] However, Raúl Castro, in his campaign diary, wrote that "faced with a general strike movement there was little we could do militarily except to offer moral support in a given zone".[189]

Interpretations of the strike of April 9, 1958, then, can be reduced to two. On the one hand, Bonachea and San Martín intimate that Castro feared a military coup in the cities, with an alliance of the urban M-26 and disaffected officers, and that Castro also feared that political hegemony of the M-26 would remain in the hands of the urban M-26.[190] The unspoken suggestion is that the guerrillas coldly promoted the strike and allowed the near-destruction of urban M-26 organizations in order to consolidate their hold on the movement. Yet, Bonachea and San Martín assume that Castro and all M-26 strategists, even those in the cities, expected the strike, urban uprising and guerrilla actions in Oriente to produce a general uprising with thousands joining the revolutionaries for the final confrontation: "This was the sort of revolutionary outcome envisioned".[191] On the other hand, Debray and Guevara argue that the general strike idea emanated from the urban M-26, that the guerrillas endorsed it through the error of "subjectivism", and that they collaborated in good faith, though they were limited in their actions by army strength and the lack of arms and fighters. If the guerrillas were counting on urban M-26 support for money, arms and supplies (and one reason advanced for the lack of arms for the urban cadres in April was that for several months they had been sending everything to the Sierra)[192] they would hardly have wished the urban M-26 to be dealt a fatal blow.

The outcome of the strike, though, was the severe weakening of the urban M-26 organizations, though they were not eliminated and played a crucial role in Las Villas and Matanzas provinces in the last weeks of fighting in 1958. The movement as a whole suffered a setback, and Batista prepared to enter the Sierra in force to destroy the guerrilla _foco_. At a time when the guerrillas in northern Oriente and in the Sierra were achieving some successes at expanding their forces by capturing weapons from the army and the _Guardia_, and receiving increased support from the urban M-26, the army was preparing to cut off their raiding and the failure of the strike limited the supplies to be sent from the cities.

In a meeting on May 3, 1958, the M-26 held a post-mortem in the Sierra. Guevara reported that the meeting was the definitive end of _llano_ leadership of the M-26.[193] The _llano_ was accused of having underestimated the regime's strength and forces and overestimating its own. Representatives of the FON, the M-26 labor organization, were criticized for having opposed PSP participation (though betrayals of M-26 militants during the strike vindicated their suspicion of the PSP).[194] The _llano_ was also accused of putschism and subjectivism. David Salvador, ex-communist and sugar worker, head of the FON, was held responsible for the exclusion of other workers' organizations from the planning of the strike.

Faustino Pérez was faulted for an overblown belief that his few, poorly-equipped and inexperienced urban militia could take and hold Havana. And René Ramos Latour was called to task for leading inexperienced militia in Santiago. All were criticized for having become used to urban tactics and applying them as the only possible methods for overthrowing Batista. Pérez and Salvador were relieved of their positions and Castro took direct command of the militias. Ñico Torres was directed to work with the PSP on planning another general strike, which he accepted reluctantly (Bonachea and San Martín claim that urban M-26 cadres saw the PSP as "to the right of Batista" and untrustworthy, rather than ideological anathema).[195] This co-operation signified more a change in attitude on the part of the PSP than an M-26 embrace of the PSP. After a visit to the Sierra in May by Carlos Rafael Rodriguez and Osvaldo Sánchez of the PSP, militants of that party increasingly joined the Rebel Army. They collaborated with the M-26 in the cities where possible, and even established their own guerrilla foco in Las Villas province, after the police burned some houses of PSP members in Yaguajay.[196]

The political outcome of the meetings was summed up by Guevara:

> The war would be conducted militarily and politically by Fidel in his double commission as Comandante-in-Chief of all forces and as Secretary-General of the Organization. The Sierra line would be followed, that of direct armed struggle, extending it to other regions and controlling the country by that means; ending some ingenuous illusions of pretended revolutionary general strikes, when the situation had not matured sufficiently to produce an explosion of that type and without preparatory work for an action of such magnitude...It was nothing more than the formalization of a reality, the political hegemony of the Sierra, a consequence of its correct position and interpretation of the facts.[197]

Debray put it more bluntly: "Thus it devolved on the Sierra to save the Revolution which had been imperilled by the city. With the failure of the strike, after it was proven to all that only the Sierra could save the Revolution, it was logical that the Sierra would assume the responsibility of leadership".[198]

The myth of the invincible guerrillas was solidified in the defeat of Batista's summer offensive. The small Rebel Army, which at that time numbered no more than four hundred,[199] defeated Batista forces variously estimated at from forty-five hundred[200] to twelve thousand.[201] The government plan was to blockade the Sierra, force the rebels away from the heights, and destroy them

between the mountains and the sea. Seven thousand new
casquitos were recruited, most of them peasants who
joined, according to Bonachea and San Martín, "because
they were better off in the barracks than cutting cane
three or four months a year and being unemployed the
rest".[202] The army spent millions on new equipment, including tanks and half-tracks, and on helicopters for
mountain assaults.[203] With artillery, naval and air support, and masses of troops, the idea was to overwhelm
the rebels.

Even so, the characteristics of the "mercenary" army which were discussed by Guevara and Castro prevented
an effective command structure and military efficiency.
Batista divided the command between the bickering generals del Río Chaviano and Eulogio Cantillo. In addition, though Cantillo was nominally in charge of the
offensive, his request for twenty-four battalions was
cut by Batista to only fourteen. The remaining troops
were to guard the coffee and sugar crops, latifundios of
Batista supporters, and to provide escort service for
the same.[204] The morale of the troops suffered as a result of this divided and uncooperative command structure. The lack of training and experience was felt
among the fresh recruits as they faced the experienced
guerrillas. Their morale was further lowered as the underground movements, including virtually all the resistance organizations, mounted a campaign of propaganda
and terror to harass them before they left the urban
centers for the Sierra.[205]

The Rebel Army itself was preparing for the defense
of the Sierra. For two months or more, recruits and veterans were trained in sniping, ambushes, marching, anti-aircraft defense, and reconnaissance (as at the Minas
del Frío school); caches of food and medicines were established and herds of cattle expropriated from latifundios were kept ready against the expected blockade.[206]
The corps of peasant messengers was supplemented by the
constant marching of the rebels across the mountains and
ravines of the Sierra, as they familiarized themselves
with the area, so that every movement of Batista's
troops could be reported quickly. New field hospitals
were prepared and several doctors joined the rebels after Radio Rebelde broadcast appeals.[207]

The actual offensive, which covered some seventy-
six days, has been thoroughly chronicled by Bonachea and
San Martín.[208] The army did what the guerrillas expected. The latter were prepared to withdraw in successive
stages, tightening their defenses with each stage, ambushing army columns and inflicting as many casualties
as possible. With the exception of the Segundo Frente
under Raúl Castro, all the columns were brought together
in the western Sierra Maestra. Castro impressed upon
the guerrillas the importance of the defeat of the of-

fensive for the future of the insurrection. He displayed his usual faith and optimism:

> This offensive will be the longest of all. After its failure, Batista will be irredeemably lost; he knows it and therefore will make the maximum effort. This is a decisive battle which is being waged precisely in the territory best known by us. We are adopting a series of measures destined to guarantee 1) organized resistance; 2) the draining and exhaustion of the adversary army; 3) the conjunction of elements and sufficient weapons to throw ourselves on the offensive as soon as they begin to weaken....The thing is to know how to make the resistance stronger each time, and this will be accomplished to the degree that they lengthen their lines and we fall back toward strategic positions. As we consider it possible that at some points they will be able to flank the Maestra, in the enclosed document we communicate the precise instructions for each case. The fundamental objectives of this plan are 1) to ready a basic territory where the organization, hospitals, shops and so forth will function; 2) to maintain Radio Rebelde on the air, a factor of utmost importance; 3) to offer the enemy greater resistance each time as we concentrate troops and occupy the most strategic points from which to launch the counterattack.[209]

The army began its pincer movement on May 24, advancing from the north; units later moved in from the south and eventually rebel territory was reduced to a tiny enclave of some four square miles.[210] Backed by what Bonachea and San Martin regard as the superb organizational efforts of Guevara ("Guevara's communications system, plus his careful preparation throughout the campaign of arms factories, field hospitals, arms depots, trenches, maps, codes and a myriad of important details making guerrilla warefare possible...")[211] the guerrillas mounted effective ambushes and counter-attacks throughout the summer. Mines and snipers would disable and halt vanguard platoons and armored vehicles, throwing columns into confusion and retreat. Constant mobility created the impression of larger numbers than were actually there, and enabled the guerrillas to avoid entrapment. All but one of the skirmishes were fought on terrain and at a time selected by the guerrillas.

One month into the campaign, on June 28, the first decisive victory occurred. An entire battalion was destroyed in a series of ambushes and assaults, resulting in casualties, prisoners and quantities of captured equipment.[212] The guerrillas immediately used the captured arms to increase their firepower.

That Radio Rebelde functioned throughout the summer was a psychological advantage noted by Castro. Nightly broadcasts by Radio Rebelde, Radio Caracas, and short-wave transmitters in Mexico and Miami were proof of guerrilla capacity to survive and struggle, even prevail, and inspired a campaign of sabotage and attacks on police in the cities, carried out by a united urban resistance. Remnants of M-26, the DR and the OA cooperated. In July, a unity Manifesto,[213] signed in Caracas with Castro's direct approval, signalled a revived broad resistance front, reflecting the co-operation of various organizations in the streets and in the mountains. It recognized the existence and contributions of DR, OA and PSP guerrilla _focos_ in Santa Clara, the Escambray Mountains, and in Pinar del Río province: "In each corner of Cuba, a struggle to the death is taking place between freedom and the dictatorship".

Frustrated in the north, the army landed a battalion on the south coast in an attempt to move the guerrillas off the heights. It was this battalion which was led by Major José Quevedo Pérez, whom Castro had known, as described in the last chapter; the operation was defeated and the battalion surrendered.[214] The Rebel Army capitalized on this victory by delivering large numbers of prisoners to the Red Cross. This, combined with Raúl Castro's kidnapping of United States nationals and Marines to protest the use of United States arms by Batista, further damaged Batista's hold on the country. Money began to flow into M-26 coffers, increasingly from the business community, industrialists and planters.

By the end of July, though not defeated, the army commanders were less sanguine about the possibilites of the offensive. General Cantillo reported to the general staff that the rebels were "very well-trained troops" numbering between one and two thousand.[215] The guerrillas had the support of "almost every inhabitant of the mountains...who act as informers and messengers". The army, on the other hand, was more than seventy-five percent "second rate", with "extremely low" morale:

> Awareness that there is no strong penalty against those who surrender or betray their unit, and that falling prisoner to the enemy ends all their problems, has sapped the will to fight through the ranks...the number of self-inflicted wounds is extraordinarily high. It is necessary to punish troops refusing to advance and to occupy their positions.

The army was disintegrating and the long-established rebel policy of humane treatment of wounded and captured soldiers was paying off. The army could not prevent the soldiers from knowing of such treatment, by the middle of the campaign.

In only one battle, that of Las Mercedes,[216], did the guerrillas suffer numerous losses. In an attempt to capture the hated Sánchez Mosquera, the rebels moved down to an exposed area. There, they took heavy casualties and it required brilliant efforts by Guevara's and Cienfuegos' units to avert disaster and the possible capture of Castro. Here, some army officers approached Castro to discuss a possible military revolt against Batista. Castro used the meetings, which lasted three days, to extricate the bulk of his forces from the trap.

After Las Mercedes, in early August, the army withdrew entirely from the Sierra, leaving great amounts of arms and material. It had been a disaster, though government censorship concealed its extent. Castro went on Radio Rebelde on August 18 and 19 to broadcast a detailed report of the campaign.[217] It was a long report filled with figures on units attacked, weapons seized and casualties incurred on both sides. It called on the ranks of the army to revolt, but warned that "if the coup is the work of opportunistic military men whose objective is to salvage their interest and look for a way out, the best possible one for the tyranny's coterie, we are resolutely opposed to such a coup".[218] Castro warned that six more months of fighting would find the army totally disintegrated. The rebels would "await the reply on the march. The rebel columns will advance in all directions toward the rest of the national territory, with nothing and no one being able to stop us...the people must ready themselves to help our fighters". He ended the broadcast with a quote from Maceo. "The revolution will be marching as long as there remains one injustice uncorrected".[219]

Without relinquishing the mobilizing revolutionary myths rooted in Cuban history and the brief life of the M-26, the Rebel Army was now its own myth. The heroic guerrilla, the martyrs resulting from twenty months of guerrilla struggle, the unity of peasants and guerrillas, agrarian reform and revolutionary justice, the ascendancy of the guerrillas as political and military vanguard; all these elements had been created through the experience of struggle in the Sierra Maestra. They sustained the drive into the plains and cities in the last four months of 1958, penetrating the consciousness of a growing number of Cubans and providing a reservoir of myths for the formation of the larger Rebel Army and the Revolutionary Armed Forces.

NOTES

1. Thomas, p. 1038.
2. Harnecker, pp. xv-xvi.
3. See Aguilar, Cuba 1933, p. 160.
4. Domínguez, p. 126.
5. Thomas, pp. 884-5.
6. E.g. those led by Rafael García Bárcena, April 1953; Ramón Barquín, April 1956; and the Cienfuegos naval mutiny, September 1957.
7. Thomas, pp. 884-5.
8. Ibid., p. 840.
9. Ibid., p. 852.
10. Carleton Beals, Great Guerrilla Warriors (Englewood Cliffs: Prentice-Hall, 1970), p. 205.
11. Thomas, p. 1039.
12. See Bonachea and San Martín, pp. 104-5, on the social composition of the Batista army.
13. Vilma Espín, in Franqui, The Twelve, p. 181.
14. Beals, p. 205.
15. Guevara, Reminiscences, p. 148.
16. Guevara, in Cuba Internacional, p. 90.
17. Cuba Internacional, p. 94
18. Batista, Cuba Betrayed, p.71.
19. Ibid., p. 82.
20. Ibid., p. 80.
21. Batista, Respuesta, pp. 65092.
22. As at the combat of Pino del Agua, in September 1957. See Guevara, Reminiscences, p. 164.
23. See the testimony of ex-Lieutenant Pedro Pascual Carrera Pérez, officer in charge at the El Uvero garrison, in Verde Olivo, 2 June 63, pp. 19-26.
24. Guevara's remarks recalled by Marzo Orozco, rebel fighter, in Cuba Internacional, p. 90.
25. Bonachea and San Martín, p. 102.
26. Ibid.
27. Carrera Pérez, p. 25.
28. Carrera Pérez, p. 25.
29. Guevara, "Qué es un guerrillero?" (February 1959), in Obra Revolucionaria, pp. 501-3.
30. Ibid., p. 501.
31. Ibid., p. 502.
32. Guevara, Reminiscences, p. 176.
33. Ibid., p. 174.
34. Ibid.
35. Guevara, Reminiscences, p. 175.
36. Ibid.
37. Ibid.
38. Guevara, "¡Qué es un guerrillero?", p. 501.
39. Ibid.
40. Ibid., p. 502.
41. Guevara, "Notas para el estudio...", p. 13.
42. Guevara, "¡Qué es un guerrillero?", p. 503.

43. Guevara, Reminiscences, p. 176.
44. Guevara, "Notas...", p. 13.
45. Guevara, "¡Qué es...?", p. 501.
46. Bonachea and San Martín, p. 102.
47. Ibid., p. 97.
48. Guevara, Reminiscences, p. 156.
49. Ibid.
50. Dubois, p. 290.
51. Castro's Radio Rebelde broadcast of August 20, 1958, cited in Dubois, pp. 290-1.
52. Castro's radio broadcast, p. 290.
53. Castro, "Instrucciones", El Cubano Libre (Sierra Maestra), No. 6 (September 1958), p. 6.
54. Dubois, p. 212.
55. Castro, Radio Rebelde broadcast, August 21, 1958, cited in Dubois, pp. 293-4.
56. Dubois, p. 288.
57. Castro, Aug. 21, 1958 broadcast, in Dubois, p. 297.
58. Castro, broadcast, cited in Bonachea and San Martín, p. 243.
59. Quevedo, cited in Taber, p. 269.
60. Castro, "They Are Losing the War" (Communiqué of July 21, 1958), in Bonachea and Valdés, pp. 389-90.
61. Letter of General Francisco Tabernilla, ex-Chief of Staff, to Batista (February 13, 1959), Bonachea and San Martín, p. 286.
62. Schulz, p. 184.
63. Frederick Engels, "Introduction" to Karl Marx, "Civil War in France", in The Marx-Engels Reader, ed. Robert C. Tucker (New York: Norton, 1972), p. 535.
64. Regis Debray, p. 53.
65. Ibid., p. 52.
66. Ibid., p. 51.
67. Guevara, Reminiscences, p. 200.
68. Bonachea and San Martín, p. 139. See also Verde Olivo 4 Aug. 63. The issue is dedicated to Frank País and contains numerous articles on his revolutionary activities.
69. Ibid., pp. 141-3.
70. Guevara, Reminiscences, p. 204.
71. Ibid., p. 98.
72. Bonachea and San Martín, p. 139, fn. 17.
73. Guevara, Reminiscences, p. 139.
74. Frank País, "Carta de Frank País a Fidel Castro, 5 July, 1957", Pensamiento Critico (Havana, 1968), p. 43.
75. Guevara, Reminiscences, p. 139.
76. Debray, pp. 113-4.
77. Debray, p. 113.
78. Schulz, p. 193.
79. Guevara, Reminiscences, p. 208.
80. Ibid., p. 210.

81. Castro, quoted in Debray, p. 69.
82. Ibid., p. 76, from a letter of 11 Aug. 57 to Celia Sanchez.
83. "Carta de Frank a Fidel", Verde Olivo, 1 Aug 65, pp. 6-7.
84. Ibid.; see also Thomas, p. 953, on the Mexico Pact.
85. Dubois, p. 166.
86. Bonachea and San Martín, p. 144, assert that Castro summoned them, as Bonachea and Valdés, p. 99. Taber, p. 154, merely mentions that they went to the Sierra. Dubois, pp. 162-3, implies both went unsummoned. Thomas, p. 953, says they "made their way to the Sierra".
87. Guevara, Reminiscences, p. 133.
88. Thomas, p. 953.
89. Text in Bonachea and Valdés, pp. 343-8.
90. Bonachea and San Martín, p. 144.
91. Bonachea and Valdés, p. 100.
92. Thomas, p. 954.
93. Guevara, Reminiscences, p. 134.
94. Ibid.
95. Ibid., p. 137.
96. Guevara, Reminiscences, pp. 136-7.
97. País, "Carta de Frank País a Fidel Castro", Verde Olivo, 1 Aug. 65, p. 7.
98. See Taber, pp. 163-5; Thomas, pp. 967-8.
99. See Thomas, p. 959; Taber, p. 167.
100. Dubois, p. 173.
101. Bonachea and Valdés, p. 102
102. See Taber, pp. 168-72; Bonachea and San Martín, p. 147.
103. See Bonachea and San Martín, pp. 148-9; Julio Camacho, "El alzamiento de Cienfuegos", Revolucion, 5, 6, 7, 8, 10 Sept. 62, p. 10. Camacho was M-26 leader in Cienfuegos.
104. See the vivid description by Taber, pp. 175-77.
105. See Dubois, p. 177: "Almost all of the 60,000 inhabitants of the city were sympathetic toward the revolt".; Bonachea and San Martín, p. 149: "The population took to the streets asking for arms".
106. Taber, pp. 177-81.
107. Guevara, Reminiscences, pp. 201-2.
108. Guevara, Reminiscences, pp. 201-2.
109. Ibid.
110. Thomas, p. 961: "According to the United States ambassador, the second in command of the CIA at the embassy had told the conspirators that any government set up as a result of a successful rising would be recognized".
111. See Guevara, Reminiscences, pp. 140-6.
112. See Taber, p. 185.

113. See Thomas, p. 972.
114. See Foner, **Antonio Maceo**, pp. 175-9.
115. See Bonachea and Valdés, p. 103; Bonachea and San Martín, pp. 162-5.
116. Excerpts from the document are reproduced in Dubois, pp. 188-90.
117. See Castro, "Letter to the Cuban Liberation Junta", in Bonachea and Valdés, pp. 351-63.
118. Castro, "Letter to the Cuban Liberation Junta", p. 352.
119. Castro, "Letter to the Cuban Liberation Junta", p. 360.
120. Letter cited in Bonachea and San Martín, pp. 168-71.
121. Bonachea and Valdés, p. 104.
122. Guevara, **Reminiscences**, p. 203.
123. Armando Olivé, Sierra fighter, in **Cuba Internacional**, p. 85.
124. Pauside Pérez, **campesino** fighter and mule-driver, in **Cuba Internacional**, p. 116.
125. Castro, "Letter to the Cuban Liberation Junta", p. 350.
126. A paper of the same name, among others, was published by Antonio Maceo in the 1890s. The Rebel Army consciously emulated this publication with the heading "El Cubano Libre once again in the **Manigua Redentora**"'in the redeeming bushland'. See Foner, **Antonio Maceo**, pp. 180-1.
127. El Cubano Libre #2, in **Cuba Internacional**, p. 91.
128. Ibid., p. 94.
129. El Cubano Libre #2, in **Cuba Internacional**, p. 94.
130. Guevara, **Reminiscences**, p. 164: "I divided the trophies among the men of my column [after the battle at Pino del Agua in September 1957]".
131. Manuel de la Cruz, **Episodios de la Revolución Cubana** (Havana: Instituto de Libro, 1967), first published in 1890. Jorge Mañach's classic biography of **Martí, el Apóstol**, 2nd ed. (Havana: Editora Popular, 1941), first published 1932.
132. Andrew St. George, "Cuban Revels", **Look**, 4 Feb. 58, p. 30.
133. "Orders to C. Cienfuegos", in Bonachea and Valdés, p. 398.
134. Cienfuegos in Cabrera Alvarez, **Hablar de Camilo**, pp. 127-8.
135. El Cubano Libre #4 (Feb. 1958), in **Cuba Internacional**, p. 117: "From that ragged and lousy 'army' of twelve men who wandered about like the only inhabitants of the highest peaks of the Maestra to our new army of six columns".
136. Guevara, **Reminiscences**, p. 199.

137. Enrique Meneses, Fidel Castro, tr. J. Halcro Ferguson (London: Faber and Faber, 1966), pp. 55-7. Meneses was a reporter for Paris-Match who spent four months with the rebels, first with Castro and then with Guevara.
138. Taber, p. 191.
139. Guevara, Reminiscences, p. 206.
140. Andrés Menés Ojeda, in Cuba Internacional, p. 111.
141. Recollections of Sergio Rodrigues, PSP contact with the Rebel Army, and of Saturnino Torres, Sierra campesino, in Cuba Internacional, pp. 112-3.
142. Ojeda, p. 113.
143. Taber, p. 208.
144. From El Cubano Libre #1, in Cuba Internacional, p. 112.
145. The threat of military coup was looming. The strike in April 1958 was a failure.
146. El Cubano Libre #1, in Cuba Internacional, p. 113.
147. Ibid.
148. El Cubano Libre #1, in Cuba Internacional, p. 113.
149. Guevara, in Cuba Internacional, p. 127.
150. Guevara, Reminiscences, p. 128.
151. Lafferté, in Cuba Internacional, p. 128. Officers of more advanced ideological understanding (of the goals of the revolution and, in fact, what a revolution was) were periodically brought in to be with the students for a time.
152. Recollection of Miguel E. Rivero, Rebel Army lieutenant, in Cuba Internacional, p. 129.
153. Guevara, in Cuba Internacional, p. 128.
154. See Taber, p. 197.
155. Ibid.
156. See Guevara, Reminiscences, pp. 228-34, and Cuba Internacional, pp. 118-120.
157. Orozco in Cuba Internacional, p. 116.
158. In Coronet, February 1958, and Look, 4 Feb. 58.
159. Dubois, p. 206: "Batista was so elated [over the news of Castro's rejection of the Miami Pact] that for the first time in months the name of Castro was permitted by censors to be used in newspaper headlines..."; p. 211: "Ambassador Smith succeeded in persuading Batista to restore freedom of the press and issue a call for presidential elections for June".
160. Guevara, Reminiscences, p. 228.
161. Dubois, p. 212; Taber, p. 213: "The components of this movement were largely from the middle and upper classes, including businessmen, manufacturers, college professors, teachers, white-collar workers and housewives".

162. The statement is reproduced in Dubois, p. 206.
163. See Castro, "On the Political Solution Offered by the Episcopate" (March 9, 1958), in Bonachea and Valdés, pp. 372-3.
164. Letter of March 6, 1958 reproduced in Dubois, pp. 220-22. Judges who issued indictments against known police killers were threatened and on March 12, Batista suspended civil rights, re-imposed censorship and removed the indictments.
165. Document of the Committee of Cuban Institutions, "To the People of Cuba" (March 15, 1958), in Dubois, pp. 225-29.
166. Taber, p. 216.
167. Document in Bonachea and Valdés, pp. 373-8.
168. Thomas, p. 988, fn. 1.
169. Bonachea and San Martín, p. 203, esp. fn. 31, and p. 214: "It can be stated unequivocally that Fidel Castro was responsible for the conception of the strike, and for its failure".
170. Guevara, Reminiscences, p. 209.
171. Debray, p. 77.
172. Ibid. See also Taber, pp. 217-19, on Castro's doubts and the feeling among militants in the spring of 1958 that a "paper dragon" of threats would be sufficient to destroy the regime.
173. Dubois, pp. 250-1.
174. Taber, p. 215.
175. Ibid., pp. 227-8.
176. Thomas, p. 990. Batista told a United States reporter that Castro had no chance of victory in a strike.
177. Bonachea and San Martín, p. 208.
178. Ibid., p. 205. Both Frank País and Faustino Pérez had extensive contacts with Protestant churches and organizations.
179. Quoted in Thomas, p. 972.
180. Ibid., pp. 988-9.
181. Ibid.
182. Bonachea and San Martín, p. 212.
183. Ibid., pp. 211-14.
184. Taber, pp. 237-8.
185. Masetti, p. 113.
186. Bonachea and San Martín, p. 214.
187. See "Diario de Osvaldo Herrera", in Cabrera Alvarez, pp. 73-92.
188. Quoted in Debray, p. 78.
189. Cited in Bonachea and San Martín, p. 214, fn. 64.
190. Bonachea and San Martín, p. 215.
191. Ibid., p. 209.
192. Ibid.
193. Guevara, "Una reunión decisiva" (first published in Verde Olivo, 22 Nov., 64), in Obra Revolucio-

naria, pp. 237-41.
194. See Bonachea and Martín, pp. 220-221 on PSP informers and their later executions by militants.
195. Bonachea and San Martín, p. 221.
196. Thomas, p. 981.
197. Guevara, "Una reunión decisiva", p. 240.
198. Debray, pp. 77-8.
199. Taber, p. 245. Taber's is the highest estimate. Thomas, p. 997, calculates less than three hundred. Guevara, Reminiscences, p. 243, wrote that there were only two hundred decent weapons among the guerrillas.
200. Taber, p. 251.
201. Bonachea and San Martín, p. 230. Guevara, Reminiscences, p. 243, speaks of "ten thousand men in the field."
202. Bonachea and San Martín, p. 229.
203. Taber, pp. 250-1.
204. Bonachea and San Martín, pp. 230-1.
205. Bonachea and San Martín, p. 229.
206. See "La Otilia", in Cuba Internacional, p. 121; See also Taber, p. 250.
207. Thomas, p. 996.
208. pp. 226-65.
209. Castro, "Report on the Offensive: Part I" (Radio Rebelde broadcast of August 18, 1958), in Bonachea and Valdés, pp. 401-2.
210. Thomas, p. 997.
211. Bonachea and San Martín, p. 260.
212. See Castro, "First Battle of Santo Domingo" (June 29 communique), in Bonachea and Valdés, pp. 382-83; See also Bonachea and San Martín, pp. 236-7.
213. Reproduced in Bonachea and Valdés, pp. 386-89.
214. See "The Battle of Jigüe" (Rebel Army communique of July 24, 1958), in Bonachea and Valdés, pp. 393-96.
215. The report is cited in Bonachea and San Martín, pp. 247-8.
216. Ibid., pp. 251-60.
217. See "Report on the Offensive", in Bonachea and Valdés, pp. 399-425.
218. Ibid., p. 413.
219. "Report on the Offensive", p. 415.

8
Fall 1958: The Expansion of Guerrilla Struggle and the Further Generation of the Rebel Army Myth

THE INVASION OF THE <u>LLANO</u>

    With the defeat of Batista's summer offensive and the ascendancy of the Sierra in M-26 leadership, the myths of the Rebel Army took on a new stature. It was a collection of myths generated by guerrilla struggle that merged with the historical myths of Cuban nationalism. The historical myths of justice, national redemption, and heroes who knew how to struggle, sacrifice and die for principles had inspired and mobilized, in turn, the Generation of the Centenary at Moncada, the <u>Granma</u> invaders and the infant Rebel Army. With their own personal sacrifices, guerrilla struggle, and political education through Sierra experiences, the Rebel Army in turn generated its own myths.

    The significance of myth-building in the course of revolutionary events is to be found in the relationship between events and the myths of a revolutionary movement. Thus in Cuba, in 1958, the myths of the Rebel Army entered the consciousness of non-combatants as the Rebel Army gained the advantage over the regular army. That which had previously maintained its grip on the minds of most Cubans was being eliminated. Debray called it "prestige". The prestige of a whole social system was rooted in the fear and respect which surrounded the armed power of the state. As long as it remained feared and respected, the majority could not be expected to speculate upon the possibilities to be opened by the elimination of the armed power of the state. But, once that power was effectively challenged and then precipitously destroyed, the myths of the Rebel Army could take hold in consciousness, preparing the mental ground for ideological transformations. Myths could then embody, as Sorel suggested, creative imagination and revolutionary projects. The frontiers of the possible would be stretched far beyond their previous dimensions. Certainly, objective conditions in Cuba, i.e. the nature of the economy and the continuing political crises of the twentieth century impinged upon consciousness and contributed to the attraction of Rebel Army myths. But, until the myths had actually inspired a successful attack on state power and made possibilities appear with their very mention, mass consciousness moved slowly.

The successes of the summer and the growing attraction of the myths of the Rebel Army were manifested in three ways. First, new recruits, both from the campesino population and from the urban resistance, joined the Rebel Army. The arms, equipment and ammunition captured from or abandoned by Batista's forces enabled the Rebel Army to expand.[1] Second, the Civic Resistance Movement grew impressively, both in militants and in sympathizers. Bonachea and San Martín calculate that, before the summer, "the urban movement had approximately ten thousand members", but that after the offensive failed, it grew by the end of 1958 to "thirty thousand who contributed cash on a regular basis".[2] The numbers of actual underground fighters, they estimate, rose from some fifteen hundred in all organizations to some "five or six thousand youths ready to engage in terrorism".[3] M-26 and DR cells, especially, began to multiply among workers, signifying new and much-expanded support for the insurrection within the working class. (As has been remarked, the PSP, with considerable influence in some unions, entered into active collaboration with the Rebel Army during the summer).[4] Money also came from the bourgeois sectors of Cuban society, as Civic Resistance organizers such as Raúl Chibás made collections from among wealthier circles.[5] Taxes on sugar production in Oriente mills levied by the Rebel Army were being collected with little resistance.[6]

Third, tacit support for the Rebel Army among churches and religious groups grew after the summer offensive. There had already been some individual priests and members of religious organizations who sided with the guerrillas before the summer offensive. The Catholic Youth Movement in Santiago, headed by Father José Chabebe, had hidden urban resistance fighters and funnelled them to the Sierra. Father Guillermo Sardiñas became the first priest to join the guerrillas in the Sierra, with the permission of the Archbishop of Havana. According to Chabebe, Castro had requested a priest.[7] Raúl Castro's tropa also had a priest, a Father Antonio Rivas, from Santiago, and radio communications with Chabebe in the same city.[8] Eventually, the Sierra column under Castro had a Protestant chaplain, and most units had priests. Religion, a part of many Cubans' lives, went with some of the fighters to the Sierra. The head of the Havana Psychiatric Hospital in the 1960s, Comandante Bernabé Orgaz, who had led a unit in the Sierra, recalled how he had said the rosary at night with his troops.9

As the struggle mounted in intensity, and especially as repression claimed the lives of students, peasants and workers, services were held in churches for those killed. Both the established churches and syncretic forms of Afro-Cuban religions, i.e. santería, became centers of emotional and spiritual resistance to the dictatorship. The guerrillas wore both Catholic medals and beaded santería necklaces. Castro was appropriated by some santería believers, and appeared in wax figurines; he himself apparently wore a Santa Barbara medal.10 There is no systematic study of the role of religious sentiments among the rebels, but the presence of priests and the probable believer status of most campesino recruits suggests, apart from such staunch atheists as Raúl Castro and Ché Guevara, that religious beliefs were not ignored or discouraged. It seems reasonable to conclude that religious sentiments among combatants were encouraged, to the extent that many fighters were believers. Their needs were seen as rights, to paraphrase Castro's remarks to Sartre, and thus efforts were made to meet those needs.

The invasion of the llano was in keeping with the merger of historically-based myths and the emerging myths of the Rebel Army. In the War for Independence, the Mambises had risen first in Oriente and established a liberated territory. They then mounted encircling attacks on Oriente cities, especially Santiago, and sent an invading column under Maceo to the western-most province, Pinar del Río. After cutting west-east communications, Maceo was to set up a Mambí guerrilla front in the countryside and eventually take Havana, in co-ordination with operations in Oriente under Máximo Gómez. Castro's sense of history and of the symbolic led him to seek a repeat of such a strategy.

But, beyond the sense of history, circumstances dictated the invasion in 1958. First of all, the extension of rebel columns "in all directions" had been announced on Radio Rebelde after the summer offensive. Secondly, as a political gesture, the timing was correct. The army, though not defeated, was suffering from low morale, conspiracies, internecine conflicts, and a loss of prestige among all social classes. The reputation of the Rebel Army among the population at large was greatly increased and morale in the guerrilla forces was higher than ever. Thirdly, there was no other means to expand Rebel Army influence across the island. Conceivably, the Rebel Army could have consolidated rural Oriente, developing the civil administration started in the Sierra and carried further by Raúl Castro in the Segundo Frente. It could have launched sabotage attacks and kept the army in its urban barracks. But this was hardly necessary, for the army had already withdrawn from the mountains and rural outposts. The crucial strategic goal of the rebels in Oriente had to be to cut communications with the west, even if they did not intend to mount attacks on other provinces.

The revolutionary myths which mobilized the Rebel Army, and its own set of myths, would not permit it to remain settled. It had to proceed in the attempt to liberate the entire country from the army and institute reforms. A political/military leadership which "can't stand injustice"[11] and which quoted Maceo ("The revolution will be marching as long as there remains one injustice uncorrected")[12] could hardly remain satisfied with its accomplishments in Oriente.

Further, the Rebel Army was not the only guerrilla _foco_ in Cuba. The DR had established itself in the Escambray Mountains of Las Villas province. A PSP _foco_, led by Félix Torres, and a "Second Front of Escambray", split off from the DR and led by Eloy Gutierrez Menoyo (a veteran of the Spanish Civil War and close to Prio's OA), were also active in Las Villas. In Pinar del Río, an M-26 guerrilla group had been established under Comandante Dirmidio Escalona, an M-26 refugee from the April 1958 repression in Havana.[13] Castro and the Rebel Army leadership, having declared their command of all M-26 _focos_ and militias, and having announced a united guerrilla effort, had to extend their hegemony over these disparate forces.[14]

Two guerrilla columns were to carry the struggle westwards; the "Antonio Maceo" column was led by Camilo Cienfuegos and the "Ciro Redondo" column was led by Guevara. The orders, long expected, came on August 18 and 21.[15] Cienfuegos was to "establish a permanent guerrilla front in Pinar del Río" and "wage the liberation war in the western part of the island". Guevara was to establish the Rebel Army in Las Villas, invite other organizations to unify in the "military effort of the Revolution" and "fight unceasingly in the central section of Cuba and to intercept the enemy until it totally paralyzes the movements of those troops throughout the island, from west to east". Like most of the M-26 and Rebel Army actions planned by Castro, the invasion appeared to be mounted against overwhelming odds. The Batista army was still well-armed and had thousands of soldiers; no cities were controlled by the guerrillas. Even the weapons windfall from the summer armed a total rebel force on only eight hundred.[16] That the guerrillas still felt the lack of arms is shown by a communiqué of September 15 to Batista's soldiers: to desert to the Rebel Army and retain full pay, so that families could be supported, "the only requisite is that he bring his weapon to us".[17] Yet, in the face of these odds, the myths of the Rebel Army sustained it in action. There was faith that the mission could be _cumplido_ 'fulfilled', in the sense of a duty fulfilled, or that they would die in the attempt. Sartre saw in this faith an exalted and existential attitude towards life: "They made a radical choice [in 1956]. One could kill them, but not bring them to submission. Thus, their new life [one of revolution] was born of this accepted death".[18] Guevara expressed this feeling of duty and the acceptance of death in addressing his column before departure: "Even if only one of us remains alive, this will ensure that the task assigned to us by Commander-in-Chief Fidel Castro will be carried out".[19]

The two commanders were granted powers approaching those of a military governor. They were to organize rebel units and name officers up to the rank of <u>comandante</u> 'major', the highest in the Rebel Army. The rebel penal code and the agrarian reform were to be applied in the territory where they established control. They were also empowered to "raise and dispose of contributions for war expenses", i.e. to impose taxes. In effect, as they dislodged the army, the guerrilla columns were to become the civil and military administration, following the pattern of the Sierra Maestra.

The political theme underlying the orders to Cienfuego and Guevara was one of unity to defeat Batista. In this respect, Castro issued a communiqué from the Sierra on September 16, addressed to exile organizations.[20] It announced the restructuring of the Committee in Exile, mainly in Florida. Haydée Santamaría was to take charge of fund-raising and all groups collecting funds, sympathetic to M-26 but not of it, were asked to "dissolve themselves": "M-26 cannot accept the proliferation of collateral organizations which carry a <u>caudillista</u> connotation, divide the effort and create confusion among the emigrés and the people". Much quoted later, during the years of crisis after 1959, Castro wrote: "Discipline is essential. Without discipline, there can be no revolutionary organization".[21] He called for a single authority to define and promote the objectives of M-26 and for a single administration of finances. In Cuban history, he said, "the best energies of the emigrés"[22] had been frustrated by division and sectarianism, and this diluted the efforts of the armed struggle. Just as the two commanders of the invasion were to unify the <u>focos</u> of Las Villas and the west, M-26 delegates named by the Sierra were to unify the exile efforts.

The exploits of the two columns, and of their commanders, became integral parts of the Rebel Army myths and, later, of the FAR, the revolutionary armed forces. It is worth reviewing some of their experiences in order to understand the generation of myth through action.

Composed of fighters long incorporated in Guevara's and Cienfuegos' units, of graduates of the Minas del Frío school, and of recent recruits, the two columns were not large. Guevara's had one hundred forty-eight fighters, while Cienfuegos' had eighty-two.[23] They left the Sierra at the end of August. Plans to travel in trucks went awry when the fuel was intercepted by the army. Heavy bombardment ensued, followed by severe tropical storms, which made the dirt roads impassable. Thus, both units had to set out on foot, their mules and horses burdened with arms and equipment, and fording swollen rivers.[24] The march across the swampy southern coast of Camagüey province, once they were out of the Sierra, was painstaking and dangerous. Great quantities of water impeded their progress, while the army set numerous ambushes and attempted to encircle them. One of Cienfuegos' lieutenants recalled that "every day the enemy threw a circle around us, which we had to avoid with cunning and a sense of strategy [they were to avoid combat until Las Villas]".[25] The difficulty of passage through Camagüey was increased by the low level of co-operation on the part of the peasantry. There had been little rebel and M-26 activity there, and the army employed terror. This made it difficult to secure guides and betrayal by campesinos was a constant threat: "The social conscience of the Camagüey campesinos in the cattle zones is minimal and we had to face the consequences of numerous betrayals".[26]

Even in the midst of water, mud, mosquitoes, ambushes, air attacks and betrayals, not all the encounters with Camagüey peasants were negative. Guevara was able to "leave the basis of a union" at a rice plantation in southeast Camagüey shortly after entering the province. He later wrote that, despite betrayals,

> in the midst of our troubles we never lacked for support from the peasants. There was always some one to serve us as guide or keep us from starving... we did not find unanimous support such as that given us by the population of Oriente...but there were always people to help us...it must be understood that their conditions of existence turned these men [on estates] into slaves. Terrified at the thought of losing their daily crust, they would inform the proprietor that we were passing through estate property, and he had nothing better to do than warn the military authorities.[27]

Physical hardships and the constant threat of annihilation wore the guerrillas down. In addition, there was some reticence on the part of the urban M-26 organizations in Camagüey to aid the columns.[28] By the time the guerrillas had been on the march for several weeks, morale had plummeted:

> The troops' morale was suffering the impact of hun-

ger and the morass of mud. We could never rest since the army was following our path with the help of airplanes. In every campesino we saw a potential chivato, in a psychological situation similar to that of the first days in the Sierra Maestra. We could not make contact with the M-26 [around Baraguá, a Camagüey town] since a pair of supposed members refused us the necessary help when I asked it. We got money, pieces of plastic [for rain protection], shoes, medicine, food and guides from some PSP members, who told me they had asked for help from M-26 for us, and were answered: 'If Ché sends us a written message, we will help him; if not, screw him'.[29]

In the last days of the trek, things appear to have been near a breaking point:

Thirst, hunger, fatigue, a feeling of impotence in the face of the encircling enemy forces, and especially a terrible foot ailment which made each step a torment, had transformed our group into an army of shadows. Day after day our physical condition deteriorated and our meals - one day yes, another day no, the third day maybe...insults, entreaties and tongue-lashings were the only way to get the weary men to advance.[30]

The situation was similar in Cienfuegos' column. Cienfuegos described some of the hardships his column experienced in a letter of October 9, 1958, addressed to Castro:

Since we left the Cauto zone [in Oriente] we have marched every single night for forty days...for fifteen days we were in water and mud up to the knees...during thirty-one days of travel across Camaguey, we ate only eleven times...After four days of total starvation, we had to kill and eat a mare from our meagre cavalry, raw and without salt.[31]

Such experiences contributed directly and substantially to the myths of the Rebel Army: the rebels had the will to endure all in order to carry out the "Cuban duty" and to prevail. Despite the hardships, the two columns arrived in Las Villas in mid-October and launched immediately into the organization and generalization of the armed struggle. As in the summer, much of their success was due to a lack of morale and inconsistent leadership in the Batista army. Although in eastern Camagüey the columns were pursued closely by an effective army commander, Colonel Suárez Suquet, both columns had experiences indicating low army morale. Guevara's column, late in September, surrounded and literally up to their necks in water, made a crossing of a raised railway, all one hundred forty-eight men, within one hundred meters of the army: "The splashing noises, impossible to avoid completely, and the full moon, made me certain that the enemy knew we were there, but the low combative level which the soldiers of the dictatorship have displayed at every juncture, made them deaf to all suspicious noises".32 Cienfuegos' <u>tropa</u>, on another occasion, slipping through frequent army patrols, heard from a captured soldier that an army detachment had seen them and heard an accidental shot, but had "not made the least effort to stop us". Cienfuegos wrote to Castro: "This is striking proof that Batista's army does not want to fight and that its morale is getting lower and lower".33 Batista would later claim that payments were made to officers in Camaguey to facilitate the rebel invasion and that many other officers believed then that the fight was lost, since the soldiers did not want to fight.34

Army leadership was confused, inefficient, disunited and mystified. Colonel Suárez Suquet was able to inflict casualties on Guevara's column in ambushes during the first two weeks of September, but was continually frustrated in his efforts to get more battalions committed to stopping the guerrillas. He charged other officers with failing to place ambushes properly, and with negligence and cowardice.35 Many officers apparently had great disdain for the guerrillas and did not feel them worth the effort. They were referred to as "rats" and "<u>guajiritos escopeteros</u>" 'little shotgun-toting peasants".36 On the other hand, some commanders believed the guerrillas very well-armed and numerous. Capitan Luís Cantón, of the Camagüey Guardia Rural, believed that several well-armed columns were in Las Villas and that "Castro is coming out of the Sierra with about fifteen hundred men to join these guerrillas and to continue marching all the way to the presidential palace".37

Other officers could not understand how the guerrillas could repeatedly evade thousands of troops and move across large stretches of territory. Competition between military districts impeded co-operation. Some districts would fail to inform the next of the passage of the guerrillas, kill some civilians, and announce a successful ambush of the rebels with "heavy casualties".38 The policy of repressing the civilian population, both urban and rural, was taken up by Colonel Suquet in an attempt to halt the elusive guerrillas. Searches of houses were ordered in an attempt to "eliminate every focus of sympathizers or persons who were known to have been imprisoned or in any way connected with the M-26-7 and who are now free on probation".39

REBEL LEADERSHIP: THE QUALITIES OF CIENFUEGOS

Luck, leadership, morale and myths carried the invading columns through the trials and dangers of Camagüey into Las Villas with surprisingly few casualties. Each of the two commanders had a core of experienced officers upon whom to rely, but the mythical proportions of Guevara and Cienfuegos, especially in the later official histories and political education of the FAR, tended to overshadow the exploits and capabilities of the others. Having already discussed the style and thinking of Guevara to some degree, I will concentrate here on Camilo Cienfuegos, perhaps the most popular rebel commander after Castro himself, by the time of Batista's fall.

Cienfuegos joined the guerrillas-in-training in Mexico on his own, travelling there from California, where he was working. It is known that he soon began to distinguish himself in combat as "El Señor de la Vanguardia" 'The Lord of the Vanguard' (Guevara's term), to the point that he was entrusted with the first rebel incursion into the llanos of Oriente in the spring of 1958.[40] There, with a column of some thirty men, he was charged with reorganizing the Bayamo and Holguín M-26, cutting communications and recruiting a campesino network.

Those around Cienfuegos recall his humor, good nature and enthusiasm.[41] He had a talent for animating the men under his command, with a touch of theater and poetry. Osvaldo Herrera, his second-in-command in Oriente,[42] recalled that Cienfuegos' personal slogan was a short verse from the poet Espronceda: "Y si muero, que es la vida? Por perdida ya la di, cuando el yugo del esclavo, como un bravo sacudí".[43] His taste for poetry and history resulted in the reading of Pablo Neruda's Canto General, José Martí's works, Miró Argenter's Crónicas de Guerra (about the 1895 War of Independence), selections from Mao's writings on the Long March, and Cuban poet Nicolas Guillén's Góngoro Cosongo to his tropa.[44] When his unit entered Palma Soriano, where José Martí was killed in 1895, Cienfuegos and several of his officers signed a document pledging their readiness to die for Cuba like Martí: "With our faces to the sun, in order to fulfill the grandiose task which he began and which death kept him from realizing...having as our witness the earth which he saturated with his blood, so much a Cuban's blood".[45] His love for song and drama manifested itself in the Sierra Maestra where, in his camp, he organized not only the nightly study circle for reading and discussing the revolutionary war, but also singing, drama and literary groups.[46]

Cienfuegos' personableness helped him establish relations with campesinos during the spring of 1958. Indefatigable, he would visit bohíos before and after sabotage missions, explaining the program of agrarian reform, distributing land by usufruct, promising a definitive distribution after the rebel victory, and setting up peasant militia groups. By the time his group was summoned back to the Sierra in preparation for the summer offensive of the army, Cienfuegos had "won the people of the zone [around Bayamo] for the revolutionary cause".47 Just as he made efforts to organize the Bayamo peasantry on the basis of agrarian reform and interventions with employers on behalf of rice plantation workers, Cienfuegos "never stopped talking to the column about the meaning of the war, the need for agrarian reform and for a radical change in the structure of the nation".48

Cienfuegos was conscious of peasant support of the rebels and the crucial difference it made to the struggle. In the middle of the summer offensive, he noted in his diary: "The people tell us they have great faith in us, that now they are secure. These words move me...Inside me there is the vow never to deceive or disappoint these men and women who trust us".49 When his column was about to leave, a large number of campesinos came to his camp to bid their sons in the Rebel Army farewell. Gifts were brought to the guerrillas, and together the national anthem and the M-26 hymn were sung50 For myth-building, this symbolized the union of peasants and guerrillas through nationalism and struggle.

With all his sociability, Cienfuegos could be strict. In one incident, just before leaving for Las Villas, a member of the unit was tried in court martial and shot. He had been taking provisions, had been warned, and was caught again. The whole column was called together to witness the execution. Cienfuegos told the assembled guerrillas: "We are and we will be implacable in fighting against those who represent a regime of oppression and of theft, and even more implacable against those who, wearing the Rebel Army uniform, shame it with dishonest acts. The conduct of the Rebel Army must always be a good example".51 After this somber incident, Cienfuegos announced the orders for the invasion, and "all responded with expressions of happiness".52

THE LAS VILLAS CAMPAIGN:
FROM COMBAT INTO THE MYTH

While the invading columns were struggling through the mud and ambushes of Camagüey, finally to reach the sanctuary of the mountains in Las Villas, the Rebel Army in Oriente mounted its own attacks. Raúl Castro was preparing to beseige Santiago in co-ordination with his brother and Juan Almeida, and his patrols ranged widely over northern Oriente, attacking remaining army and

Guardia outposts and expanding the rebel administration. Near the end of September, two successful rebel attacks took place in the foothills of the Sierra.53 Almeida's unit defeated an army battalion commanded by Colonel Nelson Carrasco, capturing the latter and inflicting twenty-five casualties. Another battalion, entrenched near Estrada Palma, was attacked by Column 12 "Simón Bolivar" under Comandante Eduardo Sardiñas. They were assisted by a unit under Capitán Pedro Miret, armed with mortars. In a fierce night-time battle, several rebel platoon leaders were killed, but sixty-seven army casualties resulted. For the first time, a rebel women's platoon, "Mariana Grajales", took part in the fighting, "withstanding the cannon fire of the Sherman tanks, firmly, without moving from their positions".54 The time of mobile column warfare had arrived for the Rebel Army.

These victories gave an impulse to Castro's confidence. He wrote to Almeida a week later that his "plan to take over the province" was near completion: "First, we will take over the countryside; within approximately twelve days all municipalities will be invaded; then we will take over and, if possible, destroy all communications routes by land, highways and the railroads".55 At this point, there was no lack of money. Yet, arms and ammunition were short. Castro authorized Almeida to organize people to "pay up to a dollar for each 30.06 or M-1 caliber bullet. It is a tempting price and we can afford it; we should not care if we spend half a million dollars on half a million bullets".56

In Las Villas, Cienfuegos and Guevara began their work of widening the war and creating effective organization. Castro judged the danger of annihilation by the army enough to cancel the Pinar del Río mission. In addition, he was aware that Guevara would need assistance in controlling the various insurrectionary focos of Las Villas. Thus, Cienfuegos received orders not to "continue the advance march until further orders. Wait and meet Ché in Las Villas. The politico-revolutionary situation there is complex, and your presence in the province is indispensable to help establish it solidly".57

Two Sierra decrees from Castro set the tone of the Las Villas campaign. As the November 3 elections approached and the candidates were announced, Castro reacted with a "no-election decree",58 calling the election a "farce...behind the back of the interests of the people in the midst of the pool of blood into which the Republic has been converted in full civil war". He forbade candidates for any elective post to participate, condemning them to penalties ranging from ten years imprisonment to execution. Rebel troops and militia were authorized to execute those who persisted in being candidates.

The other decree was a basic law of agrarian reform. Guevara described it thusly: "Though it was not complete it contained very positive inclinations. It distributed state lands, those of the servants of the dictatorship, and those of people who had obtained title by deceitful means...it gave the land to all the small tenant farmers...[the peasants] compelled the Rebel Army to establish the principle of agrarian reform in Law #3 [#One was the Rebel Army penal code, #Two, the non-election decree]".59 In keeping with the sense of history, all three laws were decreed on October 10, the anniversary of the Grito de Yara in 1868, which opened the first War of Independence.

Guevara's "Ciro Redondo" column arrived in the Las Villas mountains on October 16, a scant two and a half weeks before the elections. In a campaign to impede the elections, the guerrillas were to spread anti-election propaganda, attack army and Guardia posts, and harass communications and transport. In keeping with the agrarian focus of the Rebel Army, Guevara based this anti-election work on the application of the agrarian reform Law #Three. Even before the first school was established, Guevara wrote, "our first act was to issue a decree, establishing the agrarian reform...where small tenant farmers ceased paying rent until the revolution could decide on each case".60 Guevara later explained in a letter the dynamics of the agrarian reform, the Rebel Army and the campesinos:

> We, the leaders, explained to the defenseless campesinos how they could take up a gun and show the soldiers that an armed campesino was worth as much as the best of them; they learned that the force of one is worth nothing if not united to the force of all...we learned how revolutionary slogans must respond to the tangible desires of the people. We learned to know the people's deepest desires and how to convey them into banners of political agitation...we learned that the campesinos' desire for land was the strongest stimulant to struggle which could be found in Cuba.61

By the time the columns arrived in Las Villas, they knew that agrarian reform would generate campesino support. And the campesinos, by that time, knew that the Rebel Army represented agrarian reform. Thus, in a very short time, the Las Villas countryside was mobilized. Since by this period the possibility that the armed power of the state would be defeated was much clearer, the attraction of Rebel Army myths was stronger. The myths were already superior to the prestige of the repressive forces of the state.

There were four groups in Las Villas with whom Guevara, as the Rebel Army commander of the province, had to arrange some kind of revolutionary unity. First, the PSP: it had a *foco* of some sixty-five fighters under Félix Torres in the mountains near Yaguajay, the "Máximo Gómez" Brigade. It also had a network of experienced organizers and urban militants adept at infiltration, sabotage and communications. The PSP had held talks with Castro in the Sierra and their militants had aided the invading columns in Camagüey. Co-operation continued in Las Villas. Cienfuegos' column was met by members of Torres' unit even before they entered Las Villas, and the column proceeded to Torres' camp. Cienfuegos found it "well-organized, if poorly equipped... [and] with good people".[62] Torres put himself at the disposal of Cienfuegos, who wrote: "Soon after arriving we felt ourselves among brothers, as if in the Sierra Maestra. We were given the warmest welcome".[63] The combined units soon went into action against the army. Guevara also met with PSP members in the Escambray mountains to the south and commented that "they have shown a frank attitude toward unity, and have placed at our disposal their organization in the valleys and their guerrillas in the Yaguajay front".[64]

The second group was the DR, which had established a *foco* in the Escambray, with schools, hospitals, communications systems, fixed camps and taxes.[65] It was led by Faure Chomón and Rolando Cubelas, leaders of the assault on the presidential palace in April 1957. Some DR leaders had reservations about Rebel Army/PSP collaboration. The PSP was, as had been seen, very active in helping Cienfuegos, and a PSP member, Armando Acosta, became Guevara's chief aide.[66] However, Chomón's first concern was with the DR splinter group under Eloy Gutierrez Menoyo, which called itself the "Second Front of Escambray". Chomón wrote to Guevara that "unity cannot be accomplished with elements who are a serious threat to the purposes which inspire our struggle".[67]

Guevara had had his own troubles with Menoyo's group.[68] Approaching Las Villas, he received a letter from one of the group's commanders demanding an explanation and forbidding passage until Guevara obtained permission. Ignoring this and moving into the mountains, Guevara expected to find a cache of boots for his barefoot column, but it had been appropriated by Menoyo's guerrillas. Meetings with two of Menoyo's commanders ensued; one of them was famous in the region "for his raids on the peasants' cows"[69] and forbade Guevara to attack a town he had reserved for himself. Guevara later found out that one of the commanders had killed four men who wished to leave and join the Rebel Army. Biding his time, Guevara agreed to allow the Menoyo group to continue collecting "tribute" from area merchants and farmers in return for a free hand in establishing agrarian reform, on which the "Second Front of Escambray" seemed to have no position.[70]

Guevara was not able to achieve reconciliation between Menoyo and Chomón, nor did he expend much effort on the attempt. He was more intent on co-operating with the DR forces in defeating the army in Las Villas. In a document called the "Pact of Pedrero",[71] signed by Guevara and Rolando Cubelas in November, this co-operation was sealed. The document referred to the "purest ideals of youth struggling as brothers", the "revolutionary postulates of Frank País and Antonio Echeverría (the popular DR leader killed in the assault on the presidential palace)", and "our duty to the fatherland". It established the goal of "perfect co-ordination in military actions culminating in the synchronization of operations so that members of both M-26 and the DR will participate in combat simultaneously". Supplies and communications were to be shared, territorio libre divided into M-26 and DR zones where each had taxing powers, and collaboration on agrarian reform and the administration of justice would be pursued.

The fourth group with which Guevara had to deal was the Las Villas M-26 leadership. The provincial co-ordinator, Enquire Oltusky, and the chief of action and sabotage, Victor Manuel Paneque, were his two main interlocutors. They were more suspicious of Guevara's reliance on the PSP than were Chomón and Cubelas of the DR. Guevara apparently was adamant that unity demanded acceptance of the PSP in a united front and angrily predicted a split between himself and the M-26.[72]

Other disagreements with Oltusky centered on the nature of agrarian reform, Guevara's proposal to expropriate funds by robbing banks, and future relations with the United States. Oltusky wanted distributed land to be purchased by the campesinos. Guevara asked him why the campesinos were not disturbed by the idea of radical land reform. It was the landlords who were protesting[73] To Oltusky's refusal to carry out the order for a bank expropriation in Sancti Spiritus, Guevara responded:

> The bulk of the rebels agree with the expropriation of banks where they do not have a cent in accounts. Have you never considered the economic roots of such respect for this most arbitrary of financial institutions? Those who make their money lending the money of others and speculating with it, have no right to special consideration. The miserable sum they offer is no more than what they make in one day of exploitation, while this suffering people bleeds in the Sierra and the llano.[74]

Further, Oltusky had argued that the revolution should go easy and conceal its actions, or the United States would take offense. This ignited Guevara's scorn, according to Oltusky's own recollection of their first conversation. Guevara told him that the revolution from the "very outset must develop in a struggle to the death with imperialism. Genuine revolution cannot be concealed".[75]

The acrimony reached such a point that many urban M-26 leaders in Las Villas threatened to resign. Guevara accused them of incompetence and invited them to proceed with resignation. He never thought, he wrote to Oltusky, that "I would be boycotted by my own comrades. Now I see that the old antagonism is resurgent. The word llano has come up again and leaders who are divorced from the mass of the people advance opinions on the reactions of the people".[76] Guevara threatened to use his authority as military commander to "sweep away all the weak people". The dispute was finally settled, or rather sidetracked, by Marcelo Fernandez, M-26 national co-ordinator. Bank expropriations were called off; no M-26 leaders resigned; Oltusky promised co-operation.[77]

While Guevara carried out the various and often testy negotiations aimed at a Las Villas united front, the two rebel columns were very active. Small towns in the plains were attacked to rout the Batista administration, while remaining rural garrisons were assaulted. Guevara described the activity: "We engaged in a torrent of activity. Our columns were everywhere, reducing attendance at the polls to almost nothing. Cienfuegos' troops...paralyzed the electoral farce. Nothing could move: neither batistiano troop transports nor commercial traffic".[78] Sabotage and M-26 agitation had been effective.

In the northern parts of the province, Cienfuegos rapidly established separate units which were to expand over the countryside. The first ambush of an army patrol yielded the weapons with which Torres' PSP guerrillas were equipped.[79] The newly organized guerrilla front under Cienfuegos was efficient and complex. Each unit was responsible for organizing the rural population in its zone of operations. Peasant militias were established, along with committees handling reconnaissance and messenger services, sentry duty, supply, schools, finances and the collection of taxes from the sugar mills in the area, and propaganda. The militias were instrumental in the final capture of Las Villas towns and cities in December.[80] At the same time, urban militants with little or no guerrilla experience were incorporated into the rebel forces when they approached towns, and then were taken to a training camp, "where they were taught sabotage techniques".[81]

By the end of October, Cienfuegos' forces effectively dominated the northeastern Las Villas rural areas. Constant sabotage of railroads, highways and bridges was combined with ambushes to keep the army quartered in their barracks. Isolating these garrisons enabled the guerrillas to attack the weakest villages, take them one by one, and add to their arsenal in preparation for larger battles in December. Gálvez describes what the rebels would do in liberated villages: "They organized mass meetings explaining the reasons for fighting, where the people gave free rein to their desires for freedom, shouting, singing and crying".[82] The rebels would discuss the "electoral farce" and explain that no vehicular traffic would be allowed in the region, in order to cut off army supplies and prevent the delivery of ballot boxes.

With the aid of PSP organizer Gerardo Nogueras and the M-26 labor organization FON, Cienfuegos organized the sugar workers in all the area mills. Meetings of workers were held in nearby rebel camps and a workers' committee set up. Not only did it assist the guerrillas; it also worked to eliminate the mujalista (pro-Mujal) union leadership in the mills, hold free union elections and present demands to the management, usually for better wages and working conditions. Then the Rebel Army would come to the mill to back up the demands. In November, rebel control of the area was such that Cienfuegos' parents were able to visit him,[83] and he was "able to preside over a meeting attended by about eight hundred sugar workers from the San Agustín and Adela sugar mills".[84] At the end of the month, a meeting of five hundred workers from seven mills was held,[85] and a peasant congress of some three hundred took place. Finally, a provincial congress of sugar workers was held in the liberated town of Carrillo during the week of December 15-20.[86]

Throughout November and the first half of December, the guerrillas in Las Villas liberated villages and small towns, paralyzed transport, and established civil administration to replace the fleeing batistiano personnel. In Oriente, Castro moved from his permanent headquarters at La Plata to take Bueycito, on the northern perimeter of the Sierra. The encirclement of Santiago was proceeding, as the rebels controlled the highways, using their own land mines manufactured in the mountain camps.[87]

While Castro moved toward Santiago and engaged eighteen hundred army troops for ten days at Guisa,[88] Raúl Castro's forces moved both east and west in northern Oriente. Cities and towns taken by the rebels were bombed by Batista's air force.[89] The rebels withdrew from towns they had taken, having established militias, and called on the population to maintain order themselves: "The people must be the chief preservers of order in each liberated city and must prevent pillaging, destruction and bloodshed".[90] Revolutionary justice was promised:

> No one must take revenge on anyone. Those who have
> committed inhuman acts against the people will be
> detained and imprisoned and later tried by revo-
> lutionary courts. In the decisive moments which
> are approaching, the people must give the highest
> proof of civic sense, patriotism and a sense of or-
> der so that later no dishonorable accusation can
> be made against our revolution which, because it is
> the highest goal of the Cuban nation and the most
> extraordinary proof of the people's desire for
> peace and of their dignity, must suffer no ble-
> mish.[91]

Castro was relying on the Cuban people, a faith he had carried for years, sought to inculcate in the Rebel Army, and which he would test repeatedly after 1959.

The battles of the last two weeks of December in Oriente and Las Villas provinces were an accelerating series of confrontations with the disintegrating army. In some cities, the Batista troops, under capable officers, resisted strongly, while in others they surrendered with little or no fighting.[92] As in the September 1957 uprising in Cienfuegos, the population of liberated areas collaborated with the rebels and joined in the operations, making the fall campaigns in Oriente and Las Villas a popular insurrection. The underground was much better prepared than during the April 1958 strike; thus, when a rebel unit advanced on a guardia post, an army barracks, or a town, it was well-supplied with information and could count on the residents.

A number of events during the last two weeks of December became famous throughout Cuba and entered into the body of revolutionary myths which the Rebel Army generated. The battle for Yaguajay was one, where Cienfuegos had to spend nearly ten days besieging a well-equipped battalion commanded by an effective officer, before gaining its surrender.[93] In the myths the battle symbolized the growing military prowess of the Rebel Army and the victory of dedicated Cubans over regular units with a high degree of training and discipline. In the political education of the revolutionary military and in the popular culture promoted by the revolutionary regime, Cienfuegos became the "hero of Yaguajay"[94]

A second battle much celebrated after the victory was that of Santa Clara, the provincial capital of Las Villas. Some six thousand well-armed government troops were gathered there as rural Las Villas and its towns fell rapidly before the combined forces of the Rebel Army, the DR and Menoyo's Second Front. In taking the outlying towns of Las Villas, Guevara's forces built up a large stockpile of arms, which they gave to the ready urban and rural militias. Santa Clara became a besieged city. An armored train with hundreds of troops was sent from the city center to block the approach of the rebel troops, but was derailed by bulldozers Guevara requisitioned from the University of Santa Clara.[95] Those in the train surrendered quickly to a small rebel force under a barrage of small-arms fire and Molotov cocktails, "fraternizing with us and saying they were tired of fighting the people".[96] Actual fighting inside the city, where the government forces had retreated to strongholds like the police station, the court house and the army barracks, was either short and fierce or non-existent. Various Batista commanders fled, and the rank and file was ready to cease hostilities.[97] The fall of Santa Clara was the last decisive engagement of the revolutionary war and, before it was over, Batista had fled the country.

In Oriente, Santiago was encircled and five successive attempts by the army to break out had been defeated.[98] The rebel units were relatively untouched by these attempts, while the civilian population suffered, especially at the hands of Major Jesús Sosa Blanco, whose "progress across the country could be followed by watching the columns of smoke rising from the burning hamlets that he left behind".[99] Batista's army and air force also reduced Sagua de Tánamo, in northeastern Oriente, to rubble in nine days of battle, the army burning homes and businesses while the air force bombed[100] But in Santiago itself, the final victory, Castro's entry into the Moncada barracks was bloodless. His ultimatum to the Santiago commander, sent after he heard of Batista's flight, resulted in surrender.[101]

At the last moment, plots and conspiracies reverberated in the top ranks of the army. General Eulogio Cantillo, chief of operations in Oriente and commander of the summer offensive, tried to negotiate a coup with Castro and with Batista.[102] When the latter fled, Castro called a general strike and ordered his columns in Las Villas to move on Havana. Cienfuegos and Guevara were to take over the military bases in Havana. Castro announced that "a military junta in complicity with the tyrant, has taken power in order to assure the escape of Batista and the principal murderers and to try to block the revolutionary movement from taking power".[103] This was to be countered by the continuation of military operations by the rebels and by a general strike: "This time [as opposed to 1895] nothing and no one can impede the triumph of the Revolution". Castro was also aware that a power vacuum would result in mob action and vengeance killings, as in 1933 after the fall of Machado. Accordingly, over Radio Rebelde, he broadcast "an appeal to the people not to take justice into their own hands and to preserve order".[104] Dubois observed that the few vengeance killings which had occurred "came to an immediate halt, and all suspected torturers, assassins, and informers were arrested and imprisoned pending trial".[105]

With the flight of Batista and an atmosphere of confusion and plotting completely disrupting the army general staff, command after command surrendered to Guevara and Cienfuegos without offering resistance. Most officers were convinced some two weeks before the end that the cause was lost, as Batista made clear in <u>Cuba Betrayed</u>.[106] Their assessment of the army's fighting capacity was that it no longer existed. Thus, in Havana, Cienfuegos and Guevara, with the help of the M-26 underground, took over the military bases and maintained order. Castro made his triumphant procession the length of the island, accompanied by mass euphoria.[107]

NOTES

1. Taber, p. 269: "The weapons which were captured during the battle of Jigüe [Quevedo's battalion surrendered there] were distributed among rebel volunteers who had long been awaiting arms".
2. Bonachea and San Martín, p. 264.
3. Ibid.
4. See Schulz, pp. 342-5, for the details of Rebel Army-PSP discussions in the summer of 1958, and on the limited nature of PSP activity.
5. Bonachea and San Martín, p. 264.
6. Thomas, p. 1007; Castro, in Lockwood, p. 146.
7. Dubois, p. 164.
8. Thomas, p. 992.
9. Cardenal, p. 125.
10. Bonachea and San Martín, pp. 132-3. Santa Barbara corresponded to a <u>santería</u> war goddess.
11. Castro, in Sartre, p. 44.
12. Castro, "Report on the Offensive", p. 415.
13. See Neill Macaulay, <u>A Rebel in Cuba. An American's Memoirs</u> (Chicago: Quadrangle Books, 1970), p. 31.
14. The Caracas Pact of July 20, 1958 had named Castro the "commander-in-chief of the forces of the Revolution". See Thomas, p. 1003.
15. See "Orders to Camilo Cienfuegos" and "Che Guevara Ordered to Invade Las Villas", in Bonachea and San Martín, pp. 398 and 415-6.
16. The figure is given by Castro in Lockwood, p. 147.
17. "Proclamation to Batista's Soldiers", in Bonachea and Valdés, pp. 417-18.
18. Sartre, <u>On Cuba</u> (New York: Ballantine, 1961), p. 104.
19. Cited in Lavretsky, p. 119.
20. See "To the 26th of July Movement Committees in Exile and Cuban Exiles", in Bonachea and Valdés, pp.

419-20.
21. "To the 26th of July Movement Committees...", p. 419.
22. Ibid., p. 420.
23. Thomas, p. 1005.
24. Guevara, Reminiscences, pp. 244-5. For the "Maceo" column, see the account by Antonio Sánchez Díaz, commander of the rearguard, in Cabrera Alvarez, pp. 125-13: "Three days of cyclones and fifteen of rainstorms...destroyed our clothes and shoes".
25. Ibid., p. 131.
26. Guevara, letter to Castro of September 13, 1958, in Obra Revolucionaria, p. 256.
27. Guevara, Reminiscences, pp. 246-7.
28. See the account of Orestes Guerra, one of Cienfuegos' staff officers, in Cabrera Alvarez, p. 141.
29. Guevara, in Obra Revolucionaria, p. 257.
30. Guevara, Reminiscences, p. 248.
31. Reproduced in Franqui, The Twelve, pp. 159-174.
32. Guevara, Obra Revolucionaria, pp. 256-7.
33. Cienfuegos, in Franqui, The Twelve, p. 165.
34. Batista, Respuesta, pp. 91-2, 107.
35. See Antonio Suárez Suquet, "Reporte confidencial 41-958" (September 21, 1958) in Fuerzas Armadas Revolucionarias, Ché (Havana: Instituto del Libro, 1969), pp. 183-4.
36. See Bonachea and San Martín, pp. 272-3.
37. Luis Cantón, "Operaciones: Oct. 4, 1958", in Ché, p. 201.
38. Bonachea and San Martin, p. 276.
39. Suquet, "Confidencial: Instrucciones a los jefes de mando" (October 6, 1958), in Ché, pp. 189-90.
40. See "Diario de campaña de Osvaldo Herrera", in Cabrera Alvarez, pp. 73-99.
41. See Guevara, Reminiscences, pp. 239-40: "Camilo was happy, down-to-earth, and a joker...a man of a million anecdotes...his appreciation of people and his ability to get along with them were a part of his personality".
42. Herrera was left in Bayamo as M-26 co-ordinator, captured and committed suicide after torture, fearing he would divulge information. Cienfuegos wanted to name the invading column after him. As an alternative, Castro created the Osvaldo Herrera Order of Merit to recognize acts of valor during the invasion.
43. "And if I die, what is life? I've already given it up, the day that I shook off, like something wild, the yoke of the slave".
44. Comandante William Gálvez, "Camilo: como lo recordamos", Verde Olivo, 28 Oct. 62, pp. 4-7.
45. Document reproduced in Cabrera Alvarez, p. 106.

46. Gálvez, p. 5. Cienfuegos' position in the mythology used later in political education is that of the quintessential Cuban: culturally aware but not with a sophisticated education, with a love of life and respect for people, humorous but not cynical, and capable of encouragement of those around him.
47. See "El Guerrillero", Verde Olivo, 29 Oct. 60, pp. 7-26.
48. Ibid., p. 22.
49. Ibid., p. 24.
50. William Gálvez, "Diario de la columna 'Antonio Maceo'", Verde Olivo, 31 Nov. 63, pp. 4-8.
51. Capitán Pablo A. Cabrera (Cienfuegos' aide), "Relato", Verde Olivo, 28 Oct. 62, pp. 14-15.
52. Ibid.
53. See "The Battle of El Cerro" (September 27, 1958 communique of the Rebel Army), in Bonachea and Valdés, pp. 420-23.
54. "The Battle of El Cerro", p. 422.
55. "Letter to Major Juan Almeida" (October 8, 1958), in Bonachea and Valdés, pp. 423-6.
56. Ibid.
57. "Letter to Camilo Cienfuegos" (October 8, 1958), in Bonachea and Valdés, pp. 423-26.
58. Reproduced in Bonachea and Valdés, pp. 426-28.
59. Guevara, "Proyecciones Sociales del Ejército Rebelde", Obra Revolucionaria, p. 290.
60. Ibid., pp. 289-90.
61. Guevara, letter to Ernesto Sábato, an Argentine acquaintance, April 12, 1960, in Obras 1957-67, Vol. II (Paris: Maspero, 1970), pp. 676-80.
62. Cienfuegos in Franqui, The Twelve, p. 159.
63. Cienfuegos' diary, quoted in Lavretsky, p. 123.
64. Letter to Faure Chomón, November 7, 1958, in Ché: Selected Works of Ernesto Guevara, pp. 420-21.
65. See Bonachea and San Martín, pp. 181-5, for a description.
66. Thomas, p. 1013.
67. Faure Chomón, "Cuando el Ché llegó al Escambray", Bohemia, 15 May 60, pp. 17-19.
68. See Guevara, "Un pecado de la Revolución", Verde Olivo, 12 Feb. 61, pp. 26-9.
69. Ibid.
70. Bonachea and San Martín, pp. 186-7: "The approximately three hundred guerrillas...did not have a definite ideology, nor was the group a disciplined political organization."
71. Reproduced in Ché: Selected Works of Ernesto Guevara, pp. 41-42.
72. Thomas, p. 1013.
73. Guevara, in a letter to Oltusky, (November 3, 1958), in Obras 1957-67, Vol. II, pp. 673-4.

74. Ibid.
75. Enrique Oltusky, "Gente del llano", in Cuba: Una revolución en marcha (Paris: Ruedo Ibérico, 1967), pp. 83-4.
76. Guevara, letter to Oltusky, p. 674.
77. Bonachea and San Martín, p. 284.
78. Guevara, Reminiscences, p. 249.
79. William Gálvez, in Franqui, The Twelve, p. 148.
80. Ibid.
81. Guevara, Reminiscences, p. 249.
82. Gálvez, in Franqui, The Twelve, p. 150.
83. Gálvez, in Franqui, p. 153.
84. Bonachea and San Martín, p. 278.
85. Gálvez, ibid.
86. Bonachea and San Martín, p. 278.
87. See "Santiago de Cuba Is Surrounded" (November 2, 1958 communiqué) and "Communiqué to Paralyze Transportation" (November 9, 1958), in Bonachea and Valdés, pp. 432-3 and 435-6.
88. See "The Battle of Guisa" (December 7, 1958 Rebel Army communiqué), in Bonachea and Valdés, pp. 439-42; the descriptions of the battle in Dubois, pp. 330-31.
89. Dubois, pp. 337, 341.
90. "Orders of the Rebel Army" (November 13, 1958 Radio Rebelde broadcast), in Bonachea and Valdés, pp. 437-8.
91. Ibid.
92. Descriptions of the last battles are found in Dubois, pp. 334 ff., Bonachea and San Martín, pp. 286-301, Nuñez Jimenez, pp. 499-506, and Cabrera Alvarez, pp. 159-63.
93. See "Yaguajay", in Cabrera Alvarez, pp. 159-63.
94. See, for example, the article by Hector de Arturo, "Desde el '56", Verde Olivo, 5 Dec. 71, pp. 67-73.
95. See the "Diario de campaña" of Antonio Nuñez Jimenez, in his Geografía, pp. 501-2.
96. Ibid.
97. Ibid., p. 503: "As we entered the 'Leoncio Vidal' barracks [to propose a cease-fire] the soldiers there shook our hands and embraced us, saying that they had not been paid for three months, and asking us for canned milk, as they had not eaten for two days".
98. Taber, p. 282.
99. Ibid., p. 288.
100. Ibid.
101. Dubois, p. 351.
102. See the account of these maneuvers by Bonachea and San Martín, pp. 305-11.
103. "General Strike Proclamation" (January 1, 1959), in Bonachea and Valdés, pp. 448-9; see also "Orders to Camaguey and Las Villas Commands", pp. 447-8.

104. Cited in Dubois, p. 348.
105. Ibid.
106. Batista, Cuba Betrayed, pp. 88-123.
107. See the accounts by Taber, pp. 296-7; Dubois, pp. 359-63; Revolución, 9 Jan. 59.

9
The Institutionalization of Myths in the Political Education of the Rebel Army/FAR, 1959 to 1963

MYTHS IN THE EARLY REVOLUTIONARY
PERIOD, 1959-1963

The period after January 1959, lasting until approximately the end of 1963, when a certain security had been achieved, illustrates the dynamic of revolutionary myths as conceived in the introduction. During the insurrectionary struggle, from 1952 to 1959, revolutionary myths played a mobilizing and impelling role. An examination of the materials used in Rebel/Army/FAR political education show that the strongest myths in this period were those of Cuban history and the continuity of struggle for national redemption, of a new generation prepared to sacrifice itself for the realization of the visions of past heroes and martyrs, of the revolutionary unity of Cubans, and of the Rebel Army as the repository of revolutionary values and the hope for victory and progress. Myths did not cease, after January 1959, to mobilize Cubans for the revolutionary projects of the Rebel Army and the M-26 leadership, but they also came to function as sustaining myths.

The breakup of the apparatus of force, the Batista army and police forces, was not sufficient to guarantee either the security of the new power or the implementation of its revolutionary projects. A new and comprehensive ideology had to be communicated and accepted by the mass of the population. The essence of the myth of the Rebel Army was that it was "of the poor, by the poor and for the poor". This slogan helped to break up the class harmony that paternalism and a sense of fatalism had created, but was not enough to win ideological hegemony, for there was a competition for hegemony between three strong contenders. These were, in crude terms, the revolutionaries, the liberals, and the reactionaries. The institutionalization of revolutionary myths in both the national political culture and in the political education of the military helped to produce ideological hegemony for the revolutionary contenders.

Sorel insisted that revolutionary myths as such must give faith to the masses. In 1959, the myth of the Rebel Army had gone some way in providing that faith, but it had not yet made the masses themselves revolutionary. The role of myth in the post-1959 years was that of galvanizing the masses and building the revolutionary coalition of the Rebel Army, the <u>campesinos</u>, the working class, petit bourgeois radicals, and the PSP. Revolutionary myths had to compete with the liberal myth of reforms and representative democracy and with the reactionary myth of anti-communism. In many respects, as events moved on in the first couple of years, liberal and reactionary myths were merged. This was due in part to the winning of some liberals to the revolutionary project and to the move of others to the reactionary camp. It was also due to the eclipse of the liberal position. Two defined and contradictory alternatives eliminated any compromise. Both the myth of socialist revolution and that of counter-revolution embodied the vision of a final struggle. Sorel characterized myth as a progressive and encompassing simplification of social conflicts. Myth would embody an analysis of a situation, a faith in victory and a vision of the social relations to come. Such myths become a force themselves as, picturing a struggle between social titans, they give ever clearer form to the titans. They impart the idea of a whole people or social class in mortal combat with fore-ordained and almost metaphysically-perfected enemies. In the case of Cuba, it was <u>el pueblo cubano</u> 'the Cuban people' in <u>el cumplo de su deber</u>, carrying out a historical duty against the titans of counter-revolution, traitors and imperialism.

After January 1959, the initiatory and mobilizing revolutionary myths also became sustaining myths. Their spread, in the struggle for ideological hegemony against competing myths, especially anti-communism, the core of reactionary ideology, was greatly facilitated by the use of mass media and control of the apparatus of force. Revolutionary myths became the material of the transformation of political culture.[1] They assumed even more importance in the political education of the military, where they had to create unbending loyalty to a revolutionary process, loyalty beyond personalist bonds to individual leaders. Such different kinds of loyalties were not mutually exclusive in Cuba, since much of the appeal for loyalty was based on the personal popularity of Castro - thus the term <u>fidelismo</u>. But in the symbolism of revolutionary mythology, loyalty to Castro meant adherence to the process of revolution, a clear choice to be <u>with</u> the Revolution, as opposed to against it.

Revolutionary myths in the post-1959 period sustained the combativeness displayed during the insurrection. The notion that the fall of Batista had resolved everything had to be corrected for the revolutionary projects to move forward and to be defended against counter-revolution. Thus, the emphasis in revolutionary myths such as anti-imperialism and that of the Rebel Army as vanguard was on the continuity of struggle. It was stressed that the enemy was not dislodged, only shaken, and that its forces were being gathered for a final confrontation. Whatever form the struggle might take, the enemy would not back down. Thus, unity, loyalty and sacrifice were mandatory. The function of myth and of political education advancing revolutionary myths was to create and maintain such unity, loyalty and sacrifice.

This final chapter will examine the sustaining function of myth. The center of the discussion will be the institutionalization of revolutionary myths in the political education of the military. At the same time, the dynamics of myth, i.e. its quality of having a life of its own, to be a social force affected by other social forces and having an impact on those forces, will be explored. The nature of post-1959 revolutionary myths and their use depended in large part on the events of the 1959-63 period. Defections of Rebel Army figures, emigrations, disaffection of M-26 leaders, the struggle and eclipse of liberals and social democrats within the first cabinet, relations with both superpowers and the machinations of reactionaries and the CIA all affected the use and presentation of revolutionary myths, not only in the military but vis-à-vis the population at large. New elements of myth were added by the experiences of those years, especially those of radical reforms affecting large numbers of Cubans, and those involving violence and sacrifice. New martyrs joined those of Cuban history and the insurrectionary struggle. As imperialism mounted its offensive and as anti-communism assumed the proportions and character of a social myth, so did anti-imperialism become the commanding element of revolutionary myth. Finally, the embrace of Marxism-Leninism as an official ideology gave a comprehensive structure to the collection of revolutionary myths. This structure became a myth system, in that each myth had a specific nature and relationship with the others.

The institutionalization and dynamics of revolutionary myths in the political education of the military can be observed in a number of ways. Films, memoranda and official literature all provide evidence. I have chosen here to concentrate on four conduits of revolutionary mythology: the materials used for literacy and political indoctrination programs in the Rebel Army/FAR in the first years after January 1959; the system of political instructors during the same period; speeches and writings of the political and military leadership, usually one and the same; and the official military journal, Verde Olivo. In the case of the latter, Verde Olivo contains much information pertaining to the first three conduits of mythology. Thus, it will be used to discuss these subjects, and will also be treated as a vehicle itself.

INSTITUTIONALIZATION: REBEL ARMY RESPONSIBILITIES AND THE MANUAL DE CAPACITACIÓN CÍVICA

The basis of revolutionary power in January 1959 lay not only in the immense popularity of Castro, M-26 and the Rebel Army, but in the disintegration and destruction of the regular army. The Rebel Army leadership moved rapidly to dissolve the remnants of the army and to consolidate its hold on power by taking the potential for force into its own hands. As early as December 1957, Castro had claimed for M-26 the exclusive right to maintain order, and the Caracas Pact of all opposition groups in July 1958 had supported that claim. M-26 militia proceeded to disarm the police and maintain order in the cities. Cienfuegos and Guevara peacefully took over command of the major military compounds in Havana, Columbia and La Cabaña. The result was the total disarming of the forces of the dictatorship and the transfer of weapons into the hands of the Rebel Army. The attempt by the DR to participate in this transfer, initiated by their occupation of the presidential palace and their confiscation of some weapons upon entry of Havana, was soon ended.[2]

A political revolution by force of arms had taken place in Cuba, while the social revolution had only tentatively begun with land reform and the elimination of a few commercial middlemen in the territorio libre of Oriente and Las Villas. Although there was a tradition of radicalism and anti-imperialism in Cuba, which indicated a potential of support for revolutionary measures, there was no mass revolutionary party or working class movement. On the other hand, there was no organized and united bourgeoisie. The traditional opposition parties had been thoroughly discredited. In a situation characterized by Samuel Farber as Bonapartist,[3] in that no one social class had been able to construct political hegemony, the popularity of the Rebel Army, its possession of arms and the coherence of its leadership around the Sierra Maestra core gave it authority. With this authority, Castro placed Rebel Army figures in positions where they could control the force of arms. As he later said, "the key to this whole situation is whether the people take control of the weapons or whether the military machine remains intact with weapons in hand and the people defenseless...the prime objective is to destroy the military machine and seize its arms. Without [this] the revolution can be checked, can be betrayed and can be crushed".[4] Raúl Castro remained the virtual military governor of Oriente, with his aide Martinez Sánchez becoming Minister of Defense in the first cabinet. Huber Matos was given command in Camagüey, Calixto Morales in Las Villas, William Gálvez in Matanzas, and Dermidio Escalona in Pinar del Rio. Cienfuegos was named Chief of Staff of the Rebel Army and Díaz Lanz became head of the air force. Efigenio Ameijeiras, commander of the mobilized column in Oriente under Raúl Castro, was made the head of the national police force and, by the end of January, Sierra Maestra combatants commanded most police detachments, into which hundreds of Rebel Army soldiers had been incorporated.[5]

Almost immediately, the revolutionary myths of the Rebel Army were institutionalized in the new army. This was indicated first of all in the speeches made by Castro and Cienfuegos in the initial weeks of January. The main theme was that arms would henceforth be borne in the interests of the people and of the nation. When Cienfuegos took command of Campo Columbia, several days before Castro arrived, he addressed the regular army troops quartered there. They had been disarmed, he said, but the arms would be returned to them once criminal elements had been weeded out, "not in order to defend [individual] men but to defend national sovereignty, peace and democracy".[6] A new army, at the service of the people, Cienfuegos declared, would be formed from the Rebel Army and those elements which were "untouched by the blood spilled by the tyrant". Such a unity would guarantee "the achievement of the goals that the whole people of Cuba deserve". When Castro arrived in Havana and made his famous speech at Columbia, with the white dove settling on his shoulder,[7] he stressed the theme of Rebel Army unity with the people. It was the people who had won the war: "Every time I hear of columns, fronts or units, I think to myself, our best column, our best troops, the only ones capable of winning the war are the people. No army can defeat them".[8]

This self-identification of the guerrillas with the people, el pueblo cubano, had been a constant theme in the political education of the guerrillas. Cienfuegos had been one of its most eloquent spokesmen. During the Las Villas campaign, at the time of the congress of sugar workers, he expressed it thusly: "The people [helping us here] see the rebel invaders as legendary figures...they see in the Revolution, in M-26, the salvation and the brilliant future of Cuba...the road will be long and harsh, but we will travel it...so that those men will have, besides the freedom of the fatherland, all that they deserve; we promised it and we must redouble our efforts".[9] As on several previous occasions, Cienfuegos was impressed and moved at the faith of campesinos in the rebels: "When the guajiro with a machete in his belt and the rebel with a rifle on his shoulder embraced, the earth that they stand on, earth soaked with blood, must know that that blood was not shed in vain".

The new army, which retained the appellation Rebel Army, quickly assumed various roles: that of administration and construction in rural areas; that of revolutionary justice, in hunting down those in the Batista army and regime accused of atrocities, informing and corruption; that of anti-corruption vigilantes, ferreting out the sincecures and graft that characterized public office and the civil service; that of social arbiters, intervening in labor disputes. The leadership thought political education in the Rebel Army in these circumstances an immediate necessity, and it began, or rather continued, during the first months of the revolution.

Cienfuegos and Raúl Castro committed themselves to a program of literacy and educational superación 'upgrading' for the Rebel Army.[10] At La Cabaña, Guevara established courses of political education, which were managed by Armando Acosta, his aide in Las Villas, and Marcos Armando Rodriguez, both PSP members. Ramón Nicolau, the commissar of some three hundred Cubans who fought in the Spanish Civil War,[11] was also involved in the La Cabaña school.[12] Cienfuegos, as Chief of Staff, singled out political education as imperative. It would begin with literacy programs, as in the Sierra.[13] He inaugurated a literacy course at Campo Columbia, renamed Ciudad Liberta (Liberty City), in February, speaking to the assembled soldier-students:

> We know of your efforts to learn in the middle of war, when we had to march night after night, after long hours of fatigue the comrades wanted to learn. Many of you don't even know how to write your names. That is not important, because in a few weeks, you will all know how to read and write... and that way, you will appreciate what the duty of each of you is in regards to the fatherland...this will be an army which will be at the people's side for all their just and honorable needs.[14]

Such literacy programs as the one Cienfuegos inaugurated provided experience and models for the national literacy campaign undertaken in 1961.[15] The materials used involved capacitación cívica 'civic training', i.e "furnishing or refurnishing the minds of the students with the historical, ideological and political images which the regime felt were appropriate to the new social order".[16] The images were taken, as Cienfuegos suggested, directly from Rebel Army experiences in the Sierra. As Fagen points out, Sierra classes combined literacy training and political education in that students would read from materials with a specific political content. Much as in Paulo Freire's methods,[17] literacy materials centered around "active words" and revolutionary themes relating to the experience of the students. Indeed, Fagen writes that "out of the work in political education and literacy in the Sierra came the Armed Forces training booklet known as the Manual de Capacitación Cívica (Havana: Departamento de Instruccion, Ministerio de las Fuerzas Armadas, 1960)".[18] It was one of the bases of literacy camapign materials in 1961.

Civic training, which was integral to literacy programs in the Rebel Army and in 1961 across the whole country, is taken to be the committed imparting of political views. It is in no way neutral; rather, the aim is

> to instil...an unbounded love of the Fatherland and a feeling of solidarity with the workers and peoples of all lands in their noble struggle for a free and happy life, and teaching them to abhor imperialist wars of plunder and to work steadfastly for peace...teaching programs must help to develop a love for the people as the creators of labor and source of all social wealth. They have to indicate what is represented by the struggle against exploitation and misery...stress the underlying causes of inequality and its terrible consequences.[19]

Though these words were written after Cuba's public commitment to socialism and Marxism, such a view was fundamental to the literacy materials used in the Rebel Army before and after January 1959, with the possible exception of the term "imperialism". It would have depended on the instructors. Those in the Second Front "Frank País", for example, tended to be Marxists, as did those at La Cabaña in 1959. In this sense, the Rebel Army was the educational and political vanguard.

The actual content of the Rebel Army literacy programs which the Cienfuegos brothers,[20] Guevara and Raúl Castro sponsored in the first months of the revolution, then, can be seen through a perusal of the Manual de Capacitación Cívica[21] and another Rebel Army publication, Arma Nueva (A New Weapon).[22] The over-riding theme in these materials is that of struggle, the continuing struggle which began in the Sierra and continued after January in other forms. Each soldier who is learning to read is encouraged to see the attainment of literacy as a blow against the old society, where ignorance served the dictatorship: "To read and write is a new weapon and you should care for it as you care for your rifle".[23] This recalled Martí's aphorism about education: "Ser culto es el único modo de ser libre" 'to be educated is the only way to be free', which became a slogan of the national literacy campaign in 1961.[24] Illiteracy was seen as the enemy, correlated to the "many enemies which the Fatherland has".[25]

Arma Nueva was written simply, so that with a basic vocabulary the read would quickly be able to read sentences and paragraphs with current significance. In the first lessons on agrarian reform, for example, the readers would see the following:

> Cuba is an agricultural country. Agriculture is the base of our economy. Why is our agriculture backward? Because the peasants were not the owners of the land...[latifundios are briefly explained] Latifundismo was the cause of backwardness and of the misery of our peasants. That is why it is necessary to have land reform. It is the basic law of the Revolution. The Rebel Army will liquidate latifundistas and give the land freely to those who work it, with credits, tools and all that they need.[26]

Such lessons, vocabulary and political content were seen not long after in the literacy manuals used by hundreds of thousands of Cubans in the campaign of 1961. The teachers' manual Alfabeticemos (Let's Teach Literacy) contained short readings on topics carefully selected to convey the utmost in revolutionary sensibilities.[27]

Prefaced by short quotations from Castro, Martí and Nuñez Jimenez, selections included "The Revolution" ("Revolution means the destruction of privilege, the disappearence of exploitation, the creation of a just society"),"The Land Is Ours", "The Co-operatives", "The Right to Housing", "Cuba Had Riches and Was Poor", "Nationalization", "Industrialization", "Racial Discrimination", "Imperialism", "War and Peace", "International Unity", "Democracy" ("This system in which a rifle is given to any citizen who is ready to defend a just cause"), "Workers and Peasants", and "Health".

The Manual, as it appeared in 1960, seems to have been designed for those with an elementary degree of literacy and for use in political education classes within the FAR.[28] Like Arma Nueva and unlike Alfabeticemos and Venceremos, it was specifically directed at soldiers. It covered a wide variety of topics, many of them historical, such as the role of slavery in the sugar economay, themes from the 29th century Wars of Independence, or the history of United States interventions in Cuba. Some of its numbers, printed frequently in Verde Olivo, were written by Castro and were essays defining a specific term, such as "revolution", or "reform".

One of the first excerpts from the Manual to appear in Verde Olivo was on a theme which formed an essential part of the self-generated myths of the Rebel Army: its moral superiority over the regular army. It was a theme which was common in the Sierra and which was stressed in the first months and years after victory. Cienfuegos, on October 7, 1959, compared the two armies: "If before there was an army which abused, an army which sold itself to the worst and most powerful interests inside and outside of Cuba, today there is a rebel army, an army born of workers, born of Cuba's people, which defends workers and peasants".[29] The Manual reflected this theme in "Differences between the Professional Army and the Rebel Army".[30] The idea was to maintain and increase the combativeness of the rebel soldier via the revolutionary myth of rebel moral superiority. The formation of the professional army was seen as due to "North American intervention, which impeded the Mambí victory...[United States'] General Brooke...created the Guardia Rural, which followed the orders of latifundistas, bosses and foreign companies". The reason for such an army was clear: monopoly capital has to repress in order to maintain its exploitation, and that it cannot do for itself. Why, the reader is asked, "if the professional army had peasants, unemployed workers and humble elements, just as in the Rebel Army, did the former defend a system of oppression?" The answer provided is that the professional army was structured in such a way as to distort behavior. The officers received privileges from exploiters, and the rank and file were trained to expect booty and liberties with citizens and their property. These themes were developed by Guevara, in his Reminiscences, "Notes for the Study of the Ideology of the Cuban Revolution", "¿Qué es un guerrillero?" and "Proyecciones sociales del Ejército Rebelde". Such writings also appeared in Verde Olivo and thus became mandatory reading for those in the Rebel Army and its successor, the FAR.

Themes in the Manual, as they appeared, were often timely. Thus, in September 1960, when the country was being attacked from Florida by former batistianos, and when many defections and emigrations were occurring, the Manual dealt with the difference between revolution and reform.[31] In Latin America, "revolution" had previously meant the mere seizure of power, but "you can overthrow a system and essentially retain the same structures of property and politics". Even Batista had called his coup a revolution, the article pointed out, but revolution means "to strike until the content and structure of an obsolete social system is broken". It means the "breakup of the social relations of property which dominate at that moment...the creative dynamic of revolution engenders new conditions which meet the specific needs of the society". In other words, using fairly standard and mechanistic Marxist categories, the Cuban Revolution, the soldier was told, was a real revolution. It was going, and would continue going, as Cienfuegos said, hasta sus límites ' to its limits': "This Revolution, as in the war, has only two alternatives: win or die..."[32] Reform, for the rebel soldier, was seen in the Manual as not sufficient in the Cuban circumstances: "You cannot eliminate an evil if you do not uproot its causes".[33]

Many of the topics in the Manual were historical, reflecting the deep historical consciousness of the radical petit bourgeois elements who came from the left wing of the Ortodoxos to form M-26. Guevara, Cienfuegos, the Castros and the corps of revolutionary instructors with experience in the mountains used history to inculcate, as the UNESCO pamphlet indicated, a love of country and a radical analysis of the Cuban Republic and the revolution. Thus, the Manual presented a fairly detailed history of Cuba from pre-colonial times up to the revolution in clear language that led to the unavoidable conclusion that the revolution was necessary. The historical articles in the Manual always centered around an analysis of economic activities, in keeping with a radical point of view. Thus, the pre-colonial times were seen in terms of the different aboriginal societies' organization of production and their resulting cultures. The reader was informed that a succession of indigenous peoples had come to the island, though their origins were obscure.[34] The first known peoples, the Guanajotabeyes, lived in the west in small numbers, inhabiting caves. Their society was Stone Age with no agriculture. Nomadic, they lived on shellfish and turtles. Their successors, the Siboneyes, possibly coming from the Orinoco region of South America, had a settled agriculture, and the Taínos, after them, a more developed culture with pottery and carvings. The essential message to the rebel soldier was that the island provided for its inhabitants and that society was communal, with some hunting and fishing groups and others with agriculture. Social production and egalitarian distribution of the product were the rule, with no division of labor.[35]

Colonialism disrupted this idyllic island life, as merchant capitalism from Italian city-states searched for new sources of spices and a way to avoid Moslem control of trade routes.[36] The Manual provides a description of 15th century Spain as a dynamic arena of conflict between a rising merchant bourgeoisie, in alliance with the peasantry, and the feudal properties.[37] The coexistence of feudalism and an urban merchant class was reflected in the organization of the colony in Cuba. War on the indigenous population and the rabid search for precious metals led to the imposition of tribute payments and the repartimiento system. The authors of the Manual interpreted colonial organization as a system of wealth extraction via the labor the enslaved population.[38] The destruction of the indigenous population through war, disease and hard labor led quickly to the importation of slaves to provide for the newly-established landed class of Spaniards. This, for the Manual, was the origin of racial discrimination which plagued Cuba for centuries.[39]

Conflicts within the colony were interpreted in the Manual as based in class contradictions. Thus, the Creole/peninsular Spanish conflict was seen to have developed from the differences in approach to trade.[40] The official Spanish trade monopoly led to smuggling by the Creole tobacco and sugar growers.[41] In tobacco production, especially, with its more intensive cultivation requiring trained wage-labor and family farming, the Creole population resisted the "sharper exploitation that Bourbon reforms brought to Cuba".[42] The recurring message is that social conflicts have economic causes. A Cuban national identity is seen as having arisen from these Creole/peninsular conflicts.[43]

This concern with economics, production relations and social conflict was carried through in the Manual's series on the Cuban economy in the twentieth century. Some of the articles were again historical, in that they discussed the development of activities such as sugar cultivation over a period of centuries.[44] Others were more a cataloguing of Cuban resources. Here, the underlying theme was that Cuba was naturally rich, but its people had generally remained poor.[45] A whole series of articles on Cuba's fertility, its forests, minerals and maritime resources, obeyed this theme of the contrast between Cuba's potential and its history of exploitation and uneven distribution.

In many ways the Manual was the revolution's own unabashed self-propaganda, addressed to the rebel soldier just learning to read, a soldier often without any comprehensive view of Cuban history, geography and economy. The notion was that through superación 'upgrading, improvement', the rebel soldier could better serve the revolution and the people. If, as after May 1959, with the promulgation of the agrarian reform, the soldier was to become the administrator of the reform, and if he was to build the economy, he had to know how the condition of underdevelopment had come about. Thus, the Manual dealt in detail with the history of the economy and its distortion by colonialism and imperialism.[46] The contrast between the sad situation of the economy in the past ("before the Revolution, the economy was at the service of the exploiting national and foreign minorities")[47] and the bright future opened up by the revolution was continually being drawn. Whatever the sector of the economy covered by the Manual, the pre-revolutionary dependent and unequal structure was stressed.[48]

While the domestic exploiters received their share of blame for Cuba's relative agricultural backwardness and general rural poverty, it was imperialism that took the most abuse in the Manual. The very notion of Cuban independence before 1959 was attacked.[49] It had been a myth reinforced by the media, a myth that "the United States brought liberty" in 1898 or that "United States investments brought progress". The whole sorry truth of dependence and exploitation had been "hidden from the people". True, there had been popular discontent provoked by the exploitation, humiliation and outright crimes of imperialism, but the "Revolution was necessary for the source of evil to be seen in all its crudeness: North American imperialism".

Imperialism was seen in the Manual through a strictly Leninist conception. Surplus capital from United States monopoly interests had been invested in sugar, with United States owners becoming the newest in Cuba's history of latifundistas.[50] Likewise, Cuban industrialization had been impeded and distorted because of its domination by United States capital.[51] In mining, one of the most developed areas of the Cuban economy, the benefits had flowed to United States companies. Sixty tax-free years had been enjoyed by the United States companies and Cuba's mineral resources had played a reserve role – production increased in time of war, but minerals from the United States dominated the market at other times, resulting in layoffs of Cuban mineral workers.[52]

Politically, imperialism was allied with Cuban reactionaries, claimed the Manual.[53] As Castro had put it, Cuban exploiters had made off with the surplus value produced by Cuban workers, banking and investing it abroad "in their leisure and vices, in roulette, in trips to New York or Paris, or in palaces...where four pampered cats used to live, there are now fifty or sixty students".[54] Such elements were the allies of imperialism, and both hoped to reclaim their privileged positions, according to the Manual. It was for that reason that Cuba was being attacked, both ideologically and militarily. Imperialism hid its intentions, though, behind talk of free trade, spiritual values and democratic elections. Imperialism had criticized the revolutionary justice against criminals, claiming the executions were of "political enemies of Castro".[55] It tried to foment divisions in the revolutionary leadership through its press and tried to create conflict between religious institutions and the revolution. The Manual also charged that imperialism's own political structure, that of bourgeois democracy, was a sham. Calls for "representative democracy" were fine, as long as the realities behind the slogan remained obscure.[56] In Cuba, the political cliques had always chosen candidates close to the monopolies. Graft, vote-buying and even murder had characterized Cuban elections. What did democracy mean when the media was in the hands of the monopolies? Even in the 1960 United States elections, the Manual claimed, few knew there were more than two candidates for president. It was not the case that "all citizens had equal rights of expression". In Cuba, especially, how could all citizens be politically equal to, for example, a corporate lawyer?57

The Manual began to be published in 1960, a full year before the socialist nature of the revolution was announced. However, it can be seen from the discussion of its political content that the Manual was already anti-imperialist and influenced by Marxist concepts. Thus, one must assume that political education, from early in the revolutionary period, indeed from January 1959 on, was organized and dominated by the left wing of the Rebel Army (which was not necessarily coterminous with the PSP). It has been seen that the top leadership expected a confrontation with imperialism. The grace period before the actual CIA-backed invasion of Playa Girón in April 1961 was employed to prepare the Rebel Army ideologically and militarily. However, two considerations impinge upon this judgement. First, political education in the Rebel Army, as radical in tone as it was in the literacy programs and in the Manual, was not aimed exclusively at creating anti-imperialist convictions. It was also aimed at constructing an army with a social conscience, an army prepared to carry out land reform and innumerable construction projects, an army prepared to be involved in production, an army prepared to root out corruption, an army prepared to administer a whole series of reforms. In this sense, the Rebel Army's political education intended the creation of a "civic soldier".58 Political education in the Manual was negative only in that its purpose was to identify the enemies of the people. It was positive in that it stressed Cuba's potential. Secondly, such political education was not exclusive to the Rebel Army.59 The revolutionary leadership intended to educate a whole people, both to prepare it for coming struggles and, as a matter of principle, to equip the people with the skills necessary to build the society of the revolutionary vision. Thus, the Manual spoke of the gains of the revolution in health, education, distribution and consumption patterns, new agriculture and industry, new foreign trade patterns and culture. Land, for example, "is no longer a means of exploitation, but a source of progress and happiness".60 Economic planning would "integrate the guajiro with industrial development via higher consumption".61 Military forts had been converted into schools, projects for thousands of new classrooms and hundreds of hospitals would be undertaken by the Rebel Army.62 The emphasis was indeed upon struggle and conflict, but the main battle was for development. The hope was for national resources to be channelled into development rather than into a militarized society: "Every peso which was formerly used to buy a rifle or a bullet will be used...for a book. The moment has arrived when a work tool or a book, which were substituted by a rifle, will be taken up again by the people who liberated the country, in order to bring the greater effort to reconstruction, which this historical moment demands".[63]

REVOLUTIONARY INSTRUCTORS AND SCHOOLS OF REVOLUTIONARY INSTRUCTION

During the guerrilla struggle, as remarked in a previous chapter, schools of capacitación cívica were set up in the Rebel Army. "Tumbasiete" in the Second Front "Frank País" was the most developed example. It was considered an imperative after victory to continue and expand such schools and to provide a growing number of revolutionary instructors to manage the political education of soldiers, police and eventually the militia. One of the first schools for revolutionary instructors to be established was the "Frank País" School, named and modelled after the "Tumbasiete" academy in Oriente. That the leaders saw these schools and the task of their graduates as important is indicated by their visits to the schools. Guevara spoke to a graduating class of "civic capacitators" at the País School in October of 1960, in a period when armed counter-revolutionary bands were active in the Escambray mountains. He urged them to "try always to unite the army and the people, establish points of contact and refuse differentiation between the army and the people. Remember you come from the people, and are part of it".[64] It was this same identification with the people that the Rebel Army had experienced in the Sierra Maestra and employed to their advantage. In a time when counter-revolutionary groups were active, the Rebel Army needed unity of the people and the army to defeat them. Guevara stressed that to be like the people involved discipline and sacrifice. It was the duty of the civic capacitator to reinforce discipline by example, working harder than other soldiers, mastering military techniques and living the ideology they were propounding. Their role was to continually explain the agrarian reform, the need for industrialization, for constant study and for constant discussion. It seems that Guevara stressed these duties of the capacitators because much of the Rebel Army was inexperienced; few had had the extensive experience of the revolutionary war. The attitudes of some recruits were not politically advanced, in that they considered being a soldier a mark of their superiority and separation from the people. These attitudes, said Guevara, would make the Cuban army "just another Latin American army".[65]

As the struggle against sabotage, counter-revolutionary groups and landings mounted, to peak with the invasion at Playa Girón in April 1961, popular militias were formed. Revolutionary instructors for the militia were also trained and, after Girón, when many Cubans expected a direct imperialist invasion, Castro addressed the students at the Osvaldo Sánchez School for Revolutionary Instructors.[66] He told the students that imperialism's guerrillas and mercenaries had been defeated in the Escambray and at Girón, and that they would be defeated if they came in force, since the Cuban people were armed. But the more important weapon was a revolutionary consciousness: "An army's political consciousness, its sense of duty, its self-denial, its spirit of sacrifice, its knowledge of why it fights". The role of the revolutionary instructor was to keep the morale of the voluntary militia high, and that required that the instructor, as Guevara had said, himself have high morale. It required exemplary behavior. Revolutionary instructors had been chosen for study in the school because of their already exemplary behavior, Castro told them, and they were to be furnished with training which would keep their revolutionary consciousness higher than the norm. Much of this concern with revolutionary consciousness and the formation of a militia was likely rooted in the memory of what had happened to the reformist regime of Arbenz in Guatemala; certainly this would have been foremost in the mind of Guevara.

The training received by revolutionary instructors was centered upon "class struggle, to make revolutionaries understand the danger of counter-revolution and imperialism, so they will not fall into an easy idealism thinking that the revolution was already won".[67] The ideas was to have cadres study the course of revolutions in history, particularly that of Cuba, to read the Obra Revolucionaria (Revolutionary Writings) of Cuban leaders, in order to identify the current and potential enemies of the revolution. According to Castro, the lumpen (petty criminal and parasitical elements), the bourgeois speculators, the latifundistas, the ex-thugs in the service of Batista, and imperialism had united against the Cuban workers and peasants. It was crucial to understand both the class delineation of enemies of the revolution and that "a revolution is not a Sunday stroll, nor a bed of roses, but a sacrifice; a hard and ascetic struggle". It was necessary that revolutionary instructors impart the sense of emergency and the idea that the struggle was uneven in its progress: "It is a war which changes form; at times an armed struggle, at others a class struggle without arms, with sabotage, media campaigns, interference at the work place...a struggle in which the enemies will not tire".

"Who are your enemies and why are they your enemies?"[68] This was the central question which revolutionary instructors were to address in their activities within the Rebel Army. By 1962, revolutionary instructors were modelled after the political commissars of armies in European socialist countries.[69] A great deal was expected of them:

> You are the example, the one who never loses spirit, never tires, never weakens...you watch out for the treatment the soldier gives his equipment, for the relations the soldier has with the people, the absolute respect a revolutionary soldier must have for campesino property...your concern is with the troops, that they behave correctly everywhere...you are the guardian of ideology, of discipline, and of the moral conduct of the soldiers...You are their friend, the one who knows their problems, who orients them, who speaks to them as one from the ranks, as soldier to soldier, one who instructs them, encourages them, and raises their morale in difficult moments.[70]

And beyond these nearly super-human qualities, the revolutionary instructor was to obey a traditional principle of the Rebel Army, that of respect for the enemy, "no matter the hatred that is reasonably felt for enemies of the Fatherland". The revolutionary soldier, unlike the mercenaries and counter-revolutionaries, unlike the CIA agents sent to kill young literacy workers, " does not murder or torture...does not take the life of an enemy prisoner on his own initiative".

A series of articles appeared in Verde Olivo in 1961-2 on the topic of revolutionary instruction in the militia and in the army. Some were from talks given by visiting foreign military figures, from Viet Nam, China, Eastern Europe and the Soviet Union.[71] Others were drawn from talks by Rebel Army leaders or from the staff of the Department of Instruction, Ministry of the Armed Forces, the source of Verde Olivo. In one such article, a number of directives were given out to correct the perceived deficiencies of revolutionary instruction at the unit level.[72] Instructors had apparently been drily presenting material or merely posting written material on bulletin boards. They were urged to have collective preparatory sessions under a senior political instructor in order to master the materials themselves and co-ordinate efforts.

The materials were usually speeches or writings by Cuban revolutionary leaders, selections from Verde Olivo, Bohemia or Revolución; there was also a special text, Curso de Instrucción Revolucionaria, prepared by the Department of Instruction. Topics were usually the works of the revolution, current international events, especially official Cuban interpretations of such events, or Cuban history. Instructors were encouraged to use an outline and prepare questions to check the soldiers' understanding of the material. The use of lists of words and concepts to explain was suggested, and concentration on fundamental questions rather than details was seen as a way to make political education sessions more active. A lot was expected, in theory, of these instructors in such sessions. They were to use aids, elicit some conclusions from the group, avoid leading questions and maintain discipline in the session without becoming the center of attention. Part of the problem addressed in this article seems to have been a certain laxity in scheduling sessions, the lack of a place to hold sessions, and low levels of literacy among the soldiers.

Behind these problems lay the structure of the system of political instructors, mentioned previously. Because of the lack of trained political instructors within the expanded ranks of the Rebel Army itself, and the need for the more literate, experienced members of the Army to help fill administrative positions, most political instructors came from outside the Rebel Army and often they had little or no military training. Many of the several hundred trained in the first two years were urban M-26, PSP or DR activists. This had produced both dogmatism and a lack of understanding of the importance of political work in the army. As mentioned, this situation was changed after 1962, especially as the growth of a united political party progressed within the military. Political instructors were increasingly drawn from the military ranks and were often already officers. The political instructors had supposedly been the men ready to take command if something happened to the unit leader, yet they had little preparation or rank. This must have caused some resentment and a lack of co-operation.

Comandante José N. Causse, one of the directors of the original Tumbasiete school, inaugurated a new system of political instructors in February 1963. Addressing the new students,[73] Causse criticized the uncritical transplanting of the political commissar's role from socialist countries where conditions were very different from those in Cuba.[74] He called for a seven-month course which would be split 60%-40% between political and technical military preparation. A political instructor had to be technically equipped to fight a modern war, even though the "fundamental task [remained that of] educating the personnel of the FAR in the political doctrine which sustains our revolution, that is to say the doctrine of Marxism-Leninism".[75] At the same time, the political instructor was to "realize all those activities which tend to elevate the cultural level of our fighters, including formal education, the arts and music, i.e. to contribute to an integrated education". This conception of the role of political instructors is similar to that developed more recently in the Soviet military.76

THE ROLE AND POLITICAL CONTENT OF VERDE OLIVO IN THE POLITICAL EDUCATION OF THE CUBAN MILITARY

It has been argued throughout that the political education of the revolutionary military in Cuba was founded on revolutionary social myths. Myths were readily available from Cuban history, and the guerrilla struggle, beginning at Moncada, provided the living myths of the Rebel Army. This second group of myths has been seen conceptually as deriving from the political education of experience. In the political education of the Rebel Army/FAR after the overthrow of Batista, continuity of the two sources of myths was maintained. A flood of publications, especially the materials used in the literacy campaigns, emphasized historical continuity between the struggles of the Cuban past and the revolutionary process underway. At the same time, the revolutionary process was itself a political education which enhanced the social myths of the Rebel Army and created new ones. New martyrs and heroes issued from the first several years of the revolution and the myth of the Rebel Army as Cuba's vanguard became the myth of the Cuban nation as Latin American and Third World vanguard against imperialism.

Verde Olivo was central to the continuity of revolutionary myths in the political education of the military. Distributed to all units and read by all soldiers either directly or in study circles, Verde Olivo was the single most pervasive vehicle or political education in the military. For those who had not been in the Sierra, it attempted to instil a spirit of emulation and high regard for the Rebel Army core in the Sierra Maestra. It sought to bring the Sierra experience to new recruits and to urban M-26 veterans who joined the Rebel Army. To Sierra veterans it brought an ideological reinforcement of their guerrilla and administrative activities during the struggle against Batista. It encouraged their superación and their continued firm adherence to the revolution and to the perceived revolutionary interests of the people. The ongoing revolutionary process was interpreted and reflected in Verde Olivo, being incorporated with the revolutionary myths of the Rebel Army. Not only did Verde Olivo reflect the outstanding elements of the revolutionary process such as the struggle against counter-revolution and defections, the increasingly virulent conflict with imperialism, and the rapid development of Marxism as the official ideology; Verde Olivo was also designed to mark the cultural progress of Rebel Army members, publicize the popular achievements of the revolution, and continue the general education of the revolutionary soldier. It was a vehicle for the thought of the leadership to reach the rank and file and for the communication of socialist, international, Third World and Latin American solidarity. It was an instrument of political mobilization in that it consciously sought to inculcate revolutionary values and to elicit dedication, sacrifice and high performance from the military in the crucial period of transition between two radically different socio-economic systems.

Started shortly after the victory over Batista, Verde Olivo was an improvement over the guerrilla papers such as El Cubano Libre or the Surco. Funds, facilities and more contributors and staff made the difference. It was reorganized in the spring of 1960 and has been published weekly ever since.[77] A number of regional, divisional and even battalion-level papers supplement it, while instructional materials such as Manual and Arma Nueva were produced by its publisher, the Department of Instruction of the Ministry of the FAR. Verde Olivo, then, is the flagship of the Rebel Army/FAR propaganda and education network.

From the beginning, Verde Olivo took a radical line within the revolution. It maintained that the Rebel Army was the vanguard of the revolution, as Guevara had proposed: "The Rebel Army is the vanguard of the Cuban people...our first instrument in the struggle, our most vigorous and positive weapon".[78]

Editorials, speeches and writings of Rebel Army leaders and articles on the schools, hospitals, homes and roads built by the Rebel Army, along with pieces on the army's relations with the peasantry and workers, comprised much of the early Verde Olivo in support of the vanguard thesis. The magazine also took the offensive on the subject of communist influence in the government and the army. It followed Castro's argument that "communism is the theme which is going to be used by the counter-revolution, since there is no other pretext of greater importance, to cause harm to Cuba, to agitate or to bring about the failure of our revolution..[it is] a campaign...to recover their privileges and their power with the aid of foreigners".[79] Anti-communism had been seen as the tool of the Batista regime to divide the revolutionary forces and persuade the United States to support the dictatorship during the insurrectionary period. Thus, for example, when Cienfuegos announced the dissolution of the Bureau to Repress Communist Activities, the notorious BRAC, he referred to the organ which was "part of the stage of hatred and shame in Cuba".[80]

The leaders of the revolution and Verde Olivo quickly made their pan-American feelings known, and such internationalism was, and remains, a central theme of Verde Olivo. Castro and Guevara and a number of other

Rebel Army figures had long had anti-dictatorial sentiments and hoped to see the era of overthrows: "There were compañeros [in the Sierra]", recalled Oniria Gutierrez of Sierra Column 4, "who always said that, when we had triumphed in the struggle against Batista, it was necessary to go fight in other countries...Che said 'we all have to help each other'".[81] In Guevara's thinking, the Cuban guerrilla struggle marked the beginning of the end of dictatorships in Latin America:

> The Revolution is not limited to the Cuban nation because it has touched the consciousness of Latin America and has also alerted the enemies of our peoples...the example of Cuba provoked more unrest in all of Latin America; in all oppressed countries, the Revolution has placed the dictators of Latin America on death row because they, like foreign monopolies, are the enemies of popular government.[82]

Cienfuegos echoed the theme that Cuba was an example for other Latin American countries: "There is no doubt that in all of America the definitive era of liberation approaches...the oppressed peoples know of our identification with the liberationist cause of America...we believe that a transcendental change is occurring all over Latin America".[83] Cienfuegos saw the Rebel Army as not only knowing how to overthrow Batista, but also indirectly involved in overthrowing (by example) "other tyrannies in Latin America, because free and democratic men of America have come together and risen up, in oppressed countries, following the example of the Cuban Rebel Army to gain their freedom".[84]

One reason for this appeal to pan-Americanism was the need to generate support for the revolution in Latin America; the leaders knew that proposed reforms would unleash resistance both in Cuba and abroad: "When the foreign companies and all the 'companies' which have thousands of acres here see that the latifundio is going to be prohibited, they are going to scream. And then threats will rain down on us".[85] But this was not the only side of pan-Americanism. In June of 1959, an expedition to the Dominican Republic against Trujillo was mounted, which included Rebel Army personnel with Castro's express blessing.[86] Several other expeditions, all abortive, against Guatemala, Panama and Nicaragua, were undertaken, though not officially supported by the regime. Increasingly, as diplomatic and economic boycotts of Cuba were organized in the Organization of American States (OAS), Latin American regimes with a semblance of representative democracy also became targets and were accused of being the most comfortable allies of imperialism. Verde Olivo's coverage of Latin American concentrated on pro-Cuba demonstrations and the condemnation of dictators and "puppets". <u>Verde Olivo</u> readers were told that the peoples of Latin America, despite what their governments' actions were, enthusiastically responded to the Cuban revolution. It is easy enough, with hindsight, to argue that such pan-Americanism in <u>Verde Olivo</u> and in political education in general, was a matter of expediency and a search for a breach in Cuba's isolation. Nonetheless, the evidence exists that the leaders of the Rebel Army and many of the rank and file had deep sentiments about dictatorships in Latin America and genuinely felt solidarity with what they regarded as brother oppressed peoples.

Each measure the revolutionary government took in the first months to institute reforms was defended by <u>Verde Olivo</u> and the entire information-propaganda-education apparatus of the Rebel Army. Thus, the trials and executions of <u>Batistianos</u> were seen as positive, meeting the popular demands for justice and avoiding the mob-rule bloodletting which occurred following Machado's overthrow in 1933. The massive rent and mortgage reductions decreed in March 1959, the takeover of telephone and utility companies and the consequent rate-cuts, the takeover of the lottery system and the confiscation of Batista's properties, all of which constituted an increase in purchase power for the lower classes,[87] were presented to the Rebel Army as directly attributable to their overthrow of Batista. The reforms had been made possible because the Rebel Army was revolutionary and was of the people: this was the constant theme of many <u>Verde Olivo</u> articles and editorials.

The major reform of the first year was the promulgation of the Agrarian Reform Law of May 17, 1959. It created co-operatives, the distribution of lands over a certain maximum acreage, INRA - the National Institute of Agrarian Reform, a virtual administration in itself - some state farms, and the first attacks on <u>latifundios</u>[88] As predicted, large cattle ranchers, landowners and foreign companies protested.[89] The United States expressed its concern that the government "had not consulted with American investors before promulgating the law".[90] The propaganda apparatus of the Rebel Army was fierce in defending agrarian reform, as could be expected. Speeches defending the reform by leaders of the revolution were printed in all military organs. One such was by Cienfuegos: "It does not disturb us, that there are conspiracies, that the enemies of the revolution conspire and meet abroad to try and attack us and take away our freedom. We know that...the people, with us, will know how to bury them in the sands where they and their mercenaries disembark".[91]

As foreign and domestic criticism of the reforms, especially the agrarian reform, mounted, and as anti-communism became the repeated theme of critics, the response of the Rebel Army's propaganda apparatus became more virulent. Support of the regime by the Rebel Army, which was being taught in literacy and political education programs to see itself as the vanguard of the revolution and its first line of defense, became a matter of Cuban patriotism. Critics within the regime, such as President Manual Urrutia, Air Force Commander Pedro Díaz Lanz, and head of the Rebel Army in Camagüey, Huber Matos, all came in for harsh criticism. Leaders such as Cienfuegos began to speak about traitors: "This Revolution that we all made together, is not a Revolution of cowards, of weaklings or of traitors".[92] In the years of greatest tension, 1960-63, after Díaz Lanz defected to the United States on the grounds of the communist infiltration of the military,[93] he was depicted in the particularly vibrant political cartoons of <u>Verde Olivo</u> as a slavering toady of United States monopolies and the CIA. This image evolved from his October 1959 leaflet bombing of Havana.

The theme of patriots versus traitors, which had been part of the myth of the Rebel Army in the Sierra, emerged more as the revolution became more radical, and as it created enemies among liberals, landowners, foreign companies, professionals and even among workers and peasants. Expressing concern over the level of revolutionary consciousness in the Rebel Army, Cienfuegos cautioned that "in this army only those disposed to defend the Republic anywhere, and those who never throw mud on the memory of our dead, may remain".[94] When Urrutia criticized the agrarian reform and communist influence in July 1959, and Castro resigned,[95] the military organs condemned calls for elections, defending the "armed direct democracy" and taking the lead in the assault on Urrutia. Castro used the media to great effect in discrediting Urrutia and proceeded to call for a massive public assembly on the July 26th anniversary of the Moncada assault. Hundreds of thousands of peasants entered Havana for the meeting to support agrarian reform and call for Castro to become Prime Minister again.[96]

The period of active counter-revolution began with the first measures of revolutionary justice and rent reductions, but the agrarian reform roused the opposition of more powerful forces. Thus, a conspiracy involving Las Villas and Camagüey ranchers and Trujillo got underway in August 1959. A landing was made at Trinidad and was crushed with Rebel Army troops led personally by Castro and Cienfuegos. Then in October planes from Florida airports began to bomb sugar mills and a major defection occurred within the Rebel Army. Comandante Huber Matos, who had spoken publicly about alleged communist influence in April, June and September, resigned after Raúl Castro became Minister of Defense:

> In April 1959 I began to see pro-communist articles in <u>Verde Olivo</u>...inspired by Raúl Castro. I pro-

tested but Fidel said it did not matter. By July, I realized he was doing nothing to prevent the communits from gaining ground...I wrote a letter on October 19, 1959 saying I could not compromise my ideals by taking any part in helping to establish this new communist dictatorship.[97]

Castro, other Rebel Army leaders and Verde Olivo vilified Matos, who had told Finance Minister Rufo Lopez-Fresquet that Raúl Castro was planning to kill his brother if the communist conspiracy needed it.[98] Matos was labelled a "traitor who had obstructed the Agrarian Reform".[99] In a speech brought to the attention of all in the Rebel Army via Verde Olivo, Cienfuegos, who was placed in Matos' Camagüey command, denounced traitors to the revolution:

> There are men who were brave in the war and who today weaken, today they fear the powerful enemies of our country...those who think that sacrifice, work and difficulties ended January 1 are mistaken...we are going to achieve a true social justice; we are going to remove peasants and workers from the poverty in which those who hold the strings of counter-revolution hold them...Let those who fear the counter-revolution, who fear their planes that are again bombing us, who fear the media campaign of the enemies, let them desert...but let those who want to see this country among the first in the world stand up and say 'we are present with the Revolution'.[100]

There followed the dropping-away of liberals and social democrats in the cabinet: Felipe Pazos, Rufo Lopez-Fresquet, Manual Ray and Faustino Pérez. Guevara moved to the National Bank, new land confiscations and nationalizations occurred. Import tariffs on many United States imports were imposed. Arms purchases in the United States were denied and in Western Europe they met with little success; Cuba moved to widen trade with the Soviet Union and to secure arms there.[101]

By the time that Verde Olivo was re-organized in March 1960, relations with the United States had deteriorated to the point of breaking. "Notes from the State Department rained on Cuba", Castro later told the United Nations General Assembly,

> they never asked us about our problems, not even out of sheer pity, or because of the great responsibility they had in creating these problems. They never asked us how many died of starvation in our country, or how many were suffering from tuberculosis, or how many were unemployed...all talks by the representatives of the government of the United

States centered upon the phone company, the electric company and the land owned by American companies...they wanted 'prompt, efficient and just payment'.[102]

Flights from Florida were arriving almost daily in late 1959 and early 1960, and "millions of arrobas [and arroba is approximately eleven kilos] of cane burned...as the light planes...made their incendiary raids on the canefields".[103]

In the face of such threats and active attempts to sabotage the revolution, Verde Olivo called on patriotism. Cienfuegos' last speech,[104] on October 26, 1959, condemned the Díaz Lanz leaflet bombing of Havana, in which several people were killed and scores injured by Cuban anti-aircraft shells falling into the city. His words were reprinted throughout the next three years in Verde Olivo to help marshal revolutionary spirit. Cienguegos recalled the duty of Cubans to defend the fatherland and fulfill the duty to those fallen in the struggle against Batista:

> Those who send planes against us should not think that we will come to our knees or lower our heads. Only once will we kneel down and lower our heads and that will be the day when we make our pilgrimage to the Cuban soil which guards twenty thousand Cubans to tell them: Brothers, the Revolution is made; your blood was not shed in vain.

The Cuban military, from late 1959, expected both counter-revolutionary guerrillas and direct assaults on cities. After the October air raids, Castro announced militia training and attempted to secure weapons in Europe for the militias. The militia was to stand guard duty at all installations, such as airports, factories, sugar mills and businesses, which could be the target of sabotage, and to prepare for urban defense measures. The regular army was given intensive guerrilla training with an eye to having to withdraw into the mountains and resist a large-scale invasion.[105]

Some of the weapons the government managed to purchase in Belgium arrived aboard La Coubre in March of 1960. In a disaster reminiscent of the Maine's explosion in 1898, La Coubre blew up in Havana's harbor, killing and injuring many. Most Cubans were convinced that the CIA was responsible,[106] and Verde Olivo, in the first of its numbers after re-organization, carried photographs of the disaster and victims' denunciations of the United States. As in virtually all its numbers, Verde Olivo stressed that sacrifices were being made by soldiers and workers together in the new Cuba, whereas it had previously been "workers and soldiers fighting against each other".107

From this point on, Verdo Olivo maintained a high degree of anti-imperaialist militancy while extolling the accomplishments of the revolution. The myths of the Rebel Army were entrenched in the magazine through frequent memoirs and descriptions of battles in the Sierra, writings and speeches of figures like the Castros, Cienfuegos and Guevara. In virtually every issue there appeared quotations from Martí, and often writings and speeches from revolutionary figures and martyrs of the anti-Machado movements. A sense of Cuban revolutionary historical continuity was encouraged by articles on Cuban history, especially on the Wars of Independence. At times an issue would contain pieces on battles fought in 1868 or 1895 along with a combat encounter in 1957.

Anti-imperialism was conveyed in Verde Olivo in a variety of ways. The question of possible direct United States aggression was often brought up in editorials, interviews with commanders or units training for defense, or in speeches by Castro printed in the magazine. Care was taken to explain the actions of the United States government as motivated by economic interests: "Latin Americans, due to misunderstanding and immaturity, have been demanding that the so-called democratic United States government help us against the United States companies that exploit our countries. They do not understand that the United States government is indebted to those same interests. In the United States, the financial oligarchy governs".108 Verde Olivo was concerned to destroy Cuban illusions about United States democracy and used evidence of the repression of blacks in the United States to show how undemocratic the United States government was: "It is very American", a caption under a photograph of blacks being beaten announced, "to club them with baseball bats".109 At the same time, Verde Olivo stressed, as it still does today, that the United States government and ruling class were not the American people, with whom Cubans had every reason to feel solidarity. Rather, monopoly control of the press and financial influence over candidates made United States democracy a class rule by monopolies.

On the theoretical and polemical plane, Verde Olivo relied mostly on Guevara and Castro to explain imperialism and Cuban economic dependence. Guevara's articles, especially, were explanations of imperialism from a Leninist perspective. "Kings without crown",110 he called monopolies. His concern was to educate Cubans about the direct relationship between political and economic sovereignty: "Political power is the instrument for the economic conquest. We cannot yet proclaim before the tombs of our martyrs [a reference to Cienfuegos' last speech] that Cuba is economically independent...to win something you have to take it from someone. We have to take our sovereignty from the monopolies". Imperialism, he explained, invested abroad for profits, not to produce development. Economic struggle was just as important as the military struggle, for Guevara, and he sought to encourage a war mentality in regard to work, military training, and action against monopolies. The contradictions are there, he was saying, let us push them to their ultimate conclusion: there could be no compromise with imperialism. Castro repeated the theme that there could be no dealing with imperialism:

> Private capital does not go where it is most needed, but where it can get the biggest profits. Foreign investment capital demands conditions. Do you know what they are? The right to fire workers ...How could we think of solving our problems with solutions that have resulted in nothing for fifty years? If we did that, we would have no problems with those who have robbed us: big landlords, trusts, mining companies...but twenty thousand did not die for that.[111]

Here, the myths of the insurrectionary struggle were linked to anti-imperialism and the impending confrontation.

Verde Olivo in 1960 presented a very integrated view of the world to its readers in the army and the militia, which together comprised some hundreds of thousands. It was also available to non-military readers. Any one issue would contain a militant editorial, usually on the duplicity and machinations of imperialism, urging Cuban vigilance, in a regular column called Avanzada Rebelde (Rebel Advance). The feature Pensamiento de la Revolución (Revolutionary Thought) was usually the printing of a speech or writings of the leaders. Castro's speeches dominated Pensamiento and are a record of his extraordinary efforts and talents in the political education of a whole people. Each issue contained articles on economic projects under way or completed, army participation in rural construction projects, or a certain group of workers who had made innovations or improved productivity in spite of a lack of previously imported parts or equipment. Such articles on the economy stressed both the progress of the revolution and the unity of workers and soldiers. Usually the articles on new schools or co-operatives in the countryside stressed the same themes: progress, comparison with the odious past, and the unity of campesinos and the military. International coverage, in features like Mirando al Mundo (Looking at the World), concentrated on conditions in Third World dictatorships and on resistance to such conditions. Other articles stressed actions of international solidarity with Cuba, especially in Latin America. Sports and culture sections often were presented in the light of increased participation by Cubans, as opposed to the consumption of sports and culture by limited numbers under Batista. Reviews of movies and literature came more and more to concentrate on the political and social content of the works. Cartoons depicted fanged and unshaven Batistianos being received with open arms by top-hatted United States businessmen and politicians in Florida, their dreams of conquering Cuba being rudely interrupted by machete and rifle-wielding campesinos and workers. Defectors such as Díaz Lanz were pictured as attracted by the smell of money hung over their heads as bait by the CIA.

The major themes of the political education that Verde Olivo was conveying in 1960, in a build-up of revolutionary morale that anticipated great struggles, were the tradition of Rebel Army sacrifice and victory against great odds, the superiority of armed democracy over monopoly rule, anti-imperialism, international solidarity with Cuba, the Revolution as direct descendant of past Cuban heroes and martyrs, the necessity of unity (and thus harsh criticism of anti-communism), the reforms and gains brought by the revolution to the masses, and the unity of the military and the people. Several examples of Verde Olivo contents during 1960 will illustrate the tone of the political education contained in the magazine.

The July 17, 1960 issue opened with double-page photographs of a mass demonstration called to protest the United States' ending of the sugar quota. The caption is "We are Winning!"[112] Under the caption "With the Fatherland or Against It", an article speaks of the Ley Machete (Machete Law - nationalization) in operation against the Ley Puñal (Dagger Law - United States sugar quota restrictions). It is claimed that Khrushchev had promised military support against United States aggression and that the Soviet Union would buy the sugar.[113] In Pensamiento, Castro's June 24 speech "History Shows You Cannot Defeat a Country in Revolution"[114] is printed. Guevara's satirical column Sin bala en el directo (Missing the Target) under the psuedonym Francotirador (Sniper) compares United States media stories of Soviet missiles and submarine bases in Cuba to the 1956-69 stories. He recalls Cienfuegos's story of Soviet submarines with feet climbing Turquino Peak.[115] The editorial Avanzada Rebelde argues that the end of the sugar quota means the United States "has decided to destroy the popular Cuban government". Cubans must be prepared to turn Cuba into "a sea of fire" to destroy any invasion.[116] Eduardo Yasells, who later became the editor, contributes an article about oil. He explains that Cuba got Soviet oil cheaper than Venezuelan and ordered United States-owned refineries, with the support of Cuban technicians and the military, to process it. When they refused, the Cuban government took over the refineries.[117] Guevara, visting a military school for tank crews, says "We will win because we are only the small vanguard of an enormous army that will be built by a decided people".[118] An article by Santiago Frayle, a *Verde Olivo* staff writer, entitled "Traitor or Hero", claims that Cuba is living a moment of historical transcendence, when "to say Fatherland is to say Revolution ...the hour of direct language when every man and woman must have the notion that their only possible behavior and destiny is to be a traitor or a hero...there is no other alternative".[119] An article follows, claiming that workers now do all they can to improve productivity and to care for equipment, whereas they had no motive to do so under a system of exploitation.[120] *Mirando al mundo*, the world affairs series, reports on foreign statements of support for Cuba in the sugar controversy, including Field Marshal Montgomery and Mexico. France's crimes in Algeria are condemned.[121] An article claims that parts for buses are now being made in Cuba more cheaply than it cost to import them. Self-reliance and ingenuity are the themes.[122] Gregorio Selser's article talks of long-suffering victims of McCarthyism in the United States, House Un-American Activities Committee hearings, and democracy's hypocrisy.[123] An interview with American playwright Arthur Miller in the *Sunday Times* is reprinted, wherein Miller claims the United States Army stopped McCarthy, not the left. McCarthyism, he says, existed before and since McCarthy's death.[124] Sports and cultural reviews follow, and the magazine ends with political cartoons and a photo-essay on FAR members building homes for *campesinos* in the Sierra Maestra. Martí is quoted: "An army that sits still will crumble".[125]

By October 1960, counter-revolutionaries were active in the Escambray and militia units were sent to "clean" the area. The October 22, 1960 issue of *Verde Olivo* reflects this struggle. The first article reports the executions of some "mercenary invaders" and prison sentences for others. The stress is on co-operation between the FAR and the militia.[126] Photographs of military equipment marked "US Army Property" are published.[127] A speech by Castro is reported, comparing the Cuban with the French and Russian revolutions. He speaks of stages, alternate paths, and nuances of the revolutionary process.[128] The *Avanzada Rebelde* editorial repeats the theme of Cuba's legacy of underdevelopments: "The Cuban economic structure until the Revolution was merely the instrument of a few powerful national and foreign monopolies which controlled the political gangs which held power".[129] Such monopolies "have now dedicated themselves to thwarting the plans of the Revolutionary Government to increase production". Their sanctions and conspiracies justify the expropriation of another three hundred eighty-two firms: "Before they destroy us we have to destroy them. It is a struggle for survival by a people against those who wish to dominate them again". Let such powers conspire, Avanzada says, "but they know the Cuban people are alert, scrutinizing the horizon, ready to defend with a rifle, body to body, even with our teeth the sacred right of liberty; Patria o Muerte 'Fatherland or Death' is no idle slogan; it is a philosophy of life".

In Pensamiento, another Castro speech is presented, wherein he discusses the mobilization, using a rhetorical style of questions and answers:

> Imperialism and reaction are on the offensive. The Revolution defends itself. Is the Revolution on the defensive? Yes, it is on the defensive. Is it a mistake to say the Revolution is on the defensive? No, it is no mistake, because it is, simply, obedience to a permanent law of history and revolutions: stages of advance, stages of struggle; counter-revolutionary offensives, revolutionary counter-offensives...It is the same as occurred many times during the war...does it mean that our counter-attack will liquidate the imperialist offensive? No. It will liquidate the first manifestations, but imperialism will continue...There will be more extensive struggles, there will be greater defeats for the enemies of the Revolution...Why didn't we send the Rebel Army to deal with the groups of esbirros 'thugs'? Because the army is training for larger and more important battles... in order to combat the Escambray groups, we mobilized the Escambray militias;...and why did we refrain from giving news of our victories? So that we could wait and collect more of their weapons... the glorious soldiers of imperialism ran from us... there Kennedy, Nixon and the other imperialists have their hopes dashed...We didn't use heavy arms or planes. We have kept them for when the big boys come, those training in Guatemala and on Swan Island...We have been extremely generous...we don't want to have to shoot these people, but he who kills by iron must die by it, he who wants to kill his own countrymen with foreign iron deserves no other punishment than to die by it.[130]

An article on the training of sailors on a cruiser talks of their "familiarization with the life of the people and the different works of the Revolution. They climb the Sierra, and go to the countryside to see the campesinos' life".[131] There follows an article describing Máximo Gómez' machete charges against the Spanish in 1868-74.[132] José M. Hornos, a frequent contributor on Spain, talks of United States bases there and says Franco, the friend of Hitler, is now the friend of Eisenhower.[133] An article on Laos holds that the country is in revolutionary ferment.[134] A book review on El Pequeño Ejército Loco (The Crazy Little Army) compares Augusto Sandino of Nicaragua with Castro and Cuba and brings in Bolívar and San Martín.[135] A section from the Manual is included, tracing racial discrimination to slavery.[136]

    In these issues, it is not a siege mentality that prevails. Rather, a mixture of optimism, fierce determination and humor[137] is to be found in the repetition of the major themes. Sacrifice and the possibility of individual death is set in the context of inevitable victory and the dynamics of concrete gains for Cuba's people. Stereotypes of imperialists and Batistianos or gusanos 'worms' (those who emigrated or hoped to emigrate) make them almost laughable enemies. Cartoons of top-hatted capitalists, a surprised golfer Eisenhower and unshaven, hulking, gorilla-like Batistianos training in Florida and Guatemala reinforce the message of articles and speeches against imperialism, its Cuban allies and plots. The cartoon figures have changed little since 1960, as the contemporary cartoons of Nuez in Granma show. Differences between imperialists are rarely discussed. Kennedy's election in 1960 is seen as merely a change of cliques.[138] Latin American governments which follow the United States line in the San José, Costa Rica OAS meeting in 1960 are seen as puppets.[139] The OAS is the "Department of Colonies" for the United States, "created to facilitate juridically direct or indirect United States intervention in the internal affairs of any American state which refuses to bow down".[140] Photographs of Costa Rican police surrounding the OAS meeting to keep away any "illegal demonstration" and photographs of alleged FBI agents taping speakers at the meeting are produced to support this conception of the OAS. Guevara's article argues that the OAS meeting showed that 1) Latin American governments are not representative; anti-American and pro-Cuban demonstrations had occurred in the countries of the delegates; 2) Cuba is the goose with the golden eggs, since its revolution provoked tidbits of aid from the United States; and 3) the Latin American bourgeoisies are incapable of confronting imperialism.[141]

    Part of the Verde Olivo staff's idea of political education was to have the FAR and militia learn about the rest of the world. As relations with the Soviet Union and other socialist countries increased in 1960 and 1961, more and more articles about such countries and their armies appeared. These came from foreign sources as well as from Cubans familiar with the countries or reporting on journeys made there as official representatives, soldiers or technicians in training, or exemplary workers. In the October 1, 1960 issue, for example, there appeared a review of Alexander Bek's book Men of Panfilov on the defense of Moscow in the fall and winter of 1941.[142] FAR personnel were encouraged to read Soviet authors by the inclusion of short stories and reviews in Verde Olivo, and by the publication of various Soviet works in Spanish. More and more articles appeared favorably comparing Soviet military and economic accomplishments with those of the capitalist giants.[143] Admiration was expressed for the military establishments of such countries as the German Democratic Republic.[144]

The embrace of a revolutionary social myth by an individual leads him or her to the dilemma of commitment. Myth, as Sorel argued, gives social contradictions very clear outlines and leaves a person with a choice between two diametrically opposed alternatives. In a revolution, sooner or later the majority must choose; remaining neutral becomes a very difficult luxury and is perceived by the already committed of either camp as indicating sympathy for the other. Thus, the emphasis in 1960-63 was on the choice between hero or traitor, between participation or emigration, between being with the revolution or against it. Political education in the revolutionary military of Cuba always tended to push the individual towards total commitment. Once the myths were established through experience and indoctrination, their role in political education was even more the delineation of positions and the gaining of the individual's commitment to the revolution. Verde Olivo was a prime vehicle for producing this commitment. Coming out weekly, it was read by the entire military as a matter of course.[145] Part of the revolutionary instructor's role was to make sure it was read and discussed. Such a frequent and militant bolstering of the revolution had a major role to play in creating revolutionary commitment among the troops and militia. Each week's events were reviewed for the reader in such a way as to give near-exclusive coverage to their interpretation by the revolutionary leadership.

The message of Verde Olivo to the FAR was that the armed struggle of the Rebel Army had made the choice between revolution or newly-entrenched imperialism possible.[146] Armed struggle had created the conditions in which a mass change of consciousness was possible. In such a transitional period, it was imperative that massive efforts be made to impel such a mass change of consciousness. The national bourgeoisie, Verde Olivo readers were told, was incapable, despite certain conflicts of interest with imperialism, of leading this mass change of consciousness. Thus, that class was eclipsed in the first Cuban cabinet and came to support counterrevolution. They were forced to choose, as Guevara put it, between "those who love the people and those who hate the people".[147] Verde Olivo thus took the created myth of guerrilla struggle, the myth of the Rebel Army, combined it with the myth of national redemption and the cumplo del deber cubano (the Cuban duty to martyrs of the past and of the present) and sought to create the myth of a guerrilla people, a people in arms. For such a people, in arms, with the FAR as vanguard, no historical gates could long remain closed. Thus, the long-term Cuban slogan Venceremos 'We Shall Win'. Patria o Muerte (Fatherland or Death) had expressed the revolutionary devotion and willingness to sacrifice in the guerrilla struggle. Venceremos expressed the sense of a victory won and others to come.

The first victory to come was that at Playa Girón in mid-April 1961. The counter-revolutionaries in the Escambray had already been contained, though fighting continued into 1963. The popular militias, backed by the FAR, had done their job of "cleaning" well. Verde Olivo presented major reports on the clean-up after the main pockets of resistance had been defeated. Those who died in the campaign became martyrs in the struggle against imperialism.[148] Lists of the arms supplied by air drops from the United States were published and the weapons displayed in Havana, with their prominent "US Army" markings. Pictures and diaries of counter-revolutionaries, now known as gusanos 'worms' were published in Verde Olivo to show their low morale in the face of the militia and the FAR: "There is nothing to eat", wrote one gusano on February 26, 1961, "and we can't approach any houses. Fidel has many militia men. We've lost contact with the others. We see only the militia".[149] Castro had boasted in January 1961 that the militia and the FAR would make Escambray the most revolutionary part of Cuba and, by late March, the clean-up was well advanced, with new schools, hospitals, literacy classes, roads and hygiene programs underway.[150] Counter-revolution would no longer be able to take advantage of backwardness in the area and the lgeacy of what Verde Olivo called the corrupt leadership and opportunism of the "Second Front of Escambray" during the struggle against Batista.[151]

The national literacy campaign, about to be launched, had been a subject in Verde Olivo for some weeks when the invasion came. The first literacy workers were already in the countryside in a pilot project. Verde Olivo underlined the unity between these young volunteers and the FAR, especially when Conrado Benítez, a young urban volunteer, was tortured, hung and mutilated after his death at the hands of Batistianos.[152] Attacks in Verde Olivo on curas falangistas 'falangist priests' began at this point, since a priest had encouraged Benítez' killers and other priests had been allowing their churches and homes to be used for meetings of gusanos.[153]

With this victory in the Escambray, the revolutionary leadership felt some security and expressed publicly its confidence in the Cuban people's ability to repulse the expected invasion. Verde Olivo's photo-essays concentrated on FAR preparedness, under the slogan Si Vienen, Quedan! 'If They Come, They Will Stay!'[154] This confidence was tested starting April 15, when warplanes supplied to gusanos by the CIA attacked bases in Santiago and Havana. Repulsed by "young campesinos and workers in the anti-aircraft batteries, they fled, some right to Miami International Airport".[155] On the 17th, the landing of some "1300-1500 mercenaries, supported by Yankee air power and navy"[156] took place. Within seventy-two hours, it had been thoroughly defeated in hard fighting and all but a few were captured.

Verde Olivo has never ceased to hold up this example of the intentions of the United States government and to caution the FAR and all Cubans that the United States government has not fully laid to rest the idea of direct aggression. However, perhaps the best coverage of the events in Verde Olivo came immediately after the attack. "We answered the barbarous aggression with iron and fire and we shall win", Verde Olivo announced on April 23. The immediate logic of the attack was presented to the FAR and the militia: "The barbarians came to take from us the land that the Revolution delivered to campesinos and co-operative farmers, to take from us the new factories of the people, the mines and sugar mills, to take from our children the schools that the Revolution has opened to them all over the country, to take away dignity from the black men and women of Cuba, to take their new jobs from the workers".[157] Imperialism had attacked, said Castro on April 16 when burying the victims of the bombing attacks, "because we have made a socialist revolution under their very noses".[158] This was the famous public declaration that the revolution was socialist, forever after debated by North American social scientists trying to plumb the psychological depths of Castro's mind, sense of timing and embrace of Marxism: "This socialist revolution of the poor, by the poor and for the poor we shall defend with weapons".

As in all of Verde Olivo's numbers, especially in the periods of shortages and rationing, the central theme in the reporting of the Playa Girón invasion was that of the revolutionary unity of Cubans. A revolution was in progress that benefited workers and peasants, the majority, it was repeated, and thus workers and peasants defended the revolution against both internal and external enemies. The heroes of the invasion battles were common people. Castro expressed this sentiment even before the invasion was launched, in his radio broadcast eulogy for those killed in the bombing. Pointing to rifles being distributed to the militia, he said: "What hands are those which lift these arms? Are they not workers' hands? Are they not peasant hands? Are they not creative hands? Humble hands of the people? And who forms the majority of the people, millionaires or workers? Exploiters or the exploited? The privileged or the humble?"[159]

Verde Olivo stressed this theme of popular support and participation. In the issue which gave details of the crushing of the invasion, the front cover was a drawing of two arms, one holding a heavy wrench, the other holding a Belgian FAL automatic rifle. The back cover showed people in line for rationed goods, their cartoon mental balloons containing figures with rifles. The caption was "the sacrifice of those who fell was greater. Think about this when you are in the line-ups that the imperialist blockade has produced".[160] Pictures of civilian women near Playa Girón lying dead from strafing attacks along the roads were published, as were pictures of children wounded in the bombing and strafing raids on Havana, April 15. One of the young cadets in the FAR military school hit by the attack became a martyr of the revolution: he had dramatically written "Fidel" with his own blood on a piece of wood as he lay dying. The caption under his photograph in Verde Olivo was a line from the Cuban national anthem: "Do not fear a glorious death, since to die for the Fatherland is to live".[161]

In the following weeks, Verde Olivo published numerous articles and interviews with militia and FAR combatants at Girón. Much was made of the fact that Castro and other Rebel Army leaders took direct part in the fighting.[162] Guevara, Universo Sánchez and Julio García Oliveira, from the original Rebel Army, were all wounded.[163] All possible connections with Girón were drawn by Verde Olivo: the military attacks on the young Bolshevik Revolution by European states, the United States and Japan were compared to the invasion.[164] The role of the rearguard in the cities (the Committees for the Defense of the Revolution, neighborhood vigilance and political education groups, were already active) and the maintenance of industrial and agricultural production were praised.[165] The victory was seen as a direct homage to the ideals of Martí and the Mambises of 1868-98: "Today when the Fatherland has fought and is fighting the hardest battle against the forces of imperialism is when the glorious struggle of our mambises receives its well-deserved homage".[166] Cuba's militias were compared with those of Viet Nam, stressing the revolutionary nature of the countries dominated by imperialism.[167]

The morale and sacrifices of the Cuban defenders at Girón were contrasted with the character of the invaders, and the direct involvement of high United States officials like Secretary of Sate Dulles[168] and the CIA, dubbed the "Central Agency of Yankee Cretins",[169] was played up. The former were seen as mostly tools of those who stayed behind in Miami, though their combat leaders were seen as <u>latifundistas</u> and ex-torturers of the Batista regime. The social background of the invaders was covered by <u>Verde Olivo</u> to show the counter-revolutionary nature of their intentions:

> <u>Latifundistas</u>, 100; middle landowners, 24; owners of rental housing, 67; merchants, 112; industrialists, 35; ex-soldiers of the tyranny, 194; people of leisure, 179; high government employees, 236; <u>lumpen</u> (petty criminals), 112...these are the people who came, representing the rest, who were the owners of everything else. These mercenaries truly represented their class...None of these types fought against the tyranny in the Sierra Maestra... what better historical lesson, what better proof of the Marxist theory of class struggle can there be?[170]

On television, Castro visited the captured invaders and debated with them. It was proposed that Cuba would not hold any executions, but would send them back to Florida in return for five hundred tractors which Cuba regarded as partial indemnity for the physical damage caused. Lives, it was said, could not be replaced: "only the happiness of the people can repay such losses".[171] Castro also proposed an exchange of prisoners: the "mercenaries" would be traded for Puerto Rican independence fighters imprisoned in the United States, political prisoners in Guatemala and Nicaragua, and anti-fascists in Spanish jails.[172] Nothing came of this. Eventually, some United States corporations, ostensibly acting independently of the government, sent some tractors and medicines, and the "mercenaries" were sent to Florida after more than a year of imprisonment. Castro remarked that they had been sent back because of the generosity of the Revolution and because the Cuban people could defeat any number of such "mercenary" forces. Cuban security was "in our weapons, in our fighters, in our heroic people".[173]

CONCLUSION

The institutionalization of revolutionary social myths in the political education of the military, as well as in that of the national political consciousness, was marked by the victory over imperialism at Girón and by the announcement that the revolution was socialist and Marxist. With the defeat of counter-revolutionaries by the militia in the Escambray mountains, these former events had created a larger social myth with an appropriate set of heroes. The heroes were the Cuban people in general, and the peasantry and working class in particular. They were embodied in the FAR and the militia and had come to the stature of social myth through post-insurrectionary experiences. The Rebel Army remained the vanguard, but was now seen as the small motor which had started the large engine of the Cuban revolutionary process.

The official embrace of Marxism in 1961 provided a comprehensive structure for the collection of revolutionary social myths which, at all times during the insurrection and subsequent revolution played a crucial role in the political education of the revolutionary military. The myths together became more cohesive and operated as a system under the all-encompassing myth of the Cuban Socialist Revolution. However, it would be a mistake to claim that the embrace of Marxism was an arbitrary choice from among alternative ideologies made by a small leadership clique in the Rebel Army - the Castros and Guevara. It would also be an exaggeration to see the embrace of Marxism as a conscious ploy to attract Soviet defense and trade commitments. Unfortunately, even the most sober studies of the Cuban revolution suggest, first, that Marxism was the arbitrary choice of Fidel Castro,[174] and second, that the embrace of Marxism was a betrayal, a trick played on the Cuban masses who awaited the delivery of social justice and national redemption by free enterprise.[175]

There is a strong body of evidence and reasoned thought that in this age of industrial societies and imperialism, i.e. the dominance of monopoly capital and international hierarchies of dependence, exploitation and privilege, an age in which class conflict often upstages other historical forces, social revolution and projects of radical reforms, especially in so-called underdeveloped countries, necessarily take on a socialist and Marxist character. In the case of Cuba, perhaps the work of James O'Connor best expresses the underlying dynamics which made the Cuban revolution socialist.[176] This notion of course somewhat distorts the original Leninist view of the making of a socialist revolution. Lenin saw the struggle for a vanguard party as prior to insurrection and armed struggle, so that the overthrow of bourgeois power would be accomplished by the working class, led by a Marxist party. Even so, the Bolsheviks were themselves hard-pressed to keep up with the tide of revolutionary consciousness and demands made by the Petrograd working class and the czarist army conscripts.

In Cuba, the struggle against a dictatorship and generally against perceived social injustice opened up more possibilities as it progressed. It was almost as if those who overthrew Batista were surprised to find so much power for change in their hands when the armed forces of the state, the classic support of any prevailing set of social and production relations, disintegrated.

It was as though action had stripped away a complete layer of the textured social reality to reveal unexpected possibilities and opportunities. Some of the possibilities were not totally unexpected, such as the confrontation with imperialism. Certainly Guevara and the two Castros had some notion that imperialism would soon be an overt enemy. But that socialism would definitely be the path reforms would take and that Marxism would achieve ideological hegemony, though not in the way the PSP might have expected or desired, was not, evidently, appreciated by even the most astute observers. Certainly, once the revolution, in the form of radical reforms, was underway, a great kinship with the major revolutions of history was felt, and a long familiarity with Marxist categories and concepts lent itself to the view of the Cuban situation as one of class struggle. But this is not enough basis upon which to speculate the Marxism, like a mole, was secretly burrowing in the plans of the leadership from before Moncada. For an ideology to achieve hegemony it must be able to articulate the political vision of more than a clique.

At some point, one must decide whether indeed class struggle was the fundamental energy of the Cuban revolution. The decision that class struggle is the case may then in fact not take shape as a declaration of Marxist principles. It might, in the case of Cuba, merely be the formation of the social myth of the Rebel Army and the reform program "of the poor, by the poor and for the poor". Only later, upon reflection, does Marxism come into the Cuban picture as a comprehensive explanation of the process. As Guevara wrote some seven months before the revolution's self-denomination as Marxist, "the laws of Marxism are present in the events of the Cuban Revolution, independently of whether its leaders profess or know of those laws from a theoretical point of view".[177]

Even before socialism was proclaimed to be the nature of the revolution and Marxism-Leninism to be its ideology, the political education of the military was dominated by Marxist categories and concepts. As Huber Matos had charged, <u>Verde Olivo</u> was Marxist-influenced. However, it was not as he originally suspected, that the "communism" influencing <u>Verde Olivo</u> was Soviet Marxism in the sense that Western Cold War ideology saw Marxism as conspiratorial, imported and subversive. The PSP had no exclusive rights to the language of Marxism; the left wing of the Ortodoxos which organized to resist Batista's regime in 1952-53 spoke of class struggle and social justice, of exploitation and foreign domination. Many of the M-26 cadres during the insurrectionary war were to the left of the PSP. Official Marxist ideology was appreciated in theory while the practice of the PSP was severely criticized. Some cadres were anti-communist because the PSP was a communist party. Marxism in the revolution as a whole surpassed the thinking and practice of the PSP. There is no doubt that the PSP members involved in the political education of the Rebel Army/FAR had an effect, but the course of events and the dynamic of a reform program in a dominated and dependent country where the bourgeois apparatus of force had been eliminated and the people armed must also be credited with the early appearance of Marxist categories and concepts in political education.

Marxism provided a comprehensive explanation of politics to the makers of political education for the Rebel Army/FAR. Thus, through the years of intense confrontations with imperialism and counter-revolution, from the Agrarian Reform Law of May 1959 through Girón in April 1961, the counter-revolutionary groups under arms in 1960-63 in different parts of the country, the missile crisis in October 1962, to the unending series of assassination plots against Castro, the CIA's arming, funding, training and landing of "mercenaries" and counter-revolutionaries, and the trade and diplomatic boycotts, <u>Verde Olivo</u> explained events consistently in Marxist terms. All the revolutionary social myths of the insurrectionary period were brought under the aegis of the over-riding social myth of the Cuban Socialist Revolution. Through this focus, for example, all heroes of the past were heroes of the socialist revolution: "Camilo [Cienguegos] would not have been Camilo without the Revolution, without the opportunity of combat... [because of the Revolution] there are thousands, tens of thousands, hundreds of thousands of Camilos in the people".[178] Cienfuegos was seen as not only of the people, but from the working class, the fundamental force behind the whole of the revolutionary process: "Our entire revolutionary process, which has unfolded in distinct stages, with moments of advance and triumph and with painful moments of retrocession, is linked to the progress of the workers' movement in Cuba".[179]

The social myths which fired the imagination of those assaulting Moncada and which sustained them through prison, exile, the <u>Granma</u> landing, combat in the Sierra and the 1958 campaigns against the Batista army became part of the official myth system projected in the political education of the military after January 1959. Cuban history, with its lengthy struggle against Spanish colonialism in the 19th century, formed the myth of national redemption. The 20th century myth of national redemption focused on the anti-Machado struggle and the anti-corruption platform of Eddy Chibás. Through the lens of Marxism, figures such as Martí and Maceo were seen as precursors of the anti-imperialist struggles of the 20th century. The Rebel Army and Castro were claimed to be direct intellectual and spiritual descendants of the <u>Mambises</u> and 19th century national leaders: "The Cuban Revolution is the product both of the life and work of Martí, Maceo and others and of Marxism-Leninism. Fidel has assimilated the revolutionary humanism of Marti, the combative boldness and honesty of principles of Maceo, and the anti-imperialist intransigence of both with the theory and scientific practice of Marxism-Leninism".[180] The anti-imperialist and pro-working class sentiments of Maceo and Martí were referred to in every Verde Olivo article on the two men.[181] Similarly, heroes and martyrs of the anti-Machado struggle and the 1933 revolution such as Julio Antonio Mella and Antonio Guiteras were exalted as precursors and influences on the Rebel Army and the revolution.

The social myth of continuous struggles for national redemption embraced by Eddy Chibás and then by the fledgling M-26 had set the stage, in the Verde Olivo view, for the newest and most glorious era of Cuban history, that of the anti-Batista insurrection and socialist revolution. During the struggle against Batista, the martyrs of Moncada, the Granma, the attack on the presidential palace, the naval mutiny and uprising at Cienguegos, and M-26 dead in the cities all entered the pantheon of Cuban heroes. Cuban martyrology was seen as one continuous historical endeavor for liberation and social justice. The sacrifice of Frank País was equated with the sacrifice of Jose Martí. As such sacrifices had contributed to the guerrillas' morale in the Sierra so they would now symbolize the morale of the FAR and militia confronting imperialism and counter-revolution.

In this newest period of Cuban history when the myth of national redemption had been realized through sacrifice, especially the sacrifices of the "Generation of the Centenary" and young Cubans in general, the myth of the Rebel Army played a strong role in the political education of the military. The new myth was a created myth, from the perspective of Cubans, in 1959-63, rather than one inherited from history and embellished by continuity. It was a myth in which the heroes were still young and alive, in which those who had died creating it were fresh in the memory of the survivors and victors. The myth included revolutionary morale and discipline and superiority over the Batista army, all regular armies of Latin America in the service of oligarchies and imperialism, and the forces of the CIA and imperialism. The myth included the notion of militant combativeness, translated to mean that vigilance, combativeness and sacrifice were the only means to confront imperialism, the support and direct successor of Batista. It included the primacy of action and armed struggle against dictatorship and injustice over traditional parliamentary opposition parties. And the myth of the Rebel Army carried a class analysis in its core, in that it claimed that the Rebel Army was of the peasantry, working class and radical students, an army not dominated by bourgeois ideology or turned aside by the attractions of corruption. It had come from the people, as Verde Olivo and revolutionary leaders stressed repeatedly, and would remain of and for the people. And finally, the myth of the Rebel Army upheld the superiority of the Sierra over the llano in the official view of the insurrection, notwithstanding the inclusion of urban fighters both in the revolutionary government and in the martyrology.

The myth of the Rebel Army became, in Verde Olivo and in the formal political education of the FAR and militia, the ideal to be emulated in the struggle against imperialism. The Rebel Army was seen as the vanguard of the Cuban people's drive to national redemption and to the reforms which inaugurated socialism, reforms which Marxism's comprehensiveness gave the sanction of Martí and Maceo. National redemption led to confrontation with imperialism and the interests of the Cuban bourgeoisie and these latter were equated with Batista's regime and historical injustices. The new and more comprehensive myth of the Cuban Socialist Revolution contained an analysis of Cuban history and of conflicting interest, and identified the enemies of national redemption and of the Rebel Army as the enemies of the Cuban people and their revolution. It provided a framework for the political education of military bodies recruited from the peasantry and working class and radicalized petite bourgeoisie; it was used to create and expand revolutionary consciousness, the perceived sine qua non for the defense of the Revolution. The myths of national redemption and the Rebel Army, on the one hand, and of the Socialist Revolution, on the other, fed into and sustained each other. Batista was imperialism. The Rebel Army was the Cuban people.

NOTES

1. The phrase is Richard Fagen's. See Fagen, The Transformation of Political Culture in Cuba.
2. Thomas, p. 1069. It was ended largely by Castro's January 8 eloquence in arguing for unity, and by public support for Castro in his call to the DR to give up the palace and its arms.
3. See Farber, pp. 235-37.
4. Castro, speech of December 2, 1961, in Revolución (Havana).
5. See Schulz, pp. 404-5.
6. Cienfuegos, speech of January 4, 1959, in Cabrera Alvarez, p. 167.
7. See the descriptions in Dubois, p. 363; Bonachea and San Martín, p. 330.
8. Castro, in Revolución, 10 Ja. 59.

9. Cienfuegos' letter of November 19, 1958 to Castro, in Pérez Tarrau, pp. 59-61.
10. See "El pensamiento revolucionario de Camilo", Verde Olivo, 29 Oct. 60, p. 69.
11. See Norberto Fuentes, "Cubanos en la guerra civil española", Cuba Internacional, 112, March 1979, pp. 30-35.
12. Thomas, p. 1082.
13. Verde Olivo, 17 Sept. 59, p. 12, speaks of an 80% rate of illiteracy in the Rebel Army on January 1, 1959.
14. Cabrera Alvarez, p. 174.
15. See Kozol's study of the literacy campaign in Children of the Revolution, pp. 1-96.
16. Fagen, Cuba: The Political Content of Adult Education, p. 12.
17. See Paulo Freire, Pedagogy of the Oppressed (New York: Herder and Herder, 1971).
18. Fagen, The Transformation..., p. 240.
19. Comisión Nacional Cubana de la UNESCO, Cuba y la conferencia de educación y desarrollo económica y social (Havana: Editorial Nacional, 1962), p. 25.
20. Osmani Cienfuegos, the Marxist elder brother of Camilo, became the head of military education programs.
21. Hereafter referred to as Manual.
22. Specifically aimed at illiterates.
23. "Arma Nueva", Verde Olivo, 27 Marc. 60, p. 62.
24. Fagen, The Transformation..., p. 240, fn. 11.
25. "Arma Nueva", Verde Olivo, 27 Mar. 60, p. 62.
26. Ibid.
27. Much of Alfabeticemos is to be found in Fagen, The Political Content..., pp. 23-56. The reader used by literacy students, Venceremos (We Shall Win), was a shorter and simpler version of Alfabeticemos.
28. Those who were illiterate would have the Manual read to them in study circles.
29. Cienfuegos, in Cabrera Alvarez, pp. 179-80.
30. Verde Olivo, 3 Sept. 60, p. 25.
31. "Revolución y reforma" (Manual), Verde Olivo, 10 Sept. 60, pp. 13-14.
32. Cienfuegos, speech of October 21, 1959, criticizing those "who weaken [Huber Matos, Díaz Lanz, Urrutia] before the powerful enemies of the Fatherland", in Cabrera Alvarez pp. 180-81.
33. Cienfuegos' speech of May 11, 1959, in Verde Olivo, 10 Sept. 60, p. 14.
34. "Los Indocubanos" (Manual), Verde Olivo, 18 June 61, pp. 23-4.
35. Lección I: Historia de la propiedad de la tierra en Cuba", (Manual), Verde Olivo, 12 Nov. 60, p. 81.
36. "El descubrimiento" (Manual), Verde Olivo, 25 June 61, p. 7.
37. "La conquista" (Manual), Verde Olivo, 2 July

61, p. 15.
38. "El Siglo XVI: pacificación y repartimientos" (Manual), Verde Olivo, 9 July 61, pp. 15-16.
39. "Lección V: el perjuicio racial y la discriminación del negro" (Manual), Verde Olivo, 22 Oct. 60, pp. 61-2.
40. "El comercio exterior" (Manual), Verde Olivo, 28 May 61, p. 71.
41. "El siglo XVII y la primera mitad del siglo XVIII" (Manual), Verde Olivo, 23 July 61, pp. 71-2.
42. "Las luchas de los vegueros" (Manual), Verde Olivo, 30 July 61, p. 58.
43. See "Aparición de la nacionalidad cubana" (Manual), Verde Olivo, 20 Aug. 61, pp. 20-21.
44. See "Desarrollo de la industria azucarera" (Manual), Verde Olivo, 12 March 61, p. 71.
45. See, for example, "Riquezas naturales de Cuba" (Manual), Verde Olivo, 8 Jan. 61, p. 19.
46. "El desarrollo económico de Cuba" (Manual), Verde Olivo, 1 Oct. 60, p. 35.
47. "El desarrollo económico de Cuba" (Manual), Verde Olivo, 1 Oct. 60, p. 35.
48. See, for example, "El ganado vacuno" (Manual) Verde Olivo, 9 April 61, p. 21: "85% of cattle farmers had only 25% of the livestock, while 2% had 42.4% of the livestock".
49. "Caracter patriótica de la Revolución Cubana" (Manual), Verde Olivo, 17 Sept. 60, p. 49.
50. "El latifundio" (Manual), Verde Olivo, 19 Nov. p. 27.
51. "Industrialización" (Manual), Verde Olivo, 18 Dec. 60, p. 41.
52. "La riqueza minera" (Manual), Verde Olivo, 26 Feb. 61, p. 41.
53. "Lección VI: fuerzas revolucionarias y contra-revolucionarias" (Manual), Verde Olivo, 29 Oct. 60, p. 35.
54. Castro, "El esfuerzo de los trabajadores", Verde Olivo, 5 Mar. 61, pp. 46-7.
55. "Los pretextos con que se ataca a la Revolución" (Manual), Verde Olivo, 5 Nov. 60, p. 35.
56. "Caracter democrático de nuestra Revolución" (Manual), Verde Olivo, 15 Oct. 60, p. 33.
57. Ibid.
58. The term is from Jorge Dominguez. See his Cuba: Order and Revolution, pp. 341-78.
59. See Richard Jolly, Appendix A, "The Political Content of Cuban Education, 1962", in Dudley Seers, ed., Cuba: The Economic and Social Revolution (Chapel Hill: University of North Carolina Press, 1964), pp. 346-69.
60. "Caracter patriótico de la Revolucion Cubana" (Manual), Verde Olivo, 1 Oct. 60, p. 35.
61. "El desarrollo económico de Cuba" (Manual),

Verde Olivo, 1 Oct. 60, p. 35.
62. "El desarrollo cultural de Cuba" (Manual), Verde Olivo, 8 Oct. 60, p. 17.
63. Cienfuegos, interviewed by Bohemia, 22 Feb. 59, in Cabrera Alvarez, p. 171.
64. Guevara, in Verde Olivo, 15 Oct. 60, pp. 11-13.
65. Ibid.
66. Castro, in Verde Olivo, 21 May 61, pp. 38-9.
67. Castro, "Para el enemigo: la mano dura, la destrucción dondequiera que nos salga al paso", address to the School of Revolutionary Instructors, Verde Olivo, 8 July 62, pp. 38-40.
68. Castro, "El instructor revolucionario es el mejor colaborador del jefe de la unidad", Verde Olivo, 1 Oct. 61, pp. 22-24.
69. Dominguez, p. 365, remarks that before 1963 most political instructors were not drawn from the army. Many were civilian political activists and students, often lacking in military training. This was changed in 1963.
70. Castro, "El instructor revolucionario...", p. 24.
71. See, for example, "El trabajo ideológico en las compañias del ejército", talk by a Chinese director of political education in the People's Liberation Army, Verde Olivo, 21 Jan. 62, pp. 74-75.
72. "Algunas indicaciones sobre las clases del curso de instrucción revolucionario en el programa de preparación combativa de las FAR", Verde Olivo, 16 Feb. 62, pp. 23-4.
73. Causse, "El trabajo político ya la preparación combativa", Verde Olivo, 17 Feb. 63, pp. 4-7.
74. See Col. G. Kravchum, "The Main Stages of Development of Soviet Military Pedagogy, 1918-1920", in Col. A. M. Danchenko and Co. I. F. Bydrin, eds. Military Pedagogy: A Soviet View (Moscow, 1973), tr. and pub. by United States Air Force (Washington: United States Government Printing Office, 1976-0870-00352), pp. 46-55.
75. Causse, op. cit., p. 6.
76. See the various essays on contemporary (post-1960) Soviet military pedagogy in Danchenko and Vydrin.
77. I have used numbers published after the re-organization because of their much greater availability.
78. Guevara, "Social Ideals of the Rebel Army", Speech of January 27, 1959, in Che: Selected Works, eds. Bonachea and Valdés, p. 203.
79. Castro, "The Position of the Revolution in the Face of Communism", April 2, 1959 television interview, in Political, Economic and Social Thought of Fidel Castro (Havana: Editorial Lex, 1959), Appendix, pp. 213-29.
80. Cienfuegos, speech of February 18, 1959, in Pérez Tarrau, pp. 68-9.

81. In *Cuba Internacional*, May-June 1970, p. 139.
82. Guevara, "Social Ideals...", p. 204.
83. Cienfuegos, speeches of February 22 and 27, 1959, in Pérez Tarrau, pp. 69-70.
84. Cienfuegos, speech of June 27, 1959, to the Revolutionary Military Police, in Cabrera Alvarez, pp. 178-9.
85. Castro, "Speech to Shell Oil Company Workers", February 8, 1959, in *Political, Economic and Social Thought*, p. 187.
86. See Thomas, p. 1228.
87. See Edward Boorstein, *The Economic Transformation of Cuba* (New York: Monthly Review Press, 1968), pp. 22-3; Robin Blackburn, "The Economics of the Cuban Revolution", in James Nelson Goodsell, ed. *Fidel Castro's Personal Revolution in Cuba: 1959-73* (New York: Knopf, 1975), pp. 134-50.
88. See Andres Bianchi, "Agriculture - The Post-Revolutionary Development", in Seers, pp. 100-160.
89. Thomas, p. 1223.
90. Boorstein, p. 26; See *New York Times*, 12 June 59 for text of the diplomatic protest.
91. Cienfuegos, speech of June 27, 1959, in Cabrera Alvarez, p. 178.
92. Cienfuegos, speech of July 5, 1959, to a peasant association meeting, in Pérez Tarrau, p. 74.
93. See Thomas, p. 417.
94. Cienfuegos, speech of May 11, 1959 to Rebel Army recruits bound for Sierra training camps, in Pérez Tarrau, p. 72.
95. See Taber, p. 322; Thomas, pp. 1230-32.
96. Thomas, pp. 1234-5.
97. Matos in Lorrin Philipson, "Huber Matos, the Undefeated", *National Review*, 20 Feb. 81, pp. 153-58.
98. Thomas, p. 1244.
99. Ibid.
100. Cienfuegos, 21 Oct. 1959, in Cabrera Alvarez, pp. 180-83.
101. These approaches had begun in the spring of 1959 and were accelerated in the fall. See Andrés Suárez, *Cuba: Castroism and Communism 1959-1966* (Cambridge: MIT Press, 1967), pp. 82-5.
102. Castro, speech to UN General Assembly, September 26, 1960, in *Fidel Castro Speaks*, eds. Martin Kenner and James Petras (New York: Grove Press, 1969), pp. 12-13.
103. Taber, p. 324.
104. The next day, the small plane carrying Cienfuegos disappeared, leaving no trace of the survivors. The speech appears in *Verde Olivo*, 29 Oct. 60, p.79.
105. Luis Baez and Norberto Fuentes, "Milicias Nacionales Revolucionarias: nace un ejército", *Cuba Internacional*, Oct. 1979, pp. 12-17.

106. Thomas, pp. 1269-70.
107. <u>Verde Olivo</u>, 27 Mar. 60, p. 36.
108. Interview with Capitán Emilio Aragones, national M-26 co-ordinator, in <u>Verde Olivo</u>, 3 April 60, p. 4.
109. Ibid., p.39.
110. Guevara, "Soberanía política e independencia económica", <u>Verde Olivo</u>, 3 April 60, pp. 58-62.
111. Castro, speech of February 24, 1960, to the Cuban Labor Federation, in <u>Verde Olivo</u>, 24 April, 60, pp. 12-13.
112. <u>Verde Olivo</u>, 17 July 60, pp. 4-5.
113. <u>Ibid</u>., pp. 6-8.
114. Ibid., p. 10.
115. Ibid., p. 12.
116. <u>Verde Olivo</u>, 17 July 60, p. 13.
117. <u>Yasells</u>, "Se quedaron sin refinerías y nosotros no nos quedamos sin petróleo", Ibid., pp. 14-18.
118. Ibid., p. 22.
119. Ibid., pp. 22-23.
120. Osvaldo Ortega, "Un aporte mas de la clase trabajadora", Ibid., pp. 24-25.
121. Verde Olivo, 17 July 60, pp. 27-31.
122. Ibid., pp. 32-3.
123. "¿Existe la libertad de conciencia en Estados Unidos?", Ibid., pp. 38-9.
124. Ibid., p. 39.
125. Ibid., p. 60.
126. "Vencen ejército y milicias juntos", <u>Verde Olivo</u>, 22 Oct. 60, pp. 4-5.
127. Verde Olivo, 22 Oct. 60, p. 7.
128. Ibid., pp. 10-11.
129. Ibid., p. 23.
130. <u>Verde Olivo</u>, 22 Oct. 60, pp. 28-9.
131. <u>Ibid</u>., pp. 32-4.
132. Ibid., pp. 39-41.
133. <u>Verde Olivo</u>, 22 Oct. 60, p. 42.
134. <u>Ibid</u>., p. 54
135. Ibid., p. 58. 19th century independence leaders in Latin America.
136. Ibid., p. 61.
137. See Osvaldo Ortega, "Eisenhower: Ocho años de Golf, garrote y guerra", <u>Verde Olivo</u>, 29 Jan. 61, pp. 22-27.
138. <u>Verde Olivo</u>, 19 Nov. 60, p. 7.
139. <u>Guevara</u>, "La OEA, los gobiernos sumisos, y Cuba", Verde Olivo, 5 Nov. 60, pp. 8-17.
140. "OEA - cinco años de intrigas", <u>Verde Olivo</u>, 27 Aug 60, pp. 4-7.
141. Guevara, "La OEA...". p. 16.
142. <u>Verde Olivo</u>, 1 Oct. 60, pp. 36-7.
143. <u>See interview</u> with Faure Chomón, ambassador to the Soviet Union, Verde Olivo, 29 Jan. 61, pp. 28-31.
144. See <u>Verde Olivo</u>, 12 Feb. 61, pp. 30-33.

145. See Eduardo Yasells, "Compañias de milicias serranas", <u>Verde Olivo</u>, 16 July 61, pp. 50-54.
146. See Guevara, "Cuba: ¿excepción histórica or vanguardia en la lucha anti-colonialista?", <u>Verde Olivo</u> 9 Mar. 61, pp. 22-29.
147. Guevara, "Cuba: ¿excepcion...?", <u>Verde Olivo</u> 9 Mar. 61, p. 26.
148. See Verde Olivo, 26 Mar. 61, p. 20.
149. "Vida y final de una banda en el Escambray" excerpts from the diary of Julián Oliva Cuellar, <u>Verde Olivo</u>, 9 Mar. 61, p. 30.
150. Verde Olivo, 26 Mar. 61, pp. 9, 20.
151. See Guevara, "Un pecado de la Revolución", <u>Verde Olivo</u>, 12 Feb. 60, pp. 26-29, wherein Guevara discusses the actions of the Second Front, a breakaway from the DR led by Eloy Gutierrez Menoyo.
152. Kozol, pp. 11-12.
153. Verde Olivo, 26 Mar. 61, pp. 4-6. The priest was caught by the militia. See also Osvaldo Dorticós, "No escriben pastorales contra el analfabetismo", <u>Verde Olivo</u>, 19 Feb. 61, p. 32; Castro, "Para nosotros hay un gran culto, que es el culto a la justicia", <u>Verde Olivo</u> 16 April 61, pp. 32-3.
154. <u>Verde Olivo</u>, 22 Jan. 61, pp. 4-6.
155. <u>Verde Olivo</u>, 23 April 61, p. 3.
156. Eduardo Yasells, "Primera derrota del imperialismo en América", <u>Verde Olivo</u>, 30 April 61, pp. 6-14.
157. Verde Olivo, 23 April 61, p. 3.
158. Ibid., p. 7.
159. Castro, "Avanzada Rebelde", <u>Verde Olivo</u>, 23 April 61, p. 27.
160. Verde Olivo, 30 April 61.
161. <u>Verde Olivo</u>, 23 April 61, p. 9.
162. Verde Olivo, 30 April 61, p. 8.
163. Verde Olivo, 23 April 61, p. 9.
164. See Orlando Conteras C., "La conspiración contra la URSS", <u>Verde Olivo</u>, 7 May 61, pp. 42-6.
165. "La lucha de la retaguardia", <u>Verde Olivo</u>, 21 May 61, p. 12.
166. "Avanzada Rebelde", <u>Verde Olivo</u>, 21 May 61, p. 16.
167. Interview with Lt. Col. Le Thuc Lich of Viet Nam's militia, <u>Verde Olivo</u>, 21 May 61, pp. 18-21.
168. <u>Verde Olivo</u>, 7 May 61, p. 77.
169. <u>Verde Olivo</u>, 23 April 61, p. 29.
170. Castro, "La victoria se forjó antes de la batalla", <u>Verde Olivo</u>, 5 May 61, pp. 18-32.
171. Manual Navarro Luna, "La indemnización", <u>Verde Olivo</u>, 11 June 61, pp. 12-13.
172. Ibid.
173. Castro, <u>Verde Olivo</u>, 13 June 61, p. 22.
174. Thomas, pp. 1236-7, writes that Castro first

adopted "humanism", then toyed with nationalism à la Nasser, and finally "decided he could afford to be authoritarian as well as radical", i.e. Marxist.

175. See Theodore Draper, <u>Castro's Revolution: Myths and Realities</u> (New York: Praeger, 1962) and <u>Castroism: Theory and Practice</u> (New York: Praeger, 1965); Loree Wilkerson, <u>Fidel Castro's Political Programs from Reformism to Marxism-Leninism</u> (Gainesville: University of Florida Press, 1965), esp. pp. 82-92.

176. See O'Connor, passim.

177. Guevara, "Notas para el estudio de la ideología de la Revolución Cubana", <u>Verde Olivo</u>, 8 Oct. 60 p. 12.

178. Castro, "Avanzada Rebelde", <u>Verde Olivo</u>, 10 Dec. 61, p. 17.

179. Osvaldo Dorticós, "A luchar por el triunfo final de nuestra Revolución Socialista", <u>Verde Olivo</u>, 10 Dec. 61, pp. 18-20.

180. E. Vazquez Candela, "Martí anti-imperialista: hombre de su momento", Verde Olivo, 27 Jan. 63, pp. 35-7.

181. See, for example, Julio Antonio Mella, "Glosando el pensamiento de Martí", <u>Verde Olivo</u>, 27 Jan. 63 pp. 30-31; in the same issue, Teniente Carlos Diaz, "Jose Martí y el partido revolucionario", pp. 32-34; E. Vazquez Candela, op.cit.; Juan Marinello, "Maceo: lider ya masa", <u>Verde Olivo</u>, 10 Dec. 61, pp. 12-15.

Selected Chronology of Events

August 5, 1951	Ortodoxo leader Eddy Chibás' suicide
March 10, 1952	Military coup by Fulgencio Batista
July 26, 1953	"Generation of the Centenary" attacks Moncada Barracks in Santiago
May 15, 1955	Moncada attackers, including Castro, released from Presidio prison
July 5, 1955	Castro goes to exile in Mexico
December, 1955	Sugar workers' strike
November 30, 1956	Attempted M-26 insurrection in Santiago
December 2, 1956	Landing of the *Granma* in Oriente
December 5, 1956	Army ambushes rebels at Alegria de Pío
January 17, 1957	Successful rebel attack at La Plata
February, 1957	Herbert Matthews of the *New York Times* visits the rebels in the Sierra Maestra
March 13, 1957	Student Directorio Revolucionario attacks the Presidential Palace
May 28, 1957	Successful rebel attack on El Uvero ends period of nomadism

July 30, 1957	Frank País' death in Santiago sparks general strike
September 5, 1957	Popular uprising and mutiny in Cienfuegos
February 24, 1958	Radio Rebelde broadcasts begin
March 10, 1958	Second Front "Frank País" initiated by Raúl Castro
March 14, 1958	United States arms embargo
April 9, 1958	Frustrated general strike
June 26, 1958	Kidnapping of United States citizens in Oriente
Summer, 1958	Batista's offensive in Sierra Maestra
August-October 1958	Guevara and Cienfuegos lead Rebel Army invasion of llano
November 3, 1958	Elections held by Batista, largely disrupted
November-December 1958	Las Villas and Oriente campaigns liberate towns and cities
January 1, 1959	Batista flees; revolutionary general strike
April 17-19, 1961	CIA-sponsored invasion at the Bay of Pigs is defeated

Bibliography

Aguilar, Luis E. *Cuba 1933. Prologue to Revolution.* Ithaca: Cornell University Press, 1972.
Alexander, Robert J. *Communism in Latin America.* New Brunswick: Rutgers University Press, 1957.
Alroy, Gil Car. "The Peasantry in the Cuban Revolution" In: *Cuba in Revolution*, pp. 3-17. Ed. Rolando Bonachea and Nelson Valdes. New York: Doubleday, 1972.
Alvarez Cabrera, Pablo. "Relato". *Verde Olivo* (28 October 1962): 14-15.
Autores varios. Mártires del Moncada. Havana: Ediciones R, 1965.
Aybar de Soto, José M. *Dependency and Intervention. The Case of Guatemala in 1954.* Boulder: Westview Press, 1978.
Baez, Luis, and Fuentes, Norberto. "Milicias Nacionales Revolucionarias: nace un ejército". *Cuba Internacional* (October 1979): 12-17.
Batista, Fulgencio. *Cuba Betrayed.* New York: Vantage Press, 1962.
_____. *Piedras y leyes.* Mexico: Ediciones Botas, 1962.
_____. *Respuesta.* Mexico: Ediciones Botas, 1960.
Beals, Carleton. *Great Guerrilla Warriors.* Englewood Cliffs: Prentice-Hall, 1970.
Bek, Alexander. *The Volokolamsk Highway.* Moscow: Foreign Languages Press, 1953.
Berlin, Isaiah. *Against the Current. Essays in the History of Ideas.* Ed. Henry Hardy. London: Hogarth Press, 1979.
Bianchi, Andres. "Agriculture. The Post-Revolutionary Development". In: *Cuba: The Economic and Social Revolution*, pp. 100-160. Ed. Dudley Seers. Chapel Hill: University of North Carolina Press, 1964.
Blackburn, Robin. "The Economics of the Cuban Revolution". In: *Fidel Castro's Personal Revolution in Cuba: 1959-73*, pp. 134-150. Ed. James N. Goodsell. New York: Knopf, 1975.

Bonachea, Ramón L., and San Martín, Marta. *The Cuban Insurrection. 1952-1959.* New Brunswick: Tranaction Books, 1974.

Bonachea, Rolando, and Valdés, Nelson. "Introduction". In: *Revolutionary Struggle. Volume I of the Selected Works of Fidel Castro.* Ed. Rolando Bonachea and Nelson Valdés.

Boorstein, Edward. *The Economic Transformation of Cuba.* New York: Monthly Review Press, 1968.

Cabral, Amilcar. *Unity and Struggle. Speeches and Writings.* Tr. Michael Wolfers. London: Heinemann, 1980.

Cabrera Alvarez, Guillermo. *Hablar de Camilo.* Havana: Instituto del Libro, 1970.

Camacho, Julio. "El alzamiento de Cienfuegos". *Revolución* (5, 6, 7, 8, 10 September 1962): 10.

Camus, Albert. *The Rebel.* Tr. Anthony Bower. New York: Knopf, 1961.

Cardenal, Ernesto. *Cuba.* Tr. Donald D. Walsh. New York: New Directions, 1974.

Castro, Fidel. "Avanzada Rebelde". *Verde Olivo* (10 April 1961): 27.

———. "Comunicado de la comandancia general del Ejército Rebelde". *Bohemia* (19 June 1959): 42-6.

———. "El Esfuerzo de los trabajadores". *Verde Olivo* (5 March 1961): 46-7.

———. "El instructor revolucionario es el mejor colaborador del jefe de la unidad". *Verde Olivo* (1 October 1961): 22-4.

———. *History Will Absolve Me.* New York: Lyle Stuart, 1961.

———. "Instrucciones". *El Cubano Libre*, 6 (September 1958): 6.

———. *La historia me absolverá.* Havana: Ediciones Populares, 1961.

———. "La victoria se forjó antes de la batalla". *Verde Olivo* (5 May 1961): 28-32.

———. "Para el enemigo: la mano dura, la destrucción dondequiera que nos salga al paso". *Verde Olivo* (8 July 1962): 38-40.

———. "Para nosotros hay un gran culto, que es el culto a la justicia". *Verde Olivo* (16 April 1961): 32-3.

———. *Fidel Castro Speaks.* Ed. Martin Kenner and James Petras. New York: Grove Press, 1969.

———. *Political, Economic and Social Thought of Fidel Castro.* Havana: Editorial Lex, 1959.

Castro, Raúl. "VIII anniversario del 26 de Julio". *Verde Olivo* (16 July 1961): 3-10.

———. "Operacion anti-aérea". *Verde Olivo* (15 September 1963): 32-8.

Casuso, Teresa. *Cuba and Castro.* Tr. Elmer Grossberg. New York: Random House, 1961.

Causse, José N. "El trabajo político y la preparación combativa". Verde Olivo, (17 February 1963): 4-7.
———. "Relato: El Segundo Frente Oriental 'Frank País'". Verde Olivo (24 March 1963): 5-6.
Charzat, Michel. Georges Sorel et la revolution au XXme siècle. Paris: Hachette, 1977.
Chomón, Faure. "Cuando el Che llegó al Escambray". Bohemia (15 May 1960): 17-19.
Chomsky, Noam, and Herman, Edward S. The Washington Connection and Third World Fascism. Vol. I: The Political Economy of Human Rights. Montreal: Black Rose Books, 1979.
Comisión de Orientación Revolucionaria del Partido Unido de la Revolución Socialista Cubana. Relatos del asalto al Moncada. Havana: Ediciones Populares, 1964.
Comisión Nacional Cubana de la UNESCO. Cuba y la conferencia de educación y desarrollo económica y social. Havana: Editorial Nacional, 1962.
Conte Agüero, Luis. Cartas del Presidio. Anticipo de una biografía de Fidel Castro. Havana: Editorial Lex, 1959.
———. Eduardo Chibás, el adalid de Cuba. Mexico, 1955.
Contreras, Orlando C. "La conspiración contra la URSS". Verde Olivo (7 May 1961): 42-6.
Coser, Lewis. Continuities in the Study of Social Conflict. New York: Free Press, 1967.
Cuba: una revolución en marcha. Paris: Ruedo Ibérico, 1967.
Cuza, José L. "Combate del centro industrial de Moa". Verde Olivo (14 July 1963): 18-24.
Danchenko, A. M., and Vydrin, I. F., ed. Military Pedagogy. A Soviet View. Moscow, 1973. Tr. and pub. by United States Air Force. Washington: US Government Documents Printing Office, #0870-00352, 1973.
de Arturo, Hector. "Desde el '56". Verde Olivo (5 December 1971): 68-70.
Debray, Régis. Revolution in the Revolution? New York: Grove Press, 1967.
de la Cruz, Manual. Episodios de la revolución cubana. 1890" rpt. Havana: Instituto del Libro, 1967.
Desnoes, Edmundo, ed. La sierra y el llano. Havana: Casa de las Americas, 1961.
———. Punto de vista. Havana: Instituto del Libro, 1967.
Diaz, Carlos. "José Martí y el partido revolucionario". Verde Olivo (27 January 1963): 32-4.
Dominguez, Jorge I. Cuba. Order and Revolution. Cambridge: Belknap Press, 1978.
Dorticós, Osvaldo. "A luchar para el triunfo final de nuestra revolución socialista". Verde Olivo (10 December 1961): 18-20.

Dorticós, Osvald. "No escriben pastorales contra el analfabetismo". Verde Olivo (19 February 1961): 32.
dos Santos, Theotonio. "The Structure of Dependency". In: Readings in US Imperialism, pp. 225-236. Ed. Kuang-tih Fann and Donald Hodges. Boston: Porter Sargent, 1971.
Draper, Theodore. Castroism: Theory and Practice. New York: Praeger, 1965.
———. Castro's Revolution: Myths and Realities. New York: Praeger, 1962.
Dubois, Jules. Fidel Castro. Rebel-Liberator or Dictator? New York: Bobbs-Merrill, 1959.
Duvallon, G. "Tumbasiete: una escuela revolucionaria". Verde Olivo (27 March 1960): 12-15.
Dze-dong, Mao. Selected Works, Vols. I, II, IV. Beijing: Foreign Languages Press, 1965.
Engels, Frederick. "Introduction to Karl Marx's 'The Civil War in France'". In: The Marx-Engels Reader, pp. 526-537. Ed. Robert C. Tucker. New York: Norton, 1972.
Fagen, Richard. The Political Content of Adult Education in Cuba. Stanford: Stanford University Press, 1964.
———. The Transformation of Political Culture in Cuba. Stanford: Stanford University Press, 1969.
Fanon, Frantz. The Wretched of the Earth. Tr. Constance Farrington, New York: Grove Press, 1964.
Farber, Samuel. Revolution and Reaction in Cuba. Middletown: Wesleyan University Press, 1976.
Foner, Philip. Antonio Maceo. New York: Monthly Review Press, 1977.
Franqui, Carlos. Diary of the Cuban Revolution. Tr. Georgette Felix, Elaine Kerrigan, Phyllis Freeman, Hardie St. Martin. New York: Viking Press, 1980.
———. The Twelve. Tr. Albert Teichner. New York: Lyle Stuart, 1968.
Freire, Paulo. Pedagogy of the Oppressed. New York: Herder and Herder, 1971.
Fuentes, Norberto. "Cubanos en la guerra civil española". Cuba Internacional (March 1979): 30-35.
Fuerzas Armadas Revolucionarias. Ché. Havana: Instituto del Libro, 1969.
Gadea, Hilda. Ché Guevara: años decisivos. Mexico: Aguilar, 1972.
———. Ernesto. A Memoir of Ché Guevara. Tr. Carmen Molina and Walter Bradbury. New York: Doubleday, 1972.
Galvez, William. "Camilo: como lo recordamos". Verde Olivo (28 October 1962): 4-7.
———. "Diario de la columna 'Antonio Maceo'". Verde Olivo (31 November 1963): 4-8.

García, Calixto. "Nuestro deber era permanecer firmes a la orientación trazada por nuestro comandante en jefe". Verde Olivo (1 December 1963): 4-5.
García Salvatecci, Hugo. Georges Sorel y José Carlos Mariátegui. Lima: Ubicación Ideológica del Amauta, 1979.
Giap, Vo-nguyen. People's War, People's Army. New York: Praeger, 1962.
Gillin, John. "Ethos Components in Modern Latin American Culture". In: Contemporary Cultures and Societies of Latin America, pp. 503-517. Ed. Dwight B. Heath and Richard N. Adams. New York: Random House, 1965.
Gimenez, Armando. Sierra Maestra. La revolución de Fidel Castro. Buenos Aires: Editorial Lautaro, 1959.
Goldenberg, Boris. The Cuban Revolution and Latin America. New York: Praeger, 1965.
Goodsell, James N., ed. Fidel Castro's Personal Revolution in Cuba: 1959-73. New York: Knopf, 1975.
Guevara, Ernesto. Ché: Selected Works of Ernesto Guevara. Ed. Rolando Bonachea and Nelson Valdés. Cambridge: Massachusetts Institute of Technology Press, 1969.
⎯⎯⎯. "¿Cuba: excepción historica o vanguardia en la lucha anti-colonialista?" Verde Olivo, (9 March 1961): 22-9.
⎯⎯⎯. "La OEA, los gobiernos sumisos, y Cuba". Verde Olivo (5 November 1960): 8-17.
⎯⎯⎯. "Notas para el estudio de la ideología de la revolución cubana". Verde Olivo (10 December 1960) 10-14.
⎯⎯⎯. Obra Revolucionaria. Ed. Roberto Fernandez Retamar. Mexico: Ediciones Era, 1967.
⎯⎯⎯. Obras 1967-67, Vol. II. Paris: Maspero, 1970.
⎯⎯⎯. Reminiscences of the Cuban Revolutionary War. Tr. Victoria Ortiz. New York: Monthly Review Press, 1968.
⎯⎯⎯. "Soberanía politica e independencia económica". Verde Olivo (3 April 1960): 58-62.
⎯⎯⎯. "Un pecado de la revolución". Verde Olivo (12 February 1961): 26-9.
Harnecker, Marta. Cuba: Dictatorship or Democracy? Westport: Laurence Hill, 1980.
Hernandez, Melba. "Siempre supimos que el asalto al Moncada culminaría en la victoria". Verde Olivo (28 July 1963): 29-32.
Horowitz, Irving L. Radicalism and the Revolt Against Reason: The Social Theories of Georges Sorel. London: Routledge and Kegan Paul, 1961.
Iglesias, Joel. "Junto al Ché". Verde Olivo (13 October 1968): 37-42.

Isaacs, Harold R. *The Tragedy of the Chinese Revolution*. 2nd rev. ed. Stanford: Stanford University Press, 1961.
James, Daniel. *Che Guevara*. New York: Stein and Day, 1969.
Jolly, Richard. "The Political Content of Cuban Education, 1962". In: *Cuba: The Economic and Social Revolution*, pp. 346-69. Ed. Dudley Seers. Chapel Hill: University of North Carolina Press, 1964.
Kochanek, Stanley. "Perspectives on the Study of Revolution and Social Change". *Comparative Politics*, 5, 3 (April 1973): 313-19.
Kozol, Johnathan. *Children of the Revolution*. New York: Delacorte Press, 1978.
Lavretsky, I. *Ernesto Che Guevara*. Tr. A. B. Eklof. Moscow: Progress Publishers, 1976.
Lenin, V. I. *What Is To Be Done?* 1902; rpt. Beijing: Foreign Languages Press, 1975.
Llerena, Mario. *The Unsuspected Revolution*. Ithaca: Cornell University Press, 1978.
Lockwood, Lee. *Castro's Cuba, Cuba's Fidel*. New York: Macmillan, 1967.
Lowy, Michel. *The Marxism of Che Guevara*. Tr. Brian Pearce.
Lusson Battle, Antonio. "Relato de la columna 17 'Abel Santamaría'". *Verde Olivo* (24 March 1963): 7-8.
Macaulay, Neill. *A Rebel in Cuba. An American's Memoirs*. Chicago: Quadrangle Books, 1970.
Malraux, André. *Man's Hope*. Tr. Stuart Gilbert and Alastair MacDonald. New York: Random House, 1938.
Mañach, Jorge. *Martí, el apóstol*. 1932; rpt. 2nd ed. Editora Popular, 1941.
Mariátegui, José Carlos. *El alma matinal*. 1925; rpt. Lima: Biblioteca Amauta, 1972.
──────. *Ideología y política*. Lima: Biblioteca Amauta, 1971.
Marinello, Juan. "Maceo: lider y masa". *Verde Olivo* (10 December 1961): 12-15.
Martí, José. *Cuba, nuestra America y los Estados Unidos*. Ed. Roberto Fernandez Retamar. Mexico: Siglo XXI, 1973.
──────. *Obras completas* Vols. I and II. Havana: Editorial Lex, 1931.
──────. *Our America*. Ed. Philip Foner. New York: Monthly Review Press, 1977.
Martin, Lionel. *The Early Fidel. Roots of Castro's Communism*. Secaucus: Lyle Stuart, 1978.
Marx, Karl. "The 18th Brumaire of Louis Napoleon". In: *The Marx-Engels Reader*, pp. 436-525. Ed. Robert C. Tucker. New York: Norton, 1972.
Masetti, Jorge. *Los que luchan y los que lloran*. Buenos Aires: Editorial Jorge Alvarez, 1969.

Matthews, Herbert L. *Castro, a Political Biography*.
London: Allen Lane, The Penguin Press, 1964.
───. *Revolution in Cuba: An Essay in Understanding*.
New York: Scribner's Sons, 1975.
───. *The Cuban Story*. New York: George Braziller, 1961.
Mella, Julio Antonio. "Glosando el pensamiento de Martí". *Verde Olivo* (27 January 1963): 30-1.
Meneses, Enrique. *Fidel Castro*. Tr. J. Halcro Ferguson. London: Faber and Faber, 1966.
Merle, Robert. *Moncada, premier combat de Fidel Castro*. Paris: Hachette, 1965.
Miret, Pedro. "Un grupo verdaderamente heroíco". *Verde Olivo* (29 July 1962): 6-7.
Montané Oropesa, Jesús. "Del 26 de julio de 1953 al 15 de mayo 1955 - días de combate". *Verde Olivo* (28 July 1963): 19-23.
───. "El estilo de trabajo de los combatientes del Moncada y de Bayamo". *Verde Olivo* (19 July 1964) 8-9, 52.
───. "La Generación del Centenario libra sus primeros combates". *Verde Olivo* (29 July 1962): 8-11.
Montaner, Carlos Alberto. *Informe secreto sobre la revolución cubana*. Madrid: Ediciones Sedmay, 1976.
Navarro Luna, Manuel. "La indemnización". *Verde Olivo* (11 June 1961): 12-13.
North American Congress on Latin America. *Guatemala*. Berkeley: NACLA, 1974.
Nuñez Jimenez, Antonio. *Geografía de Cuba*. Havana: Editorial Lex, 1959.
O'Connor, James. *The Origins of Socialism in Cuba*. Ithaca: Cornell University Press, 1970.
Ortega, Osvaldo. "Un aporte más de la clase trabajadora". *Verde Olivo* (17 July 1960): 24-5.
───. "Eisenhower: ocho años de golf, garrote y guerra". *Verde Olivo* (29 January 1961): 22-7.
País, Frank. "Carta de Frank País a Fidel Castro, 5 de julio, 1957". *Pensamiento Crítico* (July 1968): 43.
───. "Carta de Frank País a Fidel Castro". *Verde Olivo* (1 August 1965): 7.
Pérez, Faustino. "A diez años del Granma". *Verde Olivo* (11 December 1966): 21-4.
Pérez Tarrau, Gabriel. *Cronología de un héroe*. Havana: Gente Nueva, 1976.
Philipson, Lorrin. "Huber Matos, the Undefeated". *National Review* (20 February 1981): 153-58.
Ponce Diaz, José. "Recuerdos del ataque". *Verde Olivo* (28 July 1963): 15-17.
Reed, John. *Ten Days that Shook the World*. New York: Bonie and Liveright, 1919.
Reyes Trejo, Albredo. "Del Moncada a las montañas". *Verde Olivo* (30 July 1972): 24-33.

Rodriguez, Rodolfo. "Porque Fidel Castro no fue asesinado al capturarlo el ejército en Oriente". Bohemia (8 March 1959): 63, 112.
Roig de Leuchsenring, Emilio. Martí, anti-imperialista. 2nd ed. Buenos Aires: Hemisferio, 1962.
———. Conclusiones fundamentales sobre la guerra libertadora cubana de 1895. Mexico: Colegio de Mexico, 1945.
———. Los problemas sociales en Cuba. Havana: Imprenta el Ideal, 1927.
Rojas, Marta. La Generación del Centenario en el Moncada. Havana: Ediciones R, 1964.
Rojo, Ricardo. My Friend Ché. Tr. Julián Casart. New York: Dial Press, 1968.
Roque Nuñez, Roberto. "Relato". Verde Olivo (1 December 1963): 14-15.
St. George, Andrew. "Cuban Rebels". Look (4 February 1958): 30.
———. "Why We Fight". Coronet (February 1958): 80-86.
Sánchez Pinares, Antonio. "Días de lucha". Verde Olivo (13 October 1968): 27-33.
Sandino Rodriguez, José Q. "Operación Captura". Verde Olivo (15 September 1963): 10-15.
Sarabia, Nydia. "René Ramos Latour, comandante en la ciudad y en la Sierra". Verde Olivo (4 August 1963): 25-6, 43-6.
Sartre, Jean-Paul. Sartre on Cuba. New York: Ballantine Books, 1961.
Schulz, Donald. "The Cuban Revolution and the Soviet Union". Ph.d. diss. Ohio State University, 1977. Ann Arbor: University Microfilms, 1977. #77-24, 698.
Seers, Dudley, ed. Cuba: The Economic and Social Revolution. Chapel Hill: University of North Carolina Press, 1964.
Sorel, Georges. From Georges Sorel. Essays in Socialism and Philosophy. Ed. and tr. John L. Stanley. New York: Oxford University Press, 1976.
———. Reflections on Violence. Tr. T. E. Hulme. London: Allen and Unwin, 1925.
———. The Illusions of Progress. Ed. and tr. John and Charlotte Stanley. 1908; rpt. Berkeley: University of California Press, 1969.
Suárez, Andrés. Cuba: Castroism and Communism. 1959-1966. Cambridge: Massachusetts Institute of Technology Press, 1967.
Suárez Blanco, Pepe. "Relato de un combatiente del Moncada". Verde Olivo (29 July 1962): 83-5.
Suchlicki, Jaime. University Students and Revolution in Cuba, 1920-1968. Coral Gables: University of Miami Press, 1969.
Taber, Robert. M-26, Biography of a Revolution. New York: Lyle Stuart, 1961.

Thomas, Hugh. *Cuba, or The Pursuit of Freedom*. London: Eyre and Spottiswoode, 1971.
Tosca, Gonzalez. "Escuelas". *Verde Olivo* (5 December 1971): 84.
Traven, B. *General From The Jungle*. Tr. Desmond Vesey. New York: Hill and Wang, 1974.
Trotsky, Leon. *Military Writings*. New York: Merit Publishers, 1969.
Tucker, Robert C., ed. *The Marx-Engels Reader*. New York: Norton, 1972.
Valdés, Nelson. "Revolution and the Institutionalization in Cuba". *Cuban Studies*, 6, 1-2 (January and July 1976): 1-37.
Vazquez Candela, E. "Martí anti-imperialista: hombre de su momento". *Verde Olivo* (27 January 1963): 35-7.
Vernon, Richard. *Commitment and Change. Georges Sorel and the Idea of Revolution*. Toronto: University of Toronto Press, 1976.
von Clausewitz, Karl. *On War*. Ed. and tr. Michael Howard and Peter Paret. Princeton: Princeton University Press, 1976.
Weyl, Nathaniel. *Red Star Over Cuba*. New York: Devin-Adair, 1961.
Wilkerson, Loree. *Fidel Castro's Political Programs from Reformism to Marxism-Leninism*. Gainesville: University of Florida Press, 1965.
Wise, David, and Ross, Thomas. *The Invisible Government*. New York: Random House, 1964.
Yasells, Eduardo. "Compañías de milicias serranas". *Verde Olivo* (16 July 1961): 50-54.
_____. "Entrevista: recuerdos sobre Frank y Daniel". *Verde Olivo* (4 August 1963): 4-13.
_____. "Primera derrota del imperialismo en America". *Verde Olivo* (30 April 1961): 6-14.
_____. "Se quedaron sin refinerías y nosotros no nos quedamos sin petróleo". *Verde Olivo* (17 July 1960) 14-18.
_____. "Siete años". *Verde Olivo* (1 December 1963): 9-11.
Yglesias, Jose. *In The Fist of the Revolution*. New York: Pantheon Books, 1968.
Zeitlin, Maurice. *Revolutionary Politics and the Cuban Working Class*. New York: Harper Torchbooks, 1970.

NEWSPAPERS CONSULTED

Diario de la Marina (Havana)
Revolución (Havana)

MAGAZINES CONSULTED

Coronet (February 1958)
Cuba Internacional (May-June 1970, March, October 1979)
I. F. Stone's Weekly (April 22, 1957)
Libre (Paris) (September-November 1971)
National Review (20 February 1981)
Look (4 February 1958)
Verde Olivo

Index

ABC Radical, 40
Academia Abel Santamaría, 64. See also Isle of Pines Presidio
Acción Nacional Revolucionaria, 77. See also Frank Pais
Acción Revolucionaria Guiterista, 27, 29. See also bonches
Acosta, Armando, 213, 230
Agostini, Jorge, 76
Agramonte, Roberto, 40, 58, 107
Alcalde, Oscar, 39, 64
Alegria de Pío, 110-114, 127
Alfabeticemos, 232
Almeida, Juan, 111, 112, 139, 146, 178, 183, 210, 211
Alvarez, Pio, 25
Ameijeiros, Efrigenio, 112, 145, 229
Arma Nueva, 231, 232, 243
Arrostía, Rev. Cecilio, 78
Artemisa group, 33-35, 78
Barquín, Col. Ramón, 83, 96
Barrera Pérez, Major, 118
Batista, Fulgencio, 1, 4, 6, 16, 18, 19, 23, 24, 26, 32, 33, 35, 36, 39, 65, 66, 76, 79, 83, 95, 96, 107, 129, 145, 146, 166, 173, 187-189, 227, 233, 242, 264
  and amnesty of Moncada attackers, 67
  on Fidel Castro, 130
  and Fidel Castro's Moncada defense, 56-59
  and Cantillo negotiation, 218
  and censorship in 1954, 66
  and censorship in 1958, 183
  and "civic dialogue", 83
  and coup of 1952, 23, 30-31
  and Cuban economy, 95
  and elections of 1954, 65-67
  and elections of 1958, 185, 211
  flight of, 181, 219
  and Isle of Pines visit, 64
  and Mexican authorities, 85, 96, 97
  and Moncada assault, 51, 52
  and Sergeants' Revolt of 1933, 157, 173
  on summer offensive, 159
Batista's army, 160, 161, 179, 181, 183, 185, 187, 219
  bombing of Oriente, 216, 218
  civic action program, 160
  corruption in, 158
  dissent in, 83. See also Ramon Barquín
  favoritism in, 157, 158
  and Las Villas campaign, 216, 217

Castro, Fidel (cont'd)
  in Mexico, 77-80, 83, 85, 96-98
  and the Moncada assault, 40, 50-63
  and the Moncada trial, 54-63
  and Movimiento de Liberacion Radical, 76
  and Movimiento Nacional Revolucionario, 76
  and Frank País, 77, 169-171
  and Partido Ortodoxo Cubano (ortodoxos), 30, 74, 75, 82, 83
  and Partido Socialista Popular, 97
  and the peasantry, 138
  on Playa Girón, 259
  and Prío Socarrás, 81, 83
  in prison, 63-67
  procession to Havana, 219
  and José Quevedo, 165, 166, 191
  and Radio Rebelde, 164, 165, 180, 191, 192
  and Rebel Army recruits, 117
  and revolutionary justice, 133, 217, 218
  and Santiago campaign, 216, 218
  and Son Los Mismos, 32
  speech at Campo Columbia, 229
  speech at Osvaldo Sanchez School, 239
  on 1958 Batista summer offensive, 164, 189-192
  and Pepito Tey, 77
  at United Nations, 247, 248
  in the United States, 79, 81
  and urban M-26, 168
  and "Zarpazo!", 32
Castro, Manolo, 29
Castro, Raúl, 64, 170, 179, 181, 183, 189, 203, 210, 246, 247
  and El Surco, 143
  and general strike of 1958, 186

Castro, Raúl (cont'd)
  and Grant Wollam, 148
  and June 1958 kidnapping, 147-149
  in Mexico, 78, 98, 99, 112
  and political education of Rebel Army, 230, 231
  and revolutionary justice, 142
  and Santiago campaign, 216, 229
  and Segundo Frente Oriental "Frank País", 139-149
Casuso, Teresa, 81, 93, 97
  and Fidel Castro, 98
  and Prío Socarrás, 98
Catholic Church, 52, 147, 171, 183, 184, 202
  and Rebel Army, 202
Cayo Confites expedition, 28
Céspedes, Manuel, 40, 58, 107, 111
del Río Chaviano, Col. Alberto, 51, 54, 58, 75, 158
  and corruption, 158
  and Moncada assault, 51, 54
  and summer offensive, 189
Chenard, Fernando, 39
Chibás, Eddy, 16, 28-33, 39-44, 56, 74, 86, 96, 107, 262
Chibás, Dr. Raúl, 74, 117, 171, 202
Chivatos, 113, 114, 119, 128, 130, 159. See also mayorales
Chomón, Faure, 30, 177, 213. See also Directorio Revolucionario
CIA, 227, 248
Cienfuegos, Camilo, 99, 111, 112, 134, 139, 179, 186, 246
  in Havana, 219, 228, 229
  internationalism of, 244
  and invasion of llanos, 179, 204-209
  and last speech, 248

Cienfuegos, Camilo (cont'd)
  and Las Villas Campaign,
    211, 213, 215, 216, 229
  leadership of, 209, 210
  and PSP, 215, 216
  and peasants, 209, 210
  and political education of
    Rebel Army, 229-231
  and Santa Clara campaign,
    217
  on treason, 246, 247
  and Yaguajay campaign, 217
"Civic Dialogue" of 1955,
  81-83, 94-96
"Civic Soldier", 122
Clausewitz, Karl von, 52, 53, 161
Collado, Abilio, 94
Committees for the Defense of the Revolution, 17
Conte Agüero, Luis, 64-67
Corintia expedition, 118, 119
Cotubanaba Henriquey, Enrique, 177. See also Miami Pact
Cowley, Major Fermín, 112, 146, 159, 181
Cubelas, Rolando, 213, 214. See also Directorio Revolucionario, Pact of Pedrera, Faure Chomón

Dalmau, Mario, 86, 89
Debray, Regis, 167, 169, 186-188, 201
de la Serna, Celia, 88
de la Torriente Bran, Pablo, 38
del Pino, Rafael, 98
de Varona, Tony, 177. See also Miami Pact
Diaz Cartaya, Agustín, 64
Diaz, Julio, 35, 97. See also Artemisa Group
Diaz Lantz, Pedro, 229, 246, 248, 251
Diaz Tamayo, General Martin, 51
dignidad, 38, 93
Directorio Estudientil Universitario (DEU), 25

Directorio Revolucionario (DR), 30, 82-84, 94, 95, 117, 191, 217, 241
  and Escambray foco, 202, 213
  and Miami Pact, 175, 177
  and plot against Batista, 82, 117, 173

Echeverría, José Antonio, 30, 74, 82. See also Directorio Revolucionario
El Acusador, 32, 33, 36, 37. See also Son Los Mismos
El Cubano Libre, 121, 137, 178, 180-182, 184, 243
"El deber Cubano", 16, 26, 39, 111, 226, 256
El Surco, 143, 181, 243
El Uvero, 119, 127, 160
Escalona, Dirmidio, 204, 229
Espín, Vilma, 116, 158

Fanon, Frantz, 3, 13
Federación Estudientil Universitaria (FEU), 28, 74, 82, 94. See also José A. Echeverría
  and Batista coup, 29, 31
  and Fidel Castro, 28
Fernandez, Marcelo, 215
Figueroa, Maria Antonia, 77. See also Juventud Ortodoxa
Freire, Paulo, 231
Frente Obrero Nacional (FON), 185, 187, 216. See also General Strike
Fuerzas Armadas Revolucionarias (FAR), 3, 24
  and myth, 18
  and political education, 31, 52, 56, 60, 109, 119, 149, 209, 227, 233, 242, 256, 260, 262, 264

Gadea, Hilda, 86, 89, 91, 93, 97
Gálvez, William, 229
García, Calixto, 86, 112

García, Guillermo, 118, 119
García, Barcena Ramon, 35, 52. 76. See also Movimiento Nacional Revolucionario
García, Reynold, 95
General Strike of 1958, 181, 184-187
Generation of the Centenary, 16-18, 35, 36, 41, 49, 52, 53, 60, 149, 201, 263
Gómez, General Máximo, 58, 111, 175, 179, 203
Gómez García, Raúl, 32, 36, 39. See also Son Los Mismos
Gonzalez, Cándido, 55, 97
Gramsci, Antonio, 13
Granados, Alberto, 88
Granma, 17, 80, 87, 94, 98, 107, 108, 110, 111, 168, 177, 201, 262
Grau San Martín, Ramón, 23, 25-28
 and Batista coup, 32
guajiros, 111, 113-120, 131, 135, 138, 149
Guardia Rural, 112, 115, 120, 128-130, 135, 140, 158-161, 167, 183, 187, 208, 211. See also chivatos
Guatemala
 Arbenz government in, 86, 90, 91
 Ché Guevara in, 89-92
Guerra, Eutimio, 114, 115, 137. See also revolutionary justice
Guevara, Alfredo, 28
Guevara, Ernesto 'Ché', 86-94, 112, 169, 170, 179, 181, 243, 260, 261
 and agrarian reform, 118-120, 135-137, 162, 212
 and anti-imperialism, 150, 181
 in Bolivia, 88, 89
 and Fidel Castro, 92, 93
 and Cuban emigrés, 92
 and El Cubano Libre, 180, 181. See also El Cubano Libre

Guevara, Ernesto Che (cont'd)
 at El Uvero, 119, 127
 and José Manuel Fortuny, 91
 and 1958 general strike, 184-187
 in Guatemala, 89-92
 in Havana, 228
 and internationalism, 244
 at La Mesa, 136-138
 at La Plata, 113
 and Las Villas campaign 211-215
 and literacy program, 116
 on llano M-26, 170-173, 188, 215. See also llano
 and invasion of llanos, 204-209
 and Marxism, 90
 in Mexico, 91-99
 and Minas del Frío School, 180, 182. See also Minas del Frío
 and morale, 161-163, 177, 206, 207
 and Enrique Oltusky, 214, 215. See also Pact of Pedrero
 and peasantry, 114, 115, 119, 120, 135-138
 and Playa Girón, 258
 and political education of Rebel Army, 120, 121, 182, 231-233, 238
 on Ciro Redondo, 178
 and revolutionary justice, 218
 and santería, 119, 203. See also santería.
 and "Second Front of Escambray", 213, 214. See also "Second Front of Escambray"
 on Sierra Manifesto, 172. See also Sierra Manifesto.
 and Jorge Sotús, 117
 and summer offensive of 1958, 190
Guitart, Renato, 39, 50, 77. See also Movimiento Nacional Revolucionario

Guiteras, Antonio, 27, 28, 39, 40, 263
Gutierrez, Alfonso, 78
Gutierrez,Menoya, Eloy, 204, 213, 214, 217
Gutierrez, Oniria, 120, 121

Hart, Armando, 35, 76. See also Movimiento Nacional Revolucionaria
Hernandez, Melba, 32, 37, 55, 65, 74. See also Son Los Mismos, Moncada trial
Herrera, Osvaldo, 209
Hymn of July 26, 64, 97, 109, 210. See also Hymn of Liberty.
Hymn of Liberty, 55

Iglesias, Joel, 120, 178
Ingenieros, José, 38
Isle of Pines Presidio, 63-67, 74. See also Academia Abel Santamaría

Joven Cuba, 40
Junta de Liberación Cubana, 175-177, 179, 183. See also Miami Pact
Juventud Ortodoxa, 35-37, 76, 77, 86. See also Partido Ortodoxo Cubano Socialista, 28, 30. See also Partido Socialista Popular

Labrandero, Daniel Martin, 95
La Calle, 73, 76, 80. See also Luis Orlando Rodriguez
Lafferté, Capitán Evelio, 182. See also Minas del Frio
La Plata, 113, 114
Lenin, Vladimir I., 1, 2, 38, 66, 67
llanos leadership, 17, 110, 122, 135, 170, 172, 173, 179, 182, 186-188, 215. See also M-26
llanos invasion, 203-217

Llerena, Mario, 35, 76. See also Movimiento Nacional Revolucionario, Movimiento de Liberación Radical
Lopez, Antonio Ñico, 86, 92, 94, 177
Lopez,Fresquet, Rufo, 247
Lusson Batlle, Antonio, 142

Maceo Antonio, 15, 17, 40, 58, 74, 107, 179, 203, 204, 263
Machado, Antonio, 24-26, 28, 31, 41
Machado, Manuel, 78
Mambises, 49, 62, 108, 163, 179, 203, 258, 262
Mao Dze-dong, 3, 160
"Mariana Grajales" platoon, 211
Marianao group, 35
Mariátegui, José Carlos, 9, 13, 17
Márquez, Juan Manuel, 80
Marrero, Pedro, 39
Martí, José, 15-17, 29, 37-39, 41, 56, 58, 62, 65, 75, 77, 79, 80, 107, 111, 145, 146, 231, 262, 263
Martinez Sánchez, Augusto, 142. See also revolutionary justice.
Marx, Karl, 1, 12, 13
Marxism-Leninism, 18, 19, 38, 122, 227, 241, 263
Mas Martín, luis, 28
Masetti, Jorge, 90, 128, 129, 136, 137, 186
Masferrer, Rolando, 27, 29, 31, 40, 159
Matos, Huber, 117, 229, 246, 247, 261
Matthews, Herbert, 114, 116, 122, 129
Mayorales, 113, 114, 128, 130, 134. See also chivatos, Guardia Rural
Mella, Julio Antonio, 25, 28, 40, 146, 263
Menendez, Jesus, 28
Mestre, Armando, 64

'Mexico Pact', 83, 94, 171
Miami Pact, 175-177. See
    also Junta de Liberacion Cubana
Milicianos, 181
Military Intelligence Service (SIM), 94, 97, 161
Minas del Frío School, 180, 182, 189, 205
Miret, Pedro, 36, 64, 75, 77, 85, 98, 211
Moncada, 31, 32, 36, 38, 39, 49, 52, 108, 262
    anniversary of, 246
    and Artemisa group, 35
    and chibasistas, 30, 96
    and myth, 16-18, 149, 201
    trial, 52-63, 67, 74-77
    veterans in Costa Rica, 80, 81
    veterans in Guatemala, 92
Montané, Jesus, 32, 39, 64, 85. See also Son Los Mismos
Montecristi group, 81
Morales, Calixto, 112, 229
Mosquera, Sánchez, 118, 129, 159, 178, 181, 192
Movimiento 26 de Julio (M-26)
    anti-imperialism in, 146
    and "Civic Dialogue", 82, 83. See also "Civic Dialogue"
    disaffections in, 227, 247
    and fund-raising, 78, 84, 191, 205
    and general strike, 185-187. See also general strike
    and Granma expedition, 109
    and las Villas campaign, 214, 215
    and llano-Sierra dispute, 110, 169-172, 201, 264
    See March 1958 meeting
    and Mario Llerena, 76
    and March 1958 meeting, 184
    in Mexico, 84-86, 94
    and Miami Pact, 175, 176
    and Moncada assault, 50-53, 56

Movimiento 26 de Julio (M-26) (cont'd)
    and Movimiento Nacional Revolucionario, 35
    and Organización Auténtica (OA), 173
    and Partido Ortodox Cubana, 82, 94, 96
    and Partido Socialista Popular (PSP), 188, 261
    and peasant network, 112
    political independence of, 81
    and Prío Socarrás, 78, 81
    urban, 19, 115, 116, 127, 142, 166-168, 173, 179, 186, 187, 202, 206, 219, 241
    in Washington, D. C., 147
Movimiento de Liberación Radical, 76. See also Mario Llerena
Movimiento Nacional Revolucionario, 35, 52, 76. See also Ramón Garcia Bárcena
Movimiento Socialista Revolucionario, 27-29. See also bonches
Mujal, Eusebio, 24, 95, 173, 185, 186
Mujalism, 24, 109, 216
Muñoz Monroy, Dr. Mario, 40
Nicolau, Ramón, 230
Nivaldo Causse, José, 144, 241. See also Tumbasiete

October crisis, 17
Oltusky, Enrique, 214, 215
Organización Auténtica (OA), 173, 191
Organization of American States (OAS), 244
Orlando Rodriguez, Luis, 76. See also La Calle
Osvaldo Sanchez School, 239

Pact of Pedrero, 214. See also Rolando Cubelas
País, Frank, 30, 77, 81, 95, 109, 116, 117, 127, 142

País, Frank (cont'd)
168-173, 263. See also
Movimiento Nacional
Revolucionario
Paneque, Victor Manuel, 214
Partido Autentico Cubano,
24, 25, 28, 32, 35, 41
51, 54, 73
Partido Comunista Cubano, 56
140. See also Juventud
Socialista, Partido
Socialista Popular (PSP)
Partido Ortodox Cubano (Or-
todoxos), 16, 18, 28-33,
35, 36, 50, 51, 54, 65,
73-79, 82, 83, 94, 96,
117. See also Juventud
Ortodoxa
Partido Socialista Popular
(PSP), 24, 26, 28, 31,
41, 51, 54, 65, 95, 97,
144, 188, 191, 202, 204,
213, 226, 241. See also
Juventud Socialista,
Partido Comunista Cubano
Patria, 181
Pazos, Felipe, 117, 171, 175
177, 247
Pena Diaz, Felix, 142, 144
Pérez Dámera, 28. See also
Cayo Confites
Pérez Serantes, Monsignor
Enrique, 51
Pérez, Crescencio, 110, 111,
114, 118, 127. See also
precaristas
Pérez, Faustino, 35, 76, 78,
111, 112, 115, 184, 186,
188, 247
Pérez, Floro, 25
Pérez, Comandante Moisés,
182. See also Minas
del Frío
Peurifoy, William, 91. See
also Guatemala
Pino, Orquidea, 78
Playa Girón, 17, 239, 257-
259
political education, 6, 7,
99, 107-109, 121, 122,
149, 181, 182, 225, 227,
230, 251, 254
political instructors, 241

precaristas, 110, 114-117,
121, 127, 135, 138
Prío Socarrás, Carlos, 23,
30, 31, 39, 54, 58, 59,
67, 78, 79, 81, 83, 95,
96, 98
Quevedo, Major José, 165,
166, 191
Ramirez, José, 144
Ramos Latour, René, 143, 168
169, 179, 185, 188
Rebel Army, 179, 181, 202,
227, 228, 230, 237, 238,
243, 244, 260, 264
and Batista's summer off-
ensive, 188-192, 201
and desertion, 115
literacy programs in, 231
and llano invasion, 203-
218
and Moncada, 53, 60
and political education,
52, 60, 108, 109, 119,
249, 229-231, 238, 242,
245
political leadership of,
6, 19, 24, 31, 35, 49
priests in, 202
santería in, 203. See
also santería
social myth of, 3, 99, 100
122, 162, 167, 172, 179,
192, 201-205, 225-229,
233, 246, 249, 263, 264
and theory of contrasting
morales, 161
and treatment of prisoners
165
and treatment of wounded,
113, 160, 166
Redondo, Ciro, 35, 112, 177,
178. See also Artemisa
group
revolutionary instructors,
239-241
revolutionary justice, 129-
132, 142, 216-218, 245.
See also Chivatos,
Augusto Martinez San-
chez, Humberto Sorí
Marín
Risquet, Jorge, 144. See
also Tumbasiete

Rivera, Diego, 97
Rodriguez, Carlos Rafael, 188
Rodriguez, Lester, 77, 109, 175
Rodriguez, Marcos Armando, 230
Rodriguez, Rene, 112
Rojo, Ricardo, 90, 91
Roque Nuñez, Roberto, 109

Saavedra, Angel, 147
St. George, Andrew, 118, 179, 183
Salvador, David, 187, 188. See also Frente Obrero Nacional (FON)
Sánchez, Celia, 110, 116
Sánchez Amaya, Fernando, 35. See also Movimiento Nacional Revolucionario
Sánchez, Martinez, 229
Sánchez, Miguel, 84, 85
Sánchez, Osvaldo, 188
Sánchez, Universo, 112
Santa Coloma, Boris Luis, 32. See also Son Los Mismos
Santa Rosa, 85, 86, 93-96
Santamaría, Abel, 32, 35-38. See also academia Abel Santamaría, Son Los Mismos
Santamaría, Haydée, 32, 38, 40, 53, 54, 74, 109, 116, 205. See also Son Los Mismos
Santería, 119, 121, 203
Sandiñas, Comandante Eduardo, 211
Sardiñas, Capitán Lalo, 133. See also revolutionary justice
"Second Front of Escambray" 204, 213, 214, 217. See also Eloy Gutierrey Menoyo
"Sierra Manifesto", 171, 172, 175
Siqueiros, David, 97
Smith, Earl, 172
Smith, Jose, 85

Sociedad de Amigos de la República (SAR), 81, 83
Son los Mismos, 32
Sorel, Georges, 8-15, 17, 18, 109, 161, 201, 226, 255
Sorí Marín, Dr. Humberto, 132
Sosa, Elpidio, 39
Sosa Blanco, Major Jesús, 146, 159, 218
Soto, Lionel, 18, 29. See also Bell of Demajagua
Sotus, Jorge, 117
Suarez, José, 35. See also Artemisa group
Suarez, Blanco, Pepe, 37, 64. See also Juventud Socialista
Suarez, Suquet, Col. 207, 208
Superación, 230, 235, 242

Tabernilla, General Francisco, 158
Tey, Pepito, 77, 109. See also Movimiento Nacional Revolucionario
Tizol, Ernesto, 39
Toledano, Lombardo, 97
Torres, Felix, 104, 213
Torres, Nico, 188
Trapote, Victor, 78
Trejo, Raúl, 25, 40
Tró, Emilio, 27
Trujillo, Rafael, 28, 33, 83, 95, 244, 246
Tumbasiete School, 144, 145, 238, 241

Union Insurreccional Revolucionaria (UIR), 27-29. See also bonches
University of Havana, 24-26, 32, 35
Urrutia, Lleó, Dr. Manuel, 177, 246

Valdes, Ramiro, 35, 96. See also Artemisa group
Verde Olivo, 228, 232, 233, 240, 242-264
Wars of Independence, 24, 25

Wars of Independence
 (cont'd)
 58, 203
 and Rebel Army military
  code, 132
Welles, Sumner, 26
Westbrook, Joe, 35. See
 also Movimiento Nacional Revolucionario
Weyler, General Valeriano, 58
White, Harold, 89
Wieland, William A., 149
Wollam, Grant, 148

Zelaya, Alfonso, 97
Zenón Acosta, Julio, 116